Bert
Collecte

Lindbergh's Flight, The Baden-Baden Lesson on Consent, He Said Yes/He Said No, The Decision, The Mother, The Exception and the Rule, The Horatians and the Curiatians, St Joan of the Stockyards

The Lehrstücke or short 'didactic' pieces, *Lindbergh's Flight*, *The Baden-Baden Lesson on Consent*, *He Said Yes/He Said No*, *The Decision*, *The Exception and the Rule* and *The Horatians and the Curiatians*, were written during the years 1929 to 1933, a crucial period of creativity and political experiment for Brecht. Rejecting conventional theatre, they are spare and highly formalised, drawing on traditional Japanese and Chinese theatre. They show Brecht in collaboration with the composers, Hindemith, Weill and Eisler, influenced by the new techniques of montage in the visual arts and seeking new forms of expression.

The Mother, a longer play, again with music by Eisler, based on the novel by Gorky, is a story of dawning political consciousness told with irony and narrative drive. Its central character is one of Brecht's great female roles.

St Joan of the Stockyards, full of pastiche and parody, is a battle of good and evil set in a mythical Chicago. As a big drama for the established professional theatre, it occupies a special position both in Brecht's oeuvre and in the theatre of his time.

The volume, edited and introduced by John Willett, includes Brecht's own notes and all the important textual variants.

Bertolt Brecht was born in Augsburg on 10 February 1898 and died in Berlin on 14 August 1956. He grew to maturity as a playwright in the frenetic years of the twenties and early thirties, with such plays as *Man equals Man*, *The Threepenny Opera* and *The Mother*. He left Germany when Hitler came to power in 1933, eventually reaching the United States in 1941, where he remained until 1947. It was during this period of exile that such masterpieces as *Life of Galileo*, *Mother Courage* and *The Caucasian Chalk Circle* were written. Shortly after his return to Europe in 1947 he founded the Berliner Ensemble, and from then until his death was mainly occupied in producing his own plays.

BRECHT COLLECTED PLAYS
Series Editors: John Willett, Ralph Manheim and Tom Kuhn

Brecht Collected Plays: One
Baal
Drums in the Night
In the Jungle of Cities
The Life of Edward II of England
A Respectable Wedding
The Beggar or The Dead Dog
Driving Out a Devil
Lux in Tenebris
The Catch

Brecht Collected Plays: Two
Man equals Man
The Elephant Calf
The Threepenny Opera
The Rise and Fall of the City of Mahagonny
The Seven Deadly Sins

Brecht Collected Plays: Three
Lindbergh's Flight
The Baden-Baden Lesson on Consent
He Said Yes/He Said No
The Decision
The Mother
The Exception and the Rule
The Horatians and the Curiatians
St Joan of the Stockyards

Brecht Collected Plays: Four*
Round Heads and Pointed Heads
Dansen
How Much Is Your Iron?
The Trial of Lucullus
Fear and Misery of the Third Reich
Señora Carrar's Rifles

Brecht Collected Plays: Five
Life of Galileo
Mother Courage and her Children

Brecht Collected Plays: Six
The Good Person of Szechwan
The Resistible Rise of Arturo Ui
Mr Puntila and his Man Matti

Brecht Collected Plays: Seven
The Visions of Simone Machard
Schweyk in the Second World War
The Caucasian Chalk Circle
The Duchess of Malfi

Brecht Collected Plays: Eight*

* *in preparation*

BERTOLT BRECHT

Collected Plays: Three

Lindbergh's Flight
translated by John Willett

The Baden-Baden Lesson on Consent
translated by Geoffrey Skelton

He Said Yes/He Said No
adapted from the translation by Arthur Waley

The Decision
translated by John Willett

The Mother
translated by John Willett

The Exception and the Rule
translated by Tom Osborn

The Horatians and the Curiatians
translated by H. R. Hays

St Joan of the Stockyards
translated by Ralph Manheim

Edited and introduced by John Willett

Methuen Drama

METHUEN WORLD CLASSICS

10 9 8 7 6 5

This edition first published in Great Britain in 1997
by Methuen Drama
11–12 Buckingham Gate, London SW1E 6LB
by arrangement with Suhrkamp Verlag, Frankfurt am Main

Reissued with a new cover 1998

Acknowledgement is due to George Allen & Unwin (Publishers) Ltd for permission to publish the translation and adaptation made by Brecht of Arthur Waley's English translation of *Taniko* from *The Nō Plays of Japan.*

A CIP catalogue record for this book is available from The British Library
ISBN 0 413 70460 2

Typeset by Wilmaset Ltd, Birkenhead, Merseyside
Printed in Great Britain by Cox & Wyman Ltd, Reading, Berkshire

Contents

Introduction

WEIMAR AT THE END OF ITS ROPE

Both politically and culturally 1929 was a crucial year for Europe and the United States, above all for Germany. The Weimar Republic was a fragile, if vibrant institution, and as soon as the American economy crashed that autumn its remarkable decade of liberal government and Socialist local administration was doomed. German unemployment, from nearly three million at the start of the year, rose to five million by the end of 1930. Increasingly the new Chancellor Heinrich Brüning bypassed parliament and ruled by presidential decree. Hitler's National Socialist Party emerged from the Bavarian fringe, allied itself with the Nationalist Right and began its steep climb to power, first in local and Land elections, then in the Reichstag elections of autumn 1930, when it won the second largest number of seats. The following year there were a number of bank crashes, and the last major Socialist stronghold, the Prussian Provincial government, was seized in a coup by the Right. The Left tamely surrendered.

Already there were signs, too, of a cultural backlash. Part of this was due to economic retrenchment: the closure of Klemperer's Kroll Opera in mid-1931, for instance, and the ending of the great modern replanning schemes in Frankfurt and Berlin. Part was ideological, enforcing the anti-modernist tastes of militant Nazis like Wilhelm Frick and the architect Paul Schultze-Naumburg in Thuringia, Alfred Rosenberg with his 'Militant League for German Culture' and the master builder Adolf Hitler himself. Part however was no longer specifically German but due to the Zeitgeist: the return to conventional forms in Austria, the ending of the Soviet engagement with modern art and architecture, the dissolution of all existing Russian arts organisations and the increasing imposition there of 'Socialist Realism' with its nineteenth-century models. Except in the Scandinavian countries, Holland, Switzerland and Czechoslovakia, the modernist excitement that had prevailed in central Europe for the second, relatively prosperous half of the 1920s was everywhere becoming stifled or at best dying down.

In September 1929, just before Wall Street's Black Monday, there were two notable failures in the Berlin theatre. One was the Piscator production of *The Merchant of Berlin* by the ex-Dadaist Walter Mehring, with sets by Moholy-Nagy and music by the Schönberg pupil Hanns Eisler. The other was the Hauptmann/Weill/Brecht gangster play *Happy End*. Piscator closed his theatre, went on tour with a play about abortion, briefly took over a more downmarket house with an actors' collective, then in 1931 moved to Moscow to make a film. Brecht however was already setting off on a more radical track, where both Weill and Eisler had become involved in what was one of the most hopeful and original movements of an otherwise disastrous time. Perhaps if he had been less committed to this new direction – philosophically as well as artistically committed, that is – the playwright would have worked harder to rescue *Happy End*, whose basic idea, as well as its song texts, seems to have originated with him. But now he was much too interested in his new tasks to rewrite and overhaul Hauptmann's script as he would previously have done. The result was that, for much of the three years (inclusive) from *The Threepenny Opera* to *The Mother*, his primary work was taking place outside the established Berlin theatre. The aim for Brecht, as also for Eisler, was what both men saw as a new or alternative 'apparatus'.

* * *

This apparatus was partly a matter of new cultural technologies, derived from the experiments of previous years, which were now supplementing, if not actually replacing, the traditional 'establishment' of opera houses, subsidised or commercial theatres and what Eisler termed 'the bourgeois concert business'. There was the radio, a 1920s medium which had started to perform specially written plays, song cycles and cantatas under the leadership of some outstanding producers and administrators; already Kurt Weill had been commissioned by Frankfurt Radio to set a cycle of Brecht poems as a *Berlin Requiem* for the tenth anniversary of Rosa Luxemburg's murder in 1929; while other specialists in broadcasting included the conductors Hermann Scherchen and Jascha Horenstein. There was the sound film, and the early synchronisation experiments before the real breakthrough of sound-on-film in 1928/29. And there was also a new concern with the social/educational aspects of the arts; notably the involvement of the amateur singer, actor, photographer or musician who got his pleasure from performing, along with the schoolchildren who were being encouraged to practise an art rather than study art history or music 'appreciation'. All this had begun to stimulate the avant-garde musicians: Milhaud in France; Hindemith, Weill, Eisler and Dessau in Germany; Shostakovitch in Soviet Russia; Antheil in the USA. Its real laboratory or think-tank was not the radical theatre but the German 'Neue Musik', with its festivals first at Donaueschingen, then from 1927 on at Baden-Baden and finally in 1930 in Berlin. Hindemith and Heinrich Burkard were the leaders, Schott of Mainz the interested publishers, 'Gebrauchsmusik' and 'Gemeinschaftsmusik' the catchwords – Applied Music and Community Music, as opposed to music for consumers. The notion of 'Lehre', meaning teaching or doctrine, was inherent in the second.

While what is now seen as the mainstream modernism, represented in the International Society for Contemporary Music, was primarily concerned with new forms and systems, more or less irrespective of accessibility, the 'New Music' was interested in the economic constraints and new inventions that underlay the German 'Neue Sachlichkeit' in all the arts – from architecture to cabaret – while at the same time building on a national tradition of education through art which went back to the Renaissance. It was socially and economically alert, technically curious, although (like Hindemith himself) broadly unpolitical, and among its practitioners before Hitler came to power were such varied partnerships as Hindemith and Gottfried Benn, Ernst Toch and the novelist Alfred Döblin, Wilhelm Grosz and Béla Balázs, Edmund Nick and Erich Kästner. In France too there were the collaborations of Milhaud with Cocteau and Paul Claudel. In 1927 the Baden-Baden Festival turned its ears to the short opera – as against the full-scale 'opera of the times' (or 'Zeitoper') intended for the traditional grand opera apparatus and audience. Weill was prominent among those interested. Through his work as a critic for Radio Berlin he had just begun a collaboration with Brecht, and as a spin-off from their work on a full opera the two men now contributed the jazzy music theatre piece, the 'Little' (or 'Songspiel') *Mahagonny*. This was new in scale, idiom, casting (Lotte Lenya, no diva she), staging (in a boxing ring) and intelligibility of the text.

In 1929 the set subjects (as it were) included works for radio, with Ernst Hardt of the Westdeutscher Rundfunk in Cologne as an interested patron, and a new extension of the Gemeinschaftsmusik developed by Hindemith with the guilds of amateur singers in 1928. This was the origin of an up-to-date cantata-like form. Eisler composed a seventeen-minute 'radio cantata', *Tempo der Zeit*, to a text by 'David Weber' (i.e. Robert Gilbert, a successful writer of lyrics). Walter Goehr set Lion Feuchtwanger's pseudo-American poems *Pep*. And Brecht, whose initial contribution Hindemith had clearly valued, wrote the texts for two linked works on the topical subject of the first flights across the Atlantic, that of the American Charles Lindbergh in May 1927, which became world famous, and that of the French airmen Nungesser and Coli some twelve days earlier, which had failed. Here was the origin of the modern 'Lehrstück' or didactic piece.

* * *

The first of these, to music by Weill and Hindemith, was *Lindbergh's Flight*, which was presented under the heading of 'original music for radio' and staged and broadcast accordingly. The other, to music by Hindemith only, was called by him 'lehrstück' (with a lower-case 'l'), then published later by Brecht as the *Baden-Baden Lehrstück vom Einverständnis* (meaning consent or agreement, a concept of self-sacrifice that became important to the writer for the next three or four years). Both works underwent substantial revision, as we have tried to indicate in our texts. The Lindbergh piece was to have been composed entirely by Weill, who however ran out of time so that Hindemith – a very rapid worker – came in to fill the gaps. After the performance Weill completed his own setting, which was then published; then Brecht made changes before his text was published separately, now with the subtitle 'A Radio Lehrstück for Boys and Girls'. Prior to this, too, the music of the *lehrstück* had been published (with due notification) by Schott before Brecht made his alterations. In neither case did the composer set all the revisions and additions which the writer made – so that there is not really a 'final' version of either.

During 1929 two new elements entered the story. The first was Brecht's traumatic witnessing of the May Day demonstrations in Berlin, when the police – who were still under the Social-Democratic Prussian administration – intervened forcibly and some thirty demonstrators were killed: an experience that is supposed to have impelled him towards the Communist Party. This was some three months before the Baden-Baden performances, though it may have influenced the subsequent revisions, notably the changing of the individual aviator in each case into a collective plural: 'The Lindberghs', 'The Airmen'. The second was his introduction to the cool formality and detached narrative of the Japanese Nō theatre, which may already have been in the air at Baden-Baden, since Weill knew Milhaud, who was a close friend and collaborator of Claudel. As a French diplomat in the Far East this great poet had seen many Nō productions and had one of his short mime plays staged with Japanese music in the Tokyo Royal Theatre. Now he and Milhaud were planning the production of *Christophe Colomb*, which Claudel had begun to write in 1927, the year of Lindbergh's crossing. Its première would be in the Berlin State Opera in 1930, and would include some use of film.

The decisive event, however, was Elisabeth Hauptmann's reading of Waley's *The Nō Plays of Japan*, a book also known to Claudel, which an English friend gave her in the winter of 1928/29. She was translating some of these when Kurt Weill consulted her about a possible text for a school opera he had been asked to write for the 'Neue Musik''s 1930 Berlin festival. The play called *Taniko or The Valley-Hurling* seemed to meet his needs, so he then asked Brecht (who apparently had not yet read it) to adapt it for him. Enough of Waley's style and feeling for language remained to determine those of the German version, and as a result our translation sets out from Waley's beautiful English, adjusted to Weill's music as well as to Brecht's changes and additions. Once again however the music has in effect been left somewhat stranded by the revisions of the text. As we show, the text printed in all the main Brecht editions is a modified version which takes account of the objections raised by liberals and the Left to the starkly authoritarian nature of the Consent or Agreement which the original play seemed to propose.

In the earlier version used at the première the figure of the Boy who goes off to the mountains, endangers his companions and has to be killed, struck some critics as being too much the exemplary model of a well-disciplined conformist, a throwback to the Kaiser's army of 1914 (or forward to the Third Reich of 1933). In response, Weill made some effort to assimilate Brecht's revisions, though not all his additional music seems to have survived. But in addition to this revised *He Said Yes* Brecht also made a counter-play with a changed ending, where the Boy says 'No' and refuses to be killed. Called *He Said No*, it is based on the unrevised text and was not set to music at all, with the result that Brecht's suggestion of performing the 'Yes' and 'No' versions together can only be fulfilled if the music is dropped.

* * *

The pairing of *He Said Yes* and *He Said No*, however 'dialectically' it may be interpreted today, was not at all what Brecht had originally intended. For Eisler, whose collaboration with the poet had so far been limited to the odd song (like the 'Abortion Ballad' in 1929), now claimed to be appalled by the 'feudalism' of *He Said Yes* when he read it, and accordingly persuaded Brecht to write a 'concretisation' of the same theme. In this, he later said, he was approaching Brecht as 'an emissary of the working class', in other words a more experienced and knowledgeable Communist. So the plan for the 1930 Berlin 'Neue Musik' was at first that Weill should contribute *He Said Yes*, as arranged with the organisers, while Brecht and Eisler would submit the 'counter-play' *Die Massnahme – The Decision* (also known as *The Expedient* or *The Measures Taken*). Whether this new work would have been ready in time is far from certain, but in the event its submission was refused, and while Weill then loyally withdrew his school opera for production outside the festival, the writing and rehearsal of *The Decision* took roughly half the year, and they were never actually seen/heard antithetically.

This was in spite of the fact that Brecht now seemed much clearer about what he was doing, and despite all the discussions that took place both with the participants and with the Party critics there was for the first time no radical reworking of the script. It was also the first of this whole batch of works to be labelled 'Lehrstück' from the outset – though a Lehrstück that, according to the note to the *Versuche* edition, set out 'to practise a particular attitude of intervention'. In other words *The Decision* maintained Brecht's interest in 'Einverständnis', which now became the conscious, rational self-sacrifice of an underground agitator, relating to what could be a real political situation. This idea of 'intervention' was conspicuously new. It was linked to that of a proletarian revolution, like the hopes of the growing Communist electorate in the towns.

Eisler was involved, as Brecht so far was not, in the new Communist culture which had been growing up around the activities of Willi Münzenberg, member of the Comintern, organiser of the IAH or International Workers' Aid, master of a whole stable of Left papers and publishing houses, sponsor of the agitprop group Kolonne Links and of Mezhrabpom-Film in Russia and its German distributors Prometheus. Through bodies such as these, the German Communists had started, from 1927 on, to build their own apparatus for the arts under an IfA or committee for Workers' Culture. Eisler was already an active contributor, as composer for the 'Red Megaphone' agitprop group and music critic for the Party press. Attempts were made to capture the huge German Worker-Singers federation, with its half a million members, for the kind of politically militant music which he had begun to write, and three of its big Berlin choral groups took part in *The Decision* under one of its conductors, Karl Rankl. A new Communist leadership actually took over the corresponding Workers' Theatre organisation, the DATB, with Wilhelm Pieck's son as its secretary. A breakaway section of the Volksbühne together with the Young Actors' Group, a professional collective which had emerged from Piscator's collapse, would support Brecht in his work on *The*

Mother and *The Round Heads and the Pointed Heads* after his didactic phase was over.

The Decision was a new experience for its author, in that the rehearsals under the direction of the Bulgarian film director Slatan Dudow (who had been studying in Moscow) involved general discussions of the political issues involved. According to a report by the Soviet writer Sergei Tretiakov, who saw the Berlin production in the winter of 1930/31, Eisler told him that it was

> not just a musical work for performance to listeners. It is a special kind of political seminar about questions of party strategy and tactics. Members of the chorus will discuss political questions at rehearsals, but in an interesting and memorable form. The Lehrstück is not intended for concert use. It is rather a means of striving to educate students of Marxist schools and proletarian collectives . . .

This was substantially different from the 'Neue Musik''s idea of exercising amateur performers and their audience in the ideas of a community. It reflects a rapidly changing time, when revolution seemed to be around the corner and Hitler a minor problem.

* * *

Largely because of its Eisler songs, which would be sung by the German Left from 1932 on, wherever they might be, *The Mother* is often treated as some kind of sequel to *The Decision*. And certainly the situation in Germany was not improving while Brecht and Eisler worked on it in the second half of 1931, following the somewhat ungenerous reaction of the Party critics to their earlier work. In a sense the background was the same. But this was not a Lehrstück so much as a piece for professional actors which had started out, in its originator Günter Weisenborn's hands, as a project for the Berlin Volksbühne with its 2000-seat theatre. It was never to be a simple platform piece, even if Caspar Neher's 1932 sets, with their dismountable framework of gas piping, were made to be easily moved to wherever the proletarian audience might be. The play was both mobile and 'epic' in that it covered some twelve years of Russian history in a succession of tightly conceived scenes. It came nearer to agitprop than any other of Brecht's works; it centred on an outstanding character, one of the great roles of his wife Helene Weigel; and only a few narrative short cuts seem to reflect the Japanese influence which was so important for the other didactic plays. If in later years the ways of staging the Lehrstücke have become more and more remote from the theatre, productions of *The Mother* on the other hand have moved steadily closer to convention, starting with the 1951 production of the Berliner Ensemble. The remarkable thing was that following the Prussian government's 1931 ban on agitprop for political meetings its early German performances could take place at all.

One reason for its particular interest for us today is that in 1935 it was performed by Theatre Union, one of the principal Left theatres in New York in the days of the New Deal. Here things appear to have gone wrong all along the line. The theatre board thought of Gorky as a Realist, even a Socialist Realist perhaps, and expected a corresponding version of the play. They seem to have taken Brecht on trust as a progressive and friend of Russia; they clearly had no idea that his adaptation of this Socialist classic had been aimed at a German proletarian audience in a desperate time. Hence he was against conventional dramaturgy, and against being truthful to the Russian background; and if his text appealed for revolutionary action it was not to attack Tsarism, but to overthrow capitalism in its local form. Worse still, he was going to fight for what he regarded as 'his' play, and somehow managed to get himself brought over to New York to do so, although this had not been part of the arrangement. Once there he expected to be able to enforce compliance through the Communist Party hierarchy, not realising how little say they had. He had no idea how to impress and cajole the American theatrical Left, and to make matters worse he seemed to have a dreadful influence on Eisler, who *had* been invited and normally got on well with Americans of averagely liberal views. The damage caused by this interesting exercise not only seems to have put the Theatre Union out of business; it also left scars which would affect Brecht's reception when he arrived in Los Angeles as a refugee six years later. As a study in comparative theatrics the episode is possibly unique.

* * *

Brecht had written two more Lehrstücke by 1935, the year of the two most formative visits of his prewar exile: the one to Soviet Russia and the other to New York. He had left Germany a month after Hitler became Chancellor in 1933, when the Reichstag Fire was a sign to many of the opposition that the last vestiges of the Weimar democracy would now be swept away by the Nazi Brown- and Blackshirts. So, not surprisingly, neither work would be performed where the author could get to it: *The Exception and the Rule* by amateurs in Palestine in 1938, then in Paris in the 1950s; *The Horatians and the Curiatians* not at all. All the same he still labelled the former of these a 'Lehrstück', and counted both of them at one time or another under that head. The better play is surely the first, which is thought to reflect the Chinese theatre rather than the Japanese. The *Horatians and the Curiatians* however is interesting for two reasons connected with Brecht's 1935 visit to Moscow. One was that he linked it too with the performance which he saw by the Chinese actor Mei Lan-fang, from which he drew some important conclusions for his new theory of 'Verfremdung' or Alienation. The other was that unless Eisler (his intermediary) was pulling his leg, it was written in response to a commission from the Red Army to write a play for children. The fact that Eisler, now a music figurehead for the Comintern, failed to compose anything for either work suggests that he took the commission less seriously than Brecht.

If the excitement of the Lehrstück phase from 1929 to 1932 – with collaborators ranging from the immensely fertile but apolitical Hindemith to the militant Communist Eisler – did not last beyond the work on *The Mother*, the relative isolation of Brecht's subsequent exile in Scandinavia gave him the impetus and the occasion to sort out some of his theoretical ideas. And in the course of so doing he would open the door to confusion, if not conscious mystification. Part of the trouble was that he only now started thinking about 'Lehrstücktheorie', as it has come to be called, when he laid down that 'the' Lehrstück needs no audience, that it teaches by being performed and not by being seen, that it should really be considered a 'Lern-' rather than 'Lehr-' (or teaching) piece, that new scenes can be interpolated in *The Decision* and that the required acting style is the same as for the epic theatre. The drawback to this reconsideration of the term is that what he was aiming to achieve with one piece may be thought today to apply to them all. Principles laid down for specific circumstances at a particular time are taken as general.

Thus the idea that *He Said Yes* and *He Said No* must be performed together was something that he himself never saw realised; it was not what the children involved with the play actually asked for; nor (to judge from Albrecht Dümling's researches) was it in fact a response to the Karl Marx School students as Brecht's notes allege. Again, the ruling on performances of *The Decision* which Brecht sent to the Swede Paul Patera in the days of the Cold War – and which was still being inexplicably applied some three decades later – appears to mean logically that barely anybody in the hundreds attending the première, whether as audience or as performers, can have learnt anything at all from that work. This too is a mystification. On top of that, these general Lehrstück rules are applied by their modern interpreters to incomplete works of Brecht's like the *Fatzer* scheme, which he never classed as such. The essential musical component, the work of great modern composers, is largely overlooked. And from this uneven theoretical pudding

– which never figured in the *Messingkauf* or his aesthetic *summa*, the *Short Organum* – a modern form of learning experience is evolved, remote from its roots and closer to today's Performance Art.

All this is an obstacle to the full realisation of some highly interesting works. The music gets dropped, new music gets written, or maybe improvised. After which the play as conceived by writer and composer is at best only half there. In the case of *The Mother* this may be because Eisler, unlike Weill, never got the use of his music made obligatory for all would-be producers. In the case of *The Decision* it is because full-scale productions prior to the 1998 centenary have been barred throughout the European mainland, turning it effectively into an introspective student exercise or at best a piece of fringe theatre, whereas it should emerge as perhaps the greatest music theatre work of modern times. There is still no commercial recording of it and no score is published. Less deliberately, the Hindemith *lehrstück* was long blocked by both collaborators, and even now is only rarely performed. *He Said No* is without music. *He Said Yes* is played less often than it should be, partly because of the pretence that the two texts are best performed together, partly because of Lotte Lenya's idea that the didactic form was imposed by Brecht on a reluctant Weill. Only *Lindbergh's Flight* is open to an authentic performance, though even here the edge of the work has been slightly dented by Brecht's heavy-handed amendments. The fact is, surely, that this writer's remarkable sense of topicality should not be crudely updated to fit our own situations at the end of the twentieth century. It can now be seen historically, in relation to a turning point in world events which is still of immense relevance to us all. Then, but only then, it speaks to the modern audience with all the originality and force that we find in his greatest poems.

* * *

What we have in this group of works is a concern with new audiences and new means of expression that focused the writer's creativity during the precarious months from the Wall Street crash to the Reichstag Fire. Part of its origins lay in his work with Kurt Weill on *The Threepenny Opera* and *Mahagonny*, pieces which however had been aimed essentially at the Berlin West End and conceived in terms of the stage apparatus as they found it there. Now, thanks to his experience with the 'Neue Musik' and its amateur singers, he proved to be addressing a different public, working with a different collaborator in Hanns Eisler and becoming involved in the very different conceptual world of Communist politics. Could he have made this shift any earlier? Most of the radical, revolutionary-minded German writers, artists and musicians of his generation had been politicised by their experiences of the First World War and the inconclusive mid-European revolutions that followed Lenin's lead in October 1917. Brecht was too sceptical for this, and the new ideas to which he committed himself in the mid-twenties were theatrical rather than baldly political. May Day 1929 helped to change him, but at the same time it was thanks to his earnings from *The Threepenny Opera* (including its film version, which was about to follow) that he was able to spend most of those four years concentrating on uncommercial tasks. Such windfalls were, he wrote, 'my only means of doing my work, much of which can be shown not to pay (e.g. *He Said Yes*, *The Decision*, *The Baden-Baden Lesson*, *The Reader for Those Who Live in Cities*, the *Keuner* stories and so on) without the damaging influence of the great financial institutions.'

Even while *The Threepenny Opera* was still running, its producer E. J. Aufricht had started pressing for another work of the same kind and for the same theatre; so Brecht, Weill and Elisabeth Hauptmann combined to plan a second light satirical entertainment for completion in the summer holidays of 1929. *Happy End*, with its English title and Runyon-style story, was written by Hauptmann and had memorable songs by Brecht and Weill. But this time Brecht, while providing the plot (which would pit 'the worst criminal in all Chicago' against 'the proverbial Salvation Army lass'), lost interest after the spring and did little or nothing to pull the show together. The result, in the new climate of social and economic crisis, was an almost instant failure: Brecht disowned all responsibility except that for the songs, Hauptmann's role as author was hidden under a pseudonym, and the wreckage might well have been swept under the mat in favour of the new Lehrstücke with their minimal staging. Nevertheless between them the 'Brecht collective' saw enough good material in *Happy End*, even aside from Weill's music, to want to rework it as a major play for the orthodox theatre and some of its most admired actors. And so, while Brecht himself became caught up in the new genre, Hauptmann and their amateur boxer friend Emil Hesse-Burri started to make a fresh assault on the scheme for a full-scale epic on the subject of the 'cold Chicago' of Frank Norris's novel *The Pit*, such as had already underlain Brecht's *Joe P. Fleischhacker from Chicago* project announced in Piscator's book *The Political Theatre* that same year.

The ambience for this play was again that which had served for *In the Jungle* (1923) and Brecht's even earlier 'Epistle to the Chicagoans', with its opening lines

> The laughter on the slave markets of the continents
> Formerly confined to yourselves

Must utterly have shaken you, the cold in the regions of the fourth depth
Will have soaked into your skin . . .

Behind this there was *The Jungle* itself (1905), with Upton Sinclair's 'muck-raking', blood-smeared images of that city's meat industry: so much more striking than the wheat market as an object of big business and its manipulations. There were the many biblical allusions. There was the Salvation Army, which had already figured in Georg Kaiser's expressionist play *From Morn to Midnight*, and as the background to Brecht's 'Exemplary conversion of a grog-seller' which Weill and he had used in *Happy End* for the 'Brandy-peddler's Song'. Hauptmann herself had written a Salvationist story, called 'Bessie So-and-so' and set in San Francisco in 1906; she herself was photographed in that Army's uniform. Moreover there were the pastiche Army songs too which might be re-used, such as the Salvationists' opening chorus (into which Weill had woven a snatch of the 'Internationale') and the final 'Hosanna Rockefeller' (a satire on the great millionaires which would later be omitted from *Happy End*'s piano score and from its published text).

* * *

The first, largely complete version of *Saint Joan of the Stockyards* was hammered out in the course of 1930, in between work on the Lehrstücke and the film of *The Threepenny Opera*; and with this the collective's long search for the major play at last became focused on one main project. A year later a revised and duplicated script was made available by Bloch-Erben, the agents; then in 1932 it was published with further revisions in Brecht's series of grey paperbound *Versuche*. The decisive preliminary step here was the merging of the 'proverbial Salvation Army lass' with the classic militant figure of Jeanne d'Arc, canonised by the Vatican in 1920 and now anglo-americised by Brecht as Joan Dark. This idea goes back perhaps to Reinhardt's production of Shaw's *Saint Joan* (at a time when Brecht was a Reinhardt assistant), but also surely to the same author's *Major Barbara*, itself written a year after Sinclair's *The Jungle* (to which Shaw refers more than once), and incorporating an anticipation of the Joan-Mauler relationship in father-daughter terms. As Hauptmann used to say, Brecht was a 'name fetishist', and it may be worth noting that Barbara and Johanna (or Joan) were two of his favourite names.

The radical transformation of this project probably took place in the summer holidays of 1930, which Brecht, Burri and Hauptmann spent in the South of France at Le Lavandou (where much of the work on *The Threepenny Opera* had been done two years earlier); after which the Berlin magazine *Tempo* first publicised the new theme and its title, along with the name of Carola Neher who would play the lead. Some of the undated early typescripts had featured another noteworthy character – God, who appears in a number of episodes as a slightly querulous old man puffing his cigar, an embarrassing guest of the Salvation Army, whose shadowy presence in the play has been somewhat ignored (some extracts are given on pp. 420–27, and it is just possible that he survives by an oversight as the Old Man of p. 279). Till then the dialogue had been mainly in prose, but now the new passages of austere rhymeless verse – including some fine long speeches and the sequence of Joan's 'Voices' in scene 11 – seem to accord with those in the Lehrstücke.

Around the same time, too, the collective began to introduce the high-flying literary parodies that characterise the quasi-Elizabethan opening scene and eventually come thick and fast at the end. One cause for this ironic change of tone and rhythm is no doubt the relationship with Schiller's Shakespearean *The Maid of Orleans* (of 1801), while another might well be Brecht's work on a version of *Hamlet* – for the same radio producer as *Saint Joan of the Stockyards* – at the end of January 1931. Finally there are Mauler's Goethe allusions following Joan's death, which bear out the play's intention (as a covering note of 1932 has it) to 'show the present stage of development of Faustian Man' – that divided character so often found in Brecht's writings.

* * *

Ever since its release to German theatre managements a mere year and a half before Hitler took power, Brecht's Joan of Arc play has occupied a special, almost mythical position both in his own oeuvre and in the theatre of his time. Here at last was what he had been aiming for, a big drama for the established professional theatre, whose tragic theme was of instant relevance both in Germany and in the depressed Middle West. Touched early on with Brecht's new-found Marxism, it had developed politically in step with its author, first so as to express the cyclical pattern of industry as posited in *Das Kapital* – end of prosperity, over-production, crisis and stagnation – and then (at a late stage of revision) to refer specifically to the Communists; this too was of interest, at least to the writer's admirers. And yet the resultant play was, and even today still is, something of a mystery, for its only recorded performance in Brecht's lifetime was in the much shortened radio version broadcast from Berlin in April 1932. As the radio critic of the (always supportive) *Berliner Börsen-Kurier* put it,

> One day it will rank among the most memorable, and at the same time disgraceful landmarks of modern cultural history that the theatre had to leave

> it to radio to communicate one of the greatest and most significant plays of our time.

The recurrent question left behind was twofold: First, how would this play work in performance? And secondly, if it was really such a remarkable work, why were the theatres not falling over one another to put it on?

Some idea of the kind of performance that Brecht had in mind can be got from the unpublished recording of the 1932 broadcast, which featured his two preferred stage protagonists: Carola Neher as Joan and, as Pierpont Mauler the meat king, the powerful Fritz Kortner, who had been the yellow-skinned Shlink of *In the Jungle* in 1924. Here Kortner speaks conventionally (for that time), but Neher adopts a strange, disjointed way of speaking which sounds like the description of Peter Lorre's 'syncopated' speech in the State Theatre's famous but short-lived *Man equals Man*: it must surely have been suggested to her by Brecht. Others in the cast seem likewise to have been his own choice: in fact the list on p. 418 reads like a small roll-call of Brecht actors, including three who would rejoin him after 1948, as well as his wife Helene Weigel. Which composer might have provided the music we do not know, but his designer Caspar Neher (unrelated to Carola) sketched a few sets and incidents for the play: notably a kind of three-sided box on a smallish stage, with a free-hanging banner in mid-stage showing images of Joan and other characters.

This certainly suggests a production envisaged for a specific theatre, and some German directors did put in for the rights despite the imminence of Hitler's Reich. Gustav Gründgens later recalled doing so, though no written record has been found; Heinz Hilpert asked for it for the Berlin People's Stage; Piscator offered to form a special company, making an agreement in April 1932 to link its performance with that of his own adaptation of Dreiser's *An American Tragedy*. Berthold Viertel planned a travelling production based on Vienna; while the Mannheim National Theatre is said also to have applied. At Darmstadt, whose regional (Land) theatre had given the world premières of *Man equals Man* and the revised *In the Jungle of Cities*, Gustav Hartung and Kurt Hirschfeld actually announced a production, only to be overwhelmed by protests both in the press and in the city council; under Hitler they emigrated to Switzerland, where Hirschfeld played an important part in the production of the big exile plays.

In 1934 Sergei Tretiakov in Moscow supervised the publication of three of Brecht's *Epic Dramas* in Russian translation: *The Mother*, *The Decision* (both with Eisler) and *Saint Joan of the Stockyards*; Brecht hoped vainly that this would lead to a Soviet production, and had already drawn Tretiakov's attention to the availability of Carola Neher, who had just emigrated to the USSR. By the end of 1972 the play had still not been produced there. There was some prospect of a production by the Prague Nové Divadlo in the early thirties, but this fell through, as did Thorkild Roose's proposed production at the Copenhagen Royal Theatre, for which a contract was made in 1935 (though it seems that Ruth Berlau, who was involved in the negotiations, may have performed some scenes with left-wing amateurs). Next a slightly revised text was published by the exiled Malik-Verlag in the year of the Munich Agreement; at one point this was to have been illustrated by George Grosz. From then on the whole project went underground until after the end of the Second World War, when Brecht made his first return to Berlin from emigration. Then, just a week after the triumphant opening of his production of *Mother Courage*, he wrote to Gustav Gründgens (who had been Goering's Intendant of the Prussian State Theatre and was now rehabilitating himself under Adenauer as Intendant at Düsseldorf) to say curtly

> Berlin NW7, 18.1.49
>
> Dear Mr Gründgens,
> You asked in 1932 for permission to perform Saint Joan of the Stockyards. My answer is yes.
> Yours
> bertolt brecht

– to which Gründgens telegraphed back a fortnight later:

> SCARED TO DEATH BY LETTER – BUT DELIGHTED YOU REMEMBER AND GRATEFUL DESPATCH BOOK SOONEST
> BEST GREETINGS
> GUSTAV GRÜNDGENS

This was a generous if slightly wry gesture by the playwright to the original of Klaus Mann's (and Istvan Szabo's) *Mephisto*, and Gründgens reciprocated by warmly praising the play and saying he was trying to get Kortner for the Mauler part and his own wife Marianne Hoppe for Joan. However, it was another ten years before the production – the play's world première – actually took place in Hamburg, to whose Deutsches Schauspielhaus Gründgens and Hoppe had meanwhile moved. One reason certainly was that Kortner, who was anyway less forgiving than Brecht, felt offended at not having been asked to direct his friend's play. In the event Brecht's daughter Hanne Hiob played Joan and got excellent notices. By then Brecht had been dead for nearly three years.

* * *

Given the 'dark times' through which he lived, it was not unusual for Brecht's works to take several years, if not decades, to realise. His poems are perhaps the most striking example; such a high proportion of them remained stashed away among his papers until after his death. But in the case of his plays there is also a clear difference between those which were written quickly, out of a well-formed initial conception, and those which were being continually rewritten, developed, chopped and changed. It is not always easy to guess which of the ensuing works fell into which category, let alone to say that the one is generally 'better' or bigger or more successful than the other. Thus both *Man equals Man* and *The Good Person of Szechwan* took years to evolve from a quite remote starting point, whereas *The Threepenny Opera* and *Happy End* were generated under high pressure, and *Mother Courage* and *The Caucasian Chalk Circle*, for all their scale and length, appear to have been written rapidly in a single draft which took relatively little revision. There was an interesting exception to both categories in the shape of *Fear and Misery of the Third Reich*, which was loosely accumulated by stitching together some two dozen separate playlets and sketches.

But *Saint Joan of the Stockyards* was special, in that the years of work devoted to it spanned not only great changes in Brecht's writing style and political convictions but also a transformation of the 'apparatus' for which it was intended. The new Left apparatus that could embrace music theatre, revue and political sketch was right for the new forms which Brecht was evolving with Weill and Eisler, but the great narrative play for the established theatre turned out to be a vain pursuit for the avant-garde at least so long as the 1930s lasted. Thus the next such work, the adaptation of *Measure for Measure* that was begun in 1931 and finished up as *The Roundheads and the Pointed Heads*, could not be performed in Germany, and only briefly elsewhere; *Saint Joan of the Stockyards* not at all. And when the opportunity returned in Switzerland during the Second World War these two plays were already on Brecht's back shelf.

The first-named has remained there, with the exception of Eisler's songs. The second has had a number of productions since Gründgens's première, notably by Benno Besson at different German and Swiss theatres; by the Berliner Ensemble in 1968 (a production that unhappily led to the replacement for a time of Manfred Wekwerth by Ruth Berghaus as artistic director); by Giorgio Strehler at the Piccolo Teatro in 1970; and by the Haiyuza Theatre in Tokyo in 1965. In North America it has had student productions, while in Dublin and London it was produced, also in the 1960s, with Siobhan McKenna under the direction respectively of Hilton Edwards and Tony Richardson. In the 1970s a production by the Glasgow Citizens with Di Trevis followed. None of them has securely established this work in the world repertoire, and *Saint Joan of the Stockyards* remains something of an unsolved problem.

* * *

The obvious problems throughout have been the size of the cast and the scale of the setting, which virtually confine it to schools and colleges or to the subsidised theatre. At the same time it has been faulted by critics on both sides of the now crumbled Wall, on two main grounds. On the one hand there is no character to personify 'the workers', and Brecht's attempts to built up the husband-eating Mrs Luckerniddle as such by successive small revisions only made matters worse. 'But how can this be changed?' Ernst Schumacher reported the playwright as saying in the last year of his life –

> Suppose I turn the leader of the workers into Joe, A Union Official or Bill, A Communist, and give him a clear-cut personality, won't I be changing my drama about Joan's petit-bourgeois reformism into an entirely different play? And how can I convey the masses except by a chorus? Of course things can't stay as they are if we decide to stage it. The workers' representatives must have a personality, that's obvious. I'll have to do some thinking about that.

Secondly, it was felt, especially in the West Germany of the 'economic miracle', that the play is in any case no longer very relevant to the modern industrial working class (or 'workforce', to use a less question-begging word). And true enough, Chicago around 1900 – the date given on the original stage script and followed by the Berliner Ensemble – or Berlin in 1931, when that script was made, were both of them remote from the relatively well-situated and well-organised, much less class-conscious workers in those cities today, while the great monopolies are becoming more and more international.

Powerful as it is, therefore, did Brecht's vision become out of date? Yes, perhaps, if we think only of its conscious preoccupation with the class war. But there is a lot more to this play, and much of it is vividly conveyed. It reminds us that, even after the various economic miracles, we still have depths in modern society, and people who sink to the bottom of them; there are still the poor and disadvantaged who feel the bitter cold, rejects now of what used to be the welfare state who have been thrown back into an unfeeling 'community' on the make. Animals are still slaughtered under disgusting circumstances, with more and more of the younger generation drawn to protest, whether by passive vegetarianism or by active concern with animal rights. Factory foodstuffs, battery feeding, artificial additives and adulteration have become topical issues; industrial accidents have changed their nature but are no less dangerous for that; pollution of the environment is a widespread concern that runs across traditional political boundaries. The association of all these things with the profit motive is clear. Meanwhile the ownership of great industries and the continuance or closing down of the companies involved in them is decided by the taking-over and manipulation of shares on the stockmarket.

Religion too has only partly changed its role. If the main branches of organised Christianity are no longer so supportive of the dominant economic order as they once were, there is nevertheless still an active fundamentalist and evangelist fringe that preaches enjoyment of worldly goods in return for social submissiveness. 'Blessed are the consumers', it might be said. And all questions concerning God can always be argued. Such are some of the aspects of our nineties that are still latent in Brecht's Saint Joan story, as well as in the force and irony with which it is narrated. Perhaps they are only waiting to be brought out. True enough, the 'battle between good and evil' is not so simple as its author at first suggested – but was it ever? The divided self of Faustian Man proves to be more confusingly subdivided than most Marxists thought – but isn't it all the more fascinating for that? One way and another the challenge to actors and directors remains, and with it the future of Brecht's most perplexing play.

JOHN WILLETT

Chronology

1898 10 February: Eugen Berthold Friedrich Brecht born in Augsburg.
1917 Autumn: Bolshevik revolution in Russia. Brecht to Munich university.
1918 Work on his first play, *Baal*. In Augsburg Brecht is called up as medical orderly till end of year. Elected to Soldiers' Council as Independent Socialist (USPD) following Armistice.
1919 Brecht writing second play *Drums in the Night*. In January Spartacist Rising in Berlin. Foundation of German Communist Party (KPD). Rosa Luxemburg murdered. April–May: Bavarian Soviet. Summer: Weimar Republic constituted. Birth of Brecht's illegitimate son Frank Banholzer.
1920 May: death of Brecht's mother in Augsburg.
1921 Brecht leaves university without a degree. Reads Rimbaud.
1922 A turning point in the arts. End of utopian Expressionism; new concern with technology. Brecht's first visit to Berlin, seeing theatres, actors, publishers and cabaret. He writes 'Of Poor BB' on the return journey. Autumn: becomes a dramaturg in Munich. Première of *Drums in the Night*, a prize-winning national success. Marries Marianne Zoff, an opera singer.
1923 Galloping German inflation stabilised by November currency reform. In Munich Hitler's new National Socialist party stages unsuccessful 'beer-cellar putsch'.
1924 'Neue Sachlichkeit' exhibition at Mannheim gives its name to the new sobriety in the arts. Brecht to Berlin as assistant in Max Reinhardt's Deutsches Theater.
1925 Field-Marshal von Hindenburg becomes President. Elisabeth Hauptmann starts working with Brecht. Two seminal films: Chaplin's *The Gold Rush* and Eisenstein's *The Battleship Potemkin*. Brecht writes birthday tribute to Bernard Shaw.
1926 Première of *Man equals Man* in Darmstadt. Now a freelance; starts reading Marx. His first book of poems, the *Devotions*, includes the 'Legend of the Dead Soldier'.
1927 After reviewing the poems and a broadcast of *Man equals Man*,

Kurt Weill approaches Brecht for a libretto. Result is the text of *Mahagonny*, whose 'Songspiel' version is performed in a boxing-ring at Hindemith's Baden-Baden music festival in July. In Berlin Brecht helps adapt *The Good Soldier Schweik* for Piscator's high-tech theatre.

1928 August 31: première of *The Threepenny Opera* by Brecht and Weill, based on Gay's *The Beggar's Opera*.

1929 Start of Stalin's policy of 'socialism in one country'. Divorced from Marianne, Brecht now marries the actress Helene Weigel. May 1: Berlin police break up banned KPD demonstration, witnessed by Brecht. Summer: Brecht writes two didactic music-theatre pieces with Weill and Hindemith, and neglects *The Threepenny Opera*'s successor *Happy End*, which is a flop. From now on he stands by the KPD. Autumn: Wall Street crash initiates world economic crisis. Cuts in German arts budgets combine with renewed nationalism to create cultural backlash.

1930 Nazi election successes; end of parliamentary government. Unemployed 3 million in first quarter, about 5 million at end of the year. March: première of the full-scale *Mahagonny* opera in Leipzig Opera House.

1931 German crisis intensifies. Aggressive KPD arts policy: agitprop theatre, marching songs, political photomontage. In Moscow the Comintern forms international associations of revolutionary artists, writers, musicians and theatre people.

1932 Première of Brecht's agitational play *The Mother* (after Gorky) with Eisler's music. *Kuhle Wampe*, his militant film with Eisler, is held up by the censors. He meets Sergei Tretiakov at the film's première in Moscow. Summer: the Nationalist Von Papen is made Chancellor. He denounces 'cultural bolshevism', and deposes the SPD-led Prussian administration.

1933 January 30: Hitler becomes Chancellor with Papen as his deputy. The Prussian Academy is purged; Goering becomes Prussian premier. A month later the Reichstag is burnt down, the KPD outlawed. The Brechts instantly leave via Prague; at first homeless. Eisler is in Vienna, Weill in Paris, where he agrees to compose a ballet with song texts by Brecht: *The Seven Deadly Sins*, premièred there in June. In Germany Nazi students burn books; all parties and trade unions banned; first measures against the Jews. Summer: Brecht in Paris works on anti-Nazi publications. With the advance on his *Threepenny Novel*, he buys a house on Fyn island, Denmark, overlooking the

Svendborg Sound, where the family will spend the next six years. Margarete Steffin, a young Berlin Communist, goes with them. Autumn: he meets the Danish Communist actress Ruth Berlau, a doctor's wife.

1934 Spring: suppression of Socialist rising in Austria. Eisler stays with Brecht to work on *Round Heads and Pointed Heads* songs. Summer: Brecht misses the first Congress of Soviet Writers, chaired by Zhdanov along the twin lines of Socialist Realism and Revolutionary Romanticism. October: in London with Eisler.

1935 Italy invades Ethiopia. Hitler enacts the Nuremberg Laws against the Jews. March–May: Brecht to Moscow for international theatre conference. Meets Kun and Knorin of Comintern Executive. Eisler becomes president of the International Music Bureau. At the 7th Comintern Congress Dimitrov calls for all antifascist parties to unite in Popular Fronts against Hitler and Mussolini. Autumn: Brecht with Eisler to New York for Theatre Union production of *The Mother*.

1936 Soviet purges lead to arrests of many Germans in USSR, most of them Communists; among them Carola Neher and Ernst Ottwalt, friends of the Brechts. International cultural associations closed down. Official campaign against 'Formalism' in the arts. Mikhail Koltsov, the Soviet journalist, founds *Das Wort* as a literary magazine for the German emigration, with Brecht as one of the editors. Popular Front government in Spain resisted by Franco and other generals, with the support of the Catholic hierarchy. The Spanish Civil War becomes a great international cause.

1937 Summer: in Munich, opening of Hitler's House of German Art. Formally, the officially approved art is closely akin to Russian 'Socialist Realism'. In Russia Tretiakov is arrested as a Japanese spy, interned in Siberia and later shot. October: Brecht's Spanish war play *Señora Carrar's Rifles*, with Weigel in the title part, is performed in Paris, and taken up by antifascist and amateur groups in many countries.

1938 January: in Moscow Meyerhold's avant-garde theatre is abolished. March: Hitler takes over Austria without resistance. It becomes part of Germany. May 21: première of scenes from Brecht's *Fear and Misery of the Third Reich* in a Paris hall. Autumn: Munich Agreement, by which Britain, France and Italy force Czechoslovakia to accept Hitler's demands. In

Denmark Brecht writes the first version of *Galileo*. In Moscow Koltsov disappears into arrest after returning from Spain.

1939 March: Hitler takes over Prague and the rest of the Czech territories. Madrid surrenders to Franco; end of the Civil War. Eisler has emigrated to New York. April: the Brechts leave Denmark for Stockholm. Steffin follows. May: Brecht's *Svendborg Poems* published. His father dies in Germany. Denmark accepts Hitler's offer of a Non-Aggression Pact. August 23: Ribbentrop and Molotov agree Nazi-Soviet Pact. September 1: Hitler attacks Poland and unleashes Second World War. Stalin occupies Eastern Poland, completing its defeat in less than three weeks. All quiet in the West. Autumn: Brecht writes *Mother Courage* and the radio play *Lucullus* in little over a month. November: Stalin attacks Finland.

1940 Spring: Hitler invades Norway and Denmark. In May his armies enter France through the Low Countries, taking Paris in mid-June. The Brechts hurriedly leave for Finland, taking Steffin with them. They aim to travel on to the US, where Brecht has been offered a teaching job in New York at the New School. July: the Finnish writer Hella Wuolijoki invites them to her country estate, which becomes the setting for *Puntila*, the comedy she and Brecht write there.

1941 April: première of *Mother Courage* in Zurich. May: he gets US visas for the family and a tourist visa for Steffin. On 15th they leave with Berlau for Moscow to take the Trans-Siberian railway. In Vladivostok they catch a Swedish ship for Los Angeles, leaving just nine days before Hitler, in alliance with Finland, invades Russia. June: Steffin dies of tuberculosis in a Moscow sanatorium, where they have had to leave her. July: once in Los Angeles, the Brechts decide to stay there in the hope of film work. December: Japanese attack on Pearl Harbor brings the US into the war. The Brechts become 'enemy aliens'.

1942 Spring: Eisler arrives from New York. He and Brecht work on Fritz Lang's film *Hangmen Also Die*. Brecht and Feuchtwanger write *The Visions of Simone Machard*; sell film rights to MGM. Ruth Berlau takes a job in New York. August: the Brechts rent a pleasant house and garden in Santa Monica. Autumn: Germans defeated at Stalingrad and El Alamein. Turning point of World War 2.

1943 Spring: Brecht goes to New York for three months – first visit since 1935 – where he stays with Berlau till May and plans a wartime *Schweik* play with Kurt Weill. In Zurich the

Schauspielhaus gives world premières of *The Good Person of Szechwan* and *Galileo*. November: his first son Frank is killed on the Russian front.

1944 British and Americans land in Normandy (June); Germans driven out of France by end of the year. Heavy bombing of Berlin, Hamburg and other German cities. Brecht works on *The Caucasian Chalk Circle*, and with H. R. Hays on *The Duchess of Malfi*. His son by Ruth Berlau, born prematurely in Los Angeles, lives only a few days. Start of collaboration with Charles Laughton on English version of *Galileo*.

1945 Spring: Russians enter Vienna and Berlin. German surrender; suicide of Hitler; Allied military occupation of Germany and Austria, each divided into four Zones. Roosevelt dies; succeeded by Truman; Churchill loses elections to Attlee. June: *Private Life of the Master Race* (wartime adaptation of *Fear and Misery* scenes) staged in New York. August: US drops atomic bombs on Hiroshima and Nagasaki. Japan surrenders. Brecht and Laughton start discussing production of *Galileo*.

1946 Ruth Berlau taken to hospital after a violent breakdown in New York. Work with Auden on *Duchess of Malfi*, which is finally staged there in mid-October – not well received. The Brechts have decided to return to Germany. Summer: A. A. Zhdanov reaffirms Stalinist art policies: Formalism bad, Socialist Realism good. Eisler's brother Gerhart summoned to appear before the House Un-American Activities Committee. November: the Republicans win a majority in the House. Cold War impending.

1947 FBI file on Brecht reopened in May. Rehearsals begin for Los Angeles production of *Galileo*, with Laughton in the title part and music by Eisler; opens July 31. Brecht's HUAC hearing October 30; a day later he leaves the US for Zurich.

1948 In Zurich renewed collaboration with Caspar Neher. Production of *Antigone* in Chur, with Weigel. Berlau arrives from US. Summer: *Puntila* world première at Zurich Schauspielhaus. Brecht completes his chief theoretical work, the *Short Organum*. Travel plans hampered because he is not allowed to enter US Zone (which includes Augsburg and Munich). Russians block all land access to Berlin. October: the Brechts to Berlin via Prague, to establish contacts and prepare production of *Mother Courage*.

1949 January: success of *Mother Courage* leads to establishment of the Berliner Ensemble. Collapse of Berlin blockade in May followed by establishment of West and East German states. Eisler,

Dessau and Elisabeth Hauptmann arrive from US and join the Ensemble.

1950 Brecht gets Austrian nationality in connection with plan to involve him in Salzburg Festival. Long drawn-out scheme for *Mother Courage* film. Spring: he and Neher direct Lenz's *The Tutor* with the Ensemble. Autumn: he directs *Mother Courage* in Munich; at the end of the year *The Mother* with Weigel, Ernst Busch and the Ensemble.

1951 Selection of *A Hundred Poems* is published in East Berlin. Brecht beats off Stalinist campaign to stop production of Dessau's opera version of *Lucullus*.

1952 Summer: at Buckow, east of Berlin, Brecht starts planning a production of *Coriolanus* and discusses Eisler's project for a *Faust* opera.

1953 Spring: Stalin dies, aged 73. A 'Stanislavsky conference' in the East German Academy, to promote Socialist Realism in the theatre, is followed by meetings to discredit Eisler's libretto for the *Faust* opera. June: quickly suppressed rising against the East German government in Berlin and elsewhere. Brecht at Buckow notes that 'the whole of existence has been alienated' for him by this. Khrushchev becomes Stalin's successor.

1954 January: Brecht becomes an adviser to the new East German Ministry of Culture. March: the Ensemble at last gets its own theatre on the Schiffbauerdamm. July: its production of *Mother Courage* staged in Paris. December: Brecht awarded a Stalin Peace Prize by the USSR.

1955 August: shooting at last begins on *Mother Courage* film, but is broken off after ten days and the project abandoned. Brecht in poor health.

1956 Khrushchev denounces Stalin's dictatorial methods and abuses of power to the Twentieth Party Congress in Moscow. A copy of his speech reaches Brecht. May: Brecht in the Charité hospital to shake off influenza. August 14: he dies in the Charité of a heart infarct.

1957 *The Resistible Rise of Arturo Ui*, *The Visions of Simone Machard* and *Schweyk in the Second World War* produced for the first time in Stuttgart, Frankfurt and Warsaw respectively.

Lindbergh's Flight

A radio 'Lehrstück' for boys and girls

Collaborators: ELISABETH HAUPTMANN, KURT WEILL

Translator: JOHN WILLETT

Characters:

CHARLES LINDBERGH [THE LINDBERGHS]
THE RADIO, *also representing*: America, New York City, the Ship, the Fogbank, the Snowstorm, Sleep, Europe, the Fishermen, Sounds (Water, Engine, a Vast Crowd)

Most of this text was set to music by the author's collaborator Kurt Weill. Due to pressure of time, some numbers had been composed by Hindemith, then re-set by Weill. Extra material added by Brecht later to form part of the work, but not set to music, is distinguished by use of a different typeface. Scenes are numbered as in the German published text. Where the musical version differed, its scene numbers are added in round brackets. Square brackets indicate cuts. For subsequent changes, including alterations of the title, see Editorial Notes.

1

CHALLENGE TO EVERYBODY

RADIO:

The world community is asking: please rehearse
The ocean flight of Captain Lindbergh
By all of you, together
Singing the music
And reading off the text.

Look, here is your machine.
Get in!
All of Europe is waiting for you
You'll make your name.

LINDBERGHS:

I am getting into my machine.

2

THE AMERICAN PRESS PRAISES LINDBERGHS' CAREFREE ATTITUDE

AMERICA (RADIO):

Is it true what they say, that all you are taking
Is your straw hat; so you
Embarked like a fool? With that
Old crate you mean to
Fly the Atlantic?
With no companion to navigate you
With no compass and without water?

3 (2)

INTRODUCING THE AIRMAN CHARLES LINDBERGH

LINDBERGH:

My name is Charles Lindbergh
My age is no more than twenty-five

Grandfather came from Sweden
Myself I am American.
As for my machine, I selected it myself.
It flies at rather more than 130 miles per hour
We named it *Spirit of St Louis*
The Ryan Aircraft Works down in San Diego
Took no more than sixty days to build it.
And sixty more days have I spent with maps and sea-charts
As I drew up my flight plan.
I'm flying alone.
And sooner than a second man I'll take more gas.
My aircraft hasn't got any radio.
I'm flying with a first-rate compass.
These past three days I have been waiting on the weather
But I'm afraid that the weather forecasts
Are not good and won't get better:
Fog in all coastal districts and gales over the sea.
I cannot afford to go on waiting.
Now I'm getting in.
I'll take the risk.

[3

DEPARTURE OF THE AIRMAN CHARLES LINDBERGH FROM NEW YORK ON HIS FLIGHT TO EUROPE]

LINDBERGH:

I shall have with me
First a couple of torches
And 1 coil of rope
Then 1 roll of sticking plaster
And 1 knife
And 4 red flares too
Protected by rubber tubing
And 1 watertight container with matches in
1 big can containing water, likewise a service water bottle
And also 5 emergency rations issued to me from US Army stores, each of them sufficient for one day, or longer in a crisis.

I shall have with me
1 large sailor's needle and 1 chopper
And 1 hacksaw and
1 pneumatic raft.
I'm flying now.
It's now twenty years since Blériot
Became a hero, for
Having flown a wretched thirty kilometres
Across the English Channel.
I shall be flying
Three thousand.

4

THE CITY OF NEW YORK INTERROGATES THE SHIPS

NEW YORK CITY (RADIO):
New York City calling:
This morning at eight o'clock
One of our people took off here, heading
Over the ocean
He was flying off to Europe.
For seven hours now he's been on his way
We've had no report from him
So we are asking
All shipping, would they tell us
If he's been seen?

LINDBERGHS:
If I do not get there
I shall never be seen again.

SHIP'S RADIO (*Chorus*):
Calling New York: *Empress of Scotland*
49 degrees 24 minutes latitude north by 34 degrees 78 minutes longitude west:
A short while ago we could hear
Through the cloudbank the sound
Of an engine
Some distance above us.

Due to the fog there, we were
Not able to locate it
But we think it might be
That this was your airman
In his aeroplane
Spirit of St Louis.

LINDBERGHS:

Nowhere a ship, and
Now here comes the fog.

5

DURING MOST OF HIS FLIGHT THE FLIER HAD TO BATTLE WITH FOG

FOGBANK (RADIO):

I am the fogbank and I am feared by
All who would conquer the ocean.
Here comes the first man of our second millennium
Who wants to fly around in the air.
What kind of man are you?
But we are going to make sure that
No one in future flies round in our air here!
I am the fogbank!
You – turn back!

LINDBERGH:

[Like the hell I will!]
What you have just said
Calls for reflection.
If you get denser, maybe I really shall
Turn back.
If there is no prospect
I'll give up the struggle.
If it's do or die
You can count me out of that.
As it is
I shan't turn back yet.

FOGBANK (RADIO):

So far you feel tall, but
You don't know you're dealing with me.
So far you've seen there were waves under you
And known
Your right hand from your left. But
Just you wait another day and one more night
Till you see no waves and you can see no sky
Nor your controls, nor
Your first-class compass.
Best grow older, and you will
Realise who I am:
I am the fogbank.

LINDBERGH:

[I'm not frightened of you.]
Seven men built my machine in San Diego
Often twenty-four hours without a break
Using a few metres of steel tubing.
What they have made must do for me
They have done their work, I
Carry on with mine, I am not alone, there are
Eight of us flying here.

FOGBANK (RADIO):

At present you are barely twenty-five.
What about when you are
Twenty-five plus another night, after just one more day
You'll be more frightened.
For tomorrow and during a thousand years, there will still be this ocean
Air and fogbanks
But you'll not be
There to see it.

LINDBERGH:

So far it's been day. But
The night will fall soon.

FOGBANK (RADIO):

For ten hours I have been fighting a man who
Has been flying round the air. That's something
Has not been seen for these past thousand years. I found

No way of bringing him down
It's up to you now, snowstorm!

LINDBERGHS:

Here you come
Snowstorm!

6

THAT NIGHT THERE CAME A SNOWSTORM

SNOWSTORM (RADIO):

For this past hour I've had in me a man
A man who has an aeroplane!
Sometimes he flew over me
Sometimes so close to the water!
For the past hour I've buffeted him
Down to the water and up to the heavens
Nowhere can he keep steady, but he
Will not be brought down.
First falling upwards
Then climbing downwards.
He is weaker than a tree by the seashore
Flimsy as a leaf off its branch, but he
Will not be brought down.
It's hours since this wretched man glimpsed the moon
Or could see his own hand
But he will not be brought down.
I have been loading his plane with icicles
So the weight may topple it downwards
But the ice breaks off the plane and
He'll not be brought down.

(6b)

LINDBERGH:

I can't go on
I'm heading for the water:
Who would imagine

There were icicles up here!
Three thousand metres at one point my height was, and
Three metres down, skimming the water.
Everywhere the storm rages on
With everywhere ice and fogbanks.
Why was I so foolish as to start this?
Now I'm afraid of dying.
Now I'm being brought down.
Four days before me two other pilots
Started out flying the ocean like me
And since then the water has drowned them
And I too shall be drowned.

7

SLEEP

SLEEP (RADIO):
Sleep, Charlie
The dreadful night
Now is over. The storm's
Blown out. Go to sleep, Charlie
The wind will bear you.

LINDBERGH:
[I must not sleep.
I'm not exhausted.]
The wind is no help to me
The water and the air are against me, and I
Am their enemy.

SLEEP (RADIO):
Only for a minute, just let your head
Droop towards the joystick. Let your eyes close for one brief instant
You've a wakeful hand.

LINDBERGH:
[I must not sleep.
I'm not exhausted.]
Often twenty-four hours without a break

My comrades in San Diego
Built this machine. Let me
Be no worse than them. I
Must not sleep.

SLEEP (RADIO):

So far to go. Best have a rest
Think of the meadows of Missouri
The river, the house
Which is your homestead.

LINDBERGH:

I'm not exhausted.

[8

IDEOLOGY

LINDBERGHS:

1

Many say time is ancient
But I always knew this was a new time.
I tell you it is no accident
That for twenty years buildings have shot up like bronze mountains
People move each year expectantly to the cities.
And on the laughing continents
The word gets round that the great and awful ocean
Is a tiny puddle.
Today I am making the first flight across the Atlantic
But I am convinced: by tomorrow
You will be laughing at my flight.

2

Yet it is a battle against what is backward
And a strenuous effort to improve the planet
Like dialectical economics
Which will change the world from the bottom up.
So now
Let us battle with nature
Till we ourselves have become natural.
We and our technology are not natural as yet

We and our technology
Are backward.
The steamship competed with the sailing ship
Which had left the rowing boat far behind.
I
Am competing with the steamship
In the struggle against what is backward.
My airplane, weak and tremulous
My equipment with all its defects
Are better than their precursors, but
In flying, I
Struggle with my airplane and
With what is backward.

3
So I struggle with nature and
With myself.
Whatever I may be and whatever idiocies I believe
When I fly I am
A true atheist.

During ten thousand years, unimpeded
Where the waters grew dark in the sky
Between light and twilight, there arose
God. And in the same way
Over the mountain tops, whence the ice came
Did ignorant people, incorrigible
Glimpse God, and in the same way
In the deserts he arrived in a sandstorm and
In the cities he was produced by the disorder
Of the different classes, for there are two kinds of men, thanks to
Exploitation and ignorance; but
The revolution abolishes him. Yet
Build roads through the mountains and he disappears.
Rivers drive him out of the desert. The light
Shows up voids and
Scares him away at once.

Therefore take part
In the battle against what is backward

In the abolition of the other world and
The scaring away of any kind of god, where-
Ever he turns up.

Under more powerful microscopes
He collapses.
Improved equipment
Is driving him from the skies.
The clearing-up of our cities
The removal of poverty are
Causing him to vanish and
Chasing him back to the first millennium.

4
Thus there may still remain
In our improved cities confusion
Which comes from lack of knowledge and resembles God.
But the machines and the workers
Will battle against it, and you too
Take part in
The battle against what is backward.]

[9

WATER

LINDBERGHS:
Once more
The water's getting closer.
NOISE OF WATER (RADIO)
LINDBERGHS:
I must
Gain height! This wind
Thrusts me down.
NOISE OF WATER (RADIO)
LINDBERGHS:
That's better now
But what's this? The joystick
Won't respond. Something
Is not right. What's that

Noise in the engine? Now
We're losing height again.
Stop!

NOISE OF WATER (RADIO)

LINDBERGHS:

My God! That
Nearly did for us!]

10 (8)

THROUGHOUT HIS FLIGHT THE ENTIRE AMERICAN PRESS KEPT SPEAKING OF LINDBERGH'S LUCK

AMERICA (RADIO):

All America thinks
Captain Lindbergh's flight
Across the ocean must succeed.
Despite the bad weather forecasts and
The very faulty state of his vulnerable aircraft
Everybody in the States believes
He's going to get there.
'Never', declares one paper, 'has a man
From our country seemed
Such an embodiment of our good fortune.'
When the fortunate crosses the ocean
Even the tempests hold their peace.
If the tempests cannot restrain themselves
The plane will keep going.
If the plane can't keep going, then
The man will win through.
And suppose that he loses
Then good fortune will win.
That's the reason why we believe
That the fortunate get there.

11 (9)

THE THOUGHTS OF THE FORTUNATE

LINDBERGH *speaking quickly and softly, without expression*:
Two continents, two continents
Are expecting me! I
Must get there.
Whom are they expecting?
Even the man they are not expecting
Must get there!
Courage is nothing, but
Getting there is everything.
He who flies out over the sea
And is drowned, is a damned fool, for
One does drown at sea.
Therefore I must get there.
Winds are thrusting me down and
Fog stops me steering, but
I've got to get there.
Yes, my airplane
Is weak, and weak my head, but
Over there they are expecting me, saying
He'll get here, and so
I must get there.

12 (10)

SO HE FLIES, WROTE THE FRENCH PRESS, WITH STORMS ABOVE HIM, SEA ALL AROUND HIM AND BENEATH HIM THE SHADE OF NUNGESSER*

EUROPE (RADIO):
Heading for our continent
Over the past twenty-four hours
Flies a man.
When he gets here

*See Introduction, page xii.

We shall see a speck in the heavens
Start to grow larger
Look like an aircraft
Execute its descent
And out of it will step down on the grass a man.
We're sure to recognise him
From the picture they put in the magazines beforehand.
But we're afraid he won't
Get here. The storms
Will drown him in the salt water
His engine will go dead on him
And he will never find his destination.
That's why we all believe
That we shall not see him.

13 (11)

LINDBERGH'S DIALOGUE WITH HIS ENGINE

ENGINE (RADIO) *running.*
LINDBERGH:
Now it's not all that far. The time
Has come to pull ourselves together
We two.
ENGINE (RADIO) *running.*
LINDBERGH:
Have you got enough oil?
Will the gasoline see us through?
What's your temperature?
How do you feel?
ENGINE (RADIO) *running.*
LINDBERGH:
Ice is no problem now.
If you were worried by the fog, that's my affair.
Get on with your business
Keep ticking over.

ENGINE (RADIO) *running.*

LINDBERGH:

Let me remind you, we two were airborne even longer
Back home there in St Louis.
It is not all that far now. First there's
Ireland, then comes Paris.
Are we going to make it?
We two?

ENGINE (RADIO) *running.*

14 (12)

AT LAST, NEARING SCOTLAND, LINDBERGH SIGHTS FISHING-BOATS

LINDBERGH *speaks*:

Those are fishing-boats
They'll know
Where the island is.
Hey, where
Is England?

FISHERMEN (RADIO):

I heard someone shout.
Who would be shouting?
Something's humming
In the air!
What can be humming?

LINDBERGH *speaks*:

Hey, where
Is England?

FISHERMEN (RADIO):

Look, there's
Something up there flying!
That is an airplane!
But how can there be a plane?
A device composed of canvas
Tied to iron, how can that
Fly over water?

Even a fool
Wouldn't dare go up in it
He would fall down and
Drown in the water.
Just the wind is
Sure to write it off. And where's the man
Could stand so long a spell at its controls?

LINDBERGH *speaks*:
Hey, where
Is England?

FISHERMEN (RADIO):
But take a look at least!
What good is looking
When we know it can't happen?
Now it's flown past.
I agree that it
Can't happen.
But all the same, it did.

15 (13)

ON THE AIRFIELD AT LE BOURGET NEAR PARIS, AT 10 P.M. ON THE EVENING OF 21 MAY 1927, A VAST CROWD IS AWAITING THE AMERICAN AIRMAN

EUROPE (RADIO):
He's coming!
In the heavens
There's a speck
Getting bigger. It is
An airplane.
Now it's going to land.
Out of it on the grass steps a man
And we
Recognise him: it is
Lindbergh.
The storm had no power to drown him
Nor the water

His engine kept on turning, and he
Has found his destination in us.
He really has got here.
He has found his destination in us.

16 (14)

ARRIVAL OF THE AIRMAN CHARLES LINDBERGH AT LE BOURGET AIRFIELD OUTSIDE PARIS

Orchestra only.

LINDBERGH *speaks*:
I am Lindbergh. Please carry me
To a dark shed, so that
No one sees my
Natural weakness.
But tell my comrades in the Ryan works at San Diego
That their work was good
Our engine held out
Their work has no flaws.

17 (15)

REPORT ON THE UNATTAINABLE

LINDBERGH, TWO SOLOISTS *and* CHORUS (RADIO):
At that time, when humanity
Began to know itself
We fashioned carriages
Of iron, wood and glass
And in these we went flying.
And that with a velocity that no hurricane
Has been known to ever exceed.
And such was our motor
Strong as a hundred horses, though
Smaller than a single one.
Ages long all things fell in a downward direction
Except for the birds themselves.

On the oldest of tablets
No one has come on drawings
Of human beings flying through the air.
Only we, we have found the secret.
Near the end of the third millennium, as we reckon time
Our artless invention took wing
Pointing out the possible
While not letting us forget:
The unattainable.
To this our report is dedicated.

The Baden-Baden Lesson on Consent

Collaborators: SLATAN DUDOW, ELISABETH HAUPTMANN

Translator: GEOFFREY SKELTON

Characters:

THE AIRMEN [THE CRASHED AIRMAN *and* THE THREE MECHANICS]
THE LEADER OF THE CHORUS
SPEAKER
THREE CLOWNS
CHORUS
THE CROWD

Seven scenes or numbers from this work were set to music by Paul Hindemith for performance at the Baden-Baden music festival in 1929 under the title 'Lehrstück'. As in the parallel case of *Lindbergh's Flight*, the additional material introduced later by Brecht, but not set to music, is distinguished by use of a different typeface. Scene numbering is that of the final eleven-scene script; figures in brackets are those of Hindemith's score, where the order of scenes from 3 on is not the same as ours. Apart from scenes 7 (Instruction) and 8 (Examination) all other scenes after scene 3 were new, so that there is no music to them. And Brecht shifted some of the others, and made the clown scene become part of scene 3. Throughout, the Airman now became plural, a collective figure performed by four singers: three mechanics and one pilot.

On a platform corresponding in size to the number of participants the Chorus is positioned at the back. The orchestra is on the left. In the left foreground there is a table at which the conductor of the singers and instrumentalists, the Leader of the Chorus songs and the Speaker sit. The singers of the Airmen's (or Mechanics') parts sit at a desk in the right foreground. [The offstage orchestra should be as far away in the hall (gallery) as is possible.] To clarify the scene the wreckage of a plane can be placed on or beside the platform.

I (I)

THE STORY OF FLIGHT

[CHORUS] THE FOUR AIRMEN *report*:
At that time, when humanity
Began to know itself
We fashioned carriages
Of iron, wood and glass
And in these we went flying.
And that with a velocity that no hurricane
Has been known to ever exceed.
And such was our motor:
Strong as a hundred horses, though
Smaller than a single one.
Ages long all things fell in a downward direction
Except for the birds themselves.
On the oldest of tablets
No one has come on drawings
Of human beings flying through the air.
Only we, we have found the secret.
Near the end of the second millennium, as we reckon time
Our artless invention took wing
Pointing out the possible
Without letting us forget:
[The unattainable.]
The yet-to-be-attained.

2 (1 continued)

THE CRASH

THE LEADER OF THE CHORUS *addresses the Crashed Airman*:
Fly no longer.
Now no more do you have need of swiftness.
The lowest piece of earth
Is now high
Enough for you.
Lie there still and be
Content.
Not high above our heads
Not far from us
And no more in motion
But immobile
Tell us who you are.
THE CRASHED AIRMAN *answer[s]*:
I was sharing in the researches of my comrades.
As our airplanes grew ever better
We flew yet higher and higher
The oceans were soon mastered
And even the mountains humbled.
I had been seized with the fever
Of building cities, and of oil.
And all my thoughts were of machines and the
Attainment of ever greater speed.
I forgot in my exertions
My own name and identity
And in the urgency of my searching
Forgot the final goal I sought.
But I beg you
To come to me and
To give me water
And place a pillow under my head
And to assist me, for
I do not wish to die.
THE CHORUS *turns to the Crowd*:
Hearken: a man calls you

To assist him.
In the heavens
He went flying, and
Now to earth has fallen
And will not perish.
So he's calling to you
To assist him.
And here
We have a beaker of water and
A pillow.
Now you must tell us
Whether we should assist him.

[VOICES, *repeated by the Crowd*:
Why should we now assist him?
He has not given us assistance.]

THE CROWD *answers the Chorus*:
Yes.

CHORUS *to the Crowd*:
Have they assisted you?

CROWD:
No.

THE SPEAKER *turns to the Crowd and says*:
Across the body of the dying man the question is considered: whether men help each other.

3 (2)

INQUIRY: DO MEN HELP EACH OTHER?

First Inquiry

THE LEADER OF THE CHORUS *comes forward*:
One of our kind went sailing across the sea, and
There he discovered an unknown continent.
But many came after
And built there in that place mighty cities, with
Boundless effort and cunning.

CHORUS:
The price of bread did not get cheaper.

[CROWD:

Tear up the pillow!]

THE LEADER OF THE CHORUS:

One of our kind once made an engine in which the
Pressure of steam made a wheel turn, and that was
The mother of many more engines
Yet many men laboured a lifetime to
Make them perfect.

CHORUS:

The price of bread did not get cheaper.

[CROWD:

Empty the water out!]

THE LEADER OF THE CHORUS:

Many of us have been drawn to meditate
On the passage of the earth through the solar system
And on a man's inner feelings and the laws
Governing all people, and the properties of air
And the fish in the ocean.
Very many
Great things they have discovered.

CHORUS:

The price of bread did not get cheaper.
Rather
Did poverty and need increase within our cities
And long years have passed since
Anyone knew what a man is.
For instance, while you flew above
Creatures like you crawled on earth
Nothing like men.

[CROWD:

Tear up the pillow, thrown the water away!

THE LEADER OF THE CHORUS:

And so he is not to be assisted?

CHORUS:

Let us tear up the pillow
And empty the water out.
The Speaker tears up the pillow and empties the water out.]

THE LEADER OF THE CHORUS *turns to the Crowd*:

So does one man help another?

CROWD: No.

Second Inquiry

THE LEADER OF THE CHORUS *turns to the Crowd*:
Look on our pictures and then say
One man helps another!
Twenty photographs showing how human beings slaughter one another in our times are shown.

THE CROWD *shouts*:
No man helps another.

Third Inquiry (6)

THE LEADER OF THE CHORUS *turns to the Crowd*:
Watch now our clowns' scene, in which
Some men help another man.

Three Clowns mount the platform. One of them, called Mr Smith, is a giant. They speak very loudly.

CLOWN 1: Lovely evening today, Mr Smith.

CLOWN 2: What do you say to the evening, Mr Smith?

SMITH: I don't find it at all lovely.

CLOWN 1: Wouldn't you like to sit down, Mr Smith?

CLOWN 2: Here is a chair, Mr Smith. Why don't you speak to us any more?

CLOWN 1: Can't you see? Mr Smith wants to gaze at the moon.

CLOWN 2: Tell me, why are you always crawling up Mr Smith's arse? You're inconveniencing Mr Smith.

CLOWN 1: Because Mr Smith is so strong; that's why I crawl up his arse.

CLOWN 2: Me too.

CLOWN 1: Please, Mr Smith, come and sit with us.

SMITH: I'm not feeling well today.

CLOWN 1: Then we must try and cheer you up, Mr Smith.
The scene continues without music.

SMITH: I don't think I can be cheered up any more. *Pause.* How does my complexion look?

CLOWN 1: Rosy, Mr Smith, nice and rosy.

SMITH: Really? And I thought I was looking rather pale.

CLOWN 1: How extraordinary! You say you think you are looking rather pale. Now I come to look at you, I must say I think you do look a little pale.

CLOWN 2: In that case you should take a seat, Mr Smith, looking as you do.

SMITH: I don't feel like sitting today.

CLOWN 1: No, no – no sitting. Whatever you do, don't sit. Better remain standing.

SMITH: Why do you think I should remain standing?

CLOWN 1 *to Clown 2*: He mustn't sit down today, otherwise he'll never be able to get up again.

SMITH: Oh, God!

CLOWN 1: See? He knows it himself. That's why Mr Smith prefers to remain standing.

SMITH: Do you know, I rather think I've got a pain in my left foot.

CLOWN 1: Bad?

SMITH *suffering*: What?

CLOWN 1: Is it hurting much?

SMITH: Yes, it's hurting a good deal.

CLOWN 2: That's what comes of standing.

SMITH: Shall I sit down, then?

CLOWN 1: No, no, you mustn't. We must avoid that at all costs.

CLOWN 2: When your left foot starts hurting you, there's only one way: off with the left foot.

CLOWN 1: And the sooner, the better.

SMITH: Well, if you think –

CLOWN 2: No doubt about it.

They saw off his left foot. Music plays.

SMITH: A stick, please.

They give him a stick.

CLOWN 1: There. Can you stand better now, Mr Smith?

SMITH: Yes, on the left side. But you must give me back my foot. I wouldn't like to lose it.

CLOWN 1: As you please – if you don't trust us.

CLOWN 2: We can go away, if you like.

SMITH: No, no. You'll have to stay now. I can't walk on my own.

CLOWN 1: Here's your foot.

Smith puts it under his arm.

SMITH: Now I've lost my stick.

CLOWN 2: But you've got your foot back.

Both laugh loudly.

SMITH: Now I really can't go on standing. The other leg is beginning to hurt.

CLOWN 1: What did you expect?

SMITH: I don't want to put you to more inconvenience than is absolutely necessary, but without that stick I find things rather difficult.

CLOWN 2: By the time we pick up the stick, we can just as well saw the other leg off, if it's hurting you so much.

SMITH: Yes, maybe that would be better.

Music plays. They saw off his other leg. Smith falls down.

SMITH: Now I'll never be able to stand again.

CLOWN 1: That's terrible, and just when we didn't want you to sit at any price.

SMITH: What?!

CLOWN 2: You can't stand up any more, Mr Smith.

SMITH: Don't say that. I can't bear it.

CLOWN 2: Say what?

SMITH: That.

CLOWN 2: That you can't stand up any more?

SMITH: Can't you keep your mouth shut?

CLOWN 2: No, Mr Smith, but what I can do is unscrew your left ear. Then you won't be able to hear me saying that you can't stand up any more.

SMITH: Yes, maybe that would be better.

They unscrew his left ear. Music.

SMITH *to Clown 1*: Now I can't hear you any more. *Clown 2 goes over to the other side.* My ear, please. *Growing angry*: And while you are about it, the other leg too. This is no way to treat a sick man. I demand the immediate return of all missing parts to their rightful owner, which is myself. *They put the other leg under his arm and lay the ear in his lap.* If you think you can play tricks with me, then you are utterly mistaken. – What's the matter with my arm?

CLOWN 2: It's because of all that useless junk you're carrying around with you.

SMITH *softly*: Yes, that'll be it. Couldn't you take it off me?

CLOWN 2: Yes, or we could take off the arm. That would certainly be better.

SMITH: Yes, please, if you think –

CLOWN 2: Of course.

They saw off his left arm. Music.

SMITH: Thank you. It's kind of you to take so much trouble over me.

CLOWN 1: There, Mr Smith, now you've got everything that belongs to you. Nobody will be able to rob you now.

They place all the amputated limbs in his lap. Smith examines them.

SMITH: Funny, my head's so full of unpleasant thoughts. *To Clown 1*: Say something nice, will you?

CLOWN 1: With pleasure, Mr Smith. Would you like to hear a story? There were these two men coming out of a pub, arguing furiously. Then they began to pelt each other with bits of horse-shit. One of them got a lump right in the mouth. So he says: 'Right, that stays there now till the police arrive.'

Clown 2 laughs. Smith does not laugh.

SMITH: That's not a nice story. Can't you tell me something nice? I told you, my head's full of unpleasant thoughts.

CLOWN 1: No, Mr Smith, I'm sorry, but apart from that story there is really nothing I could think of telling you.

CLOWN 2: But we could of course saw off the top of your head, to let those stupid thoughts out.

SMITH: Yes, please, maybe that will help.

They saw off the upper part of his head. Music.

CLOWN 1: How does that feel, Mr Smith? Is that easier?

SMITH: Yes, much easier. Now I feel much, much easier. Only – my head feels rather cold.

CLOWN 2: Then why not put on your hat? *Bawling*: Hat on!

SMITH: But I can't reach.

CLOWN 1: Would you like your stick?

SMITH: Yes, please. *Fishing for his cap*: Now I've dropped the stick. I can't reach my hat. And I'm feeling so terribly cold.

CLOWN 2: Maybe if we were to screw your head right off?

SMITH: Well, I don't know.

CLOWN 1: Oh, come on.

SMITH: No, really – I just don't know anything any more.

CLOWN 2: All the more reason, then.

They screw off his head. Music. Smith falls over backwards.

SMITH: Stop! Someone, put a hand on my brow.
CLOWN 1: Where?
SMITH: Someone, hold my hand.
CLOWN 1: Which one?
CLOWN 2: Are you feeling easier now, Mr Smith?
SMITH: No, I'm not. There's a stone sticking into my back.
CLOWN 2: Now really, Mr Smith, you can't have everything.
Both laugh loudly.
(End of the Clown Number.)

THE CROWD *shouts*:
No man helps another.
THE LEADER OF THE CHORUS:
Shall we tear up the pillow?
CROWD:
Yes.
THE LEADER OF THE CHORUS:
Shall we empty the water out?
CROWD:
Yes.

4

HELP REFUSED

CHORUS:
So they are not to be helped.
We tear up the pillow, we
Empty the water out.
The Speaker now tears up the pillow and empties the water out.
THE CROWD *reads out*:
Here for sure you have seen
Help of some kind
Given here and there within conditions
As yet indispensable, of
Force.
And still we advise you to meet cruel
Reality
Even more cruelly and

To lay aside the claim
Together with the conditions
That give rise to the claim. Thus
Not to count on help:
To refuse help requires force
To obtain help requires force also.
As long as force reigns help can be refused
When force no longer reigns, there is no need of help.
So you should not demand help, but abolish force.
Help and force form a single whole
And this whole must be altered.

5

CONSULTATION

THE CRASHED AIRMAN:
Comrades, we
Are about to die.
THE THREE CRASHED MECHANICS:
We know we are about to die, but
Do you know it?
Listen, then:
You will die for certain.
Your life will be stripped from you
Your achievement wiped out
You die alone
No one else is concerned
You die finally
And so must we too.

6

CONTEMPLATION OF THE DEAD

THE SPEAKER:
Contemplate the dead!
Ten photographs of dead bodies are shown. The Speaker then

says: 'Second contemplation of the dead', *and the photographs are shown again.*

After the contemplation of the dead, THE CRASHED AIRMEN *begin shouting:*

We cannot die!

[(4)

LOOK ON DEATH

From the centre of the Chorus a dancer comes slowly forward and performs a dance of death. As the music ends, the Airman cries out:

AIRMAN:

I cannot die!

CHORUS *to the Airman:*]

7 (5)

INSTRUCTION

THE CHORUS *turns to the Crashed Airmen:*

We have no help to give you.
Just a book, just a single thought, just a word of guidance
Can we give you on your way.
Die
But still seeking, seeking
And in seeking learn truth.

AIRMAN:

I have but little time:
Not enough for much learning.

CHORUS:

Though your time is short
Still it is enough
For the way of truth is easy.

The Speaker steps forward from the Chorus, a book in his hand. He goes to the Crashed Airmen, sits down and reads from the commentaries.

THE SPEAKER *reading*:

1. He who takes something away will keep hold of something. And he from whom something has been taken will also keep hold of it. And he who keeps hold of something will have it taken away.

Whoever of us shall die, what does he lay aside? Surely he does not lay simply his table or his bed aside. He of us who dies knows this: I lay aside all that exists. I give away more than I have. Whoever dies lays aside the street which he knows, but also that which he does not know; the treasures that he has and also those that he does not have; poverty itself; his own hand.

Yet how shall he who is not practised lift up a stone? How shall he lift up a large stone? How shall he who has not learned to lay aside, lay aside his table or – even more – lay aside everything that he has and everything that he does not have? The street which he knows, and also that which he does not know; the treasures that he has and also those that he does not have; poverty itself; his own hand?

[AIRMAN *sings*:

So I learn to see:
What I have done was wrong.
Now I learn to see that a man
Must lie prostrate and not strive
For heights, nor depths, nor yet velocity.

THE SPEAKER *reading*:]

2. When the thinking man was overtaken by a great storm, he was seated in a large carriage, taking up much room. The first thing that he did was to descend from his carriage. The second was to take off his cloak. The third thing was that he laid himself down on the ground. Thus he conquered the storm in his smallest dimension.

AIRMAN *addresses the Speaker*:

Did he thus outlast the storm?

[CHORUS *and* CROWD] THE SPEAKER:

In his smallest dimension he outlasted the storm.

THE CRASHED AIRMEN:

In his smallest dimension he outlasted the storm.

THE SPEAKER *continues*:

3. Encouraging a fellow-being to face up to his death, the thinking man bade him lay his goods aside. When he had laid them all aside, there remained to him only his life. Lay yet more aside, said the thinking man.

[CHORUS *and* CROWD:

Lay yet more aside.

THE SPEAKER *continues*:]

4. When the thinking man conquered the storm, he did so because he recognised the storm and agreed to it. Thus, if you wish to conquer death, you may conquer it by recognising death and agreeing to it. But let whoever has the wish to agree hold on to his poverty. Let him not cling to objects. For objects can be taken away, and then there is no agreement. Similarly, let him not cling to life. For life can be taken away, and then there is no agreement. Nor should he cling to his thoughts. For thoughts too can be taken away, and there too there is then no agreement.

8 (7)

EXAMINATION

The Chorus examines the Airmen in the presence of the Crowd.

i

CHORUS:

How high then were you flying?

[AIRMAN] THE THREE MECHANICS:

Unimaginably high was I flying.

CHORUS:

How high then were you flying?

[AIRMAN] THE THREE MECHANICS:

Over twelve thousand feet was I flying.

CHORUS:

How high then were you flying?

[AIRMAN] THE THREE MECHANICS:

Fairly high was I flying.

CHORUS:

How high then were you flying?

[AIRMAN] THE THREE MECHANICS:

I raised myself but little over the earth's surface.

[CROWD] THE LEADER OF THE CHORUS *turns to the Crowd*:

He raised himself but little above the earth's surface.

THE CRASHED AIRMAN:

I flew unimaginably high.

CHORUS:

And he flew unimaginably high.

ii

CHORUS:

Was your deed acclaimed?

[AIRMAN] THE THREE MECHANICS:

No, it was not enough acclaimed.

CHORUS:

Was your deed acclaimed?

[AIRMAN] THE THREE MECHANICS:

It was acclaimed.

CHORUS:

Was your deed acclaimed?

[AIRMAN] THE THREE MECHANICS:

It was enough acclaimed.

CHORUS:

Was your deed acclaimed?

[AIRMAN] THE THREE MECHANICS:

I for my deed was vastly acclaimed.

[CROWD] THE LEADER OF THE CHORUS *to the Crowd*:

For his deed he was vastly acclaimed.

THE CRASHED AIRMAN:

I was not enough acclaimed.

CHORUS:

And he was not enough acclaimed.

iii

CHORUS:

Who are you?

[AIRMAN] THE THREE MECHANICS:

We are those who have [I am he who has] flown across the ocean.

CHORUS:

Who are you?

[AIRMAN] THE THREE MECHANICS:

We are ones [I am the one] like yourselves.

CHORUS:

Who are you?

[AIRMAN] THE THREE MECHANICS:

I am no one.

THE LEADER OF THE CHORUS *to the Crowd*:

They are no one.

THE CRASHED AIRMAN:

I am Charles Nungesser.

CHORUS:

And he is Charles Nungesser.

iv

CHORUS:

Who waits for you now?

[AIRMAN] THE THREE MECHANICS:

Many over the sea wait for us [me] now.

CHORUS:

Who waits for you now?

[AIRMAN] THE THREE MECHANICS:

Our fathers [My father] and our mothers [my mother] are awaiting us [me] now.

CHORUS:

Who waits for you now?

[AIRMAN] THE THREE MECHANICS:

No one is waiting now.

THE LEADER OF THE CHORUS *to the Crowd*:

[He is no one, and] no one waits for him now.

v

CHORUS:

Who therefore dies when you die?

[AIRMAN] THE THREE MECHANICS:

We [He] whose deed was acclaimed too much.

CHORUS:

Who therefore dies when you die?

[AIRMAN] THE THREE MECHANICS:

We [He] who raised ourselves [himself] but little from the ground.

CHORUS:

Who therefore dies when you die?

[AIRMAN] THE THREE MECHANICS:

We [He] whom no one waits for.

CHORUS:

Who therefore dies when you die?

[AIRMAN] THE THREE MECHANICS:

No one.

CHORUS:

Now you [he] have [has] seen it:
No one dies when he dies.

[CROWD:

Now he has seen it:
No one dies when he dies.

CHORUS:

Now is his smallest dimension attained.

CROWD:]

Now is their [his] smallest dimension attained.

THE CRASHED AIRMAN:

But I with my flight
Reached my greatest dimension.
However high I flew, none flew
Higher.
I was not enough acclaimed, I
Cannot be acclaimed enough
I flew for nothing and for nobody.
I flew for flying's sake.
No one awaits me, I
Do not fly towards you, I
Fly away from you, I
Shall never die.

9

FAME AND DISPOSSESSION

CHORUS:

But now
Show what you have achieved.
For only
Achievement is real.
So now lay aside the engine
Wings and undercarriage, everything
With which you flew and
Together made.
Lay it aside.

THE CRASHED AIRMAN:

I will not lay it aside
What is
The aircraft without the airman?

THE LEADER OF THE CHORUS:

Take it!

The aircraft is carried off to the opposite corner of the stage by the Crashed Airman. During the dispossession, the CHORUS *acclaim the Crashed Airmen*:

Rise up, airmen, you have changed the earthly laws.
Ages long all things fell in a downward direction
Except for the birds themselves.
On the oldest of tablets
No one has come on drawings
Of human beings flying through the air.
Only you found the secret.
Near the end of the second millennium, as we reckon time.

THE THREE CRASHED MECHANICS *suddenly point to the Crashed Airman*:

Look, what is that?

THE LEADER *quickly, to the Chorus*:

Begin the 'Completely Unrecognisable'.

CHORUS *groups around the Crashed Airman*:

Completely unrecognisable to us
Has now become the face

Of him who
Needed us as we
Had need of him: for such
Was he.

THE LEADER OF THE CHORUS:

This
Holder of a function
Though but self-assumed
Took from us what he needed, and
Denied us that of which we had need.
Thus his face
Was extinguished with his function:
He had but one.

Four members of the Chorus discuss him over his body.

THE FIRST:

If he was here –

THE SECOND:

He was here.

THE FIRST:

What was he?

THE SECOND:

He was no one.

THE THIRD:

Had he been someone –

THE FOURTH:

He was no one.

THE THIRD:

How did one bring him into sight?

THE FOURTH:

By giving him something to do.

ALL FOUR:

By calling on him he comes into existence.
When one changes him he is there.
Who needs him recognises him.
Who finds him useful enlarges him.

THE SECOND:

And still he is no one.

CHORUS *all together, to the Crowd*:

What lies there functionless

Is no longer human.
Die now, you No-Longer-Man!

THE CRASHED AIRMAN:

I cannot die.

THE THREE MECHANICS:

Man, you have dropped out of the flow.
Man, you were never in the flow.
You are too big, you are too rich
You are too self-contained.
That is why you cannot die.

CHORUS:

But
He who cannot die
Will yet die.
He who cannot swim
Will yet swim.

10 (3)

THE CHORUS SPEAKS TO THE CRASHED AIRMAN

CHORUS:

One of our kind
In his body, face and his thinking
To us all akin
Must now take leave of us, for
He has been branded overnight and
Since this morning has his breath been stinking.
See how his flesh decays, and his face which
Once we knew, is now strange to us.
Come, speak to us now, we await
From the usual place the sound of your voice. Speak!

He speaks not. Not a word from
His mouth. Be not afraid, for you
Must go now. Go at once!
Do not look round, go
Away from us.

II

AGREEMENT

CHORUS *addressing the Three Mechanics*:
You, however, who have shown you agree to the flow of things
Do not sink back into the void.
Do not dissolve like salt in water, but
Dying
Rise to your death
As you worked at your work
By revolutionising a revolution.
So in your dying do not
Observe death's demands
But accept from us the charge
To rebuild our aircraft.
Begin!
So as to fly for us
To the place where we have need of you
And at the necessary time. For
We call on you
To march with us, and with us
To change not only
An earthly law, but
The basic law
Accepting that all must be altered
The world and all mankind
Above all, the disorder
Of human classes because there are two kinds of people
Exploitation and ignorance.

THE THREE MECHANICS:
We agree to the alteration.

CHORUS:
And we request you:
Alter our engine and improve it.
Also increase safety and speed
And in the swifter outset do not forget the goal.

THE THREE MECHANICS:
We improve engines, safety and

Speed.

CHORUS:

Then lay them aside.

THE LEADER OF THE CHORUS:

March on!

CHORUS:

Having improved the world, then
Improve the improved world.
Lay it aside.

THE LEADER OF THE CHORUS:

March on!

CHORUS:

If in improving the world you have fulfilled truth, then
Fulfil this fulfilled truth.
Lay it aside!

THE LEADER OF THE CHORUS:

March on!

CHORUS:

In altering the world, alter yourselves!
Lay yourselves aside!

THE LEADER OF THE CHORUS:

March on!

He Said Yes/He Said No

Opera for schools

(after the Japanese play *Taniko or The Valley-Hurling* by Zenchiku, as translated into English by Arthur Waley)

Collaborators: ELISABETH HAUPTMANN, KURT WEILL

Translator: ARTHUR WALEY *from the Japanese, adapted to Brecht's text by* JOHN WILLETT

Characters:

THE TEACHER
THE BOY
THE MOTHER
THE THREE STUDENTS
THE FULL CHORUS

Note: This version follows the text of Universal-Edition's piano score of 1930 (UE 8206). Additional passages from Brecht's *Versuche* edition of 1931 are indicated and appended as notes numbered 1 to 14; we know that two of them were set by Weill, but there is no trace of music for the others. Other changes from Waley are however included and form part of the work. The ten episodes correspond to the musical 'numbers' in the score.

He Said Yes

ACT ONE

1

THE FULL CHORUS:

Nothing is more important to learn than agreement.
Many can say yes; at the same time there is no agreement.
Many are not even asked, and many
May be agreeing to error. Therefore:
Nothing is more important to learn than agreement.

2

The Teacher in Space 1, the Mother and the Boy in Space 2.

THE TEACHER: I am a teacher. My school is at a temple in the town. And there I have a pupil who has lost his father; he has only got his mother to care for him. I am on my way to see them so I may say farewell to them, for I shall very soon be starting to make a journey to the mountains.[1] *He knocks at the door.* May I please come in?

THE BOY: Who is there? It's the Master who's come, the Master who has come out to see us!

THE TEACHER: Why has it been so long since you came to my classes at the temple?

THE BOY: I have not been able to since my mother fell ill.

THE TEACHER: I had no idea. Kindly tell her at once I am out here.

THE BOY *calls to Space 2*: Mother, the Master is here.

THE MOTHER *from Space 2*: Ask if he would kindly come in.

THE BOY: Kindly step through this door.

3

The Boy and the Teacher both enter Space 2.

THE TEACHER: It's a long time since I last saw you. Your son says you have caught the illness. Tell me now, are you better?

THE MOTHER: There's no need for you to worry because of my illness. It is a thing of no importance.[2]

THE TEACHER: I am glad that you say so.[3] I have come here so I may say goodbye to you, because I shall be leaving shortly to make an expedition to the mountains.[4] There is a town beyond the mountains with some outstanding teachers.

THE MOTHER: Oh, a scientific[5] mountain-climbing! Yes, indeed; they tell me that many very famous doctors live there; but I have also been informed that it can be a dangerous pilgrimage. So do you mean to take my child there with you?

THE TEACHER: It is not a journey a young child is fit to make.

THE MOTHER: [6] I hope you will come back in safety, sir.

THE TEACHER: Now I must go. Farewell to you.

BOY *and* MOTHER: Farewell to you.

4

THE BOY: I've something to tell you.

THE TEACHER: What will you tell me?

THE BOY: That I will set out for the mountains too.

THE TEACHER:

It is as I said to your mother
This is such a difficult and
Dangerous excursion. You could not possibly
Join us. And besides:
How could you think of
Abandoning your mother's bedside?
Of deserting your mother who is not well?
You stay here! There's
No question of your coming with us.

THE BOY:

It's because of my mother's illness that
I know I must go with you, to seek out

Those doctors in the town beyond the mountains, and
Ask them for medicine and consultation.

THE TEACHER: Then I shall have to speak to your mother again.
The Teacher goes back into Space 2. The Boy listens at the door.

5

THE TEACHER: I have come back once again to tell you that your son says he intends to come with us. So I have said that he cannot leave you by yourself here, cannot leave you with your illness; that the journey's dangerous and difficult. I said it was quite impossible for him to come with us. But he replied that he has to get to the town that lies over the mountains to seek medicine for his mother's illness, and consultation.

THE MOTHER: Well, I have listened to all your words. I cannot question what my boy said to you – that he'd gladly go along with you on this dangerous mountain trip. So come in, my son!
The Boy enters Space 2.
Ever since the day when your
Father was torn from us
I've had no one else beside me.
I've never known you
Fade from my thinking or be out of my eyesight
Any longer than I'd need to
Get your breakfast
See your clothes were kept tidy, and
Look after the money.

THE BOY: It is all as you say . . . Yet there's nothing can outweigh my sense of duty as I see it.

THE BOY, THE MOTHER, THE TEACHER:
I shall (he will) make this very difficult dangerous journey
To relieve your (my, her) illness
To the town beyond the mountains
Seeking for medicine and for consultation.

6

THE FULL CHORUS:
They realised there was no plea
Could be strong enough to move him.
Then the Master and the mother said together
With one voice:

THE TEACHER, THE MOTHER:
O see how deeply he's agreeing!
Many will be found agreeing to error, but he
Would not give agreement to her illness, and
Insisted that illness has to be cured.

THE FULL CHORUS:
The mother said however:

THE MOTHER:
Now I have no more strength left;
If it must be, then
Go with the Master.
But be swift, but be swift
Put risk behind you and come back.

ACT TWO

The door has been removed. The right half of the acting area is filled by a raised platform, with steps leading up to it. To the left, in Space 1, a sign says 'Mountain Path'. To the right (upper level), a sign saying 'Mountain Peak'. The stage is empty.

7

THE FULL CHORUS:

The members of the expedition
Now have reached the mountains
And the Master is one of the climbers
And the boy too.
The boy was not fit for the exertions of the journey:
He overstrained his heart
Which longed for the order to turn back homeward.

At dawn when he saw the peaks looming up above
Laboriously towards the hills he
Dragged his feet.

8

Enter in Space 1 the Teacher and the Three Students, followed by the Boy bearing a jug.

THE TEACHER: We have climbed so fast to get here. Already we're at the first hut. We will stay here a little, we'll call a halt and stay a little.

THE THREE STUDENTS: We'll obey you.[7]

THE BOY: I must tell you something.

THE TEACHER: What will you tell me?

THE BOY: That I do not feel well.

THE TEACHER: Stay! Such things may not be said by those who travel to perform a task like ours. Perhaps you are exhausted because you are not used to climbing. Lie down here and rest. Recover a little. *He mounts the platform.*

THE THREE STUDENTS: It seems that this young boy is ill with climbing. So let us try asking the Master about it.

THE FULL CHORUS: Yes. You do that!

THE THREE STUDENTS *to the Teacher*: It seems to us that this young boy is ill with climbing. What's wrong with him? Are you so anxious about him?

THE TEACHER: He's not feeling well. Otherwise I see nothing much wrong with him. He seems exhausted by climbing. He can lie here and rest: recover from his climb.

THE THREE STUDENTS: Does this mean you are not so anxious about him?

The Teacher says nothing. Long pause.

THE THREE STUDENTS:[8]

Listen. The Master has just said
That this boy was merely tired out with climbing.
But now he is looking very strange.
Once past the hut you reach the narrow ridge.
That will call for both hands clinging on to the rock face
If one's to cross it.[9]
We cannot carry stragglers.
Should we not follow the mighty Custom and
Hurl his body down to the valley?

They call down to Space 1, holding their hands to their mouth like a funnel:

Are you ill from climbing?

THE BOY: No. You see me standing here. Would I not have sat down if I were really ill?

Pause. The Boy sits down.

9

THE THREE STUDENTS: We'd better go and tell the Master. Sir, when we asked you about the boy you told us he'd become exhausted, become exhausted with climbing. But he now is looking very strange. Also he has sat down.[10] And here is something we say with dread: since ancient times the Custom has been that all those who fail the climb should be thrown into the valley.

THE TEACHER: What, you would hurl this child down into the valley?

THE THREE STUDENTS: Yes, that's what we say!

THE TEACHER: A mighty Custom, true. I tell you I cannot gainsay it. Although the Custom demands too that he who fails has to be asked if the others must turn back for his sake. I find that my heart is weighted down by pity for that creature. I shall now approach him and shall tell him tenderly of this great Custom.

THE FULL CHORUS: Yes, you do that!

THE THREE STUDENTS *standing with their faces turned towards one another*:

So now let us ask him: does he demand
That we turn back just for his sake?
But we say, suppose he does
Even so we shan't turn back
But shall hurl him into the valley.[11]

THE FULL CHORUS:

They wanted to ask him: did he demand
That they turn back just for his sake?
But they said: suppose he did
Even so they'd not turn back
But would hurl him down to the valley.[12]

10

The Teacher has gone down to the Boy in Space 1.

THE TEACHER: Listen to me.[13] There's been a law here from ancient times that if anyone's taken sick on such a journey, into the valley's depths he must be hurled – which means instant death. But the same Custom prescribes that the one with the sickness be asked: should we turn back again for that reason? And moreover the Custom says that the sick man must reply: no, you should not turn back.

THE BOY: I understand.

THE TEACHER: Do you want us to turn back home for your sake?

THE BOY: No, you should not turn back.

THE TEACHER: [14] So do you want to be treated just like everyone else?

THE BOY: Yes.

THE TEACHER *calls up*: Come on down here! He says yes to me. It's what the Custom wants him to reply.

THE THREE STUDENTS: He says yes to us. It's what the Custom wants him to reply.

They carry the Boy up to Space 2.

You should lean your head against our arm.
Do not strain too hard.
We'll carry you carefully.

The Three Students stand before the Boy at the further edge of the platform, shielding him.

THE BOY *out of view*:

I knew quite well that if I made this journey
I might forfeit my life to make it.
I was thinking of
My dear mother
That drove me on to join you.
Take then my jug
Fill it with a healing draught
Bring it to my mother
When you return home.

THE FULL CHORUS:

At that his friends took the jug
And they sighed for the ways of the world
And the bitterness of its practices
And then they threw him down.
Foot to foot they stood in a knot
Close up by the edge of the valley
And hurled him down the cliff
With averted eyes, blindly
No one guiltier than his neighbour
And clods of earth after
And likewise great flat stones they flung.

Later additions and substitutions by Brecht (not included in the 1930 piano score)

1 And this is because an epidemic has broken out here, and several great doctors live beyond the mountains.

2 **For the Mother's lines substitute:** I am sorry to say I am no better, because so far nobody knows a medicine with which to treat it.

3 **For the Teacher's first sentence substitute:** Something must be found.

4 **For his fourth sentence substitute:** Tomorrow I shall undertake a journey to the mountains, to get medicine and consultation.

5 **For 'scientific' substitute:** Aid

6 **Insert:** Good.

7 **Insert:** *They mount the platform in Space 2. The Boy holds back the Teacher.*

8 **Insert:** *to one another.*

9 **From here to the end of section 8 substitute:**

Let us hope he is not ill.
Since if he can go no further we shall have
To leave him here.
They call down to Space 1, holding their hands to their mouth like a funnel:
We will ask the Master.

Then the first three lines of section 9 follow, down to 'sat down'.

10 **From here substitute as follows for the five lines ending 'I cannot gainsay it':**

THE TEACHER: I see that he has become ill. Try to carry him across the narrow ridge.

THE THREE STUDENTS: We will try that.

Stage effect: The Three Students try to carry the Boy across the narrow ridge. The players must construct the narrow ridge out of platforms, ropes, chairs and so on, in such a way that the Three Students are able to cross it on their own, but not when carrying the Boy.

THE THREE STUDENTS: We cannot carry him across, and we cannot stay by him. Whatever happens we must go on, as a whole town is waiting for the medicine that we are to collect. It is a dreadful thing to say, but if he cannot walk with us we shall have to leave him lying here in the mountains.

THE TEACHER: Yes, perhaps you will. I cannot gainsay you. But I think it is right

11 **For the Students' last line substitute:** But shall leave him there and go further.

12 **Similarly with the last line of the Full Chorus.**

13 **After the Teacher's 'Listen to me' at the start of section 10, substitute for his two lines down to 'Custom prescribes':** Because you are ill and can go no further, we must leave you here. But it is right

14 **Then substitute for the next four lines, up to the stage direction *They carry the Boy up to Space 2*, as follows:**

THE TEACHER: So are you consenting that you should be left behind?

THE BOY: I will think it over. *He pauses for thought.* Yes, I am consenting.

THE TEACHER *calls from Space 1 to Space 2*: He has answered as necessity demanded.

THE FULL CHORUS *and* THE THREE STUDENTS *while going down to Space 2*: He has said yes. Go on!

The Three Students remain standing.

THE TEACHER:

Go on now, no hesitation
On towards our destination.

The Three Students remain standing.

THE BOY: Let me say something: I beg you not to leave me lying here, but to throw me down into the valley, for I am frightened to die alone.

THE THREE STUDENTS: We cannot do that.

THE BOY: Stop! I demand that you should.

THE TEACHER:

You resolved to go on and leave him there
Deciding his fate is easy
Enacting it is hard.
Are you ready to throw him down into the valley?

THE THREE STUDENTS: Yes.

Weill's new setting of passages 1 and 14 have survived and are in the Weill/Lenya Archive at Yale, but if there were new settings of the others they have been lost.

He Said No

[Note: The first nine episodes of this 'counter-play' are to all intents and purposes identical with the 1930 text of *He Said Yes*, as set by Weill and given above. The substitutions and insertions which Brecht added to this later, as noted from 1 to 14, were *not* made in *He Said No*.

There is however an entirely different episode 10, which bears no relation to the music. The whole ten-episode work therefore must be treated as a play, not an opera. The new episode 10 is as follows.]

10

The Teacher has gone down to the Boy in Space 1.

THE TEACHER: Listen to me. There's been a law here from ancient times that if anyone's taken sick on such a journey, into the valley's depths he must be hurled – which means instant death. But the same Custom prescribes that the one with the sickness be asked: should we turn back again for that reason? And moreover the Custom says that the sick man must reply: no, you should not turn back. If only I could take your place, how gladly I should die!

THE BOY: I understand.

THE TEACHER: Do you want us to turn back home for your sake? Or do you consent that you should be hurled into the valley, as the Custom prescribes?

THE BOY: *He pauses for thought.* No, I do not consent.

THE TEACHER *calls from Space 1 to Space 2*: Come on down! He has not replied in accordance with the Custom.

THE THREE STUDENTS *coming down to Space 1*: He has said no. *To the Boy*: Why have you not replied in accordance with the Custom? Whoever says A must also say B. When you were asked at the start if you would consent to whatever might happen on the journey, you replied yes.

THE BOY: My answer was wrong, but your question was more so. Whoever says A does not have to say B. He can recognise that A was wrong. I wanted to fetch medicine for my mother, but now I have become ill myself and it is no longer possible. And I want immediately to turn back, as the new situation demands. I am asking you too to turn back and take me home. Your research can surely wait. If there is indeed something to be learnt beyond the mountains, as I hope, then it can only be that in a situation like ours one has to turn back. And as for the ancient Custom I see no sense in it. What I need far more is a new Great Custom, which we should bring in at once, the Custom of thinking things out anew in every new situation.

THE THREE STUDENTS *to the Teacher*: What are we to do? What the boy says makes sense even if it is not heroic.

THE TEACHER: You must decide for yourselves. But I have to tell you that you will be the object of general laughter and disgrace if you turn back.

THE THREE STUDENTS: Is it not disgraceful for him to speak for himself?

THE TEACHER: No. I see nothing disgraceful in that.

THE THREE STUDENTS: Then let us turn back, and no laughter and no disgrace shall stop us from doing the sensible thing, nor any ancient Custom discourage us from adopting a right thought.

You should lean your head against our arm.
Do not strain too hard.
We'll carry you carefully.

THE FULL CHORUS:

In this way the friends took their friend
And founded a new Custom
And a new law
And they brought the boy back.
Side by side they walked in a knot
To confront disgrace
To confront laughter, with eyes open
None more cowardly than his neighbour.

The Decision

Lehrstück

Collaborators: SLATAN DUDOW, HANNS EISLER

Translator: JOHN WILLETT

Characters:

THE FOUR AGITATORS. *They play*:

The Young Comrade • The Director of the Party House • The Two Coolies • The Overseer • The Two Textile Workers • The Policeman • The Merchant

THE CONTROL CHORUS

The text that follows is based on that of Universal-Edition's piano score of 1931 (UE 2744), which is virtually the same as that in *Versuche 4*, 1931. These contain some changes following the Berlin première on 13 December 1930. Important variants are listed on pp. 90–91. Titles and numbering of the musical numbers (Nos. 1–14) follow Eisler's piano score.

No. 1 PRELUDE

THE CONTROL CHORUS: Show yourselves! For your work has been successful. Now there's one more land where the Revolution's begun, and the lines are drawn, so militants know where they stand. We are in agreement with you.

THE FOUR AGITATORS: Stop! There's something we must tell you. We have to report the death of a comrade.

THE CONTROL CHORUS: Can you say who killed him?

THE FOUR AGITATORS: We killed him. We shot him and threw him into a lime pit.

THE CONTROL CHORUS: What could he have done that led to your shooting him?

THE FOUR AGITATORS: Often he did the right thing, sometimes the wrong thing, but in the end he became a risk to the movement. He wanted to do the right thing, and did the wrong thing.[1] We are asking for your verdict.

THE CONTROL CHORUS: Show us how it occurred, and we shall inform you of our verdict.

THE FOUR AGITATORS: We shall accept your verdict.

I

THE TEACHINGS OF THE CLASSICS

THE FOUR AGITATORS: We arrived as agitators from Moscow with orders to travel to the town of Mukden, where we were to make propaganda and reinforce the Chinese Party in the factories. We were to report to the last Party house before the frontier, and ask for a guide. In the outer office a young comrade came up to us and we discussed the nature of our mission. We will repeat the conversation.

One of them plays the Young Comrade, and they group themselves as three confronting one.

THE YOUNG COMRADE: I am the secretary of the last Party house before the frontier. My heart beats for the Revolution. The sight of injustice made me join the ranks of the militants. Man must help man. I am for freedom. I believe in the human race. And I support the decisions of the Communist Party, which is fighting for the classless society against exploitation and ignorance.

THE THREE AGITATORS: We come from Moscow.

THE YOUNG COMRADE: We were expecting you.

THE THREE AGITATORS: Why?

THE YOUNG COMRADE: We are getting nowhere. There is disorder and want, a lot of fighting and not much bread. Plenty of people with courage but not many who can read. Not many machines, and no one to understand them. Our railway engines have been driven till they are wrecks.

No. 2a RECITATIVE

THE YOUNG COMRADE: Did you bring us any railway engines?

THE THREE AGITATORS: No.

THE YOUNG COMRADE: Have you brought any tractors with you?

THE THREE AGITATORS: No.

THE YOUNG COMRADE: Our peasants still harness themselves to old-fashioned wooden ploughs. And we have nothing to put in our fields. Have you brought us any seed?

THE THREE AGITATORS: No.

THE YOUNG COMRADE: Well, at least you'll have got machine guns and ammunition for us?

THE THREE AGITATORS: No.

THE YOUNG COMRADE: There are two of us here to defend the Revolution. So you surely must have a letter from the Central Committee for us, telling us what to do?

THE THREE AGITATORS: No.

THE YOUNG COMRADE: So you mean to help us yourselves?

THE THREE AGITATORS: No.

THE YOUNG COMRADE: We live in our clothes day and night, beating off the forces of hunger, demoralisation and counter-revolution. And you have nothing for us.

THE THREE AGITATORS: That is right: we have nothing for you. But for the Chinese workers across the frontier in Mukden we have the teachings of the Marxist classics and their propagandists, the ABC of Communism. For the ignorant, to shed light upon their situation; for the oppressed, to teach them class-awareness; and for the class-conscious, the experience of the Revolution. What we are supposed to get from you is an automobile and a guide.

THE YOUNG COMRADE: So that was a bad question I asked?

THE THREE AGITATORS: No, it was a good question followed by a better answer. We know that impossible demands have been made of you, but still more is going to be demanded: one of you two will have to guide us to Mukden.

THE YOUNG COMRADE: Then I am to abandon my task which was too much for two people and will now have to be done by one. I shall go with you. Marching ahead, spreading the teachings of the Communist classics: the World Revolution.

No. 2b PRAISE OF THE USSR

THE CONTROL CHORUS:

All the world was telling of
Our misfortune.
But still there sat at our
Bare board
The hope of the numberless exploited which
Lives on water alone.
And our teacher was Knowledge, who
Behind our broken-down door
Gave clear lessons to all those present.
Once the door's been broken, we
Sit on inside, plainly visible
Whom no frost can kill off, nor hunger
Ever tireless, debating
The future of the world.

THE FOUR AGITATORS: So the young comrade from the frontier post approved the nature of our work and, as four men and one woman, we reported to the director of the Party house.

2

THE OBLITERATION

THE FOUR AGITATORS: But our work in Mukden was illegal, and so before we crossed the frontier we had to obliterate our faces. Our young comrade was in agreement. We will repeat the incident.

One of the Agitators plays the Director of the Party house.

THE DIRECTOR OF THE PARTY HOUSE: I am the director of the last Party house. I agree that the comrade from my post should go along as their guide. However, there are disturbances in the factories at Mukden, and at present the eyes of the whole world are turned on that city to see if any of us can be seen leaving the Chinese workers' huts. What is more I have been told that there are gunboats in a state of readiness on the rivers and armoured trains on the railway embankments, all ready to attack the moment one of us is seen there. So I propose that the comrades should cross the frontier as Chinamen. *To the Agitators*: You must not be seen.

THE TWO AGITATORS: We will not be seen.

THE DIRECTOR OF THE PARTY HOUSE: If anyone is injured he must not be found.

THE TWO AGITATORS: He will not be found.

No. 3a RECITATIVE

THE DIRECTOR OF THE PARTY HOUSE: Are you prepared to speak and to keep on until you stop, but to disappear before anyone looks at you, so as to conceal both those left alive and the dead too?

THE TWO AGITATORS: Yes.

THE DIRECTOR OF THE PARTY HOUSE: Then you'll be different people. You'll not be Karl Schmitt from Berlin, you'll not be Anna Kjersk from Kazan, and you'll not be Peter Savitch from Moscow; no, you'll be without either surname or mother – empty pages upon which the Revolution writes what it has to say.

THE TWO AGITATORS: Yes.

THE DIRECTOR OF THE PARTY HOUSE *gives them masks which*

they put on: Then you'll find you won't be nobodies any longer, but from that moment, probably till you vanish off the face of this planet, you will be unknown workers, Chinese, militants, and children all of Chinese mothers, yellow-skinned, speaking Chinese in dream and delirium.

THE TWO AGITATORS: Yes. *They put on their masks.*

THE DIRECTOR OF THE PARTY HOUSE: For the sake of Communism, agreeing to the forward march of the proletarian masses of every country, saying yes to the revolutionising of the world.

THE TWO AGITATORS: Yes. And the young comrade said yes. Thus he showed that he agreed to the obliteration of his face.

No. 3b SPEECH CHORUS

THE CONTROL CHORUS: All those who fight for Communism must know how to fight and how not to fight; to tell the truth and not to tell the truth; to be servile and also how not to be servile; to keep one's promises and also not keep them; how to confront a danger, how to avoid danger; to be known by sight and unknown. All those who fight for Communism have just this to be said in their favour: that they are fighting for Communism.

THE FOUR AGITATORS: We went to Mukden as Chinamen, four men and one woman, to make propaganda and to reinforce the Chinese Party by means of the teachings of the Communist classics and their propagandists, the ABC of Communism, bringing to the ignorant new light on their situation, to the oppressed class-consciousness, and to the class-conscious experience of the Revolution.

No. 4 PRAISE OF ILLEGAL ACTIVITY

THE CONTROL CHORUS:

Best of all
To raise your voices for the working class.
Loud and clearly calling on the masses to struggle
Stamping firmly on all oppressors, freeing all victims of oppression.
Useful and difficult are all those small routines

Secret and obstinate knots in
That mighty net the Party weaves
Under the rifle barrels of the bosses.
Speaking, but
Without betraying the speaker.
Winning, but
Without betraying the winner.
Dying, but
Without declaring the death.
Who would not do a lot for fame? Who
Would do as much for silence?
But it is just the poorest of all that make Honour their guest
It's out of the meanest hovel that comes forth
Irresistible Greatness.
And when Fame asks who did
The great deed, it will ask in vain.
Show yourselves
Just for an instant, you
Unknown men; you can cover your face while we
Utter our thanks.

THE FOUR AGITATORS: In the city of Mukden we made propaganda among the workers. We had no bread for the hungry, merely knowledge for the ignorant, and so we spoke of the causes of poverty: did not abolish poverty itself but spoke of abolishing its causes.

3

THE STONE

THE FOUR AGITATORS: To start with we went to the Lower City. Some coolies on the river bank were tugging a barge with a rope. But the ground was slippery. When one of them slipped and the overseer struck him we told the young comrade 'Go after them and make propaganda among them. Tell them that in Tientsin you saw boots for barge-hauliers with wooden bars underneath to stop them skidding. Try to get them to insist on boots like that. But don't let yourself become sorry for them!' And we asked 'Do you agree?' and he agreed, and hurried off, and at once let himself become sorry for them. We will show it.

Two Agitators act the part of Coolies by tying a rope to a stake and pulling it over their shoulders. One acts the Young Comrade, and one the Overseer.

THE OVERSEER: I am the Overseer. I have to get this rice to Mukden before evening.

THE TWO COOLIES: We are the coolies and we are hauling the rice barge up the river.

No. 5 SONG OF THE RICE-BARGE HAULIERS

THE FIRST COOLIE:

In the town further upstream
There'll be a bowl of rice for us.
– Only the barge we're hauling is heavy
And the water's flowing downhill.
We'll never get this barge up there.

MEN'S CHORUS:

Pull harder, men's mouths are
Waiting for the next meal.
Pull steadily, don't push
The man in front.

THE YOUNG COMRADE: How hideous to hear the lovely way these men cloak the torment of their work.

THE OVERSEER: Pull harder.

THE FIRST COOLIE:

Now night's almost come. A bunk
That would seem too cramping for a dog's ghost
Costs as much as half a bowl of rice.
And this bank is so slithery
We can't budge from the spot.

MEN'S CHORUS:

Pull harder, men's mouths are
Waiting for the next meal.
Pull steadily, don't push
The man in front.

THE SECOND COOLIE *slipping to the ground*: I can't go on.

THE FIRST COOLIE *while the coolies halt and are whipped until the fallen man picks himself up*:
We know we'll never
Survive the rope that cuts our shoulders.
The whip which he wields has seen
Four generations like us
Nor are we the last one.

MEN'S CHORUS:
Pull harder, men's mouths are
Waiting for the next meal.
Pull steadily, don't push
The man in front.

THE YOUNG COMRADE: It is hard to look at these men without being sorry for them. *To the Overseer*: Can't you see the ground is too slippery?

THE OVERSEER: What about the ground?

THE YOUNG COMRADE: Too slippery.

THE OVERSEER: Are you trying to tell me that this towpath is so slippery they can't haul a bargeload of rice?

THE YOUNG COMRADE: Yes.

THE OVERSEER: So you don't believe they need rice in Mukden?

THE YOUNG COMRADE: If these men fall down they can't haul the barge.

THE OVERSEER: Is it my job to lay stones for them all the way to Mukden?

THE YOUNG COMRADE: I've no idea what your job is but I know theirs. It's to stick up for themselves. *To the coolies*: Don't you imagine that what has been impossible for two thousand years is going to be impossible for ever. In Tientsin I saw barge hauliers with boots that had wooden bars underneath to stop them sliding. They achieved this by making a joint demand. You make a joint demand for boots like that.

THE COOLIES: Sure, we can't go on towing this barge without boots like that.

THE OVERSEER: But the rice has got to be in Mukden tonight. *He whips them, and they pull.*

THE FIRST COOLIE:
First our fathers shifted the barge from the river mouth

Just a bit upstream. And our sons will
Get to the head springs, but our place is
In between them.

MEN'S CHORUS:
Pull harder, men's mouths are
Waiting for the next meal.
Pull steadily, don't push
The man in front.

THE SECOND COOLIE: Help me!

THE YOUNG COMRADE: Are you inhuman? I'm picking up a stone and laying it in the mud. *To the coolie*: Now step on that.

THE OVERSEER: Quite right. What help are boots in Tientsin? I'd sooner have your tender-hearted comrade follow with a stone and lay it in front of anyone who slips.

THE FIRST COOLIE:
This barge bears rice. The farmer who
Sowed and gathered it was paid
With a heap of small change. Our
Payment is even less, because we
Are too many. One ox costs more.

One of the coolies slips and falls, the Young Comrade lays a stone in front of him, the coolie picks himself up.

MEN'S CHORUS:
Pull harder, men's mouths are
Waiting for the next meal.
Pull steadily, don't push
The man in front.

THE FIRST COOLIE:
Once the rice has arrived at last
And the children want to know just
Who hauled the heavy barge, they'll hear: That's
A barge that got hauled here.

One of the coolies slips and falls, the Young Comrade lays a stone in front of him, the coolie picks himself up.

MEN'S CHORUS:
Pull harder, men's mouths are
Waiting for the next meal.
Pull steadily, don't push
The man in front.

The foodstuff from downstream gets to
The eaters upstream. Those
Who hauled it have not
Had their food yet.

One of the coolies slips and falls, the Young Comrade lays a stone in front of him, the coolie picks himself up.

THE YOUNG COMRADE: I can't go on. You must insist on other boots.

THE FIRST COOLIE: He's simple, they're laughing at him.

THE OVERSEER: No, he's one of those agitators. Hold him, you men!

THE FOUR AGITATORS: And instantly he was held. And they hunted him for two days, then he met us and for a week they hunted us and him all over Mukden, and it became impossible for us to show our faces in the Lower City.

THE LEADER OF THE CONTROL CHORUS: Discussion!

No. 6a DISCUSSION

THE CONTROL CHORUS:
But is it not correct to take the side of the weaker
To help him wherever he may be –
The exploited one – in his daily sufferings?

THE FOUR AGITATORS: He was no help to the weaker, but hindered us from making propaganda in the lower part of the town.

THE CONTROL CHORUS:
We are in agreement.

THE FOUR AGITATORS: The Young Comrade realised that he had separated thinking from feeling. But we comforted him and repeated the words of comrade Lenin:

No. 6b LENIN QUOTATION (SPEECH CHORUS)

THE CONTROL CHORUS:
He's not wise who never makes mistakes.
He is wise who makes mistakes and puts them right.

No. 6c CANON ON A LENIN QUOTATION

THE CONTROL CHORUS:

He's not wise who never makes mistakes.
He is wise who makes mistakes but puts them right.

4

JUSTICE

THE FOUR AGITATORS: We set up the first cells in the factories and trained the first Party cadres, started a Party school and showed them how to produce the forbidden literature in secret. After that we worked in the textile factories, and when wages were cut a section of the workers went on strike. However, the rest of the workers continued working, and so the strike looked like being a failure. We told the Young Comrade 'Go to the factory gates and hand out our leaflets.' We will repeat what was said.

THE THREE AGITATORS: You messed things up with the coolies.

THE YOUNG COMRADE: Yes.

THE THREE AGITATORS: Did that teach you anything?

THE YOUNG COMRADE: Yes.

THE TWO TEXTILE WORKERS: Will you do better in the strike?

THE YOUNG COMRADE: Yes.

Two of the Agitators act Textile Workers and one a Policeman.

THE POLICEMAN: I am a policeman, and those in power give me my bread so I can fight discontent.

No. 7a STRIKE SONG[2]

THE CONTROL CHORUS:

Comrade, come and join us, and risk
Your penny that's worth nothing at all
Your sleeping-place that's always sodden
And your place of work which you'll lose any day.

Join us in the coming struggle!
Surely you can't want us to fail.
Help yourself by giving us help. Let
Solidarity prevail.

Solidarity or oppression? isolation or freedom?

THE YOUNG COMRADE:

Give up what you have got, comrade!
You have got nothing.

THE CONTROL CHORUS:

Comrade, come and join us. Confront their rifles
And insist you get your pay.
Once you know that you've not all that much to lose
Their police will find those rifles simply aren't effective.

Join us in the coming struggle!
Surely you can't want us to fail.
Help yourself by giving us help. Let
Solidarity prevail.

THE TWO TEXTILE WORKERS: After the last shift we go home; our wages have been cut, but we don't know what we ought to do, we just go on working.

THE YOUNG COMRADE *gives one of them a leaflet, as the other stands idly by*: Read this and pass it on. Once you've read it you'll know what you ought to do.

The First Worker takes it and walks on.

THE POLICEMAN *taking the leaflet from the First Worker*: Who gave you that leaflet?

THE FIRST WORKER: I don't know: somebody walked past and shoved it in my hand.

THE POLICEMAN *to the Second Worker*: You gave that leaflet to him. The police are looking for people distributing leaflets like that.

THE SECOND WORKER: I didn't give anyone a leaflet.

THE YOUNG COMRADE: Is it a crime to teach the ignorant to understand their position?

THE POLICEMAN: Your teachings have terrible effects. Spread them in a factory like this, and it doesn't know who it belongs to. This little leaflet is more dangerous than a battery of artillery.

THE YOUNG COMRADE: So what's in it?

THE POLICEMAN: I don't know. *To the Second Worker*: So what's in it?

THE SECOND WORKER: I know nothing about that leaflet. I didn't distribute it.

THE YOUNG COMRADE: I know he didn't.

THE POLICEMAN *to the Young Comrade*: Did you give him that leaflet?

THE YOUNG COMRADE: No.

THE POLICEMAN *to the Second Worker*: Then you gave it him.

THE YOUNG COMRADE *to the First Worker*: What are they going to do to him?

THE FIRST WORKER: He could be put in prison.[3]

THE YOUNG COMRADE: What do you want to put him in prison for, officer? Aren't you a worker too?

THE POLICEMAN *to the Second Worker*: Come along. *Hits him on the head.*

THE YOUNG COMRADE *tries to stop him*: It wasn't him.

THE POLICEMAN: Then it was you all along.

THE SECOND WORKER: It wasn't him.

THE POLICEMAN: Then the two of you were in it together.

THE FIRST WORKER: Go on, run, your pockets are stuffed with leaflets.

The Policeman knocks the Second Worker down.

THE YOUNG COMRADE *to the First Worker, pointing at the Policeman*: He's killed an innocent man, you witnessed it.

THE FIRST WORKER *attacking the Policeman*: You corrupt pig!

The Policeman draws his revolver. The Young Comrade grabs the Policeman's neck from behind, the First Worker twists his arm slowly backwards. The revolver goes off, the Policeman is disarmed.

THE YOUNG COMRADE *shouts*: Help, comrades, help! They're killing innocent bystanders!

THE SECOND WORKER *getting up, to the First*: Now we've assaulted a policeman we'll never be able to go back to the factory, and – *To the Young Comrade.* – it's all your fault.[4]

THE FOUR AGITATORS: And instead of distributing leaflets he had to hide, for they reinforced the police guard.

DISCUSSION[5]

THE CONTROL CHORUS: But is it not correct to stop injustice wherever it occurs?

THE FOUR AGITATORS: He stopped a small injustice, but the big injustice was the strike-breaking, and that continued.

No. 7b

THE CONTROL CHORUS:
We are in agreement.

5

BY THE WAY, WHAT IS A MAN?

THE FOUR AGITATORS: Daily we fought against the old organisations, against submissiveness and against despair; we taught the workers to transform their fight for better pay into a fight for power. Taught them to handle weapons and how to conduct demonstrations. Then we heard that the business community was involved in a dispute about tariffs with the English who controlled the city. So as to exploit this division among the rulers for the benefit of the ruled we sent the Young Comrade with a letter to the richest of the business men. It said 'Arm the coolies.' We told the Young Comrade 'Conduct yourself in such a way that you get the weapons.' But once the food was put on the table he couldn't keep silent. We will show it.
One Agitator acts the Merchant.

THE MERCHANT: I am the merchant. I am expecting a letter from the coolie organisation about a joint operation against the English.

THE YOUNG COMRADE: Here is the coolie organisation's letter.

THE MERCHANT: I invite you to eat with me.

THE YOUNG COMRADE: I am honoured to be permitted to eat with you.

THE MERCHANT: While they are preparing the food I will tell you what I think about coolies. Kindly sit there.

THE YOUNG COMRADE: I am most interested to know what you think.

No. 8a RECITATIVE

THE MERCHANT: Tell me why I can get things twice as cheap as the others? And tell me why my coolies work for such miserable pay.

THE YOUNG COMRADE: I've no idea.

THE MERCHANT: Because I am a shrewd man. And you are also shrewd men, for you know how to get the coolies to pay you a good income.

THE YOUNG COMRADE: We know how to. Incidentally, are you going to arm the coolies against the English?

THE MERCHANT: We'll see, we'll see. I know how one has to handle a coolie. You have to provide sufficient rice for him so he runs no risk of dying, otherwise how can he work for you. Are you with me?

THE YOUNG COMRADE: Yes, I am with you.

THE MERCHANT: That's where you've got it wrong. Because if coolies cost even less than does rice, why not go and buy myself a new one? Are you with me now?

THE YOUNG COMRADE: Yes, I am with you now. Incidentally, when will you start sending arms into the Lower City?

THE MERCHANT: Soon, soon. You ought to see how the coolies who pack my leather buy the rice in my canteen. D'you think I pay a high price for my labour?

THE YOUNG COMRADE: No, but your rice is expensive. And your labour has to be up to standard. But your rice is below standard.

THE MERCHANT: Yes, you are shrewd people.

THE YOUNG COMRADE: And are you going to arm the coolies against the English?

THE MERCHANT: We can have a look round the armoury after we've eaten. First I must sing my favourite song.

No. 8b SONG OF SUPPLY AND DEMAND

THE MERCHANT:

Rice can be had down the river.
People in the remoter provinces need their rice.
If we can keep that rice off the market
Rice is bound to get dearer.

Then the men who pull the barges must go short of rice
And I shall get my rice for even less.

THE YOUNG COMRADE: By the way, what is rice?

THE MERCHANT:

Don't ask me what rice is.
Don't ask me my advice.
I've no idea what rice is
All I have learnt is its price.

In winter time the coolies need warm clothing.
Then you must buy cotton so that
You can keep cotton off the market.
When a cold spell comes, then clothes get more expensive.
Our cotton-spinning mills pay too high wages.
And cotton's too plentiful in any case.

THE YOUNG COMRADE: By the way, what is cotton?

THE MERCHANT:

How can I say what cotton is.
How can I give my advice.
I've not the least notion what cotton is
All I have learnt is its price.

Men like these need too much feeding
And this makes a man dearer.
To provide for their feeding you need more men.
The cooks may get it done cheaper, but look at
The eaters making it dearer.
And men are in short supply in any case.

THE YOUNG COMRADE: By the way, what is a man?

THE MERCHANT:

Don't ask me what a man is.
Don't ask me my advice.
I've no idea what a man is
All I have learnt is his price.

THE CONTROL CHORUS:

He can't tell what a man is
He only knows his price.

THE MERCHANT *to the Young Comrade*: And now we will eat my good rice.

THE YOUNG COMRADE *standing up*: I cannot eat with you.

THE FOUR AGITATORS: Those were his words, and neither ridicule nor threats could induce him to eat with a man he despised; and the merchant threw him out, and the coolies were not armed.

DISCUSSION

THE CONTROL CHORUS: But is it not correct to put honour above everything else?

THE FOUR AGITATORS: No.

No. 9 ALTER THE WORLD, IT NEEDS IT

THE CONTROL CHORUS:

Whom would the just man fail to greet, if it helped him to stop
 an injustice?
What medicine tastes too nasty to save
A dying man?
How much meanness would you not commit if the aim is
To stamp out meanness?
If you'd found out how the world could be altered, what would
 you
Refuse to do?
What would you refuse to do?
Sink deep in the mire
Shake hands with the butcher: yes, but
Alter the world, it needs it!
Who are you?[6]

For some time we have listened to you less
As if judging you, more as
Men who must learn.

THE FOUR AGITATORS: Even as he left, the Young Comrade realised his mistake, and volunteered to be sent back over the frontier if we wished. We were well aware of his weakness, but we still needed him since he had many supporters among the youth organisations, and did much at that time to help us knit the Party's network together under the guns of the capitalists.

6

THE BETRAYAL[7]

THE FOUR AGITATORS: During that week the repression became exceptionally severe. All that we had left was a hideout for our printing machine and leaflets. But one morning there were major hunger riots in the city, and from the countryside too major riots were reported. On the evening of the third day, after a dangerous journey to our place of refuge, we were met at the door by the Young Comrade. And there were sacks standing in the rain outside. We will repeat the conversation.

THE THREE AGITATORS: What sacks are those?

THE YOUNG COMRADE: Those are our propaganda material.

THE THREE AGITATORS: What is supposed to be done with them?

THE YOUNG COMRADE: I have something to tell you: the new leaders of the unemployed came here today and convinced me that we must start the operation right away. So we should distribute the material[8] and storm the barracks.

THE THREE AGITATORS: Then you misled them. But tell us your reasons and see if you can convince us.

THE YOUNG COMRADE: Misery is on the increase and there is growing unrest in the town.

THE THREE AGITATORS: The ignorant are starting to realise their situation.

THE YOUNG COMRADE: The unemployed have accepted our teachings.

THE THREE AGITATORS: The oppressed are becoming class-conscious.

THE YOUNG COMRADE: They are out on the streets aiming to smash the spinning mills.

THE THREE AGITATORS: They have no experience of revolution.[9] Our responsibility is all the greater.

THE YOUNG COMRADE:

The unemployed cannot go on waiting and I
Cannot go on waiting.
There is too much misery.

THE THREE AGITATORS: But still too few militants.

THE YOUNG COMRADE: Their sufferings are monstrous.

THE THREE AGITATORS: Suffering isn't enough.

THE YOUNG COMRADE: Inside there we have seven who came to us on behalf of the unemployed; behind them stand seven thousand, and they know that unhappiness does not grow on one's skin like leprosy; poverty does not fall from above like a roof tile; on the contrary, unhappiness and poverty are men's handiwork; famine is cooked for them, but their lamentation is consumed as food. They know everything.

THE THREE AGITATORS: Do they know how many regiments the government has?

THE YOUNG COMRADE: No.

THE THREE AGITATORS: Then they don't know enough. Where are your weapons?

THE YOUNG COMRADE *showing his hands*: We shall fight tooth and nail.

THE THREE AGITATORS: That won't be enough.[10] You see only the misery of the unemployed, not that of the workers. You see only the city, not the peasants in the plains. You see the soldiers only as oppressors, not as miserable oppressed creatures in uniform. Go then to the unemployed, cancel your advice to storm the barracks, and convince them that they must join tonight's demonstration by the factory workers, while we try to convince the disaffected soldiers that they too must demonstrate in uniform alongside us.

THE YOUNG COMRADE: I told the unemployed not to forget how often the soldiers had fired on them. Am I now to tell them that they are to demonstrate alongside murderers?

THE THREE AGITATORS: Yes, because the soldiers may realise how wrong they were to fire on miserable members of their own class. You should recall comrade Lenin's classic advice not to treat every peasant as a class enemy but to make rural poverty your ally in the fight.

THE YOUNG COMRADE: Then let me ask: do the Marxist classics allow misery to be kept waiting?

THE THREE AGITATORS: They are talking about methods which deal with misery as a whole.

THE YOUNG COMRADE: So don't the classics accept the supreme importance of giving immediate help to any individual in misery?

THE THREE AGITATORS: No.

THE YOUNG COMRADE: Then the classics are crap, and I am going to rip them apart; for man, real live man, is crying out and his misery rips through the limitations of their teachings. That is why I shall launch the operation instantly and at once; for I am crying out and ripping through the limitations of their teachings.

He tears up their writings.

THE THREE AGITATORS:

Do not rip them apart! We need them
Every page of them. You must face reality.
Your revolution is hastily made and will last a single day
And tomorrow it will be strangled.
But our revolution will begin tomorrow
Conquering and altering the world.
Your revolution stops when you stop.
When you have stopped
Our revolution will continue.

THE YOUNG COMRADE: Listen to what I say. With my own two eyes I have seen that misery cannot be kept waiting. That is why I oppose your decision to wait.

THE THREE AGITATORS: You have not convinced us. So go to the unemployed and convince them that they must join in the revolutionary front. You are to treat this as an order in the name of the Party.

THE YOUNG COMRADE:

Who do you think is the Party?
Does it sit in a big house with a switchboard?
Are all its decisions unknown, all its thoughts wrapped in secrecy?
Who is it?

THE THREE AGITATORS:

We are it.
You and I and them – all of us.
Comrade, the clothes it's dressed in are your clothes, the head that it thinks with is yours
Where I'm lodging, there is its house, and where you suffer an assault it fights back.
Show us the path we must take, and we

Shall take it with you, but
Don't take the right path without us.
Without us it is
The most wrong of all.
Don't cut yourself off from us!
We can go astray and you can be right, so
Don't cut yourself off from us!

That the short path is better than the long one cannot be denied.
But if someone knows it
And cannot point it out to us, what use is his wisdom?
Be wise with us.
Don't cut yourself off from us!

THE YOUNG COMRADE: Because I am right I cannot give way. My own two eyes tell me that misery cannot wait.

No. 10 PRAISE OF THE PARTY

THE CONTROL CHORUS:
One single man may have two eyes
But the Party has a thousand.
One single man may see a town
But the Party sees six countries.
One single man can spare a moment
The Party has many moments.
One single man can be annihilated
But the Party can't be annihilated
For its techniques are those of its philosophers
Which are derived from awareness of reality
And are destined soon to transform it
As soon as the masses make them their own.

Who do you think is the Party?
Does it sit in a big house with a switchboard?
Are all its decisions unknown, all its thoughts wrapped in secrecy?
Who is it?

We are it.
You and I and them – we all are.

Comrade, the clothes it's dressed in are your clothes, the head that it thinks with is yours
Where I'm lodging, there is its house, and where you suffer an assault it fights back.

THE YOUNG COMRADE: None of that is valid now: the prospect of battle makes me reject everything that applied yesterday, I withdraw my agreement with everyone, I shall do the simple human thing. Here is an operation. I shall be its spearhead. My heart beats for the Revolution. The Revolution is here!

THE THREE AGITATORS: Be quiet!

THE YOUNG COMRADE: There is oppression here. I am for freedom.

THE THREE AGITATORS: Be quiet! You will betray us.

THE YOUNG COMRADE: I cannot be quiet, because I am right.

THE THREE AGITATORS: Right or wrong, if you speak we shall be lost. Be quiet!

THE YOUNG COMRADE:

I saw too much
Therefore I shall appear before them
As who I am, and say how it is.
He takes off his mask and shouts:
We have come to help you.
We are from Moscow.
He rips up his mask.

THE FOUR AGITATORS:

And we looked at him, and in the half-light
We saw his naked face
Human, open, guileless. He had
Ripped up his mask
And from the houses came the
Cries of the exploited: Who is
Disturbing the sleep of the poor?
And a window opened and a voice called:
Look! Foreigners! Down with the agitators!
So we were recognised
And at the same time we heard there were riots
In the Lower City, and the ignorant were waiting

In the meeting houses and the unarmed on the streets.
But he would not stop shouting.
And we struck him down
Picked him up and hurriedly departed that place.

7

EXTREME PERSECUTION AND ANALYSIS

No. 11 RECITATIVE

THE CONTROL CHORUS:

They departed that place!
Unrest was growing in the town
And yet the leaders were making their getaway.
What is your decision?

THE FOUR AGITATORS:

Wait for it.
It is easy to know the correct course
Away from the shooting
With months to spare
But we
Had five minutes to spare and
Did our thinking under the guns.

When we had got away as far as the lime pits outside the town we could hear our pursuers behind us. Our young comrade opened his eyes, heard what had happened, realised what he had done, and said: We are lost.

THE CONTROL CHORUS: In a time of utmost persecution, confusing all our ideas, militants are forced to take stock and pause, weighing the effort against the objective.

THE FOUR AGITATORS: We shall repeat the analysis.

No. 12a RECITATIVE

THE FIRST AGITATOR: We'd better escort him across the border, so we said.

THE SECOND AGITATOR: Although the masses are out on the streets now.

THE THIRD AGITATOR: And it's our job to see that they come to the meetings.

THE FIRST AGITATOR: Which all means that we cannot escort our young comrade across the border.

THE THIRD AGITATOR: If we were to hide him and he's found, then what are we to do when they identify him?

THE FIRST AGITATOR: There are gunboats in a state of readiness on the rivers and armoured trains on the railway embankments, all prepared to attack us the moment one of us is seen there. He must not be seen.

No. 12b WE ARE THE SCUM OF THE EARTH

THE CONTROL CHORUS:

When they see us going inside
The exploited man's cabin
All the exploiters get their cannon to fire
Against that cabin and our country as a whole.[11]

For when the hungry man
Groans and hits back at his torturers:
They say we must have paid
Him to groan and to hit back.

Each of our faces says
That we think exploitation is wrong.
Each warrant for us says we
Help people who are exploited.
Those who help men in despair
Rank as the scum of the earth.
We are the scum of the earth
We can't afford to let them find us.

8

THE DECISION

THE FOUR AGITATORS:

What we decided was:
In that case he must vanish, and vanish entirely

For we can neither take him with us nor leave him
Therefore we must shoot him and throw him into the lime pit, since
The lime will burn him up.

No. 13a

THE CONTROL CHORUS:
Was that the only answer?
THE FOUR AGITATORS:
With so little time we could think of no other.
Like an animal helping an animal
We too would gladly have helped him who
Fought for our cause with us.
For five minutes, in the teeth of our pursuers, we
Considered if there was any
Better possibility.
Pause.[12]
So what we decided was straightway
To cut our own foot away from our body. *It is*
A terrible thing to kill.
But not only others would we kill, but ourselves too if need be
Since only force can alter this
Murderous world, as
Every living creature knows.
It is still, we said
Not given to us not to kill. Only on our
Indomitable will to alter the world could we base
This decision.

No. 13b

THE CONTROL CHORUS:
Go on speaking, and be sure
We sympathise with you.
It was so hard to do what was correct
Nor was it you who judged him, it was
Reality.

THE FOUR AGITATORS: We will repeat our last talk.

THE FIRST AGITATOR: We should ask him if he agrees, because he was a courageous fighter.

THE SECOND AGITATOR: But even if he does not agree he must vanish, and vanish entirely.

THE FIRST AGITATOR *to the Young Comrade*: If you are caught they will shoot you, and because you will be identified our work will be betrayed. So we must shoot you and throw you into the lime pit so that the lime burns you up. But let us ask you: can you see any other way?

THE YOUNG COMRADE: No.

THE THREE AGITATORS: Let us ask you: are you in agreement? *Pause.*[13]

THE YOUNG COMRADE: Yes.

THE THREE AGITATORS: Where would yoy like us to take you? we asked.

THE YOUNG COMRADE: To the lime pit, he said.

THE THREE AGITATORS: We asked: Do you want to do it on your own?

THE YOUNG COMRADE: Help me.

THE THREE AGITATORS:

Lean your head on our arm
Shut your eyes.

THE YOUNG COMRADE *out of sight*:

And he said: For the sake of Communism
Agreeing with the advance of the proletarian masses of
All countries
Saying yes to the revolutionising of the world.

THE FOUR AGITATORS:

Then we shot him and
Threw him down into the lime pit.
And when the lime had swallowed him we
Went back to our work.

No. 14 FINAL CHORUS

THE CONTROL CHORUS:

Comrades, your work was successful.
You've helped to disseminate

Marxism's teachings and the
ABC of Communism –
For the ignorant, shedding light upon their situation
For the oppressed, class-awareness, followed
By our experience of the Revolution.
There too the revolution has begun
And the militants know where they stand in the battle.
We are in agreement with you.[14]
At the same time your report shows how much
Is needed if our world is to be altered:
Rage and stubbornness, knowledge and rebellion
Quick reactions, profound meditation
Icy patience, endless repetition
Awareness of little things and awareness of big ones:
Only studying reality's going to
Help us alter reality.

past/present switches
– they meet the Young Comrade
– they deceive with masks
– Comrade meant to spread propaganda to Coolies
– Gets a worker killed
– meets merchant
– revolutionary differences

Textual variants

1 The three lines from 'What can he have done' are new. (p. 63)

2 See Editorial Notes. In the earlier text there is no strike; and the Textile Workers sing a different chorus, starting 'Today there was again/Less money in our wage packet', which however was not set to music by Eisler and so presumably had been changed by December 1930. (p. 73)

3 In the 1931 versions this read 'He could be shot'. It was changed in the 1938 Malik edition and the 1967 *Gesammelte Werke* (or *GW*). (p. 75)

4 The rest of the scene is changed since the première, where the Agitators report (rather unclearly) that 'The textile workers came out on strike; but the coolie organisation called for the policeman to be punished, and this was done; but the strike was called off for a long time and the factory guards were increased. Everyone spoke of the murder of the innocent man, but we were driven out of the factories.' (p. 75)

5 Here the piano score differs from the *Versuche* version, which has the Agitators replying 'He could have told the coolies that they would only be able to defend themselves against the police if they got the other workers in the factory to declare their solidarity with them against the police. For the policeman had committed an injustice.' Our text is closer to that of the première. (p. 75)

6 Instead of the three concluding lines the version of the première went on:

> Stinking, vanish from the
> Freshly cleaned room! You would surely be
> The last filth you must
> Get rid of! (p. 79)

7 For scene 6, 'The Betrayal', the title was previously 'Empörung gegen die Lehre' (Discontent with the Teaching). (p. 80)

8 Previously the Young Comrade said 'We called for a general strike', to which the Agitators reply 'That is the fourth time you have betrayed us'. (p. 80)

9 Instead of the sentence about lack of revolutionary experi-

ence, the Agitators previously said 'The paths to revolution are becoming clearer'. (p. 80)

10 From here down to Lenin's remark about rural poverty is new. Previously the Agitators announced that they had consulted the coolie organisation and decided there could be no armed action till the delegates of the peasants had arrived. Then the Young Comrade spoke his line about 'With my own two eyes', leading to the first stanza of 'Praise of the Party' by the Agitators. The Young Comrade's question about the Marxist classics then followed. (p. 81)

11 The first verse of this chorus is different in the published texts. We print what Eisler set. (p. 86)

12 The first version of all omitted the rest of this speech down to 'This decision', but it was in the text of the première. (p. 87)

13 The text for the première (ii) is closer to *He Said Yes*, and the first version of all (i) closer still. So in (i) they ask the Young Comrade if he agrees, and he says 'Yes', on which they comment 'He has answered in accordance with reality'. Then when he says 'Help me' they repeat the Three Students' 'Lean your head on our arm', and after his final declaration for Communism, 'saying Yes to the revolutionising of the world', they stand 'foot to foot' as in Waley to hurl him down, 'and clods of lime after/And flat stones they flung'. In (ii) these last words are omitted. (p. 88)

14 The concluding (italicised) section of the chorus was not in the pre-1931 texts. (p. 89)

The Mother

After Gorky

Play

Collaborators: HANNS EISLER, SLATAN DUDOW, GÜNTER WEISENBORN

Translator: JOHN WILLETT

Characters:

PELAGEA VLASSOVA, *The Mother*
PAVEL VLASSOV, *her son*
ANTON RYBIN, ANDREI NACHODKA, IVAN VESSOVCHIKOV, *workers in the Suchlinov factory*
MASHA KHALATOVA, *a worker*
POLICEMAN
INSPECTOR
GATEKEEPER
KARPOV, *a worker*
THE FACTORY GUARD
SMILGIN, *a worker*
THE TEACHER, *Nikolai Vessovchikov*
PAVEL SOSTAKOVITCH (SIGORSKI), *unemployed*
WARDER
YEGOR LUSHIN, *a farm worker*
TWO STRIKE-BREAKERS
VASSIL YEFIMOVITCH, *the butcher*
THE BUTCHER'S WIFE
THE LANDLADY
THE PEASANT WOMAN
THE POOR WOMAN
THE DOCTOR
THE OFFICIAL
A woman at the copper collection point
A woman in black
A maidservant
Working woman with a child
THE STOREKEEPER (*woman*)

Numbers in brackets refer to optional choruses given on pp. 358–360.

1

THE VLASSOVAS OF ALL COUNTRIES

Pelagea Vlassova's room in Tver. (1)

PELAGEA VLASSOVA: I am quite ashamed to offer this soup to my son. But I've no dripping left to put in it, not even half a spoonful. Only last week they cut a kopeck an hour off his wages, and I can't make that up however hard I try. I know how heavy his job is, and how badly he needs feeding up. It is bad that I cannot offer my son better soup; he's young and has barely stopped growing. He is very different from his late father. He's always reading books, and has never found his meals good enough. And so he is getting more and more discontented. (2)

She pours the soup into a container and takes it over to her son. On returning to the stove she sees how her son, eyes still on his book, lifts the lid and sniffs the soup, then replaces the lid and pushes the container away.

PELAGEA VLASSOVA: He's sniffing his soup again. It's the best I can give him. And soon he'll realise I'm no good to him any more, just a burden. What use is it my eating with him, living in his room and buying my clothes out of his earnings? Presently he'll leave me. What am I to do, Pelagea Vlassova, forty-two, a worker's widow and a worker's mother? I count the pennies over and over again. I try it this way and I try it that. One day I skimp on firewood, another day on clothing. But I can't manage. I don't see any answer. (3)

Her son Pavel has picked up his cap and the container, and left. The Mother tidies the room.

CHORUS

sung to the Mother by the revolutionary workers:

Brush down his coat
Brush it again then!
Once it's had a good brushing
It'll be decently ragged.

Cook with devotion
Take no end of trouble!
If you're a kopeck short
All his soup will be water.

Work even harder than now
Cut down your expenditure
Reckon it more exactly!
If you're a kopeck short
You can do nothing.

Whatever you do
You'll still have to struggle
Your position is bad
It'll worsen.
This cannot go on, but
What is to be the answer?

As the raven who can find nothing
For her fledglings to eat
Battles helplessly with the winter blizzard
And gets no reply to her crying
You too know there's no answer
When you cry.

Vainly you work till you drop, devising ways
To replace the irreplaceable and
Taking endless trouble to afford the unaffordable.
If you're a kopeck short, hard work is not enough.
Don't think the question of why your kitchen's empty
Will get decided in the kitchen.

Whatever you do
You'll still have to struggle
Your position is bad
It'll worsen.
This cannot go on, but
What is to be the answer?

2

THE MOTHER IS CONCERNED TO SEE HER SON IN THE COMPANY OF REVOLUTIONARY WORKERS

Pelagea Vlassova's room.

Three men and a young woman, all workers, bring a duplicator. It is early morning.

ANTON RYBIN: Two weeks back, Pavel, when you joined our movement, you said we could come to your room if we had a special job on. Your place is safest, as we've never worked here before.

PAVEL VLASSOV: What are you going to do?

ANDREI NACHODKA: Print today's leaflets. The latest wage-cuts have got the workers worried. We've been handing out leaflets at the works for the past three days, and today will be crucial. Tonight there's going to be a works meeting to decide whether to put up with a cut of another kopeck or go on strike.

IVAN VESSOVCHIKOV: We've brought the duplicator and some paper.

PAVEL: Sit down. My mother will make us some tea.

They go to the table.

IVAN *to Andrei*: Wait outside and watch out for the police.

ANTON: Where's your brother?

MASHA KHALATOVA: Sidor couldn't come. He saw someone looking like a policeman following him home last night. So today he thought he'd better go straight to the factory.

PAVEL: Keep your voice down. I'd sooner my mother didn't hear us. So far I've told her nothing about all this; she's not that young, and there's really no way she could help.

ANTON: Here's the stencil.

They start working. One of them has hung a thick cloth across the window.

PELAGEA VLASSOVA *aside*: I don't like seeing my son Pavel mixing with that lot. They're no good for him. They'll get him all worked up, then drag him into something. I'm not serving tea to their sort. (4) *She goes to the table.* Pavel, I can't make tea for you. There's not enough tea. It won't be strong enough.

PAVEL: Then make us some weak tea, Mother.

PELAGEA VLASSOVA *has gone back and sat down*: Suppose I do nothing of the kind, they may start to realise I can't abide them. I just don't like having them hanging around here, speaking so quietly I can't hear a word. *She again goes to the table.* Pavel, I can't have the landlord notice people are meeting here in the middle of the night and printing things. As it is, we can't pay our rent.

IVAN: Believe me, Mrs Vlassova, there's nothing interests us more than your rent. It may not look like it, but in fact it's all we care about.

PELAGEA VLASSOVA: You don't say.

She walks back.

ANTON: I don't think your mother's very glad to see us here, eh, Pavel?

IVAN: It's so hard for her to see we have to do this so that she can buy her tea and pay the rent.

PELAGEA VLASSOVA: Talk about thick-skinned! They're carrying on as if they simply hadn't noticed. What are they up to with Pavel? He went off to the factory and was glad they had a job for him. He wasn't earning much, and in the last twelve months it's been less and less. If they're going to cut it by another kopeck, then I'd sooner give up eating. But it worries me to see him reading those books, and I don't care to have him going off to all those meetings where they just work people up when they ought to be resting. The only result will be he'll lose his job.

MASHA *sings to Vlassova*:

THE ANSWER

If you've nothing on your plate
How can you fight the oppressor
Unless you can take the State
And turn the whole thing upside down for ever?
That's the way to fill your plate.
Start now, before it is too late.

If you find that you'll always be unemployed
How can you fight the oppressor

Unless you can take the State
And turn the whole thing upside down for ever?
After the bosses' power has been destroyed
You'll find nobody need be unemployed.

If they mock your weakness as absurd
Time will apply the pressure
And you will enjoy no rest
Until all the weak join together
And march till their voice is heard.
Then you will have the last word.

ANDREI *entering*: Police!

IVAN: Hide those papers!

Andrei takes the duplicator from Pavel and hangs it out of the window. Anton sits on the papers.

PELAGEA VLASSOVA: What did I say, Pavel? Here come the police. Pavel, what are you up to? What's in those papers?

MASHA *leads her to the window and makes her sit on a chair*: Just sit there and keep quiet, Mrs Vlassova.

Enter a policeman and an inspector

POLICEMAN: Halt! Anyone moves will be shot. That's his mother, your honour, and that's himself.

INSPECTOR: Pavel Vlassov, I have to search your premises. What is this squalid gang you've gathered here?

POLICEMAN: Here's Sidor Khalatov's sister; we arrested him this morning. It's them all right.

MASHA: What's happened to my brother?

INSPECTOR: Your brother sends his best wishes; at present he's our guest. He is bolshevising our bedbugs and has collected a large following. A pity he hasn't more pamphlets.

The workers exchange glances.

INSPECTOR: Some of the cells where he is are still vacant, come to think of it. Didn't I hear you people singing a charming ditty just now? Pray don't let me interrupt you. I too am something of a musician. Just that it pains me, Mrs Vlassova, that such a song should have been sung in *your* house. Because it means that I have to search your house for the music, so that we members of the police force can join in with our crude voices. *He walks over to the divan.* For example, Mrs Vlassova, I shall have to slit your divan open. Is that what you wish? *He slits it open.*

PAVEL: No banknotes there, are there? That's because we are workers and don't earn much.

INSPECTOR: And that mirror on your wall. Does it really have to be smashed by the rough hand of a policeman? *He breaks it to pieces.* You're a respectable woman, I know. And there was nothing dubious in the divan. But what about the chest of drawers? It's a nice old piece. *He overturns it.* Well, well, nothing behind that either. Vlassova, Vlassova, decent people are never sly; you aren't sly, are you? And there's your dripping jar with a spoon in it; very touching, that jar. *Takes it off the shelf and drops it.* Dear me, it has fallen on the floor, and now it seems that there really is dripping in it.

PAVEL: Not much. There isn't much dripping in it, Inspector. And there isn't much bread in the breadbin, or much tea in the tin.

INSPECTOR: So that's a political jar after all. Vlassova, Vlassova, do you really have to get mixed up with us in your old age, with us bloodhounds? How beautifully you've washed your curtains. It isn't often one comes across that. Nice to see it. *He rips them down.*

IVAN *to Anton, who has leapt up out of fear for the duplicator*: Sit down, they'll shoot you.

PAVEL *loudly, in order to distract the Inspector*: Did you really have to throw the dripping jar on the floor?

ANDREI *to the Policeman*: Pick the jar up!

POLICEMAN: It's Andrei Nachodka from Little Russia.

INSPECTOR *goes up to the table*: Andrei Maximovitch Nachodka, weren't you in gaol once before on a political charge?

ANDREI: Yes, in Rostov and in Saratov. But the police there had some manners.

INSPECTOR *pulling the leaflet from his pocket*: Do you know the villains who are circulating these highly treacherous leaflets in the Suchlinov works?

PAVEL: We've never seen villains here before.

INSPECTOR: We'll soon shut that big mouth of yours, Pavel Vlassov. Sit straight when I'm speaking to you!

PELAGEA VLASSOVA: Don't you shout like that. You're a young man, and you haven't learnt what it is to be poor. You're a public servant. You get a fat regular salary for cutting up my sofa and finding my dripping jar empty.

INSPECTOR: It's too early to start crying, Vlassova, I should save your tears for later. Better keep an eye on that son of yours, he's going down a bad road. *To the workers*: One of these days you'll learn it doesn't pay to be sly with me.

The Inspector and the Policeman leave. The workers tidy up.

ANTON: Mrs Vlassova, we owe you an apology. We had no idea they suspected us. And now your flat has been wrecked.

MASHA: Were you very frightened, Mrs Vlassova?

PELAGEA VLASSOVA: Yes, I see Pavel's going down a bad road.

MASHA: So you think it's all right for them to wreck your place because your son is fighting for his kopeck?

PELAGEA VLASSOVA: They're not in the right, but nor is he. (5)

IVAN *back at the table*: What about getting those leaflets distributed?

ANTON: If we let just one police search stop us distributing leaflets, then we're all piss and wind. Those leaflets have got to be distributed.

ANDREI: How many are there?

PAVEL: About five hundred.

IVAN: And who's going to distribute them?

ANTON: It's Pavel's turn.

Pelagea Vlassova beckons Ivan to come to her.

PELAGEA VLASSOVA: Who's to distribute your leaflets?

IVAN: Pavel. It's got to be done.

PELAGEA VLASSOVA: Got to be done, indeed. It all comes of reading books and getting home late. Then it's working here with those machines and having to hang them out of the window. And then covering the window with a cloth. And discussing things in a whisper. Got to be done! All of a sudden there's me with the police in my house, and they're treating me like a criminal. *She stands up.* Pavel, I'm not having you distribute those leaflets.

ANDREI: It's got to be done, Mrs Vlassova.

PAVEL *to Masha*: Tell her they have to be distributed for Sidor's sake, to take the heat off him.

The workers come up to Pelagea Vlassova. Pavel remains at the table.

MASHA: Mrs Vlassova, it's got to be done for my brother's sake too.

IVAN: Otherwise Sidor could be sent to Siberia.

ANDREI: You see, if no leaflets are distributed today they'll realise it must have been Sidor yesterday.

ANTON: That's good enough reason in itself why it's got to be done again today.

PELAGEA VLASSOVA: I see that it's got to be done to save this young man you have dragged in. But what about Pavel, suppose they arrest him?

ANTON: There's not that much risk.

PELAGEA VLASSOVA: There's not that much risk, eh. You talk a fellow round and get him involved. This and that have to be done to save him. There's no risk but it's got to be done. We're under suspicion, but we have to distribute leaflets. It's got to be done, so there's not much risk. So one thing leads to another. And in the end there's a fellow on the gallows: stick your head through that noose, there's not much risk. Gimme those leaflets, I'll go and distribute them, not Pavel.

ANTON: But how will you set about it?

PELAGEA VLASSOVA: Don't you worry. I can manage every bit as well as you lot. There's my friend Maria Korssunova sells snacks there during the lunch break. I'll stand in for her today and use your pamphlets as wrapping paper.

She goes and gets her shopping bag.

MASHA: Pavel, here's your mother offering to distribute our leaflets today.

PAVEL: Argue it out between you. I'd rather not say what I think of her offer if you don't mind.

ANTON: Andrei?

ANDREI: I think she can bring it off. The workers know her and the police have nothing against her.

ANTON: Ivan?

IVAN: I agree with Andrei.

ANTON: Even if they caught her she'd have the least trouble. She's not in the movement, which means she only did it for her son's sake. Comrade Vlassov, in view of the desperate situation and the great danger to Comrade Sidor, we're for accepting your mother's offer.

IVAN: We're convinced that she runs the least risk.

PAVEL: All right.

PELAGEA VLASSOVA *to herself*: It's certainly a very bad business I've offered to help with, but I've got to keep Pavel out of it.

ANTON: Right, Mrs Vlassova, we're entrusting you with this packet of leaflets.

ANDREI: It means you'll be fighting for us now, Pelagea Vlassova.

PELAGEA VLASSOVA: Fighting? I'm not a young woman any longer, and I'm not a fighter. I'm happy if I can scrape my three kopecks together, that's enough fighting for me.

ANDREI: Do you know what's in those pamphlets, Mrs Vlassova?

PELAGEA VLASSOVA: No, I can't read.

3

Courtyard of the Suchlinov factory.

PELAGEA VLASSOVA *carrying a large basket, is outside the factory gates*: It all depends what kind of man the gatekeeper is: is he idle or pernickety? All I need do is get him to give me a pass. Then I'll wrap my wares in the pamphlets, and if they catch me I'll just say 'They were planted on me, I can't read.' *She has a good look at the Gatekeeper*. He's fat, must be idle. I'll see what he does if I offer him a gherkin. Fellows like that like eating but can't afford it. *She goes up to the gate and drops a packet in front of the Gatekeeper.* Hey, I've dropped one of my packets. *The Gatekeeper looks away.* Funny, I've gone and forgotten, all I need do is put my basket down, then I've got both hands free. When I was just going to trouble you. *To the audience*: Talk about hard-boiled! You have to keep chatting him up, then he'll do anything for a bit of peace and quiet. *She goes to the opening and talks rapidly*: Just like Maria Korssunova, ain't it, only yesterday there was me telling her: 'Do what you like but just don't you get wet feet!' But d'you think she'd listen to me? No. Went on digging potatoes and got wet feet! Next morning she feeds the goats. Wet feet! What d'you say to that? So there she is flat on her back. But instead of keeping to her bed, that same evening out she goes.

Of course it's raining, so what does she get? Wet feet!

GATEKEEPER: Can't come in here without a pass.

PELAGEA VLASSOVA: Just what I told her. You know, her and me, we're just like that – *Gesture.* – but talk of pigheaded, you never seen nothing like it. Vlassova dear, I'm sick, so you'll have to go to the factory for me and sell my food packets. There you are, Maria, says I, now you've lost your voice. But why've you lost it? Just you say wet feet to me once more, she croaks, and I'll crown you with this teapot! Did I say pigheaded?

The Gatekeeper sighs deeply and lets her in.

PELAGEA VLASSOVA: I know, I'm taking up your time.

It is the lunch break. The workers are sitting eating on boxes and so on. Pelagea Vlassova offers them snacks. Ivan Vessovchikov helps her to wrap these up.

PELAGEA VLASSOVA: Gherkins, tobacco, tea, fresh pasties!

IVAN: And the wrapping paper is the best part.

PELAGEA VLASSOVA: Gherkins, tobacco, tea, fresh pasties!

IVAN: And the wrapping paper is free.

A WORKER: Got any gherkins?

PELAGEA VLASSOVA: Gherkins, yes, here you are.

IVAN: And the wrapping paper mustn't be thrown away.

PELAGEA VLASSOVA: Gherkins, tobacco, tea, fresh pasties!

A WORKER: What's so special about what's printed on the wrapping paper? I can't read.

ANOTHER WORKER: How'm I to know what's on your wrapping paper?

FIRST WORKER: You're holding one, clever.

SECOND WORKER: Quite right, it says something.

FIRST WORKER: So what?

SECOND WORKER: Good for them, they say if we get drawn into negotiating the more fools us.

PELAGEA VLASSOVA *crosses the yard*: Gherkins, tobacco, tea, fresh pasties!

THIRD WORKER: Here they are, with the police after them and factory security tightened up, and here's another pamphlet just the same. They know what they're doing, that lot, and nobody's going to stop them. There's something in what they say.

FIRST WORKER: Well, when I see something like that I'm for it.

PAVEL: Here's Karpov at last.

ANTON: I wonder what he's got us.

KARPOV *arrives*: Are all our committee here?

The members of the works committee gather in a corner of the yard, among them Anton and Pavel.

KARPOV: We negotiated, friends.

ANTON: What's the result?

KARPOV: Friends, we have not come back empty-handed.

ANTON: Did you save our kopeck?

KARPOV: Friends, we have always laid stress on the intolerable sanitary conditions in this factory.

PAVEL: Got the kopeck?

KARPOV: The marsh outside the eastern gate is an absolute disgrace.

ANTON: So that's going to be your excuse!

KARPOV: Think of those clouds of mosquitoes every summer that drive us indoors; of the high incidence of malaria, of the persistent threat to the health of our children. That marsh, friends, can be drained at the cost of 24,000 roubles. Mr Suchlinov is prepared to take that on. The area gained would allow the factory to be extended, with a consequent increase in jobs. As you know, the prosperity of the factory means prosperity for all of us. Friends, at present it is not doing so well as we might think. We cannot ignore what Mr Suchlinov told us about our sister enterprise in Tver, whose imminent closure will mean 700 of our friends losing their jobs. We are for the lesser evil. It would be unrealistic to close our eyes to the fact that this country is facing one of the worst economic crises it has ever experienced.

ANTON: In other words, capitalism is sick and you are the doctor. So you want to accept the wage cut?

KARPOV: Our negotiations suggested no other answer.

ANTON: Then we call for negotiations with the management to be broken off, given that you cannot resist the wage cut. We reject the marsh deal.

KARPOV: I'm warning you, don't break off negotiations with management.

ANOTHER WORKER: You must realise it would mean a strike.

PAVEL: We say nothing but a strike can prevent the kopeck cut.

ANTON: The question for today's meeting is quite simple. It is:

should Mr Suchlinov's marsh be drained or our kopeck be saved? We must strike; May 1st is only a week away now, when we must try to ensure the closure of all other factories where wages are supposed to be cut.

KARPOV: I am warning you!

Sound of the factory siren. The workers stand up and go back to work. Looking back at Karpov they sing him the

SONG OF THE PATCHES AND THE COAT

If you see that our coat's in tatters
You come along and complain 'That's not good enough.
We must hurry to his rescue, do our best to help him.'
Off you go to buttonhole our boss
While we hang about and shiver.
Back you come then, triumphantly set to show off
What you've managed to win for us:
Just some makeshift patches.
  Right, we've got the patches.
  Yes, but where is
  The complete coat.

If you hear us cry out in hunger
You come along and complain 'That's not good enough.
We must hurry to his rescue, do our best to help him.'
Off you go and buttonhole our boss
While we wait and rub our stomachs.
Back you come then, triumphantly set to show off
What you've managed to win for us:
One stale crust.
  Right, we've got a stale crust.
  Yes, but where is
  The complete loaf.

We don't only need the patches
We must have a complete coat.
We don't only need a stale crust
We must have a complete loaf.
We need much more than a job or two
We must have the whole of the works
And the coalmines and the steel and

Control of the State.
Right, all that's what we must have
But what have
You to offer us?

The workers go off.

KARPOV: A strike, then!

PELAGEA VLASSOVA *comes forward*: Gherkins, tobacco, tea, fresh pasties!

KARPOV: A gherkin.

Pelagea Vlassova sells him a gherkin, and sits down to count her takings.

PELAGEA VLASSOVA *to herself*: They can't be allowed to cut wages; it's very wrong, and particularly hard on me. If wages keep going down how can I manage with Pavel? He's already so dissatisfied. (6)

KARPOV *follows her*: This is a leaflet. So you're handing them out? You realise this bit of paper means a strike?

PELAGEA VLASSOVA: A strike? How come?

KARPOV: These leaflets are calling on the workers in the Suchlinov plant to strike.

PELAGEA VLASSOVA: I know nothing about that.

KARPOV: So why are you distributing them?

PELAGEA VLASSOVA: We have our reasons. Why are our people being arrested?

KARPOV: Have you any idea what they say?

PELAGEA VLASSOVA: No, I can't read.

KARPOV: They're stirring our people up. Strikes are bad news. Tomorrow morning nobody goes to work. What about tomorrow evening? And next week? It means nothing to the firm whether we work or not, but for us it's a matter of life and death. *The Factory Guard hurries in accompanied by the Gatekeeper.* Are you looking for something, Anton Antonovitch?

FACTORY GUARD: Yes, they've been distributing leaflets agitating for a strike. I can't think how they got in. What's that you've got?

Karpov tries to hide the leaflet in his pocket.

FACTORY GUARD: What's that you're stuffing in your pocket? *He pulls it out.* A leaflet!

GATEKEEPER: So you read those leaflets?

KARPOV: Anton Antonovitch, my friend, surely we're allowed to read what we want.

FACTORY GUARD: Hah. *Seizes him by the collar to drag him away.* I'll teach you to read leaflets that call on your workforce to strike.

KARPOV: But I've done nothing. This woman here will tell you I've done nothing.

PELAGEA VLASSOVA: He's done nothing. I can swear it. He's completely innocent!

KARPOV: Let go! Let go of me!

FACTORY GUARD *beating him*: I'll learn you! Leaflets!

Factory Guard and Gatekeeper take Karpov away.

PELAGEA VLASSOVA: All the man did was buy a gherkin.

4

PELAGEA VLASSOVA GETS HER FIRST LESSON IN ECONOMICS

Pelagea Vlassova's room.

PELAGEA VLASSOVA: Pavel, today I distributed the leaflets you had given me, so as to take the heat off that young man you people had got involved. After I'd finished that, with my own eyes I had to see another innocent fellow being arrested just because he had read one of those leaflets. What is it you've got me to do?

ANTON: Thanks from us all, Mrs Vlassova, for your clever action.

PELAGEA VLASSOVA: So that's what you call cleverness? And what about Karpov, whom I and my cleverness put in prison?

ANDREI: 'Twasn't you that put him in prison. Far as we know it was the police.

IVAN: But you helped unite the workers in the Suchlinov factory. You'll have heard the strike vote was almost a hundred per cent.

PELAGEA VLASSOVA: I didn't want to make a strike; just to help someone. And I didn't help him, but got someone else into trouble. How about Sidor, how about the other one? Why are they being arrested? Because they read leaflets? Why are you striking? What did that leaflet say?

PAVEL: What do you think it said?

PELAGEA VLASSOVA: Something wrong.

ANTON: Mrs Vlassova, it seems we owe you an explanation.

PAVEL: Sit down, Mother, we'll put it on the line for you.

They get chairs and sit in a circle round Pelagea Vlassova.

IVAN: What that leaflet said, you see, was that the workers shouldn't allow Mr Suchlinov to cut the wages he pays us, just as he pleases.

PELAGEA VLASSOVA: What nonsense, how are you to stop him? Why shouldn't Mr Suchlinov be able to cut the wages he pays you, just as he pleases? Does his factory belong to him, or doesn't it?

PAVEL: It belongs to him.

PELAGEA VLASSOVA: Right. This table, for instance, belongs to me. Let me ask you: can I do whatever I want with it?

ANDREI: Yes, Mrs Vlassova, you can do whatever you want with this table.

PELAGEA VLASSOVA: Right. For instance, can I smash it into little pieces if I want?

ANTON: Yes, you can smash this table into little pieces if you want.

PELAGEA VLASSOVA: Aha. Mr Suchlinov's factory belongs to him like my table does to me, so can he do with it whatever he wants?

PAVEL: No.

PELAGEA VLASSOVA: Why not?

IVAN: Because for his factory he needs us workers.

PELAGEA VLASSOVA: And suppose he says he doesn't need you any longer?

PAVEL: You see, Mother, you have to look at it like this: at one moment he may need us, and at another not.

ANTON: That's right.

PAVEL: When he needs us we have to be there, and when he doesn't need us we're there just the same. Where else can we go? And he knows that. He doesn't always need us, but we always need him. And he takes advantage of it. Mr Suchlinov has his machines there. But they are our work tools. We haven't any others. We have no looms and no lathes; we use Mr Suchlinov's. His factory belongs to him, but if he closes it then he is taking our tools away from us.

PELAGEA VLASSOVA: Because your tools belong to him the same way my table belongs to me.

ANTON: Right, but do you think it's right that our work tools should belong to him?

PELAGEA VLASSOVA *loudly*: No! But whether or not I think it's right, they belong to him just the same. And somebody might think it's not right for my table to belong to me.

PAVEL: You see, that's where we'd say: it's not the same thing for a table to belong to you as for a factory. Course a table can belong to you, or a chair for that matter. It harms nobody. If you store it in the loft, what harm can that do? But if a factory belongs to you you can harm several hundred people. Because their work tools are in your possession, and this gives you the power to exploit them.

PELAGEA VLASSOVA: Right, so he can exploit us. Don't act as if I wouldn't have realised that after thirty years' experience. There's just one thing I didn't realise – something could have been done to stop it.

ANTON: So now we agree, Mrs Vlassova, with respect to Mr Suchlinov's property, that his factory is property in a quite different sense from, let's say, your table. He can use his property to exploit us.

IVAN: And there's another remarkable thing about his property: if he doesn't use it to exploit us it is entirely valueless to him. It is of great value to him just so long as it constitutes our tools. The moment it stops being our means of production it becomes an old scrapheap. So he and his property are dependent on us.

PELAGEA VLASSOVA: Good, but how are you to convince him that he is dependent on you?

ANDREI: It's like this. Suppose he, Pavel Vlassov, goes up to Mr Suchlinov and says 'Mr Suchlinov, without me your factory is old scrap-iron, so you can't cut my wages just as you please', then Mr Suchlinov will laugh himself silly and chuck Vlassov out. But suppose all the Vlassovs in Tver, eight hundred Vlassovs, stand there saying the same thing, then Mr Suchlinov won't laugh any longer.

PELAGEA VLASSOVA: And that is your strike?

PAVEL: Yes, that's our strike.

PELAGEA VLASSOVA: And that's what the leaflet said?

PAVEL: Yes, that's what the leaflet said.

PELAGEA VLASSOVA: A strike is bad news. What do I cook with? What about the rent? Tomorrow morning none of you go to work. What about tomorrow evening? And next week? Never mind, we can get round that somehow. But if the leaflet was only about a strike, why were the police arresting people? How does it come to be their business?

PAVEL: Yes, Mother, you tell us: how does that come to be their business?

PELAGEA VLASSOVA: If we take up our dispute with Mr Suchlinov, that's surely nothing to do with the police? You must have gone about it the wrong way. There must be a misunderstanding. People thought you were planning some violence. What you need is to show the whole city that your dispute with the management is peaceful and justifiable. That would impress them.

IVAN: It's just what we want to do, Mrs Vlassova. On May 1st, the international celebration of the workers' struggle, all the factories in Tver will be demonstrating for the liberation of the working class. And we shall carry banners calling on all of them to support our fight against the kopeck cut.

PELAGEA VLASSOVA: If you march peacefully through the streets just carrying your banners, then nobody can object.

ANDREI: We are quite sure Mr Suchlinov is not going to like it.

PELAGEA VLASSOVA: He will have to like it.

IVAN: The police will probably break up the demonstration.

PELAGEA VLASSOVA: Why should the police be on Mr Suchlinov's side? The police may be above you, but they are just as much above Mr Suchlinov.

PAVEL: So, Mother, you think the police will take no action against a peaceful demonstration?

PELAGEA VLASSOVA: Yes, that's what I think. There's nothing violent about it. You and I will never agree about violence, Pavel. You know I believe there is a God in Heaven. I want nothing to do with violence. I've been meeting it for forty years and couldn't do anything to stop it. But when I die I want at least to have done nothing violent myself.

5

REPORT ON MAY DAY, 1905

Street.

PAVEL: When we workers from the Suchlinov factory entered the market square we met up with the column of other factory workers; there must have been several thousand of them. We were carrying banners which said 'Workers, support our struggle against the wage cuts! Workers, unite!'

IVAN: We were marching in a calm and disciplined manner. Singing songs like 'Arise, ye starvelings from your slumbers!' and 'Brüder, zur Sonne, zur Freiheit'. Our factory came immediately after the big red flag.

ANDREI: Close by me marched Pelagea Vlassova, just behind her son. When we collected him first thing this morning she suddenly appeared at the kitchen door fully dressed, and when we asked where she was going she replied:

PELAGEA VLASSOVA: Coming with you.

ANTON: Many of her sort came with us, drawn to our cause by the severe winter, the wage cuts in the factories and our own propaganda. Up to the Tverskaya and the Avenue of the Redeemer we saw just a few policemen and no military, but at their junction we found ourselves suddenly faced with a double line of soldiers. The moment they saw our flag and our banners a voice shouted at us: This is a warning! Break it up! We're going to shoot. Then: Drop that flag! – Our column came to a halt.

PAVEL: But those behind kept on coming, so those in front couldn't stop and the shooting began. As the first of us fell there was total confusion. Many of them couldn't believe what they were seeing was really happening. Then the police started advancing on the main body.

PELAGEA VLASSOVA: I had gone along to demonstrate for the workers' cause. The marchers were a lot of decent people who had worked all their lives. Of course there were some desperate men among them who'd been driven to extremes by unemployment, and some that were too hungry and weak to defend themselves.

ANDREI: We were still close to the leaders and kept together even when the shooting started.

PAVEL: We had our flag, Smilgin was carrying it and we were not going to give it up, because we all of us understood how important it was that we should be the ones to be hit and brought down, and our flag, the *red* flag, should be the one they took. We didn't have to talk about it, because we wanted all the workers to see who we are and what we stand for: for the workers' cause.

ANDREI: Our opponents had to behave like wild animals. Because that's what the Suchlinovs pay them to do.

MASHA: Sooner or later everyone would see this, and our flag, the *red* flag, had to be held specially high so that they could all see it, not least the police, but all the rest too.

IVAN: And those who didn't see it would have to be told about it, that day or tomorrow or in the years to come, till the day when it would be seen again. Because we thought we knew – and many of us knew for sure at that instant – that it would often be seen *again*, from this time forward to the total transformation of all things, that flag that is on the march, our flag, the most dangerous of all in the eyes of our rulers and oppressors, the most relentless!

ANTON: And for us workers, decisive!

ALL:

Therefore you will see it
Always have to see it
With joy or revulsion
Depending on your role in this great war
Which will not ever finish except
With our side's conclusive triumph
In every town of every country
Where the workers are found.

PELAGEA VLASSOVA: On this day it was carried by the worker Smilgin.

SMILGIN: My name is Smilgin. I have been fifteen years in the movement. I was one of the first to spread revolutionary ideas in our works. We fought for our wages and improved working conditions. In the course of this I often negotiated on behalf of my colleagues with the employers. At first I saw them as enemies; then I admit I thought a different approach would help. As our power increased, I thought, we would start to be consulted. It seems that was wrong. Here I stand now, thousands stand behind me, but in front of us once again stands armed force. Are we to give up our flag?

ANTON: Don't you give it up, Smilgin! Negotiations lead nowhere, we said. And Pelagea Vlassova told him:

PELAGEA VLASSOVA: You don't have to give it up, they can't do anything to you. The police can't object to a peaceful demonstration.

MASHA: Just at that moment a police officer screamed at us: Hand over that flag!

IVAN: And Smilgin looked behind him and saw our banners behind his flag and our slogans on the banners. And behind the banners were the strikers from the Suchlinov works. And we watched to see what he, close beside us, one of us, would do with the flag.

PAVEL: Fifteen years in the movement, worker, revolutionary, on May 1st 1908, at 11 a.m. by the corner of the Avenue of the Redeemer, at the critical moment. He said:

SMILGIN: I am not handing it over! We won't negotiate!

ANDREI: Well done, Smilgin, we said. That's right. All as it should be.

IVAN: Yes, he said, and fell on his face, for by then they had shot him.

ANDREI: And four or five men came running towards us to get the flag. But the flag lay beside him. Then our quiet, level-headed Pelagea Vlassova, our comrade, bent down and took hold of the flag.

PELAGEA VLASSOVA: Give us the flag, Smilgin, I said. Give it me! I'll carry it for you. Everything is going to be different!

6

a

FOLLOWING THE ARREST OF HER SON PAVEL, IVAN VESSOVCHIKOV BRINGS PELAGEA VLASSOVA TO HIS BROTHER NIKOLAI, A TEACHER

Schoolmaster Vessovchikov's flat in Rostov.

IVAN: Nikolai Ivanovitch, I have brought Pelagea Vlassova, our friend Pavel's mother, to see you. They arrested her son because of what happened at the May Day demonstration. Then she got notice to leave her old flat, so we have promised her son to find safe quarters for her. Your flat is not under suspicion. Nobody can suggest you have anything to do with the revolutionary movement.

THE TEACHER: Yes, that's perfectly true. As a teacher I should lose my position if I had my head in the clouds like you.

IVAN: All the same, I hope you'll be able to keep Mrs Vlassova here, as she has got nowhere to go. You'd be doing a great favour to me, your brother.

THE TEACHER: I have no reason to do you a favour. I'm extremely doubtful about everything you are doing. All of it is nonsense. I often enough shown you why. But that doesn't apply to you, Mrs Vlassova. I realise your position is desperate. And anyway I need a housekeeper. As you see, my things badly need putting in order.

IVAN: Of course you must pay her something for her work, she has to send something to her son now and again.

THE TEACHER: I would only be able to pay you quite a small wage of course.

IVAN: In political matters he is as thick as a plank. But he has his human side.

THE TEACHER: Ivan, you are an idiot. Mrs Vlassova, that's the kitchen, in there is a sofa, and you can sleep on it. I see you have brought your own bedlinen. The kitchen is this way, Mrs Vlassova.

Pelagea Vlassova takes her bundle into the kitchen, and at once starts arranging it.

IVAN: My personal thanks, Nikolai Ivanovitch, and I beg you to keep an eye on her. She must not have anything more to do with politics right away. She was involved in the May Day disturbances and needs to have a rest. She's worried about what's happened to her son. I'm making you responsible for her.

THE TEACHER: You won't catch me dragging her into politics like you do.

b

SCHOOLMASTER VESSOVCHIKOV FINDS HIS HOUSEKEEPER MAKING PROPAGANDA

In the kitchen some workers are sitting round Pelagea Vlassova.

WOMAN: We've been told Communism is a crime.

PELAGEA VLASSOVA: That's not true. Communism is good for us. What is there against Communism? *She sings*:

PRAISE OF COMMUNISM

It stands to reason, anyone can grasp it. It's not hard.
If you're no exploiter then you must understand it.
It is good for you, find out what it really means.
The dullards will say that it's dull, and the dirty will say that it's dirty.
It has no use for dirt and no use for dullness.
Exploiters will speak of it as criminal
But we know better:
It's going to stop them being criminal.
It is not a madness, rather
The end of all madness.
It is not the problem
But the solution.
It is that simple thing
Which is so hard to do.

WOMAN: Why don't all the workers understand that?

SOSTAKOVITCH, *an unemployed worker*: Because they are being kept in the dark about the fact that they are exploited, and that this is a crime, and that this crime can be eliminated.

They stop talking, as the Teacher enters his room next door.

THE TEACHER: Here I come, back from the beer-house, my head ringing with arguments, infuriated once again by that fathead Sachar and his way of contradicting me all the time when of course I was perfectly right, and thankful to be in my own peaceful surroundings. I think I'll soak my feet and read the paper.

PELAGEA VLASSOVA *entering*: Why, Nikolai Ivanovitch, you're back already.

THE TEACHER: Yes, and I'd like you to prepare me a hot foot-bath. I'll take it in the kitchen.

PELAGEA VLASSOVA: What a good thing you've arrived, Nikolai Ivanovitch, such a good thing, as you must go straight out again. The lady next door was just telling me your friend Sachar Smerdyakov was here an hour ago. He couldn't leave a message as he urgently needs to speak to you personally. Catch him quickly! Catch him quickly! Think how often you've slipped up on your obligations because of your inborn love of your comforts. What's more, it's some kind of personal favour Mr Smerdyakov is asking you for. As I told you, he was here just an hour ago.

THE TEACHER: Mrs Vlassova, I've spent the entire evening with my friend Sachar Smerdyakov.

PELAGEA VLASSOVA: Oh? But the kitchen's in a dreadful mess, Nikolai Ivanovitch. The washing's hanging up to dry.

Murmur of voices from the kitchen.

THE TEACHER: That's the first time I've heard my washing talk, and – *pointing to the samovar which she is carrying* – when did my shirts start drinking tea?

PELAGEA VLASSOVA: Nikolai Ivanovitch, I have to tell you that we are having a bit of a chat over a cup of tea.

THE TEACHER: Oh. And who are 'we'?

PELAGEA VLASSOVA: They might make you feel embarrassed, Nikolai Ivanovitch. They're not very well-off.

THE TEACHER: Ha, so you're talking politics again! Is that unemployed fellow Sostakovitch one of them?

PELAGEA VLASSOVA: Yes, and his wife and his brother with his son, and his uncle and his aunt. They're very sensible people; you'd be interested in what they have to say.

THE TEACHER: Mrs Vlassova, haven't I already told you that I don't want any talk of politics in my house? Here am I, I come home exhausted from my beer-house, and find my kitchen chock-a-block with politics. I am surprised, Mrs Vlassova, very surprised indeed.

PELAGEA VLASSOVA: Nikolai Ivanovitch, I am sorry that I had to disappoint you. I was telling them about May 1st. They need to know more about it.

THE TEACHER: What do you know of politics, Mrs Vlassova? Only this evening I was telling my friend Sachar, a highly intelligent person: 'Sachar Smerdyakov, nothing on this earth is so difficult and incomprehensible as politics.'

PELAGEA VLASSOVA: You must be quite tired out. But if you had a spare moment: all of us agreed this evening that you could make a lot of things clear to us, not least about May 1st, which is so particularly incomprehensible.

THE TEACHER: I am not all that keen on an aimless dispute with Mr Sostakovitch. The most I could do would be to familiarise you with the basic principles of politics. But really, Mrs Vlassova, it worries me to see you in the company of such dubious-looking individuals. Bring along the samovar and a bit of bread and some pickled gherkins.

They take it all into the kitchen.

c

PELAGEA VLASSOVA LEARNS TO READ

THE TEACHER *in front of a blackboard*: So you want to read, do you? I can't think what use it would be to you in your position, you're a bit old to start now. But I'll do my best for Mrs Vlassova's sake. All got something to write with? These are three simple words I'm writing, 'Hat, Dog, Fish'. I'll say them again: 'Hat, Dog, Fish'. *He writes.*

SOSTAKOVITCH: What's the point of words like that?

PELAGEA VLASSOVA *sitting at the table with the three others*: Does it really have to be 'Hat, Dog, Fish'? We're old and we haven't got all that long to learn the words we need.

THE TEACHER *with a smile*: It doesn't matter what words you learn from.

PELAGEA VLASSOVA: Why not? How do you write 'Worker' for instance? Pavel Sostakovitch here would be interested in that.

SOSTAKOVITCH: We don't talk about 'Hats'.

PELAGEA VLASSOVA: He's a metalworker.

THE TEACHER: But you use those letters.

ONE OF THE WORKERS: But the words 'Class War' have letters in them too.

THE TEACHER: Right, but you have to start with the simplest, not the hardest. 'Hat' is simple.

SOSTAKOVITCH: 'Class War' is a lot simpler.

THE TEACHER: There's no such thing as Class War. Let's be clear about that.

SOSTAKOVITCH *standing up*: I can't learn anything from you if you think there's no class war.

PELAGEA VLASSOVA: You're here to learn how to read and write, and you can do that here. Reading *is* class war.

THE TEACHER: That's a lot of rubbish, in my view. 'Reading *is* class war' – what on earth does that mean? What's the point of such talk? *Writing.* So here's 'Worker'. Copy it down.

PELAGEA VLASSOVA: 'Reading *is* class war' means: once we can read and write we'll be able to write our own pamphlets and read our books. Then we can direct the class war.

THE TEACHER: Let me tell you people something. I'm a teacher, and for twelve years now I've taught reading and writing, but I have to admit: I know in my heart that it's all rubbish. Books are rubbish. They just make mankind worse. Take a simple peasant, he's a better person because he's not been spoiled by civilisation.

PELAGEA VLASSOVA: So how d'you write 'Class War'? Pavel Sostakovitch, you must keep your hand steady, or it'll shake so your writing's not clear.

THE TEACHER *writing*: Class War. *To Sostakovitch*: You must write in a straight line and not go beyond the margin. Those who don't respect the margins don't respect the law. Generation after generation has amassed piles of knowledge and written piles of books. And we have never progressed so far technically. But what has it done for us? We have never seen such confusion. The whole box of tricks should be chucked into the depths of the sea, all those books and machines into the Black Sea. Defend yourselves against knowledge! Finished yet? Sometimes I get completely drowned in melancholia. What, I ask myself, can such truly great thoughts – thoughts that encompass not just the Now but the Always and the Eternal, the Human Condition in its essence – what can they have to do with class war?

SOSTAKOVITCH: Thoughts like that are no use. As you drown you're exploiting us.

PELAGEA VLASSOVA: Shut up, Pavel Sostakovitch. Please, how do you spell 'Exploitation'?

THE TEACHER: Exploitation. That's another word only found in books. Fancy me ever having exploited anyone!

SOSTAKOVITCH: You only say that because you get none of the loot.

PELAGEA VLASSOVA *to Sostakovitch*: The W in 'Class War' is exactly the same as the W in 'Worker'.

THE TEACHER: Knowledge doesn't help. Knowledge doesn't help. Goodness helps.

PELAGEA VLASSOVA: If you don't need your knowledge, just let us have it.

PRAISE OF LEARNING
sung by the learners:

Study the simple things: nothing
Comes too late for those whose day's
About to dawn.
Study your ABC. True, it's not enough, but
Study it. Don't neglect your potential
But learn! Knowledge is essential.
You must be ready to take over.

Study, tramp on a bench!
Study, man under sentence!
Study, wife in the kitchen!
Study, man of seventy!
You must be ready to take over.
Back to the classroom, you displaced person!
Get hold of more knowledge, freezing man!
Hungry man, grab for a book: books will be your weapons.
You must be ready to take over.

Don't hesitate to question things, comrade.
Don't just accept them but
See for yourself.
What you yourself don't know
You don't know.
Check through the invoices.
You have to pay them.
Learn how to point to each single item
Ask how it came to be there.
You must be ready to take over.

PELAGEA VLASSOVA *getting up*: That's enough for today. We can't go on taking in all that much at once. Or else Pavel Sostakovitch will be having another sleepness night. Thanks from us all, Nikolai Ivanovitch. We can only tell you that your teaching us to read and write is a great help.

THE TEACHER: I can't believe that. But don't think I'm saying your opinions are worthless. I'll come back to that point at our next lesson.

d

IVAN VESSOVCHIKOV CAN'T RECOGNISE HIS OWN BROTHER

IVAN: I thought I'd see how you were doing, Mrs Vlassova, and bring you some of our leaflets. Has Pavel written?

PELAGEA VLASSOVA: Not a word. I'm very worried about him.

THE TEACHER: You don't need to worry about a man like your son.

PELAGEA VLASSOVA: The worst of it is that I never know what he is doing, or what they are doing to him. For instance I don't even know if they are giving him enough to eat and if he isn't freezing. Do you know if they get blankets in there? I'm very proud of him. Lucky me, I have a son who is needed. *She recites*:

PRAISE OF THE REVOLUTIONARY

Some get in the way.
When they've gone it's an improvement
But when he has gone you miss him.

When oppression is on the increase
Many become discouraged
But his courage grows greater.

He'll mount a campaign for a
Penny on wages and for hotter tea
And the right to control the state

He'll say to Property:
Where do you come from?
He'll ask Opinions:
Whom do you serve?

Where no one has raised a voice
You'll find him speaking
And where men live under oppression and much talk of Fate is heard
He'll see the names are published.

Where he sits at table
Dissatisfaction's sure to sit there too.
The food will be bad
And the room be found too cramping.

Wherever they chase him, there
Will come disorder, and where they've expelled him
There will unrest remain.

IVAN: Since they were arrested it's as if the earth had swallowed them up. Nobody can get to them. It's bad for the movement, for instance because Pavel is the only one who knows the addresses of those peasants who asked about our paper. And nothing is more important just now than educating the landless peasants.

PELAGEA VLASSOVA: Yes, I've often thought we should be talking to the peasants.

THE TEACHER: It'd be a lot of people to talk to: 120 million peasants, you couldn't do it. Anyway revolution's not on in this country and with these people. Your Russian won't ever make a revolution. That's something for the West. The Germans are revolutionaries, they'll make a revolution. As I was telling my friend Sachar Smerdyakov: these people are putting out a paper full of nothing but foreign words: stuff they themselves can't understand.

Ivan laughs.

THE TEACHER: So what?

IVAN: Where have you put that nice portrait of the Tsar? The room looks quite naked.

THE TEACHER: I thought I'd take it down for a bit. One gets bored, having to look at it all the time. Tell me, why is there nothing in your paper about the dreadful situation in our schools?

IVAN: I only thought – surely you can't have taken that picture down because you're bored with it?

PELAGEA VLASSOVA: Don't say that. Nikolai Ivanovitch is always wanting something fresh.

IVAN: Indeed.

THE TEACHER: Anyway I don't like being treated as an idiot. I was asking you a question about your paper.

IVAN: I can't recall anything whatever being changed in your flat, Nikolai. That frame alone cost twelve roubles.

THE TEACHER: Then I can hang the frame up again. You always treated me as if I were stupid, so that makes you stupid yourself.

IVAN: I am surprised, Nikolai Ivanovitch; your subversive talk and your belittling of our Tsar astound me. You seem to have developed into an agitator. And you have acquired such a determined look. It's positively dangerous to catch your eye.

PELAGEA VLASSOVA: Don't tease your brother. He is a very sensible person. A lot of children learn from him, so what he says about the situation matters. On top of which he has taught us to read and write.

IVAN: I hope you also learned something when you were teaching them to read.

THE TEACHER: No – I learned nothing at all. These little people have only a minimal understanding of Marxism. I don't mean to offend you, Mrs Vlassova. Naturally it's a very complex business, and it takes an educated mind to understand it. The strange thing is that the people who'll never be able to do so fall on it like hot cakes. In itself Marxism is not at all bad. It has its points, though of course there are some great gaps in it, and at some crucial junctures Marx's view of things is totally wrong. There's a lot I could say about this. Of course the economic aspect matters, but there's more to it than economics. Sociology? Yes, but I think biology will contribute just as much. My question is: does this doctrine have a place for the human condition? Humanity will never change.

PELAGEA VLASSOVA *to Ivan*: But here's somebody who has changed quite a bit, don't you think?

Ivan takes his leave.

IVAN: Mrs Vlassova, I can no longer recognise my brother.

7

PELAGEA VLASSOVA TAKES ADVANTAGE OF A VISIT TO HER SON IN PRISON TO GET THE NAMES OF THE MOVEMENT'S SUPPORTERS AMONG THE PEASANTS

Prison.

PELAGEA VLASSOVA: The warder will be watching very closely, but I've still got to find out the names of the peasants who asked about our paper. I hope I'll be able to remember all those names.

The Warder brings in Pavel.

PELAGEA VLASSOVA: Pavel!

PAVEL: How are you, Mother?

WARDER: You must sit at a distance from one another. There, and there. Talk about politics is forbidden.

PAVEL: Best talk about home, Mother.

PELAGEA VLASSOVA: Yes, Pavel.

PAVEL: You found somewhere to stay?

PELAGEA VLASSOVA: At schoolmaster Vessovchikov's.

PAVEL: Are they looking after you properly?

PELAGEA VLASSOVA: Yes. But how about you?

PAVEL: I wasn't sure if they could take care of you.

PELAGEA VLASSOVA: You've grown quite a beard.

PAVEL: Yes, I look older, don't I?

PELAGEA VLASSOVA: And then I went to Smilgin's burial. The police started hitting at people again and arrested some of them. All of us were there.

WARDER: That's political, Mrs Vlassova.

PELAGEA VLASSOVA: Really? Is it? How's one to know what to talk about?

WARDER: In that case your visits are unnecessary. You've nothing to talk about, but you come round and bother us. And it's me gets blamed.

PAVEL: Are you helping with the housework?

PELAGEA VLASSOVA: That too. Vessovchikov and me are taking a trip to the country next week.

PAVEL: The teacher?

PELAGEA VLASSOVA: No, Ivan.

PAVEL: A bit of fresh air?

PELAGEA VLASSOVA: That too. *Softly*: We need those addresses. *Aloud*: Oh, Pavel, we all miss you so.

PAVEL *softly*: I swallowed the addresses when they arrested me; I can only remember a few.

PELAGEA VLASSOVA: Oh, Pavel, how could I have imagined spending my old age like this?

PAVEL *softly*: Lushin in Pirogovo.

PELAGEA VLASSOVA *softly*: How about Krapivna? *Aloud*: What a worry you are to me!

PAVEL *softly*: Sulinovski.

PELAGEA VLASSOVA: I've been praying for you, too. *Softly*: Sulinovski in Krapivna. *Aloud*: I spend the evenings all on my own, sitting by the lamp.

PAVEL *softly*: Terek at Tobraya.

PELAGEA VLASSOVA: And schoolmaster Vessovchikov has started complaining about the mess I make.

PAVEL *softly*: And they'll be able to give you the other addresses.

WARDER: Visiting time is over.

PELAGEA VLASSOVA: Just another minute, you kind man. I'm so confused. Oh, Pavel, what's left for us old people but to crawl into a hole so we don't have to be seen? We're no use to anybody any more. *Softly*: Lushin in Pirogovo. *Aloud*: They make us realise our time is over. There's nothing ahead of us now. What we know is all finished – *Softly*: Sulinovski at Tobraya. *Pavel shakes his head.* Sulinovski in Krapivna – *Aloud*: and our experience counts for nothing. Our advice is harmful, because there's an unbridgeable ravine cuts us off from our sons.

Softly: Terek at Tobraya. *Aloud*: We go our way and you go your way. *Softly*: Terek at Tobraya. *Aloud*: We've got nothing in common. The time to come will be yours!

WARDER: But visiting time is over.

PAVEL *bowing*: Goodbye, Mother.

PELAGEA VLASSOVA *bowing likewise*: Goodbye, Pavel.

SONG
to be sung by the actor playing Pavel:

They've got all their statute books and their precedents
They've got all those police stations and prison blocks
(Not to mention other institutes and homes).
They've got all those prison warders and judges
Who earn fat pay packets and don't have any scruples.
What's the object?
Do they imagine they can get us down like that?
  Before they vanish – which we are expecting –
  They'll have come to realise
  That the whole thing's bound to be in vain.

They've got their newspapers and their printing presses
To blacken our name and reduce us to silence
(Not to speak of the statesmen they employ).
They've got those clerics and academics
Who earn fat pay packets and don't have any scruples.
What's the object?
Are they so scared of the truth coming out?
  Before they vanish – which we are expecting –
  They'll have come to realise
  That the whole thing's bound to be in vain.

They've got their tanks and artillery
They've got their machine guns and hand-grenades
(Not to speak of those rubber clubs they wield).
They've got their policemen and soldiers
Who earn thin pay packets and don't have any scruples.
What's the object?
Are their opponents as strong as all that?
  They're so sure the Lord won't reject them
  Or let them go down the drain.

But the refuse cart will collect them
And all their hesitations will have been in vain.
Neither money nor tanks will protect them
A few last screams and nothing more will remain.

8

FROM 1909 TO 1913 THE WORKERS KEPT TRYING TO WIN THE POOR PEASANTS AND AGRICULTURAL WORKERS OVER TO THE MOVEMENT

a

Country road.

As Pelagea Vlassova approaches with two workers she is met by a shower of stones. Her companions take to their heels.

PELAGEA VLASSOVA *whose head bears a great bruise, to her attackers*: Why are you throwing stones at us?

YEGOR LUSHIN: Because you're strike-breakers.

PELAGEA VLASSOVA: Strike-breakers, are they? No wonder they're in such a hurry. Where's the strike in these parts?

YEGOR: On the Smirnov estate.

PELAGEA VLASSOVA: And you are the strikers? My head says you are. But I'm no strike-breaker. I've come from Tver to see one of the workers on your estate. He's called Yegor Lushin.

YEGOR: Lushin, that's me.

PELAGEA VLASSOVA: Pelagea Vlassova.

YEGOR: Are you the one they call the Mother around Tver way?

PELAGEA VLASSOVA: That's right. I've brought copies of our paper for your lot. I didn't know you were out on strike, but it looks to me – *pointing at her bruise* – as if things are getting tough.

YEGOR: I'm sorry we threw that bruise at you. Our strike is going badly. We've got no strike fund and nothing to eat, and most of us want to disperse this evening and make separate efforts to get work on other local estates. A whole lot of strike-breakers are due to arrive first thing tomorrow. They've started slaughtering pigs and calves to feed them.

PELAGEA VLASSOVA: Who does the slaughtering?

YEGOR: Our estate butcher. The estate butcher's, the estate bakery and the estate dairy of course are not striking.

PELAGEA VLASSOVA: Why not?

YEGOR: Why should they? It's only us farm workers are getting our pay cut.

PELAGEA VLASSOVA: And haven't that lot had a cut ever?

YEGOR: Course they have, only not just now.

PELAGEA VLASSOVA: Haven't you people talked to them?

YEGOR: Wouldn't be any use. What have they to do with us? You can see how the chimney's belching smoke for the strike-breakers. They are workers and we are peasants. And peasants are peasants and workers are workers. Our estate butcher is a worker too. He used to be in a factory canteen.

PELAGEA VLASSOVA: So he won't join the strike? And you get no supper?

YEGOR: Let's have those papers; that's nothing to be surprised about.

PELAGEA VLASSOVA: Here they are. *She divides the bundle of papers in two, and gives one of them to him.*

YEGOR: What about those? Why aren't you giving us the whole lot?

PELAGEA VLASSOVA: The other half must go to the kitchen.

YEGOR: For the butcher, d'you mean? He knows what he's doing all right. You can't tell him anything he doesn't know. But he does it because otherwise he himself would get nothing to eat. That sort already knows whatever you can tell him.

PELAGEA VLASSOVA: Right, he knows it all, but it's not enough. Let me tell you something. I'm a worker myself, and I find it wrong that you've never exchanged a word with the workers here because you too know it all. You should have started by telling yourself that wherever you find a worker there's some hope left. Anyway I must take them their papers. Even though it truly is a shame that the chimney's belching smoke. *She hastens towards the kitchen.*

YEGOR: What an obstinate old lady! That sort won't recognise the real world. Peasant is peasant and worker is worker.

b

The estate kitchen.

The two Strike-breakers are sitting over their food in the kitchen of the estate and talking to the Butcher.

FIRST STRIKE-BREAKER, *munching, to the Second*: Anyone who lets his country down in the hour of peril is a bastard. And any worker who strikes is letting his country down.

THE BUTCHER *as he pounds the meat*: What d'you mean, his country?

FIRST STRIKE-BREAKER: They're Russians and we're in Russia here. And Russia belongs to the Russians.

THE BUTCHER: Oh, really?

SECOND STRIKE-BREAKER: You bet it does. Anyone who can't feel that – that meat's not quite done – there's no way of explaining it to him. But you can bash his head in.

THE BUTCHER: Right.

FIRST STRIKE-BREAKER: This table's the fatherland, the meat's the fatherland.

THE BUTCHER: But it's not quite done.

SECOND STRIKE-BREAKER: My seat here is the fatherland. And, you know – *to the Butcher* – you're a part of the fatherland too.

THE BUTCHER: But I'm not quite done either.

FIRST STRIKE-BREAKER: Everyone has to defend his fatherland.

THE BUTCHER: Yes, if it is his.

SECOND STRIKE-BREAKER: That's just base materialism.

THE BUTCHER: You arsehole!

The Butcher's Wife brings in Pelagea Vlassova, who is making much of her head injury.

THE BUTCHER'S WIFE: Come and sit down here. I'll make you a cold poultice and then you must eat something to help you get over your shock. *To the others*: Someone threw a stone at her.

FIRST STRIKE-BREAKER: Why, that's her. She came in the train with us.

SECOND STRIKE-BREAKER: It's the strikers did it. We were so worried about her.

PELAGEA VLASSOVA: It's getting a bit better.

THE STRIKE-BREAKERS: God be praised.

THE BUTCHER'S WIFE: They fight like wild animals for such rotten jobs. What a nasty bruise! *She goes to fetch water.*

PELAGEA VLASSOVA *to the audience*: How much more sympathy a bruise awakens in those who expect bruises than in those that dish them out!

FIRST STRIKE-BREAKER *pointing at the Mother with his fork*: Here is a Russian woman who's been stoned by Russian workers. Are you a mother?

PELAGEA VLASSOVA: Yes.

FIRST STRIKE-BREAKER: A Russian mother – stoned!

THE BUTCHER: Russian stones too. *To the audience*: Fancy my having to give my good soup to a shower like this. *To Pelagea Vlassova*: Why were they throwing stones at you?

PELAGEA VLASSOVA *pressing a damp rag to her bruise to cool it*: They had seen me mixing with strike-breakers.

SECOND STRIKE-BREAKER: The bastards!

PELAGEA VLASSOVA: Why bastards? I was just thinking maybe they're not bastards at all.

THE BUTCHER'S WIFE: So why did they throw stones at you?

PELAGEA VLASSOVA: Because they thought I was one.

THE BUTCHER'S WIFE: How could they think you were a bastard?

PELAGEA VLASSOVA: Because they thought I was a strike-breaker.

THE BUTCHER *with a smile*: So you think throwing stones at strike-breakers is all right?

PELAGEA VLASSOVA: That's it.

THE BUTCHER *beaming, to his wife*: Give her something to eat! At once! Give her two helpings! *He goes up to Pelagea Vlassova*: My name is Vassil Yefimovitch. *Calls after his wife*: And get the whole staff to come in. They can learn something here. *The staff appear in the doorway.* This woman was stoned by the strikers. There's a bruise on her head. Here she is. I just asked her how she got that bruise. She says: Because they took me for a strike-breaker. I ask her: So throwing stones at strike-breakers is all right? And what does she reply?

PELAGEA VLASSOVA: Yes.

THE BUTCHER: My friends, when I heard that I said: Give her something to eat! Give her two helpings! *To Pelagea Vlassova*: Why aren't you eating? Is it too hot for you? *To his wife*: D'you have to serve it when it's boiling? Is she supposed to scald her mouth?

PELAGEA VLASSOVA *pushing the plate away from her*: No, Vassil Yefimovitch, the food's not too hot.

THE BUTCHER: So why aren't you eating it?

PELAGEA VLASSOVA: Because it's been cooked for the strike-breakers.

THE BUTCHER: For whom, did you say?

PELAGEA VLASSOVA: For the strike-breakers.

THE BUTCHER: Well! If that isn't the limit! Interesting: so I'm a bastard too. Get that, I'm a bastard. And why am I a bastard? Because I'm helping the strike-breakers. *To Pelagea Vlassova*: Is that it? *He sits down with her.* But isn't striking wrong? You mean: it all depends what the strike's about? *Pelagea Vlassova nods.* You mean: their wages have been cut. But what's to say wages can't be cut? Look, everything around here belongs to Mr Smirnov in Odessa. Why shouldn't he be able to cut wages? *As the delighted Strike-breakers express their agreement*: Isn't it his money? So don't you think he should be able to set the wage at two roubles on one day and two kopecks on another? You think not? What do you think happened last year? Even my pay was cut. And what did I do about it – *to his wife* – on your advice? Nothing. And what's going to happen in September? It'll be cut again. And what am I doing wrong now? I'm ratting on people who've had a cut too and won't put up with it. So what does that make me? *To Pelagea Vlassova*: So you won't eat my cooking? I was just waiting for one decent person to say to my face that no decent person would eat my cooking. That's the last straw. I'd long ago had enough. Just one more straw – *indicating Pelagea Vlassova* – tipped the balance. It's not enough to be angry and discontented. Practical measures are needed. *To the Strike-breakers*: Tell your friend Mr Smirnov he can feed you from Odessa. He can be so kind as to cook for you himself, the pig.

THE BUTCHER'S WIFE: Don't get so worked up.

THE BUTCHER: I've worked in factory canteens, don't forget. I left because their shitty job didn't suit me. *With his wife trying to calm him down*: I thought I'd move to the country, there's some decency there, and what do I find? Another shitty hole where I'm supposed to feed strike-breakers.

THE BUTCHER'S WIFE: I suppose we can move on again.

THE BUTCHER: You bet: we'll move on. *Grandly*: Someone bring me the big pot of beans. And you fetch all the bacon. Whatever's hanging up. What's it been cooked for?

THE BUTCHER'S WIFE: You're not doing yourself any good! You're going to ruin us.

THE BUTCHER *to the Strike-breakers*: Get out, you saviours of the fatherland! We're striking. The kitchen staff are on strike! *He drives the Strike-breakers out.* I'm a butcher, and it's me, not the pigs who's supposed to get the last laugh. *With his arm around his wife's shoulders, he goes up to Pelagea Vlassova.* And now go out, find the people who stoned you, and tell them their supper is ready.

PRAISE OF THE VLASSOVAS
recited by the estate cook and his staff:

Pay respect to our comrade Vlassova, sturdy warrior.
Keen and cunning, you can trust her.
Trust her when there's a fight. Cunning to outwit our foes, keenest
Of our agitators, all her actions are small
But she's tough, we can't do without her.
And she's not alone, wherever she fights
She'll always be tough, always trusted and cunning
In Tver, Glasgow, Lyons, Chicago
Shanghai, Calcutta
All those Vlassovas of all countries, in their mole-burrows
Unknown soldiers who serve the Revolution
We can't do without them!

9

1913. FOLLOWING A LONG PERIOD OF DETENTION IN SIBERIA, PAVEL RETURNS HOME

Schoolmaster Vessovchikov's flat.

Pelagea Vlassova, Vassil Yefimovitch and a Worker are carrying a printing machine into the Teacher's flat.

THE TEACHER: Pelagea Vlassova, you cannot install a printing press here. You'd be abusing my feelings towards your movement. In principle, as you know, I am with you, but this would be going much too far.

PELAGEA VLASSOVA: If I've got you right, Nikolai Vessovchikov, you approve of our leaflets, is that it? I seem to remember you drafted the last one for the council workers yourself. But you're against them being printed? *They are setting up the press.*

THE TEACHER: No. But I'm against their being printed here.

PELAGEA VLASSOVA *offended*: We will note that, Nikolai Ivanovitch.

They continue to work.

THE TEACHER: Well then?

THE WORKER: Once comrade Vlassova's got something into her head there's nothing one can do about it. We've had a lot of trouble with her in that way. But not a soul's going to notice. The paper has got to be out by eight.

PELAGEA VLASSOVA: We'll have to print extra copies this time, because they keep getting seized. It's when they tighten up the controls that people start shrugging their shoulders and come to terms with all the filth and meanness.

The Teacher goes next door and starts reading. They begin printing and the machine is very noisy. The Teacher bursts in.

PELAGEA VLASSOVA: Rather noisy, isn't it?

THE TEACHER: You'll shake the lamp off my table! You can't possibly print illegal material here if it's going to make such a din as that.

PELAGEA VLASSOVA: Nikolai Ivanovitch, we too have noticed that it makes a bit of noise.

VASSIL YEFIMOVITCH: If we could put something under it the

neighbours wouldn't be able to hear a sound. Have you anything we could put under it, Nikolai Ivanovitch?

THE TEACHER: No, I've nothing.

PELAGEA VLASSOVA: Don't talk so loudly! – The woman next door has some felt in her drawer for the children's coats. I'll go and ask her. Don't print any more till I come back! *She goes to the neighbours'.*

THE WORKER *to the Teacher*: We're sorry you're not happy with her. Actually, when we brought her here it was so that she could get away from politics. We'd never have thought of installing an illegal press here. But she insisted.

THE TEACHER: I am very angry. I greatly disapprove of the way you exploit her, for instance. The other day I came home and had to watch her standing there with her old purse as she fished out her wretched kopecks to pay her dues.

VASSIL YEFIMOVITCH: That's right, nobody gives us anything. It's poverty makes revolutions, and what's more they cost money. The Mother's very tough about getting in subscriptions. That's another half-loaf of bread you owe us for our work, she'll say when she goes round collecting.

A knock. They cover up the machine. The Teacher opens the door.

PAVEL'S VOICE *outside*: Does Pelagea Vlassova live here? It's Pavel Vlassov.

Pavel enters.

PAVEL: Hullo, where is Mother?

VASSIL YEFIMOVITCH: She'll be back in a moment. Are they after you?

PAVEL: Yes. I have to be off to Finland this evening.

THE WORKER: Sit down here. We'll give your mother a surprise.

They seat Pavel on a chair facing the door and pose either side of him. Pelagea Vlassova comes in.

PELAGEA VLASSOVA: Pavel! *She hugs him.* He's even thinner than before! Instead of getting fatter he gets thinner! I thought they wouldn't be able to keep you for long. How did you get away? How long can you stay here?

PAVEL: This evening I'll have to move to Finland.

PELAGEA VLASSOVA: At least you can take your coat off, can't you?

Pavel takes off his coat.

THE TEACHER: I'm told you're fighting for freedom, but what about the terrible slavery you are imposing on your own party? Fine kind of freedom! Nothing but orders and compulsion!

PELAGEA VLASSOVA: You see, Nikolai Ivanovitch, it's like this. We're not opposed to those orders quite like you are. We need them more. There's more at stake for us, if you don't mind my saying so. Freedom is a bit like your money, Nikolai Ivanovitch. Since I started doling out your pocket-money you've been able to buy a lot more. If you spend less for a while, you'll then find you can spend more. You can't say that's not so.

THE TEACHER: I'll have to give up arguing with you. You're a dreadful tyrant.

PELAGEA VLASSOVA: Yes, that's how we have to be.

VASSIL YEFIMOVITCH: Did you get the felt? *To Pavel*: We've got to have the papers ready by eight o'clock.

PAVEL: Then let's go!

PELAGEA VLASSOVA *radiantly*: Start the press at once so we have more time. What d'you say to the way that Martha Alexandrovna turned me down? Her excuse was: the felt was for the children's coats. I said: 'Martha Alexandrovna, just a moment ago I saw your children coming back from school. Wearing coats!' 'Coats?' she said. 'Those aren't coats, they're patched-up rags. The kids at school laugh at them.' 'Martha Alexandrovna,' I told her, 'poor folk have wretched coats. Let me take that felt at any rate till tomorrow morning. I promise you if you let me have it, it will do more to help your children than would a smart coat.' But she wouldn't see reason, the wretch. She just wouldn't let me have it. Not a vestige of sense! *She reaches under her apron, brings out a few pieces of felt and lays them under the machine.*

THE TEACHER: So what's that then?

PELAGEA VLASSOVA: The felt of course.

They all laugh.

VASSIL YEFIMOVITCH: Then why all that complaining about Martha Alexandrovna?

PELAGEA VLASSOVA: Because she forced me to steal it, because have it we must. And it's very good for her children that papers like this should be printed. That's the honest truth.

VASSIL YEFIMOVITCH: Pelagea Vlassova, we thank you for this felt in the name of the Revolution.

Laughter.

PELAGEA VLASSOVA: I'll give it back in the morning. *To Pavel, who has sat down*: D'you want a bit of bread and butter?

VASSIL YEFIMOVITCH *at the machine*: And who's going to gather the pages?

Pelagea Vlassova goes to the machine. Pavel looks for bread.

PELAGEA VLASSOVA: Look in the bottom cupboard. The knife's in the drawer. This is Vassil Yefimovitch who joined the movement when I made my little trip to the country. He's very strict.

PAVEL: Don't worry about me, I even found a piece of bread in Siberia once.

PELAGEA VLASSOVA: You see, he's reproaching me. I'm not looking after him. I'll cut it for you anyway.

THE TEACHER: And who's going to gather the pages?

PAVEL *cuts himself a slice of bread while the others are printing*: The papers will be gathered by the mother of the revolutionary Pavel Vlassov, by the revolutionary Pelagea Vlassova. Is she looking after him? No way. Does she give him a cup of tea? Run him a bath? Kill a calf? Not for one moment. Fleeing from Siberia to Finland against the icy blasts of the north wind, the shots of his pursuers ringing in his ears, he finds no place to lay his head but in an illegal printing shop. And instead of caressing his locks his mother gathers the pages.

PELAGEA VLASSOVA: If you want to give a hand, come over here.

Pavel stations himself at the machine, facing his mother. They recite:

PELAGEA VLASSOVA:

Did they give you a bad time?

PAVEL:

All right but for the typhus.

PELAGEA VLASSOVA:

Did you at least get proper food?

PAVEL:

Yes, except when I got nothing at all.

PELAGEA VLASSOVA:

Where are you going now, then? Will it be for long?

PAVEL:

Not if you people go on working like this.

PELAGEA VLASSOVA:

Will your lot be working there too?

PAVEL:

You bet.
And it matters as much there as here.

A knock. Enter Sostakovitch.

SOSTAKOVITCH: Pavel, you must leave at once. Here are your tickets. Comrade Issay will be waiting for you at the station, with the Finnish passes.

PAVEL: I'd hoped we'd have a few hours at least. Never mind. *He puts on his coat again.*

PELAGEA VLASSOVA *takes her coat*: I'll go down with you.

SOSTAKOVITCH: No, that'd be risky for Pavel. They know you by sight, but they don't know him.

PAVEL: I'll be seeing you, Mother.

PELAGEA VLASSOVA: Let's hope I can give you your butty next time.

PAVEL: Let's hope. See you, comrades!

Exeunt Pavel and Sostakovitch.

THE TEACHER: God will help him, Pelagea Vlassova.

PELAGEA VLASSOVA: I don't know about that.

She turns back to the machine and they go on printing.

PELAGEA VLASSOVA *recites*:

PRAISE OF THE THIRD THING

People keep telling you how
A son is soon lost to his mother. Not to me:
I kept touch with mine. D'you want to know how? Through
The third thing.
He and I lived as two, but a third thing
Was shared by us both; we pursued it in common. It brought
Us together.
Often I have listened to children
When they spoke with their parents.
What a contrast it was when we two spoke
Talking about the third thing that was common to us:
That tremendous cause that is shared by so many!

How close to each other we felt when close to
The cause! How good to each other when
Close to its goodness!

10

IN THE ATTEMPT TO CROSS THE FINNISH BORDER, PAVEL VLASSOV IS ARRESTED AND SHOT

Schoolmaster Vessovchikov's flat.

CHORUS
sung to the Mother by the revolutionary workers:

Comrade Vlassova, your son
Has been shot. But
As he went to the wall where they intended to shoot him
He went towards a wall which had been built by men of his own kind
And the rifles they aimed at his breast, and the bullets
Had been made by men like himself. Merely absent
Were they therefore, or dispersed; but for him were still there
And present in the work of their hands. Not even
Those who were ordered to shoot him differed from him, or were for ever incapable of learning.
Truly he still went bound with chains, that had been
Forged by his comrades and laid by them on their comrade; yet
Closer grew the factories; as he passed by he could see them
Chimney on chimney, and since it was early dawn
For it is at dawn that they normally bring them out, there was
Nobody there, but he saw them crowded full
With that huge throng, whose numbers had always grown
And still grew.

Three women enter, bearing a bible and a pot full of food.

THE THREE WOMEN *outside the door*: When Pavel Vlassov tried to cross the Finnish border he was caught and shot. We want to forget all our differences with Vlassova and sit down with her as Christians to express our fellow-feeling for her. She has no religion, so there is nothing for her to hold on to in her sorrow.

They enter.

LANDLADY: Mrs Vlassova, you are not alone in this sorrowful time, the whole house feels for you.

Overcome by emotion the three women sit down. They sob loudly.

PELAGEA VLASSOVA *after a moment*: Take a little tea. It'll make you feel better. *She pours tea for them.* Bucks you up, doesn't it?

LANDLADY: Oh, Mrs Vlassova, you take it so calmly.

PEASANT WOMAN: But you are quite right. All of us are in God's hand.

POOR WOMAN: And God knows what he is doing.

Pelagea Vlassova says nothing.

POOR WOMAN: We thought we should see you were all right. I'm sure you're not cooking for yourself at all properly, the way things are. Here's a pot with something to eat, you just have to heat it up. *She hands her the pot.*

PELAGEA VLASSOVA: Thank you very much, Lydia Antonovna. It's very kind of you to have thought of it. Really it is so good of you all to have come.

LANDLADY: My dear Vlassova, I have also brought my bible for you in case you want to read anything. You may keep it as long as you like. *She hands Pelagea Vlassova her bible.*

PELAGEA VLASSOVA: Thank you for your kind intentions, Vera Stefanovna. But I hope you will not be very offended if I give the book back to you? When Mr Vessovchikov went off on holiday he said I could use his books. *She hands back the bible.*

LANDLADY: I only thought you probably wouldn't want to be reading your political papers just now.

PEASANT WOMAN: Do you really read them every day?

PELAGEA VLASSOVA: Yes.

LANDLADY: Mrs Vlassova, my bible has frequently been a great comfort to me.

Silence.

POOR WOMAN: Haven't you any photos of him?

PELAGEA VLASSOVA: No. I did have some. But then we destroyed them all so the police wouldn't get them.

POOR WOMAN: You so need something to remember them by.

PEASANT WOMAN: They say he was such a good-looking man!

PELAGEA VLASSOVA: Come to think of it, I have got a photo. Here's his 'Wanted' notice. He cut it out of a paper for me.

The women study the 'Wanted' notice.

LANDLADY: Mrs Vlassova, it says here that your son had become a criminal. He had no religion, and you yourself have never pretended, I mean you have never missed any chance of letting us know your opinion of our religion.

PELAGEA VLASSOVA: That's right, I've no use for it, Vera Stefanovna.

LANDLADY: And hasn't all this made you think differently?

PELAGEA VLASSOVA: No, Vera Stefanovna.

LANDLADY: So you still think that everything can be solved just by reasoning?

POOR WOMAN: I did tell you, Vera Stefanovna, that Mrs Vlassova won't have changed her views.

LANDLADY: But the other night through the wall I heard you weeping.

PELAGEA VLASSOVA: I apologise for that.

LANDLADY: There's no call to apologise, of course I didn't mean it that way. But was it reason that made you weep?

PELAGEA VLASSOVA: No.

LANDLADY: Well, you see how far reason gets you.

PELAGEA VLASSOVA: It wasn't reason that made me weep. But when I stopped, reason had something to do with that. What Pavel did was right.

LANDLADY: Why did they shoot him then?

POOR WOMAN: Were they all against him perhaps?

PELAGEA VLASSOVA: Yes, but in being against him they were against themselves.

LANDLADY: Mrs Vlassova, Man needs God. He is powerless against Fate.

PELAGEA VLASSOVA: We say that Man's fate is man.

PEASANT WOMAN: Dear Mrs Vlassova, we peasants . . .

LANDLADY *indicating her*: My relative is just here on a visit.

PEASANT WOMAN: We peasants see these things differently. You have no crops on your fields, only bread from the baker's. You only see the milk, not the cow. You pass no sleepless nights when there's thunder in the air, and what does a hailstorm mean to you?

PELAGEA VLASSOVA: I understand, and in those situations you pray to God.

PEASANT WOMAN: Yes.

PELAGEA VLASSOVA: And in springtime you have processions and public prayers.

PEASANT WOMAN: Right.

PELAGEA VLASSOVA: And then you get thunder and hailstorms. And your cow falls ill. Don't any of the peasants in your part of the world insure against bad harvests and cattle disease?

PEASANT WOMAN: I've heard tell of that.

PELAGEA VLASSOVA: Yes, insurance can help when praying has been no use. So you no longer need pray to God when it looks like thunder, but you do have to be insured. Because it helps you. Losing his importance is bad news for God. So there's some hope that this God may vanish from your minds once he has vanished from over your fields. In my young days everybody still believed he was sitting somewhere in the skies and looking like an old man. Then aeroplanes came in, and the papers started saying everything was measurable even in the sky. No more talk of a God sitting up in Heaven. Instead we now often hear talk of him being like some kind of gas, nowhere and everywhere all at once. Then we read what all the gases were made up of, and God wasn't included, so that he lost out even as part of the air and kind of blew himself away. Now they write that he means something purely spiritual, and that's most suspicious.

POOR WOMAN: So you're saying he's stopped being important because we've stopped noticing him?

LANDLADY: Don't forget, Mrs Vlassova, that God took away your Pavel for a reason.

PELAGEA VLASSOVA: The Tsar took him away, and I shan't forget the reason.

LANDLADY: It was God who took him away, not the Tsar.

PELAGEA VLASSOVA *to the Poor Woman*: Lydia Antonovna, they tell me that God, who took away my Pavel, now means to take away your two rooms as from next Saturday. Is it true that God has given you notice?

LANDLADY: I have given her notice because it's the third time she has not paid her rent.

PELAGEA VLASSOVA: So, when God sentenced you, Vera Stefanovna, to lose your rent for the third time what steps did you take? *Vera Stefanovna remains silent.* You gave Lydia Antonovna notice and put her on the street. And you, Lydia Antonovna, what steps did you take when God sentenced you to be put out on the street? My suggestion would be for you to ask the landlady to lend you her bible. Then when you are sitting there in the cold streets you can open its pages and read out to your children that they must fear God.

LANDLADY: If you had read the bible to your son oftener he would still be alive now.

PELAGEA VLASSOVA: But wretchedly alive; he had a wretched life. Why is it only death that you people are afraid of? My son wasn't all that afraid of death. *She recites:*

But he was very much frightened by the misery
Which is plain for all to see in our cities.
What terrifies us is hunger and the depravity
Of those who feel it and those who cause it.
Do not fear death so much, fear an inadequate life!

Pause.

How can it help you if you fear God, Lydia Antonovna? You should be more afraid of Vera Stefanovna. It wasn't God's inscrutable decision that snatched my son from me, but the very scrutable decision of the Tsar, and in just the same way it was Vera Stefanovna that's put you on the street because some man in a villa who has nothing to do with God has sacked you from your job. Why talk about God? They tell you that 'in his Father's house' there are many mansions, but they never tell you why so few of them are in Russia, or why this should be so.

POOR WOMAN: Give me that bible, Vera Stefanovna. In the bible it says: Love thy neighbour as thyself. Why are you throwing me on the street? Give me the bible, I can show you the place. It's plain as the nose on your face that they shot Pavel Vlassov because he was for the workers, and a worker himself. *She grabs the bible.* Give it here, I'll show you . . .

LANDLADY: You're getting no bible from me for that purpose, not for that.

POOR WOMAN: For what then? For no good one, I bet.

LANDLADY: This is the Word of God!

POOR WOMAN: Just so. Your God's no good to me if I can't see the evidence! *She tries to tug the bible away from the Landlady.*

POOR WOMAN: I want that book.

LANDLADY *holds on to it*: It's my property.

POOR WOMAN: Like the entire house, eh?

LANDLADY: Now let me show you something, where it says you must respect the property of others.

The bible is ripped to shreds.

PEASANT WOMAN *as she picks up the pieces*: Now it's torn to pieces.

PELAGEA VLASSOVA *after putting the pot of food in safety*: Better a torn bible than a spilt dinner.

POOR WOMAN: If it weren't for my faith in a Heavenly Father who makes up for everything, good and evil alike, I'd be joining Pelagea Vlassova's party today. *Exit.*

LANDLADY: Pelagea Vlassova, you see what you've done to Lydia Antonovna, and it's because he talked the same way that your son was shot, and you don't deserve any better.

She goes off with her relatives.

PELAGEA VLASSOVA: You poor things! *Calls after them*: Whatever happens I'd advise you to insure your harvest! *Sits down exhausted.* Oh Pavel!

11

FROM HER BED OF SICKNESS, PELAGEA VLASSOVA HEARS THAT WAR HAS BEEN DECLARED

Schoolmaster Vessovchikov's flat.

The Teacher has called a doctor to come and examine Pelagea Vlassova.

THE TEACHER: Don't say anything about a fee to her, I'll settle it. She has been sick and depressed ever since the death of her son. Now she has got worse. It's not so much the housework, but there was a particular sort of work which she always used to do, and now she has stopped. *To Pelagea Vlassova*: Pelagea Vlassova, I don't want to worry you. I called the doctor. I don't like the way you are breathing.

The Doctor examines Pelagea Vlassova.

PELAGEA VLASSOVA: Did they tell you I haven't any money?

The Doctor nods.

THE DOCTOR *leaves the room and shrugs his shoulders as he tells the Teacher*: Her son's death must have been a severe blow to her. She must on no account get up. She is completely exhausted. She's an old woman now. *He leaves.*

The Teacher sits down by her bed and reads a paper.

PELAGEA VLASSOVA: Anything in the paper?

THE TEACHER: War has been declared.

PELAGEA VLASSOVA: War. – What are our comrades doing?

THE TEACHER: Our five Duma representatives have been arrested for high treason and sent off to Siberia.

PELAGEA VLASSOVA: That's bad. *Pause.* If the Tsar is mobilising, us workers must mobilise too. *Pause.* I must get up.

THE TEACHER: You're on no account to get up. You are ill. And what could you do against the Tsar and his generals? *Pause.* I'm just going down to get the latest edition. Now they'll completely destroy the Party.

CHORUS
sung to Pelagea Vlassova:

Get up, the Party's under threat!
You are sick, but the Party's dying.
You are weak, but you must help us.
Get up, the Party's under threat!

You had your doubts about us
No time for doubting:
We've reached our limit.
You made complaints about the Party
Don't knock the Party when they're
About to smash it.

Get up, the Party's under threat!
Get up now!
You are ill, but we have need of you.
Don't die, for you must help us.
Don't stay away, we're off to the fight.
Get up, the Party's under threat, get up!

During this chorus Pelagea Vlassova has laboriously got herself up, dressed, taken her bag and progressed, unsteadily but with increasing speed, through the flat to the door.

12

IN THE FIRST YEARS OF THE WAR THE WORKERS DO NOT WANT TO LISTEN TO THE REVOLUTIONARIES

Street.

Pelagea Vlassova has had a bloody beating, and some workers carry her into a corner.

FIRST WORKER: What's the matter with her?

SECOND WORKER: We saw this old woman in the crowd of people cheering the troops as they marched off. Suddenly she cried out 'Down with the war, long live the Revolution!' Then the police came and beat her about the head with their truncheons. We quickly dragged her into this corner. Give her face a wipe, will you?

THE WORKERS: Hurry up and get moving, old lady, or they'll still catch you.

PELAGEA VLASSOVA: Where's my bag?

THE WORKERS: There you are.

PELAGEA VLASSOVA: I got some leaflets there. Saying something about the position of us workers in wartime: the truth about it.

THE WORKERS: You go home, old lady, and leave the truth in your bag! It's dangerous. If they catch us with it we'll be beaten and locked up. Haven't you yourself had enough?

PELAGEA VLASSOVA: No, no, you've got to be told! It's our ignorance of our position that's holding us down.

THE WORKERS: And the police?

PELAGEA VLASSOVA: They're ignorant too.

THE WORKERS: But our leaders are saying first of all we must defend our country and help to beat the Germans.

PELAGEA VLASSOVA:

What sort of leaders are they?
You're fighting side by side with the class enemy
Worker against worker.

Your organisations, laboriously built up
With the pennies of self-denial, are being broken.
Your experiences are forgotten
And forgotten is the solidarity of the workers of all countries
Their common fight against the class enemy.

THE WORKERS: None of that applies any longer. We have struck against the war in several factories. Our strikes have been beaten down. The Revolution is no longer coming. Go home, old lady, recognise the world for what it is. What you want will never, never, never happen!

PELAGEA VLASSOVA: At least you should read what we have to say about the situation. Would you? *She offers her leaflets to them.* Won't you even read?

THE WORKERS: We can see that you mean us well, but we are not accepting your leaflets. We can't run any more risks.

PELAGEA VLASSOVA: Yeees, but remember that the whole world – *she is shouting so loudly that the alarmed workers cover her mouth up* – is covered by an immense darkness, and up to now you have been the only people could be reached by Reason. Think what it will mean if you give up!

13

ANTI-WAR PROPAGANDA

Outside a Patriotic Copper Contribution Centre.

Seven women are standing before a door with a flag and a sign saying 'Patriotic Copper Contribution Centre'. Among them is Pelagea Vlassova with a small mug. A civil official arrives and unlocks the door.

THE OFFICIAL: It has just been announced that our brave troops have wrested the fortress of Przemysl from the enemy for the fourth time with unparalleled heroism. One hundred thousand dead, two thousand prisoners of war. The Army High Command has declared that schools are to be shut throughout Russia and the bells rung. Three cheers for our holy Russia, hip, hip, hooray! The counter for copper contributions will be opened in five minutes. *He goes inside.*

A WOMAN: How marvellous that our war is going ahead so well!

PELAGEA VLASSOVA: I've only got a tiny mug. That won't make more than five or six bullets. How many of those will hit the target? Perhaps two out of the six, and at most only one of them a killer. Your big cauldron should be good for at least twenty, and that lady in front, her can ought to make a shell. A shell takes out five or six men at a time. *Counts the different vessels*: One, two, three, four, five, six, seven, half a moment, that lady's got two, so it's eight. Eight! That should be enough to launch a small bayonet attack. *She gives a subdued laugh*: Hm, hm, hm. I nearly took my little mug back home again. Two soldiers ran into me – their names ought to be taken – and told me: 'Go on, give them your copper, you cow, to stop the war from ever ending!' What d'you say to that, isn't it awful? 'You two', I said, 'ought to be shot out of hand. And if my little mug', I told them, 'serves for nothing more than to shut your filthy mouths then it has not been given in vain. It should be enough for a bullet each.' For why am I, Pelagea Vlassova, giving up my little mug? I'm giving it up so the war doesn't stop!

WOMAN: What on earth are you saying? That the war's not going to stop if we hand in our copper? We're handing it in precisely so it does stop!

PELAGEA VLASSOVA: No, we're handing it in to stop it stopping!

A WOMAN DRESSED IN BLACK: No, no, once they've enough copper and can make shells, then our men out there will win much sooner. Then the war will stop!

PELAGEA VLASSOVA: Oh, once they have the shells then of course it won't stop, because they'll be able to carry on. As long as they've got ammunition they'll carry on. The other side are contributing too.

WOMAN *pointing to a sign*: 'Hand in your copper and shorten the war.' Can't you read?

PELAGEA VLASSOVA: Hand in your copper and prolong the war! That's to mislead spies.

WOMAN DRESSED IN BLACK: But why do you want the war to be prolonged, then?

PELAGEA VLASSOVA: It's because my son will become a sergeant in another six months. Two more bayonet charges and they put my son up to sergeant. And that will mean double the pay. And besides we have to get Armenia and Galicia, and we certainly need Turkey.

WOMAN DRESSED IN BLACK: What do we need?

PELAGEA VLASSOVA: Turkey. And the money we've had from France will need to be repaid. And in that way it's a war of liberation.

WOMAN: Naturally. Of course it's a war of liberation. But that doesn't mean it has to go on for ever.

PELAGEA VLASSOVA: Another six months at least.

WOMAN DRESSED IN BLACK: And you think it will last that long once they've got the copper?

PELAGEA VLASSOVA: Of course. They get the soldiers for nothing. You've a son at the front, haven't you? There you are, your son's already at the front and now you're handing over your copper. So it should be good for another six months.

WOMAN DRESSED IN BLACK: Now I'm really confused. At one moment the war's supposed to be getting shorter, then it's supposed to be getting longer. I don't know what to believe. My husband has already fallen, and my son is outside Przemysl. I am going home.

She leaves. The bells start ringing.

WOMAN: Victory bells!

PELAGEA VLASSOVA: Yes, we're winning! We give up our mugs, our cauldrons and our copper cans, but we're winning. We've nothing left to eat, but we're winning! You're either for the Tsar and his victory, or you're against him. We're winning, but we've got to win! Otherwise there'll be a revolution, that's certain. And what will come of our beloved Tsar in that case? We have to stand by him in times like these. Look at the Germans! They're already eating the leaves off the trees for their Kaiser!

WOMAN: What on earth are you talking about? A minute ago that woman took her cauldron away and left, all because of you.

A WORKING WOMAN: You didn't have to tell her that, about your wanting the war to last longer. There's nobody else wants that!

PELAGEA VLASSOVA: What? How about the Tsar? And the generals? Do you think they are scared of a war with Germany? It's 'Up and at 'em!' 'Win or die!' That's how it should be. Can't you hear those bells? You only get those for winning or dying. Why are you against the war? Who are you, anyway? We're all a better class of people here, if I'm not mistaken? But you are a worker. Are you a worker or aren't you? Admit it! You're just trying to thrust your way in here. Don't forget that there's still a certain distance between your sort and ours!

A MAIDSERVANT: You shouldn't have said that to her. She too is giving up her things for the fatherland.

PELAGEA VLASSOVA *to the Working Woman*: You can't possibly really want to stand here. What good is the war to you? It's pure humbug your standing here. We can do all right without you and your sort. This is our war! Nobody is going to object if you workers want to join in, but that doesn't give you a part in it, not by a long chalk. Go to your factory and see that they put up your wages, and don't push yourself in here where you don't belong. *To the Maidservant*: You can take her stuff for her if she really insists on handing it in.

The Working Woman hurries away.

THIRD WOMAN: Who on earth is this person doing all the talking?

FOURTH WOMAN: That's half an hour I've been listening to her driving people away.

THIRD WOMAN: You know what she is? – A Bolshevik. And quite a tricky customer! – Just don't argue with her, pay her no attention – Beware of Bolshevism, it takes thousands of different forms! – If a policeman appears they'll just arrest her!

PELAGEA VLASSOVA: You're right, I am a Bolshevik. But you are murderers, the way you queue up there. There's not an animal would surrender its young as you do: without rhyme or reason and for a bad cause. Your womb should be torn out of you. It should shrivel up and you should be barren, you in your queue. No need for your sons to return. To such mothers? They're shooting for a bad cause, so let them be shot for a bad cause. But you people are the murderers.

FIRST WOMAN *turns round*: I'll show you what you deserve, you Bolshevik!

She goes up to the Mother with a can in her hand and strikes her in the face. Another of them also turns and spits in front of her. Then the counter opens and the three women pass inside.

THE MAIDSERVANT *remains standing*: Don't bother with them.

But tell me what I ought to do. I know you Bolsheviks are against the war, but I am in service and I can't return to my masters with these copper cans. I don't want to hand them in. But if I don't hand them in, it won't have helped anyone and I shall be dismissed. So what should I do?

PELAGEA VLASSOVA: You can't do anything by yourself. Hand the copper cans in in your employers' name. In their name people like yourself will make ammunition out of them. And people like yourself will use them to shoot with. But it will be people like yourself who will decide whom to shoot at. Come along this evening to – *She whispers an address in her ear.* There'll be a worker from the Putilov factory speaking, and we'll be able to explain to you what we want our attitude to be. But don't tell that address to anyone who shouldn't know it.

14

A street.

Pelagea Vlassova heads a demonstration and carries the red flag. The Maidservant is marching alongside her.

A WORKER: As we came along the Lybin-Prospekt there were already several thousand of us. More than fifty firms were on strike, and the strikers joined us to demonstrate against the war and against Tsarist domination.

SECOND WORKER: In winter 1916/17 there were already 250,000 on strike in the factories. The inadequate wages at a time of rising prices, the shortage of foodstuffs, the despair as to the war, the despatch to the battlefields of famished workers and peasants: all this had driven them towards our Bolshevik ranks.

THIRD WORKER: We carried banners inscribed 'Down with the war! Long live the Revolution' and red flags.

PELAGEA VLASSOVA: For what a lot I, Pelagea Vlassova, a worker's widow and a worker's mother, still have to do! Many years ago, when first I felt worried to see my son no longer getting enough to eat, I just groaned. That changed nothing. Then I helped him in his fight for the extra kopeck. In those days we conducted small strikes for better wages. Now we are part of an enormous strike in the munition factories and a struggle for power in the state.

THE MAIDSERVANT: Many people say that what we want cannot ever succeed. We should be content with what we have got. The power of the rulers is impregnable. We would always be defeated. Even many workers say it will never work!

PELAGEA VLASSOVA *recites*:

Those still alive can't say 'never'.
No certainty can be certain
If it cannot stay as it is.
When the rulers have already spoken
That is when the ruled start speaking.
Who dares to talk of 'never'?
Whose fault is it if oppression still remains? It's ours.
Whose job will it be to get rid of it? Just ours.
Whoever's been beaten must get to his feet.
He who is lost must give battle.
He who is aware where he stands – how can anyone stop him moving on?
Those who were losers today will be triumphant tomorrow
And from never will come today.

THE MAIDSERVANT: Our flag was borne by a woman in her sixties. We said: 'Isn't that flag much too heavy for you? Give us the flag!' But she said:

PELAGEA VLASSOVA: No, when I feel tired I'll give it to you, dear, and then you can carry it.

FIRST WORKER: So that is how she marched with us, tirelessly, from morning till past midday.

The Exception and the Rule

Lehrstück

Collaborators: EMIL HESSE BURRI, ELISABETH HAUPTMANN

Translator: TOM OSBORN

Characters:

THE MERCHANT
THE GUIDE
THE COOLIE
TWO POLICEMEN
THE LANDLORD
THE COOLIE'S WIFE
THE LEADER OF THE SECOND EXPEDITION
THE JUDGE
TWO ASSESSORS

Translator's note on the words of the songs: These are songs, not poems. The music by Paul Dessau is now the only setting authorised by the Brecht Estate. I have therefore taken great care to attempt both an elegant representation of the sense of the original and a text that can be matched to Dessau's music. For the purposes of production, musical directors will be able to refine this matching, with the assistance of the score.

THE ACTORS:

We are here to report
The story of a journey. It was undertaken
By one who exploits and two of the exploited.
Closely observe the behaviour of these people:
Find it strange, even when ordinary
Inexplicable, even when familiar
Incomprehensible, even when it is the rule.
Even the slightest detail, however simple
You should look at with suspicion. Ask if it is needed
Especially when it is quite normal.
Please, we say to you now, do not accept
Events that happen every day as natural!
For in these times of bloody confusion
Ordered disorder, deliberate violence
Inhuman humanity –
Nothing must be called natural, so that nothing
May be thought unchangeable.

I

THE RACE IN THE DESERT

Two small parties are hurrying across the desert some way apart.

THE MERCHANT *to his two men, the Guide and a coolie carrying the load*: You've got to move faster. We must reach the outpost at Han in two days. We must be a full day ahead of the others by the time we get there. *To the audience*: I am Karl Langmann, merchant. I am travelling to Urga to sign up an oil concession. I'm not the only one with that idea. The first man there gets the deal. Because I am clever and can organise and am ruthless with my men, I have cut the time for this journey by nearly half so far. Unfortunately one of my rivals is moving as fast as I am. *He looks through his binoculars.* There. I can still see them. *To the Guide*: Why don't you make him move? I'm paying you to drive him, not to admire the view. Do you realise how much this is costing? All right, it's not your money. But if you sabotage me I'll report you to the employing agent in Urga.

GUIDE *to the Coolie*: Try to go faster.

MERCHANT: There's no guts in your voice. You'll never make a guide that way. I should have paid more for a better one. It's always worth it in the end. Why don't you beat him? I'm not for beating, but now it's needed. If I don't get there first, I'm finished. You hired your brother, admit it. A relative, that's why you won't beat him. I know you people. You're tough all right when you want to be. Beat him, or you're fired. And you can try suing me for your money. My God, they're gaining on us.

COOLIE *to the Guide*: Beat me, but not yet your hardest. It's too soon to make me work my hardest.

The Guide beats the Coolie.

SHOUTS FROM BEHIND: Hallo . . . Is this the road to Urga? Wait for us. We are friends.

MERCHANT *does not answer and does not look back*: To hell with them. March on. I've got to keep these men moving another three days. I'll drive them hard for two days and bribe them on the third. In Urga we'll see. I haven't left my rivals behind yet, but on the second night I won't rest, and by morning they'll be out of sight and I'll be at the outpost at Han a day ahead. *He sings*:

I marched all night, and that has put me ahead.
I was ruthless, so I maintained my speed.
The weak man falls behind, and the strong man pushes through.

2

THE END OF A BUSY ROAD

MERCHANT *at the entrance to Han*: This is the outpost of Han. I have arrived a full day ahead of the others. I've exhausted my men, and they don't like me for it. They have no spirit for breaking records. They're not fighters. They spend their lives crawling in the mud. They don't complain, because we still have the police, thank God, to maintain law and order.

TWO POLICEMEN *approaching*: Everything all right, sir? Any trouble on the road? Any trouble with your men?

MERCHANT: Yes, everything's all right. I've made it in three days instead of four. The road's shocking, but that won't stop me finishing the job. What are the roads like beyond Han?

TWO POLICEMEN: After this, sir, comes the uninhabited Yahi Desert.

MERCHANT: Can I get a police escort?

TWO POLICEMEN *as they walk off*: No, sir. Our patrol ends here. And you won't see another one, sir.

3

THE DISMISSAL OF THE GUIDE AT THE OUTPOST OF HAN

GUIDE: Since we spoke to the policemen on the road by the outpost, our merchant has changed. The manner he uses with us is quite different: you could almost call him friendly. It can't be that he's relaxing from the journey, because he hasn't ordered a day's rest, not even here, the last outpost before the Yahi Desert. I don't know how I can get this porter to Urga, he's exhausted already. Altogether the merchant's friendliness makes me worried. I am afraid of his scheming. He goes about deep in thought. New thoughts mean new treacheries. He plans, but it's the porter and I who have to suffer. Otherwise we lose our wages, or he leaves us stranded in the middle of the desert.

MERCHANT *approaching*: Take some tobacco. And cigarette paper. A good draw on that stuff'll make you people go through Hell, won't it? You're capable of anything for the sake of some smoke down your lungs. Well, we're lucky. Our tobacco would last us three times the distance to Urga.

GUIDE *taking it, sotto voce*: Our tobacco!

MERCHANT: Come and sit down, friend. No? A journey like this brings people together. Well, you needn't sit down if you prefer to stand. I respect your customs. Normally I wouldn't sit down with you, just as you wouldn't sit down with the porter. That's what makes the world go round. But we can have a smoke together. Can't we? *He laughs.* That's what I like about you. It's your own kind of dignity. All right, get us ready now. And check the water. I'm told there are not many waterholes in the desert. One more thing. I want to warn you about the porter. Did you see the look in his eye when you beat him? There's no good in that look. You'll have to manage him better in the next few days. We've got to go even faster. And he's a lazy brute. We'll be going through uninhabited territory, and he may show his true colours. To him, you're privileged. You earn more and you don't have to carry. That's reason enough for him to hate you. You'd be well advised to keep your distance. *The Guide goes through to the courtyard. The Merchant sits alone.* A queer lot.

The Merchant sits silent. The Guide supervises the packing. Then he sits and smokes. When the Coolie is finished he sits down and the Guide gives him tobacco and cigarette paper. The Coolie starts a conversation with the Guide.

COOLIE: The merchant speaks of a service to Mankind. He wants to raise oil from the ground and build a railway. He says he will spread prosperity. But if they build a railway here, how shall I earn my living?

GUIDE: You don't need to worry. The railway won't be here so soon. What I've heard is that when they find oil, they hide it. If they dig a hole and oil comes out they get paid money to stop it up again. That's what the merchant is hurrying to find. Not the oil, but the money for keeping quiet.

COOLIE: I don't understand.

GUIDE: Nobody understands.

COOLIE: In the desert it will be much worse. I hope my feet will last.

GUIDE: They will.

COOLIE: Are there thieves?

GUIDE: Only a few scavengers near the outpost.

COOLIE: And later?

GUIDE: When we've crossed the river Myr we follow the waterholes.

COOLIE: You know the way?

GUIDE: Yes.

The Merchant has heard voices. He approaches unseen and listens.

COOLIE: Is it difficult to cross the river?

GUIDE: Not usually at this time of year – unless it floods. And then one can drown in the current.

MERCHANT: He's actually talking to the porter. He's sitting with him. And smoking with him.

COOLIE: What happens then?

GUIDE: One may have to wait a week for the water to go down.

MERCHANT: So that's it. Advising him to delay and to value his own skin more than the expedition. This man is dangerous. He'd be on his side. He's not competent to push this thing through. Which is putting it at its most favourable. Certainly from now on it would be two against one. He's obviously afraid to handle his subordinate firmly, now that it's uninhabited territory we are coming to. I must get rid of him. *He goes to them.* I gave you the order to supervise the packing. Now we'll see how well you carry out orders. *He pulls at a strap hard, till it breaks.* Do you call that packing? To break a strap means a day's delay. Which would just suit you, delay.

GUIDE: I don't want delay. And the strap won't break, if it isn't pulled at.

MERCHANT: Are you contradicting me? Is this strap broken or not? You look me in the face and tell me this strap won't break. You're completely untrustworthy. I made a mistake in treating you people decently, it was bound to cause trouble. I can't use a guide who doesn't maintain his position. You ought to be a porter. You're not fit to be a guide. And I've good reason to believe you're actually stirring up trouble with those supposed to be under your command.

GUIDE: What reason?

MERCHANT: You'd like to know that, wouldn't you? Well, you're dismissed.

GUIDE: But you can't dismiss me in the middle of a journey.

MERCHANT: You should be thankful if I don't report you to the agent in Urga. Here are your wages up to this point. Landlord! *Landlord comes.* You are my witness that I have paid him. *To Guide*: I can tell you now, you'd better not show your face in

Urga in future. *Looks him up and down.* You'll never be anything. *Goes with Landlord to the other room.* I'm starting off right away. If anything goes wrong, you are my witness that today I set out alone – *indicating the Coolie* – with this man.

Landlord gestures that he understands nothing.

MERCHANT *disconcerted*: He doesn't understand. This means there'll be no one to say where I've gone. And the trouble is, they know there's no one.

He sits down and writes a letter.

GUIDE: It was a mistake to sit down together. Take care, that's an evil man. *Gives the Coolie his water-bottle.* Hide this bottle and keep it in reserve. He'll certainly take yours if you lose the way. How are you going to find it? I must try to explain the route to you.

COOLIE: Please don't. If we talk he may dismiss me too. But I would get nothing because I have no union like you, and no rights.

MERCHANT *to the Landlord*: Give this letter to the men who will arrive tomorrow and are also on their way to Urga. I am going on with my porter.

LANDLORD: But he's not a guide.

MERCHANT: So he does understand. He just didn't want to understand. He knows what's going on, but he won't get involved. *Harshly, to the Landlord*: Explain the route to Urga to my porter.

The Landlord goes out and does so. The Coolie nods frequently.

MERCHANT: I can see this is going to be a battle. *He takes out his revolver and cleans it. He sings*:

The sickly man dies and the strong man wins through.
What makes the earth yield up its gift of oil to Mankind?
What makes the coolie so willing to give his labour?
This oil needs a tough battle
With the earth and with the coolie.
And, as always in this fight
The sickly man dies and the strong man wins through

He enters the other yard, ready for his journey. Do you know the way now?

COOLIE: Yes, master.

MERCHANT: Then start.

Merchant and Coolie go. The Landlord and the Guide watch them.

GUIDE: I don't know if he understood the route. He understood too quickly.

4

CONVERSATION IN A DANGEROUS REGION

COOLIE *sings*:

This is the road to the town of Urga
Nothing can stop me until I reach Urga.
Thieves cannot stop me from reaching Urga.
The desert cannot stop me reaching Urga
I can eat in the town of Urga and get paid.

MERCHANT: This porter seems quite unworried. There are thieves and bandits in this area near the outpost. But he sings. *To the Coolie*: That guide – I never did take to him. One day he'd be surly, the next day he'd crawl. Untrustworthy.

COOLIE: Yes, master. *He goes on singing*:

The road is rough all the way to Urga
I hope my feet last out on the long road to Urga.
There is untold suffering on the road to Urga.
But in Urga I can rest my body and get paid.

MERCHANT: Why are you singing, tell me, and why are you so cheerful, friend? You're not afraid of thieves? I suppose you think what they could take from you is not yours. Whatever you have that could be taken is mine.

COOLIE *sings*:

And my wife waits for me in Urga.
And my small son also waits for me in Urga
And . . .

MERCHANT: I don't like your singing. We have nothing to sing about. You can be heard all the way to Urga. There's no better way of attracting bandits. You can sing tomorrow as much as you please.

COOLIE: Yes, master.

MERCHANT *going ahead of him*: He wouldn't defend himself for a moment, if anyone tried to take his pack. What would he do? It should be his duty to protect my property as his own, if it was in danger. But he never would. No breeding. He never says a word, either. That's the worst sort. I can't see what's going on inside his head. What is he plotting? He has no cause to laugh, but he laughs. Why does he laugh? Why, for instance, does he let me walk in front? He knows the route. Where is he taking me, actually? *He looks round and sees the Coolie wiping out their tracks in the sand with a cloth.* What are you doing?

COOLIE: I am wiping out our tracks, master.

MERCHANT: What for?

COOLIE: In case of bandits.

MERCHANT: Ah, in case of bandits. But it ought to be possible for someone to find where you have taken me. Where *are* you taking me? Walk ahead. *They walk on silently. To himself*: It's true, one really leaves very clear tracks in this sand. Actually it's a very good idea to wipe out our tracks.

5

THE CROSSING OF THE RIVER IN FLOOD

COOLIE: We have come the right way, master. Here is the river Myr. Usually at this time of year it is easy to cross, but if it is in flood, one can drown in the current. It is in flood.

MERCHANT: We have to cross it.

COOLIE: One may have to wait a week for the water to go down. Now it is dangerous.

MERCHANT: We shall see. We can't wait a single day.

COOLIE: Then we should find a ford, or a boat.

MERCHANT: That takes too much time.

COOLIE: But I swim very badly.

MERCHANT: The water's not so high.

COOLIE *trying it with a stick*: It is very high.

MERCHANT: Once you are in the water you'll swim all right. Because you'll have to. Try to see the whole picture, like me. Why are we going to Urga? Can't you get it into your thick skull that it's a service to Mankind to raise oil from the ground? Raising oil from the ground means a railway and the spread of prosperity. There'll be food and clothing and God knows what else. And who will have done it? Us. It depends on our journey. Think. The eyes of the nation are on you, on *you*, a little man like you. And you can hesitate to do your duty?

COOLIE *who has been bowing respectfully in the course of this speech*: I swim very badly.

MERCHANT: I am risking my life too. *Coolie bows*. I can't understand you. You're not interested in reaching Urga as fast as possible. You want to make this journey last as long as possible. You have no real interest in this journey, only in your pay.

COOLIE *standing on the bank in fear*: What shall I do? *He sings*:

1
Here is the river.
To swim across is dangerous.
Here on its bank two men are standing.
One plunges in to swim over. The other
Hesitates. Is the one courageous?
Is the other cowardly? On the far side
The first sees profit to be made.

2
Up out of danger the first man climbs
Taking new breath
Standing proud upon the other bank
Ready for his new venture
And for eating good new food.
But the other climbs up out of danger
Panting, for nothing
Except new dangers to face with less
Strength than before. Are these men both brave?
Are these men both clever?
Together they conquered the river
But they do not share the conquest.

3
'We' and 'I and you'
Are not the same at all.

We are the conquerors
But you still conquer me.

At least allow me half a day's rest. I am tired from carrying. After a rest I would be stronger.

MERCHANT: I've got a better idea. A revolver in your back. Shall we lay a bet that you get across? *He pushes him forward. To himself*: My money makes me fear the danger from bandits and ignore the danger from the river. *He speaks to music*:
This is how Man triumphs
Over the desert and the river in flood
And triumphs also over his own kind
To find oil, which Man needs.

6

A CAMP FOR THE NIGHT

In the evening the Coolie, his arm broken, is trying to put up a tent. The Merchant sits by.

MERCHANT: I've already said you needn't put up the tent today, since your arm was broken crossing the river. *The Coolie continues silently.* If I hadn't pulled you out, you'd have drowned. *The Coolie continues*. Your accident was not my fault. After all, that log could have struck me too. All the same, the accident occurred when you were on a journey with me. I just don't have much cash on me, but when we get to Urga I'll give you some money from my bank.

COOLIE: Yes, master.

MERCHANT: A short answer. He blames me with every look. How these coolies can bear you a grudge! *To the Coolie*: You can rest now. *He goes and sits a little way off.* I'm sure his injury is less worrying to him than it is to me. His sort don't care about being intact or damaged. Their ambition ends at the rim of a food bowl. They are born low and they stay low. When we fail we start again. They never start at all because they are failures from the start. Only the man born to fight succeeds. *He sings*:
The sick man will die and the strong man will fight
That's as it should be.

The strong get glory, leave the weak to their plight
That's as it should be.
If he's down let him lie, take a kick at his head
That's as it should be.
The one who wins is the one who gets fed
That's as it should be.
The feast after battle won't include the dead
How else could it be?
God gives to each his place, either servant or lord!
That's how it must be.
If you're in luck – well done. If not, it's your fault
That's as it should be.

The Coolie has approached. The Merchant sees him and is frightened.

MERCHANT: He was listening. Stop where you are. What is it?

COOLIE: The tent is ready, master.

MERCHANT: Don't creep around in the dark. I won't have that. When a man comes near me I want to hear his footsteps. Also I want him to look me in the face when I speak to him. Go and lie down, and stop busying yourself around me. *The Coolie goes back.* Stop. You'll sleep in the tent. I'll sit here. I'm used to the air. *The Coolie goes into the tent.* I'd like to know how much of my song he heard. *Pause.* What's he doing now? He's still moving about.

The Coolie can be seen carefully preparing his bed in the tent.

COOLIE: I hope he won't complain. It's difficult to cut grass with one hand.

MERCHANT: I'd be a fool not to be on my guard. Trust is foolish. This man was injured because of me, perhaps for the rest of his life. It's only to be expected that he should want to pay me back. And a strong man asleep is no better than a weak man asleep. It's a weakness to need sleep at all. It's true if I sat in the tent I wouldn't risk catching the sickness in the air. But what sickness can be as dangerous as a man can be? For little money that man marches by my side, and I have a lot of money. But the journey is equally hard for us both. When he was tired he was beaten. When the guide sat with him, the guide was dismissed. When he covered up our tracks in the sand, perhaps really because of bandits, he was shown lack of trust. When he was afraid on the bank of the river, he got a revolver in his back. How can I sleep in the same tent as that man? He can't make me believe that he'll forget all that. I wonder what he's scheming up in there now. *The Coolie can be seen quietly lying down to sleep.* I'd be a fool to go in that tent.

7

a

AT THE END OF THE TRACK

MERCHANT: Why have you stopped?
COOLIE: Master, there is no more track.
MERCHANT: Well?
COOLIE: Master, beat me if you must, but not on the arm. I don't know the way any more.
MERCHANT: But it was explained to you at the outpost at Han.
COOLIE: Yes, master.
MERCHANT: Then I asked you if you understood it, and you said yes.
COOLIE: Yes, master.
MERCHANT: And you did not understand it?
COOLIE: No, master.
MERCHANT: Then why did you say yes?
COOLIE: I was afraid of being dismissed. I only knew that one must follow the waterholes.
MERCHANT: Then follow the waterholes.
COOLIE: But I don't know where they are.
MERCHANT: Walk on, and don't fool around with me. I know that you've travelled this route before.

They go on.

COOLIE: Shouldn't we wait for the others coming behind us?
MERCHANT: No.

They go on.

b

THE SHARING OF THE WATER

MERCHANT: Where do you think you're going now? That way is north. East is there. *The Coolie goes on in that direction.* Stop. What are you thinking of? *The Coolie stops, but doesn't look at the Merchant.* Why do you avoid my eyes?

COOLIE: I thought that way was east.

MERCHANT: Right, I'll teach you a lesson in finding the way. *He beats him.* Now, where's east?

COOLIE *screams*: Not on the arm.

MERCHANT: Where is east?

COOLIE: That way.

MERCHANT: And where are the waterholes?

COOLIE: That way.

MERCHANT *furious*: That way? But you were going that way.

COOLIE: No, master.

MERCHANT: So? You weren't going that way? Were you going that way? *Beats him.*

COOLIE: Yes, master.

MERCHANT: Where are the waterholes? *The Coolie does not answer. The Merchant, trying to appear calm*: You said just now that you knew where the waterholes are. Do you know? *The Coolie is silent. The Merchant beats him and repeats*: Do you know?

COOLIE: Yes.

MERCHANT *beats him*: Do you know?

COOLIE: No.

MERCHANT: Give me your water-bottle. *The Coolie gives it.* I could now take the view that all the water belongs to me, since you've led me the wrong way. Instead, I shall divide the water out between us. Take your mouthful and then walk on. *To himself*: I lost control. In this situation I shouldn't have beaten him.

They go on.

c

MERCHANT: We've been here before. There are our tracks.
COOLIE: If we have been here before, we can't be far off our way.
MERCHANT: Pitch the tent. We've finished the water in our bottle. My own bottle is empty. *The Merchant sits while the Coolie puts up the tent. The Merchant drinks secretly from his own bottle. To himself*: He mustn't know that I still have some water. Otherwise if he has a spark of sense in his head he'll attack me. If he comes near, I shall shoot him. *He takes out his revolver and puts it in his lap.* If we can only find that last waterhole again. My throat's already dried up. How long can one last without water?
COOLIE: I must give him the bottle that the guide gave me. Otherwise, if they find us and I'm still alive but he is dead, they'll punish me.
He takes out the bottle and goes towards the Merchant. The Merchant suddenly sees him standing there and does not know if the Coolie saw him drinking or not. The Coolie has not seen him drinking. The Coolie holds out his bottle. The Merchant, thinking it is a large stone and that the Coolie is enraged and about to attack him, cries out.
MERCHANT: Put down that stone. *And he shoots the Coolie who, not understanding, still holds out the water-bottle.* Right, you brute. That's finished you.

8

THE SONG OF THE LAWCOURTS

THE ACTORS *as they prepare the scene for the court, sing*:
Behind the thieves and bandits
The law comes scavenging.
And when an innocent man has fallen
Judges, lawyers and their clerks gather round his body to condemn him.
The law will destroy
His innocence and his rights.

The words of the court at work
Cast the shadow of a slaughterer's knife.
That slaughterer's knife is quite sharp enough
Without the attachment called a verdict.

The sky goes dark. The vultures are circling above.
Starved out by the desert they have flown here.
In the courts murderers find refuge. Trackers
Gather there in safety. And here in the lawcourts
Thieves can hide their stolen goods, wrapped in a piece of
paper
On which is written the law.

9

THE COURT

The Guide and the victim's Wife are already seated in the courtroom.

GUIDE *to the Wife*: Are you the wife of the dead coolie? I am the guide who hired him. I have heard that at this trial you will ask for the merchant to be punished and for compensation. I came at once, because I have the evidence which will prove that your husband was innocent. It is here in my pocket.

LANDLORD *to the Guide*: I have heard that you have evidence in your pocket. Let me give you some advice. Leave it where it is.

GUIDE: But is it right that the coolie's wife should not be compensated?

LANDLORD: But is it right that you should be blacklisted?

GUIDE: I'll think about your advice.

The Judge enters, as do the accused Merchant and the Leader of the Second Expedition.

JUDGE: I declare this court in session. Let the wife of the dead man speak first.

WIFE: My husband was a porter for this gentleman across the Yahi Desert. Near the end of the journey this gentleman shot him. Although it will not bring my husband back to life, I claim that his murderer should be punished.

JUDGE: And also you are claiming compensation.

WIFE: Yes, because I and my small son have lost our breadwinner.

JUDGE *to Wife*: Do not feel ashamed of your material concern. It is quite proper. *To the Leader of the Second Expedition*. Behind the expedition of the merchant Karl Langmann there came a second expedition, which had been joined, after his dismissal, by the guide of the first expedition. The expedition which came to grief was sighted hardly a mile from the route. What did you find as you approached?

LEADER 2: The merchant had almost no water left in his bottle, and the coolie lay dead in the sand.

JUDGE *to Merchant*: Did you shoot the porter?

MERCHANT: Yes. He attacked me suddenly without warning.

JUDGE: How did he attack you?

MERCHANT: He wanted to strike me from behind with a stone.

JUDGE: Can you explain why he should attack you?

MERCHANT: No.

JUDGE: Did you drive your men especially hard?

MERCHANT: No.

JUDGE: Is the guide from the first expedition present?

GUIDE: I am.

JUDGE: Can you add any information?

GUIDE: In my eyes, what mattered to the merchant was reaching Urga as soon as possible, to secure an oil concession.

JUDGE *to Leader 2*: Would you say that the expedition ahead of you was travelling unusually fast?

LEADER: No, not unusually. They had a day's lead and they held it.

JUDGE *to Merchant*: You must have been forcing the pace to maintain your lead.

MERCHANT: I forced the pace not at all. That was the guide's concern.

JUDGE: Did the accused give you orders to drive the porter particularly hard?

GUIDE: I drove him no harder than usual – if anything less hard.

JUDGE: Why were you dismissed?

GUIDE: In the eyes of the merchant I was too familiar with the porter.

JUDGE: And that was forbidden? Would you say that this porter, with whom familiarity was forbidden, was difficult to handle?

GUIDE: No. He bore everything because, as he told me, he was afraid of being dismissed. He was not in a union.

JUDGE: Did he have much to bear? You must answer. And don't consider your answers too carefully. We shall arrive at the truth in any case.

GUIDE: I was only there up to the outpost at Han.

LANDLORD *to himself*: Well done, guide.

JUDGE *to Merchant*: Did anything occur later which could explain the porter's attack?

MERCHANT: No, nothing that could be laid to my account.

JUDGE: Listen here, you should not try to paint yourself whiter than you are. That is no help to your case. If your handling of the coolie was so perfect, how do you explain his hatred? Because it is only by making credible his hatred of you that you can make credible your own need for self-defence. Think well before you speak.

MERCHANT: I do have something to confess. I did strike him once.

JUDGE: I see. And from this one occasion the coolie conceived such a powerful hatred?

MERCHANT: No, but I did hold a revolver to his back when he didn't want to cross the river. And in crossing the river he did break his arm. So that also was my fault.

JUDGE *smiling*: In the eyes of the coolie.

MERCHANT *also smiling*: That's what I meant. In fact I pulled him out of the water.

JUDGE: All right. After the dismissal of the guide, you gave the coolie cause to hate you. And what about before? *To the Guide, severely*: Admit, after all, that the man hated the merchant. If one thinks about it, it's really quite understandable. What could be more natural than that this man, who is badly paid, driven into danger at the point of a gun, actually injured for the sake of another man's profit, risking his life for almost nothing, should hate the other man?

GUIDE: He didn't hate him.

JUDGE: Let us now hear the evidence of the landlord of the outpost at Han in case he can tell us something which will make clearer our picture of the merchant's relations with his men. *To the Landlord*: How did the merchant treat his men?

LANDLORD: Well.

JUDGE: Shall I clear the court? Do you fear you might lose custom if you speak the truth?

LANDLORD: No, it's not necessary in this case.

JUDGE: As you wish.

LANDLORD: He even gave the guide tobacco. And never questioned what he owed the guide when he dismissed him. Also the coolie was well treated.

JUDGE: Your outpost is the last police call on the route?

LANDLORD: Yes, after that comes the uninhabited Yahi Desert.

JUDGE: I see. So the friendliness displayed by the merchant would be rather what we might call circumstantial, indeed temporary, could we say tactical, friendliness. Just as our officers in the war adopted a more comradely attitude towards the men as the army approached the front. This sort of friendliness has no great significance.

MERCHANT: For instance he always used to sing when he was on the march. I never heard him sing once after the time I put my revolver in his back to make him cross the river.

JUDGE: Clearly he felt very bitter. It is only natural that he should. Again we can take an illustration from the time of war, when it would have been quite understandable for simple people to say to us officers: yes, you are fighting your own war, but we are fighting *your* war. In the same way the coolie could say to the merchant: you are making money for yourself, but I am making money for *you*.

MERCHANT: I have another confession to make. When we lost our way, I divided the water from one bottle between us, but the second bottle I kept for myself.

JUDGE: Did he perhaps see you drinking from the second bottle?

MERCHANT: That was what I thought when he came for me with the stone in his hand. I knew he hated me. From the moment we'd come to uninhabited territory I'd been on my guard day and night. I had to assume that he'd take the first opportunity to attack me. If I hadn't killed him when I did, he would have killed me.

WIFE: I would like to speak. He couldn't have attacked him. He never attacked anybody in his life.

GUIDE *to Wife*: It's all right. I've got the evidence of his innocence in my pocket.

JUDGE: Did anyone find the stone with which the coolie was about to make his attack?

LEADER 2: That man – *indicating the Guide* – took it from the dead man's hand.

The Guide holds out the bottle.

JUDGE: Is that the stone? Do you recognise it?

MERCHANT: Yes, that's the stone.

GUIDE: And look what is inside the stone. *He pours out water.*

FIRST ASSESSOR: It is not a stone. It is a water-bottle. He was offering you water.

SECOND ASSESSOR: It seems after all that he was not making an attack.

GUIDE *embracing the widow of the dead man*: I told you I had proof of his innocence. For once there was proof. You see, I gave him this bottle as they set out from the last outpost. The landlord witnessed it, and it's my bottle.

LANDLORD *to himself*: The fool. Now he's finished too.

JUDGE: That can't be the truth. *To the Merchant*: He's supposed to have been handing you a drink.

MERCHANT: It must have been a stone.

JUDGE: No, it was not a stone. You can see it was a water-bottle.

MERCHANT: But I couldn't have known it was a water-bottle. The man had no reason to offer me water. I wasn't his friend.

GUIDE: But he offered him water.

JUDGE: But why did he offer him water? Why?

GUIDE: He must have thought the merchant was thirsty. *The Judges smile at each other.* Probably out of common humanity. *The Judges smile.* Perhaps it was stupidity, for I don't think he had anything against the merchant.

MERCHANT: Then he must have been very stupid. The man was injured through my fault, perhaps for life. His arm. It would only be right that he should want to pay me back.

GUIDE: It would be right.

MERCHANT: For little money he marched with me, and I have a lot of money. But the journey was equally hard for both of us.

GUIDE: So he knows that.

MERCHANT: When he was tired he was beaten.

GUIDE: And wouldn't that be right?

MERCHANT: I *could* only assume that the coolie would attack me at the first opportunity. Unless I assumed he couldn't think at all.

JUDGE: What you mean is that you were right to believe that the coolie must hold something against you. So you did indeed kill someone who might well be harmless, but only because you could not have known that he was harmless. It happens sometimes with our police. They shoot into a demonstrating crowd, a harmless crowd, but they shoot because they can only believe that these people are going to drag them off their horses and lynch them. These policemen shoot out of fear. And their fear is that of the reasonable man. What you mean is that you could not have known that this coolie was an exception to the rule.

MERCHANT: One lives by the rule, not the exception.

JUDGE: So the question is: what possible ground could there be for this coolie to offer water to his oppressor?

GUIDE: No reasonable ground.

JUDGE *sings*:

The rule says: an eye for an eye.
Only fools assume the exception.
No reasonable man can expect water
To be offered by the enemy.

GUIDE *sings*:

According to the system they live by
Humanity is the exception.
All those who act with human feeling –
They are the ones who will suffer.
Protect from themselves those who seem too friendly
Prevent them from making any offers of their help.
See that cup, raised to you in thirst: so be quick to close your eyes.
Cover your ears: before you hear that groan.
Do not let your foot move: someone is calling to you for help.
You are lost, lost if you forget yourself. You
Give water to a thirsty man and
A wolf will drink.

JUDGE: We will retire to consider our judgement.

The court withdraws.

LEADER 2: Aren't you afraid they might never give you another job?

GUIDE: I had to tell the truth.

LEADER 2 *smiling*: Well, if you had to . . .

The court returns.

JUDGE: The court wishes to put another question to you. There was no way in which you gained by shooting the coolie?

MERCHANT: Quite the contrary. I needed him. He carried the maps and instruments that I needed for my contract in Urga. I couldn't carry them alone.

JUDGE: Did you not secure your contract in Urga, then?

MERCHANT: How could I? I arrived too late. I am ruined.

JUDGE: Then I shall now deliver our judgement. The court finds proved that the coolie approached his master not with a stone but with a water-bottle. This fact established, however, the court takes as more reasonable the view that the coolie was about to attack his master with the bottle, and not that he was offering him water. The porter belonged to a class of men which has, after all, grounds for supposing itself exploited. For such a man it would be a matter of common wit to defend himself in face of an inequitable distribution of the water. Indeed it might even seem a matter of justice to such people as the coolie, limited and prejudiced as their outlook is by its dependence on mere reality, to revenge themselves against their tormentor. It must be said that, in the last analysis, they have nothing to lose. The merchant belongs to a different class from that of the porter. He could only anticipate the worst. He could not credit that the porter whom he had ill-treated, as he himself has said, would offer him an act of friendship. His common wit told him that he was in the greatest danger. The isolated nature of the area must have caused him great anxiety. The distance from the police and the restraint of the law would encourage his servant to demand his share of the water. The accused therefore acted in justifiable self-defence regardless of whether he was actually threatened or merely believed himself to be threatened. In the circumstances as established it was inevitable that he should believe himself threatened. The case is therefore dismissed; and the widow's claim fails.

THE ACTORS:

There ends
The story of a journey
You have heard and you have seen.
You saw the normal, that which happens every day.
But please, we say to you now:
Even when ordinary, find it strange
Even when familiar, find it inexplicable
Even when quite normal, it must astound you
Even when the rule, recognise it as an abuse
And wherever you have recognised abuse
Put it right!

The Horatians and the Curiatians

A play for schools

Collaborator: MARGARETE STEFFIN

Translator: H.R. HAYS

Characters:

CHORUS OF CURIATIANS
CHORUS OF HORATIANS
THE THREE CURIATIAN GENERALS – *archer, spearman, swordsman*
THE THREE HORATIAN GENERALS – *archer, spearman, swordsman*
THE HORATIAN WOMEN
THE CURIATIAN WOMEN

THE MUSTERING

The city of the Horatians and the city of the Curiatians. The cities turn to their Generals.

CHORUS OF CURIATIANS:

Why do we battle among ourselves, Curiatians?
Once more
Winter is over and once again
Within our walls the conflict rages
Over the ownership of land and the ownership of the minepits.
Therefore
We have determined to arm ourselves
And in three armies
To invade the land of the Horatians
And to overthrow them totally
Appropriating all their goods above and below the ground.
They shout to the Horatians:
Submit!
Hand over your huts, farmlands and implements or else
We shall overcome you with such military strength
That none of you shall escape.

CHORUS OF HORATIANS:

The robbers come! With an enormous
Military strength they overrun the country.
They will grant us life if we surrender
What we need to live.
But why
Are we more afraid of death than hunger?
We shall not submit!

CHORUS OF CURIATIANS:

We give over troops and weapons
To our Generals.

CHORUS OF HORATIANS:

We give over troops and weapons
To our Generals.
Shoulderframes with little flags which indicate divisions of troops are fastened to the shoulders of the Generals and on black-

boards the number of soldiers is written down.

CHORUS OF CURIATIANS:

To you, General,
We give over seven cohorts of archers.

CHORUS OF HORATIANS:

To you, General
We give over seven brotherhoods of spearmen.

CHORUS OF CURIATIANS:

To you, General
We give over twelve cohorts of swordsmen.

CHORUS OF HORATIANS:

To you, General
We give over seven brotherhoods of archers.

CHORUS OF CURIATIANS:

To you, General
We give over seven cohorts of spearmen.

CHORUS OF HORATIANS:

To you, General
We give over twelve brotherhoods of swordsmen.

ALL SIX GENERALS:

Bring the weapons!
Bows, spears, swords and shields are brought.

CHORUS OF CURIATIANS:

Choose
From this rich supply of weapons
The very best.

CHORUS OF HORATIANS:

Those are your weapons.

FIRST CURIATIAN:

The bows must be good. Without good bows
I can do no fighting.
He bends the bow but it breaks.

CHORUS OF CURIATIANS:

Throw it away.
He throws it away and bends another, which holds.

FIRST CURIATIAN:

With this bow I am content.

FIRST HORATIAN, *one bow is laid before him. He bends it carefully*:

I can bend it farther but then it will break.

CHORUS OF HORATIANS:
Be content with this. We have no others.

FIRST HORATIAN:
But it won't carry far.

CHORUS OF HORATIANS:
Then go nearer the foe.

FIRST HORATIAN:
But I run a great risk.

CHORUS OF HORATIANS:
Yes.

HORATIAN WOMEN:
If the archer quarrels with his bow
There can be no fighting.

FIRST HORATIAN *quickly*:
I do not quarrel with it.

CHORUS OF HORATIANS *as two spears are brought to the Second Horatian*:
Here is your spear and here
Is a Curiatian spear. You can see
They are equally long and equally heavy.
And you, too
Are a match for your opponent, spearman.

CHORUS OF CURIATIANS:
Bring new spears.

The Second Curiatian is given a much longer spear. Five great shields are brought to the Third Curiatian warrior. He goes from shield to shield and tries to pierce them with his sword. Three are pierced through. He chooses one of the last two.

THIRD CURIATIAN:
The sword has grown dull.

CHORUS OF CURIATIANS:
Here is a new one.

Third Curiatian pulls a horsehair from his helmet and cuts it with his sword.

THIRD CURIATIAN:
With this sword and shield I am well equipped.

THIRD HORATIAN *as two shields are laid before him – one small, one big*:
I will try this to make sure.

He pierces the big one through and turns to the small one.

CHORUS OF HORATIANS:

Wait, you have tried it! The undamaged one
Is made of the same metal. But the first shield
Was held incorrectly.

A warrior holds the shield aslant while a second warrior thrusts at it so that the blow glances off.

THIRD HORATIAN:

I understand. Since it is not proof
Against a straight thrust
I must make sure to receive
Only glancing blows.

CHORUS OF HORATIANS:

Shall we mend the big shield for you?

THIRD HORATIAN:

No, I shall take the small one.
It is splendidly light.

He takes it.

I am content with this shield.
I can move faster with it. And I know the sword.
I forged it myself. It is as good
As I could make it.

CURIATIAN AND HORATIAN WOMEN:

Now go. Not all of you
Will come back to us.

CURIATIAN GENERALS:

Do not weep! Prepare the victory wreaths
In advance. We shall return
Laden with much booty.

CURIATIAN WOMEN:

We shall count the days until you come to us.
Your place at the table, your place in bed
Will be empty.

HORATIAN GENERALS:

But how shall the fields be tended
How shall the workshops be kept going without us?

HORATIAN WOMEN:

Do not trouble yourselves.
The fields will be tended. Only make sure

That we reap the harvest.

CHORUS OF HORATIANS:

To balk the attack
To avoid the submission and the theft
Of our huts, farmlands and implements
We have determined, O Horatians
To advance with three armies.
We shall fight
Until our opponents are totally overthrown.

I THE BATTLE OF THE ARCHERS

THE HORATIAN:

Yesterday evening
My opponent reached the position
I had planned for.
I have so planned it
That he must come from behind a mountain
In order to attack me. And so
There is little distance between us
As it has to be on account of my bow.
Now I am waiting for the sun.
It must be to my advantage.

THE CURIATIAN:

I await my opponent
Among mountains that are strange to me
And I do not know how near he may be
However, I have no wind against me
And my bow is good.
I wait for the sun.

BOTH CHORUSES:

The archers have reached their positions.
When it is light, the battle begins.

THE WARRIORS:

It is getting light.

The warriors bend their bows. An actor carries in a spotlight on a stick which represents the sun. He carries it very slowly across the stage. His passage from left to right must last as long as the fight. As the sun rises over the Horatian's mountain, he is in shadow, his opponent in the light.

THE CURIATIAN:

Oh, the sun blinds me!
I cannot aim and my opponent
Remains in darkness. He is covered
By the shadow of the mountain.

First volley of arrows. The blinded Curiatian shoots too high. The Horatian hits him in the knee. The Curiatian draws out the arrow.

I am hit and my opponent
Is not hit.
I had forgotten that the sun not only lights up
But blinds as well.
I needed light to aim
But it came from his direction.
My position is bad.
Since my knee is shattered, my opponent
Can keep me in this bad location.

CHORUS OF CURIATIANS:

What have you lost?

The Curiatian shows how many he has lost by taking two little flags from his shoulderframe and throwing them away. The Chorus of Curiatians speaks to their man as they erase two cohorts from the board.

You have lost two cohorts
Out of your seven.
But your weapon is good.
As always
Time is in our favour.
Take no risks.
In the end
Better weapons will prevail.

THE HORATIAN:

My bow does not carry far enough.
But my opponent is blinded by the sun
And my arrow
Has at least shattered his knee.
My position is good.

CHORUS OF HORATIANS *to their man*:
Why have you stopped fighting? A good position
Does not stay good for ever. We shall be worse off
If we do not better ourselves. Inevitably
The sun moves across the heavens. Irrevocably
Morning becomes midday.

THE HORATIAN:
With a volley of arrows I intended to shoot down
The man with the sun in his face.
But I did not kill him with the first arrow
He is only wounded, and now
Has retreated behind his stone
And fights no more. But the sun travels
And my mountain shadow grows shorter
And I have retreated from the enemy
So that my arrow can no longer reach him.

CHORUS OF HORATIANS:
It is too bad
That your bow is a poor one. But we have no better.
Throw it away! Fight with your fists!
You must fight with every means you have.
At least do something!

THE HORATIAN:
I do not agree with you. After all
I have already hindered the enemy
With my bow.
I am an archer, not a prizefighter.
It was already noon
When your message reached me, now
I, too, am in sunlight.
And so I shall shift to a spot
From which I can hit the man
Who is blinded. Now comes
The second volley of arrows.
The sun has now travelled between the two mountains so that both warriors are in sunlight.

THE CURIATIAN:
The sun comes from behind the mountain. The enemy
Has advanced and is now in sunlight. Perhaps

I can hit him now.

THE HORATIAN:

Come out, you robber!
Shoot off your arrow! Oh!
I cannot see! The sun
Blinds me as well.
Second volley of arrows. Both go too high.

THE HORATIAN *and* THE CURIATIAN *each to his own Chorus*:

The second volley is over.
We have both failed to hit.

CHORUS OF CURIATIANS *to their man*:

But you have gained
An advantage.

THE HORATIAN:

Inevitably
The sun travels across the heavens. Irrevocably
Morning becomes midday. Now what shall I do?
If I was blinded when the sun was at high noon
My enemy must also be blinded still.
Then I can advance
As I was advised, and even
Fight with my fists.
He takes a step forward to the left, stops, covering his eyes with his hand. He speaks to his Chorus.
I tried to advance. But now
The sun is already behind the second mountain.
The enemy is in shadow. I
Am wholly in sunlight.
At nightfall I took your advice, forgetting
You gave it at midday.
The sun is now behind the second mountain, so that now the Curiatian with his third arrow can deliver the mortal shot.

THE CURIATIAN:

Victory! My last arrow
Has hit!
In the course of a day my disadvantage
Has become an advantage.
Now that I have the advantage
My better bow prevails.

CHORUS OF CURIATIANS:

Victory! A whole army of our opponents
Is destroyed. Five cohorts of archers
Are now free for the final battle. After a short rest
They shall move to the east
In order to join our other armies.

CHORUS OF HORATIANS:

After its last message, that it did not wish
To engage the enemy again, we have heard nothing
Of our army. We must conclude
That it was destroyed.
It clung to one position
It clung to one weapon
And it clung
To one plan. But inevitably
The sun travelled across the heavens. Irrevocably
Morning became midday and midday became nightfall.
To the Wife of the Horatian:
Woman, no more news
Comes from your husband. But in the city of the enemy
We hear a victory celebration. We conclude
The archer has fallen.
The Wife is dressed in widow's weeds.
Erase seven brotherhoods from the number of soldiers!
Where they were, they are no more.
The plan, begun with them
Must be carried out by others.
The seven brotherhoods of archers are erased.
The enemy advances into our valleys.
In the track of the army
Travel the overseers.
Those who shed their blood now pay for it.
The fruitful farmland
Now produces no more than a stony waste
For the enemy carries off the corn.
The farmer
Wipes the sweat from his eyes
But he who has the sword
Eats the bread.

2 BATTLE OF THE SPEARMEN

CHORUS OF HORATIANS:
The enemy marches into our mountains.
He travels through ravines
Along a rushing river.
You must stop him, spearman!

THE HORATIAN:
I have seen him press forward. His spear
Is enormous. In open fight
I cannot stop him.
If you agree to it
I shall overpower him
Without running into danger myself. But to do it
I have a long march before me
And I have
But little time.

CHORUS OF HORATIANS:
We are agreed that you should
Spare the army. We have lost
One already.
But stop the enemy!

Seven Conversions of a Spear

By a difficult march over the mountains the Horatian approaches the enemy at a spot where the mountains extend to the edge of the road. As he climbs, he leans on his spear.

THE HORATIAN:
I climb the mountain. The spear
Is my stick. It is my third foot
The foot that never gets hurt
The foot that never grows tired.
One tool has many uses.
He reaches a crevasse in the mountains.
But how shall I go on? Here is a crevasse.
When I was a boy, I hung from an oak limb
And swung over a brook into a garden
Where there were apples. My spear was once

An oak limb.
In this way I shall cross the crevasse.
One tool has many uses.
He lays it over the crevasse and crosses hand over hand.

CHORUS OF HORATIANS:
The enemy falls upon our valleys.
Stop the enemy!

FIRST HORATIAN:
But how shall I go on? I have crossed
The crevasse but here is a snowdrift.
How can I tell how deep it is?
My spear shall be my measuring stick.
One tool has many uses.
He measures the depth of the snowdrift.
But how shall I go on? The snowdrift.
Is too deep for me. And the other cliff edge
Is higher than this one.
Again I look at my spear.
I say it shall be my vaulting pole.
One tool has many uses.
He vaults over.

CHORUS OF HORATIANS:
The enemy advances! He drives off
Our herds.
Hasten! Stop the enemy!

THE HORATIAN:
But how can I go on? Here is a ridge.
It is narrower than my foot. All my efforts
Will be in vain if this ridge holds me back.
I shall walk along it. With my spear
I shall keep my balance. Its weight which was often
Too great as I climbed, I now
Make use of and I say
One tool has many uses.
He walks along the ridge, using the spear as a balancing pole.

CHORUS OF HORATIANS:
The enemy approaches
Our minepits.
Stop the enemy!

THE HORATIAN:

I have arrived. I lean
Over the cliff edge. Below me
Runs the road that my enemy shall march over.
I shall crush him beneath rock fragments.
With my spear I can loosen them.
One tool has many uses.
He loosens rock fragments.
My spear is my crowbar.
It holds back the rockpile until my enemy is under it.
With a pressure of my fingers
I shall crush my enemy.
My spear has preserved me.
He prepares a small avalanche.
My enemy is not yet there.
And I am tired from running.
He sits down to wait.
And I lean back, knowing
I dare not sleep. And I am not too exhausted
To act, but I am too exhausted to do nothing.
And I fall asleep.
He sleeps. The Curiatian comes in sight. He marches slowly forward. While the Horatian sleeps, he passes the danger point.

THE HORATIAN:

And I wake up and again
Lean over the cliff edge
And looking down I see
That the enemy has already passed by
The spot where I intended to strike at him.
My hurry that brought me to the goal
Exhausted me. And so
I cannot carry out the plan.

CHORUS OF HORATIANS:

Our spearman has completed a great march
And overcome all obstacles
But exhaustion
Repaid him for all his efforts.
Worse than a lost battle
Is wasted effort.

Arise, spearman
And forget what you have done. Once more
Throw yourself against the enemy
But with less hope.

THE HORATIAN:

I can do no more
I have done my share.

CHORUS OF HORATIANS:

What you have done amounts to nothing.
If you had lain in the grass and counted clouds
Things would have been no worse for us.
You have done much
But you have not stopped the enemy.

THE HORATIAN:

Then was it all wrong?
All that I did?

CHORUS OF HORATIANS:

No. But you have not finished.
Stop the enemy!
You, who devised so much
Think of something new.
You, who expended so much effort
Bestir yourself again.
Stop the enemy!
All that you have accomplished
Will add to your fame if you stop the enemy.
But you shall get no credit
If you do not stop him.
Seven labours amount to nothing
But if you perform the eighth
And stop the enemy
You shall be acclaimed for eight labours.

THE HORATIAN:

I agree.
So I get to my feet once more.
The way I took to get here
I take back.
The fight I thought hopeless
I shall fight.

As the following chorus is recited, the Horatian descends. He moves the rock fragments back. He withdraws his spear, he measures the snowdrift and vaults it, he crosses the crevasse, hand over hand, he climbs down the mountain. A snowstorm overtakes him and in his great hurry he has losses. He loses one little flag in the snowdrift, another on the ridge, another falls into the crevasse.

Now go back the same way!
You have lost time. Lose no more!
You are weakened. Now do twice as much!
Snowfalls and storm
Add to your discouragement.
The man with victory in sight
Overcomes many difficulties, but it is hard
To encounter the old ones afresh
On the way back. Or after a defeat
With redoubled courage to redouble your cleverness
Only to return to the starting point
Of all your efforts.
Each device leads back, each handhold
Only erases a mistake and yet
Fighting your way back steadily
Is a part
Of the new advance.

THE HORATIAN:

I have succeeded. I have come back
To the starting point. I see only
One chance for me in battle
Since my spear is too short.
The result of my plan is uncertain
To carry it out difficult.
In no other way
Can I stop my foe.
Indeed, for this plan
My spear is too long. Though I cannot
Lengthen it
I can shorten it.

He breaks it in two, throws one half of it away and goes off.

CHORUS OF HORATIANS:

But we erase
Three brotherhoods of archers
Now lying in the snow and crevasses.
And we place our hopes
In the army that has shrunk.

The Ride on the Flood

THE CURIATIAN: I am marching through a river valley. There is a mountain on one side of me and a river on the other. The mountain is insurmountable and the river is impassable since further on there is a mortally dangerous waterfall. And I cannot be attacked from the front because my spear is so long that my enemy cannot reach me.

The Horatian comes down the river on a raft. He is rowing with his spearbutt.

Now I see my enemy on my right hand, coming down the river on a raft. I cannot see that he has any weapons. He is coming down very fast. But I cannot turn my spear around between the rock walls. It is too long. He suddenly raises the raftpole from the water and throws himself upon me.

THE HORATIAN:

And I come travelling down the flood
Toward the great waterfall.
And my spear is my raftpole.
One tool has many uses.
And now, as I reach my enemy
It is a spear again
And I thrust with it.

THE CURIATIAN: And with the full force of the river which he rides like a mighty horse, he thrusts the spearbutt into my body as he glides by. I go down. My opponent is destroyed. The falls must have drowned him. I am badly wounded and lie motionless in the narrow pass. I had forgotten that the river was not impassable but rather passable at the cost of a man's life and so my position was not unassailable but assailable at the cost of a man's life. So my enemy has fallen but I am badly wounded.

CHORUS OF CURIATIANS:

What have you lost?

The Curiatian shows how many he has lost as he takes five of his little flags from his shoulderframe and throws them away.

CHORUS OF HORATIANS:

The spearman has fallen.
We erase five brotherhoods from the number of the soldiers.
Where they were, they are no more.
The plan, begun with them
Must be carried out by others.

Five brotherhoods are erased and the Spearman's Wife is dressed in widow's weeds.

WIFE OF THE SPEARMAN:

How did he fight?

CHORUS OF HORATIANS:

He stopped the enemy.
He completed two marches
And overcame all obstacles.
At the last he rode on the river and added
The great strength of the river
To his small strength.
But the river that flung him at his enemy
Flung him away again. For a long time
We saw him rowing. As far as the waterfall
He struggled to reach the shore. Then the waterfall
Drowned him at last. He did not kill his enemy
But he left a weakened foe
For his comrades in the fight.

CHORUS OF CURIATIANS *as they erase five cohorts from the board*:

Five cohorts out of seven have fallen.
But we are certain to win. Unconquerable
Our army presses forward. Our opponent
Has been seized by despair. He runs
To meet our arrows and throws himself into the water.
The booty is immense. Cease your quarrelling
Over the ownership of the land and the new minepits, Curiatians
By tomorrow the final battle will take place
In which we shall have three armies

Against our enemy's one.

HORATIAN WOMEN:

Our men fall like slaughtered cattle.
When the butcher reaches them, they fall.
One made good plans but fell. The other
Showed courage and fell. And we
We are glad of the plans and the courage and weep.
We were content that they fought.
If we weep, it is because they fell
Not because they fought. Alas, he
Who returns is the victor
And when there is no victory, none return.

CHORUS OF HORATIANS:

The robbers come!
The fight still rages and already
They carry off ore from the minepits.
With the cries of their warriors
Stricken to death, are mixed
The commands of the overseers.

3 THE BATTLE OF THE SWORDSMEN

THE HORATIAN: For two days I have been holding my opponent in check. As he is too heavily armoured, I am waiting until the archer and the spearman can reach me.

The Curiatian throws the broken spearbutt of the second warrior and the bow of the first at his feet.

THE CURIATIAN:

Your brothers are destroyed. Surrender!

THE HORATIAN: I know the spear and I know the bow. My comrades in battle must have been destroyed as the Curiatian says. Then I must attack quickly in spite of his armour or he will be joined by his archer and his spearman.

THE CURIATIAN:

I thought to frighten him out of attacking with the news.
But now I see I have provoked him to attack.

THE HORATIAN:

I will fall upon his flank.

He steps to one side and sees the other two armies, hitherto hidden behind the Curiatian. They are marching up, the Spearman decked with victory wreaths, the Archer decked with victory wreaths and laden with booty, both of them now armed with swords.

It is too late. They are almost here.

THE CURIATIAN SWORDSMAN *shouts to the Spearman*:

Draw your sword and hasten! The battle begins!

THE CURIATIAN SPEARMAN:

Marching along a river
In a narrow pass, I drowned my enemy.
Seven brotherhoods were overthrown. In spite of my losses
And the disorder of my supply train
I hurry in to the final battle.
He shouts behind him:
The battle begins. Hasten, archer!

THE CURIATIAN ARCHER:

I am coming.
Between two mountains
In unknown territory
At the third volley
I overthrew my enemy.
Before nightfall, his last army
Will be defeated.

THE CURIATIAN SWORDSMAN:

I am stronger than my opponent by seven cohorts.

THE HORATIAN SWORDSMAN:

I cannot attack. I am too heavily outnumbered.
He asks the Chorus:
What shall I do?

CHORUS OF HORATIANS:

In spite of the bravery of our armies
Our knowledge of the battleground
And our employment of all means of defence
We have lost two battles. Two armies
Are destroyed. Two out of three women
In our city
Wear widow's weeds.
Your brotherhoods, swordsman

Are our last reserves:
You have waited for reinforcement.
Wait no longer. None will come.
In your hands
Are our farmlands, herds and workshops.
Between us and the robbers
There is no one but you.

THE HORATIAN:
They are moving up
With their superior numbers
They will utterly destroy me.
They come against me with three swords
A threefold sword arm.
And how shall I stand my ground?
My shield is poor.

CHORUS OF HORATIANS:
Don't give a foot of ground!
Your weapons
Cannot be helped. Now
Use them. The number of the enemy
Cannot be reduced. Stand firm.
Throw yourself upon them. Destroy . . .
Alas, what are you doing?
The Horatian has begun to run away.

CHORUS OF CURIATIANS:
Victory! The enemy
Has taken to his heels.
Pursue him, Curiatians!

THE CURIATIAN SWORDSMAN:
After him! At the sight of our superior numbers
The enemy has taken to his heels.
After him or he will escape us!

CHORUS OF HORATIANS:
Make a stand! He does not hear us!
Our last man
Has given up the fight. Our best defender
Has been corrupted by the enemy.
The Horatian Swordsman tries to reassure them with a motion of his arm as he runs.

Don't deny it! Why are you running away?

CHORUS OF CURIATIANS:

Surrender! Hand over the keys of your city!
Don't let him escape, Curiatians.

THE CURIATIAN SPEARMAN *to the Swordsman*:

Don't let him escape!
You can still run!

The three Curiatian armies begin the chase but they cannot all move forward with the same speed. The badly wounded Spearman lags behind. The slightly wounded Archer passes him but still lags.

CHORUS OF CURIATIANS:

How fast he runs!
He cannot save himself but he turns his defeat
Into disgrace.
He has not even enough courage
To merit an elegy
Sung by his own people.

THE HORATIAN SWORDSMAN:

I am glad my shield is light.
I can run better.

CHORUS OF HORATIANS:

He mocks us!

THE CURIATIAN SWORDSMAN:

I am running
As fast as I can. My shield
Is heavy.

THE HORATIAN SWORDSMAN:

And I can run
As fast as you can.
Run faster!
Or I shall escape you!

CHORUS OF HORATIANS:

Erase his brotherhoods of men!
Where they were, they are no more.
The plan, that depended on them . . .

As the number of swordsmen is half erased, he turns in a little half circle and comes back at the Curiatian. During the chase the pursuers have been separated.

Wait! He has turned around. He is coming back!
He attacks!

CHORUS OF CURIATIANS:

He attacks!
And our swordsman
Is out of breath. His shield
Was heavy. And our archer
Could not catch up!

CHORUS OF HORATIANS:

Our archer shattered his knee.
And he is hindered by his boots, his helmet and his knapsack.

CHORUS OF CURIATIANS:

And our spearman also lags behind!

CHORUS OF HORATIANS:

Our spearman has torn his side.

The Horatian Swordsman beats the untried Curiatian Swordsman after a short fight. Then he runs back at the Archer.

CHORUS OF CURIATIANS:

The swordsman has fallen.
Erase twelve cohorts
From the number of soldiers
Where they were . . .

The Horatian has reached the Archer, beaten his sword out of his hand and cut him down. Then he runs on.

The archer has fallen as well. And the enemy
Rushes on. The pursuit
Has separated the pursuers. The flight
Was an attack. Only the spearman
Remains, he's badly wounded.

The Horatian has reached the Spearman and brings him down without trouble.

Erase nineteen cohorts! Where they were
They are no more. The plan, that depended on them
Now no one can carry out.

The three Curiatian Wives are then dressed in widows' weeds. The nineteen cohorts are erased.

CHORUS OF HORATIANS:

Victory! Your stratagem, swordsman
Divided the enemy and your strength

Overthrew them.

THE HORATIAN SWORDSMAN:

I saw the archer marching along
Laden with booty and the spearman marching along
Without booty. And I saw that the swordsman had no victory wreath.
I knew, too, that they would throw themselves upon me.
And I saw the swordsman look behind him
Seeing one with a victory wreath, the other laden with booty.
Then I knew that what came upon me like *one* army
Had once been three divisions and could again
Be cut in three. And I saw
How one was strong, one limped
And the third crawled. And I thought
Three can still fight
But only one can run.

CHORUS OF HORATIANS:

The robbers have been beaten back.
Our archer employed unsuccessfully
The great machine of nature
Which is always moving. But our spearman
With the river and the flood and his spearbutt made himself
Into a great projectile.
And our swordsman saw
How a unity can be split up when it is in motion.
His stratagem divided the enemy
And his strength overthrew him.
Our archer weakened his enemy.
Our spearman wounded him badly.
And our swordsman completed the victory.

Saint Joan of the Stockyards

Collaborators: H. BORCHARDT, E. BURRI, E. HAUPTMANN

Translated by RALPH MANHEIM

Characters

JOAN DARK, *lieutenant in the Black Straw Hats*
PIERPONT MAULER, *meat king*
CRIDLE/GRAHAM/LENNOX/MEYERS, *meat packers*
SLIFT, *a broker*
MRS LUCKERNIDDLE
GLOOMB, *a worker*
PAUL SNYDER, *major in the Black Straw Hats*
MARTHA, *a Black Straw Hat*
JACKSON, *a lieutenant in the Black Straw Hats*
MULBERRY, *a landlord*
A WAITER
Meat Packers
Wholesalers
Stockbreeders
Brokers
Speculators
Black Straw Hats
Workers
Labour Leaders
The Poor
Detectives
Newspapermen
Newsboys
Soldiers
Passers-by

I

THE MEAT KING PIERPONT MAULER RECEIVES A LETTER FROM HIS FRIENDS IN NEW YORK

Chicago, Stockyards.

MAULER (*reading a letter*): 'It has come to our attention, dear Pierpont, that the meat market has been severely depressed of late. And the tariff barriers in the south have withstood all our attacks. It therefore seems advisable, dear Pierpont, for you to drop the meat business'. This tip has just come to me from my dear friends in New York. But here's my partner.

He hides the letter.

CRIDLE: Why so gloomy, dear Pierpont?

MAULER:

Remember, Cridle, how the other evening
As we were walking through the stockyards
We stopped to look at our new processing machine.
Remember, Cridle, that big blond steer
Looking so dumbly skyward as the blow
Descended. I felt as if that blow had fallen on me.
Oh, Cridle. Oh, what a bloody business we are in.

CRIDLE:

The same old weakness? I find it hard to believe
That you, a giant among meat packers
King of the stockyards, before whom butchers tremble
Should faint with anguish over a big blond steer.
Don't mention this to anyone, I beg you.

MAULER:

O faithful Cridle!
I shouldn't have gone down to that slaughterhouse.
For seven years I'd kept away, ever since
I went into business. I can't bear
It any longer. I'm giving up
This bloody business before the day is out.
You take my share. I'll sell it to you cheap.

I'd soonest sell it to you, for no one else
Is so much part and parcel of the business.

CRIDLE:

How cheap?

MAULER:

Old friends like us won't haggle
Over a little thing like that.
Suppose we say ten million.

CRIDLE:

That wouldn't be too much if it weren't for Lennox
Who battles us for every can of meat
Who spoils the market with his bargain prices
And will sink us if he doesn't go down first.
Until he falls – and you alone can fell him –
I won't accept your offer. Until then
You'll have to keep your crafty brain at work.

MAULER:

No, Cridle, the groaning of that steer
Will live forever in my heart. This Lennox
Must be destroyed at once, for I'm determined
To give up butchering and live in virtue.
Come, Cridle, and I'll tell you how to hasten
Lennox's fall. But then you'll have
To take this hateful business off my hands.

CRIDLE:

If Lennox falls.
They go out.

2

a

THE COLLAPSE OF THE BIG PACKING PLANTS

Outside the Lennox plant.

THE WORKERS:

We, the seventy thousand workers at the Lennox packing plants
Can't live a single day more on our wretched wages.
Yesterday we took another big pay cut
And today again they've posted a notice, saying:
Anyone who isn't satisfied with
The wages here can leave.
Okay, let's leave, the whole lot of us, and fuck
Their daily shrinking wages.
Silence
This work has long filled us with loathing
This plant has been a hell to us and only
The cold terrors of Chicago
Have kept us here. But now
A twelve-hour day no longer
Gets us a plate of hash or
The cheapest pair of pants. So
We might as well walk out and
Kick the bucket right away.
Silence.
Who do they think we are? Do they expect us
To stand out here like cattle, ready
For anything? Do they
Take us for blockheads? We'd sooner starve. Come on, we're
Getting out of here.
Silence.
Say, it's six o'clock gone by.
Why don't you open up, you bloodsuckers? Your
Cattle are here, you butchers, open up!

They knock.
Maybe we've been forgotten.
Laughter.
Open up! We
Want to get into
Your stinkholes, your filthy kitchens
To cook your greasy
Meat for the dinners of the rich.
Silence.
We demand at least
Our same old wage, low as it is, at least
A ten-hour day, at least . . .

A MAN (*passing*):
What are you waiting for? Don't you know
That Lennox has shut down?
Some newsboys run across the stage.

THE NEWSBOYS: Meat king Lennox forced to shut down! Seventy thousand workers high and dry! M. L. Lennox crushed by cut-throat competition of Pierpont Mauler the meat king and philanthropist.

THE WORKERS:
Christ!
Hell itself
Has closed its gate in our face!
We are lost. The ruthless Mauler
Has grabbed our exploiter by the throat and
We are choking!

b

P. MAULER

Street.

THE NEWSBOYS: Chicago Tribune. Extra! P. Mauler, meat king and philanthropist, attends opening of P. Mauler Hospital, biggest and most expensive in the world.
Mauler passes with two men.

A PASSER-BY (*to another*): That's P. Mauler. Who are those men with him?

THE OTHER: Detectives. They're guarding him in case somebody tries to strike him dead.

c

TO ASSUAGE THE MISERY OF THE STOCKYARDS, THE BLACK STRAW HATS SALLY FORTH FROM THEIR MISSION HOUSE: JOAN'S FIRST DESCENT INTO THE DEPTHS.

Outside the headquarters of the Black Straw Hats.

JOAN (*at the head of a shock troop of Black Straw Hats*)
In a dark time of cruel confusion
Of ordained disorder
Of systematic lawlessness
Of dehumanized humanity
When in our cities the turmoil never ceases:
Into such a world, resembling a slaughterhouse
Summoned by rumours of impending violence
Hoping to stop the brute force of the short-sighted workers
From smashing their tools and
Destroying their livelihood
We propose to bring back
God.
Diminished in glory
Almost despised
No longer admitted
To the places where real life is lived –
Yet the sole salvation of the lowliest!
We have therefore decided
To beat the drum for Him
To get Him a foothold in the slums
To make His voice resound in the stockyards.
To the Black Straw Hats:
This campaign of ours
Is undoubtedly the last of its kind. The last attempt
To set Him up again in a crumbling world
Using the lowliest to do so.
They march out to the beating of drums.

d

THE BLACK STRAW HATS WORKED IN THE STOCKYARDS FROM MORNING TO NIGHT, BUT WHEN NIGHT FELL THEY HAD ACCOMPLISHED NEXT TO NOTHING.

Outside the Lennox packing plant.

A WORKER: There's a big swindle under way in the meat market. It looks like we'll have to go hungry until the fight is over.

OTHER WORKERS: The light's on in the offices. They're counting their profits.

The Black Straw Hats enter. They put up a sign saying: 'A bed for the night 20 cts. With coffee 30 cts.'

THE BLACK STRAW HATS (*singing*):

Watchful, be watchful
We've seen you, man going down
We've heard your appeal for rescue
Seen the girl about to drown.
Stop all these motorcars, hold up that tram
We shall prevent you from sinking, we do give a damn.
Wait until we arrive!
Take courage now, my brothers, we'll see that you survive!
There's hope for every sinner
You'll eat a decent dinner
You have to stay alive.
So never say that nobody can change things
That inequality is ours from birth.
If you'll agree with us it's time for action
And all decide to sweep it from the earth
We'll order the tanks to move up here
And warships will mobilize
And bombers will blacken the skies
So that you, my brother, get a bowl of soup for supper.
And don't forget that the poor are
The mightiest army of all.
And now we must go forward
And everyone answer our call.
'Tenshun! Fix bay'nets! Beat the drum!

Courage, all those who were sinking! Look this way! Here we come.

While still singing, the Black Straw Hats start handing out their little tract, 'The War Cry', spoons and bowls of soup. The workers say 'Thank you'. Then they listen to Joan's speech.

JOAN: We are soldiers of God. Because of our hats people call us the Black Straw Hats. Wherever conditions are unsettled and violence threatens, we come marching with our drums and banners, to remind people of God, whom they've all forgotten, and lead their souls back to Him. We call ourselves soldiers, because we're an army, marching as to war against crime and poverty, for those are the powers that are trying to drag us down. (*She starts ladling out the soup.*) There you are. Get some hot soup inside you. After that things will look entirely different, but kindly spare a thought for the one who provides it. Once you start thinking, you'll see there's only one solution: to look up and not down. To put yourself in line for a good berth up top and not down below. To try and be first up top and not down below. Now you see how much reliance can be placed in earthly happiness. None at all. Trouble comes like rain that nobody makes but it comes all the same. See what I mean? Where do your troubles come from?

A SOUP EATER: From Lennox & Co.

JOAN: Maybe Mr Lennox has worse worries than you do right now. What have you got to lose? His losses come to millions!

A WORKER: There's not much fat in this soup, but there's plenty of wholesome water, and you've got to admit it's good and hot.

ANOTHER WORKER: Shut up and enjoy the banquet! Listen to the heavenly message or they'll take your soup away.

JOAN: Quiet! Tell me this, dear friends; why are you poor?

A WORKER: Okay, you tell us.

JOAN: I will: it's not because you're not blessed with earthly goods – which don't come everybody's way – but because you have no feeling for the higher things. That's why you're poor. The earthly joys you chase after, a bit of food, a nice place to live, a movie show – these are crude sensual pleasures. God's word is a higher, finer, more spiritual joy. I bet you can't think of anything sweeter than whipped cream. Well, the word of God is even sweeter. Oh, how sweet it is! It's like milk and honey, and in it ye dwell as in a palace of gold and alabaster. O ye of little faith, the birds under heaven have no 'Help Wanted' ads, and the lilies of the field have no jobs, and yet He feeds them because they sing His praise. You all want to get to the top. But what kind of place do you call the top, and how do you expect to get there? All right. We Black Straw Hats have a very practical question to ask you: What does a man need to get to the top?

WORKER: A stiff collar.

JOAN: No, not a stiff collar. Maybe you need a stiff collar to get ahead in the world, but before God you need a lot more, an entirely different kind of halo, and you men haven't even got a celluloid collar to your name, because you've completely neglected the inner life. So how do you expect to get to the top – or what you in your folly call the top? By brute force? As if anything but destruction were ever accomplished by violence. You think you'll get a paradise on earth by fighting for it. But I say unto you: fighting won't get you a paradise, it will get you chaos.

A worker runs in.

THE WORKER:

There's a job open!
At No. 5 Plant, it pays wages, and
It's calling you!
The place looks like a shithouse.
Run!

Three workers leave their full soup bowls and run away.

JOAN: Hey, you, where are you running so fast? When you're being told about God! I guess that's something you don't care to hear about!

A BLACK STRAW HAT: We're out of soup.

THE WORKERS:

They're out of soup.
It was watery, there wasn't much of it. But it was

Better than nothing.

All turn away and stand up.

JOAN: Stay where you are, it doesn't matter. The Lord's soup will never run out.

THE WORKERS:

When will you finally
Open your crawling cellars
You butchers of men?

Groups form.

A MAN:

Now how will I finish paying for the cute little damp little cottage
Where twelve of us live? Seventeen
Installments I've paid and now the last is due.
They will throw us out on the street and never again
Will we see the trampled ground with the parched yellow grass on it
And never again will we breathe
The familiar contaminated air.

A SECOND MAN (*around whom a group has formed*):

Here we stand with hands like shovels
And necks like fork lifts, wanting to sell
Our hands and necks
And no one buys them.

THE WORKERS:

And our tools, a mountain
Of steam hammers and cranes
Locked behind walls!

JOAN:

Hey, what is this? Why, they're turning their backs!
Fed your bellies, eh? Thanks for coming. Why have you stayed this long?

A WORKER:

For the soup.

JOAN:

We will carry on. Sing!

THE BLACK STRAW HATS (*singing*):

March straight into the fight
Into the thickest of the fray!

And sing with all our might. It is still night
But bright will be the dawning day
And our Lord Jesus is on his way.

A VOICE (*from the rear*):
There's still some jobs open at Mauler's.
The workers go out except for a few women.

JOAN (*gloomily*):
Pack up the instruments. Did you see how they all beat it when the soup ran out?
Those people rise no higher than
The rim of a bowl. They
Believe in nothing but what
They hold in their hands – if they believe in hands.
Living from minute to minute insecurely
They cannot rise from the lowest depths
Where only hunger can capture their attention. No
Song can move them, no word
Reaches them down there.
(*To the bystanders*:) We Black Straw Hats feel as if we had a starving continent to feed with our spoons.
The workers come back. Shouts in the distance.

THE WORKERS (*front*): What's that shouting? A gigantic river of humanity from the direction of the packing plants!

VOICE (*from the rear*):
Mauler and Cridle are closing down too!
The Mauler plants have shut their gates!

THE RETURNING WORKERS:
Running for work we met halfway
A river of desperate men
Who had lost their jobs. They started
Asking us about jobs.

A WORKER (*front*):
O God! Another column from over there!
Endless! Mauler too
Has closed. Where are we to turn?

THE BLACK STRAW HATS (*to Joan*): Let's go. We're wet and frozen stiff. We've got to eat.

JOAN: First I've got to find out who's to blame for all this.

THE BLACK STRAW HATS:

Hold it! Don't get involved in that! They'll chew
Your ears off. Their minds are low.
They're lazy. Lazy and greedy. They haven't had
One higher impulse since the day they were born!

JOAN: I want to know. (*To the workers.*) Now tell me. Why are you running around this way? Why are you out of work?

THE WORKERS:

Bloodsucking Mauler is locked in battle
With penny-pinching Lennox. That's why we're starving.

JOAN:

Where does this Mauler live?

THE WORKERS:

Where cattle are bought and sold, in
A big building, the Livestock Exchange.

JOAN:

I'm going to see him, because
I've got to know.

MARTHA (*one of the Black Straw Hats*):

Don't get involved in that! Ask many
Questions and you'll get many answers.

JOAN:

Never mind. I want to see this Mauler
Who's at the bottom of so much misery.

THE BLACK STRAW HATS:

In that case, Joan, your future looks black to us.
Don't get involved in earthly strife.
It will engulf you
Your purity won't last, and soon
Your bit of warmth will perish in
The all-pervading cold.
Goodness departs from those who leave
The comforting hearth fire.
Striving downward step by step
In search of an answer never to be found
You will vanish in the muck!
For muck is what gets heaped upon those who
Ask incautious questions.

JOAN:

I want to know.

The Black Straw Hats go out.

3

PIERPONT MAULER FEELS THE BREATH OF ANOTHER WORLD.

Outside the Livestock Exchange.

Joan and Martha are waiting down below; above, the meat packers Lennox and Graham in conversation. Lennox is chalky-white. The sound of the Livestock Exchange behind them.

GRAHAM:
Alas, good Lennox, what a bitter blow
Vile Mauler has struck you. Irresistibly
The monster rises, making merchandise
Of nature itself, selling the air we breathe.
That man could sell us the food we ate for dinner
Squeeze rent from houses that caved in long ago
Coin money from rotten meat, and if you stoned him
I'll wager he would turn your stones to gold.
So consuming is his greed, such second nature
His unnatural passion has become to him
That he himself would not disown it.
You see, he's soft, he has no love of money, he
Can't bear the sight of misery, can't sleep at night.
So go to him, and in a half-choked voice
Say: Mauler, look at me. Mauler, take your
Hands from my throat. Think of your old age.
That'll stop him. He may even burst into tears.

JOAN (*to Martha*):
You alone, Martha, have come
Here with me. All the others
Have left me with a warning on their lips
As if I were going to my death – strange warning!
Thank you, Martha.

MARTHA: I too warned you, Joan.

JOAN: And came with me.

MARTHA: But will you recognize him, Joan?

JOAN: Never fear, I'll recognize him.
Cridle appears above.

CRIDLE:
Well, Lennox, there's an end to your undercutting.
You're finished. I'll shut down and wait for
The market to pick up. I'll clean up the premises
And oil my knives and put in some of those new
Processing machines that save a pretty penny
In wages. New contraption. Pretty fancy.
The pig rides up on a conveyor belt
Of wire netting to the topmost floor
And there the butchering begins. The pig
Plunges almost unaided, landing on
The knives. Not bad, eh? See, the pig
Butchers itself, converts itself to sausage.
From floor to floor descending, first forsaken by
Its hide, to be fashioned into leather
Then parting with its bristles, used for brushes
And lastly casting off its bones – which give us bone meal –
It's forced by gravity into the can
That's waiting down below. Not bad, eh?

GRAHAM:
Not bad. But where's your outlet for that can?
Accursed times! The market's ruined, glutted
And business, once so thriving, at a standstill.
Fighting over a constipated market
You drove the prices down by undercutting each other
Like buffaloes which, fighting, trample the grass they're fighting over.
Mauler comes out with Slift his broker and group of packers. Behind him two detectives.

THE PACKERS:
The question is who can hold out longest.

MAULER:
Lennox is sunk. (*To Lennox*:) You're through. Admit it.
And Cridle, I expect you now to take
Over the plant as we agreed you would
Once Lennox fell.

CRIDLE:
Yes, Lennox is through, but so is the thriving market.
Therefore, dear Mauler, you will have to come
Down on the price of your stock. Ten million is too steep!

MAULER:
What's that! The price
Is right here in the contract! Lennox, look!
Is this is a contract? Does it state a price?

CRIDLE:
Yes, but this contract was drawn up in good times.
Does it say anything about a slump?
What can I do on my own with a packing plant
When nobody's buying a single can of meat?
Ah, now I know why you couldn't bear to see
Them kill a steer: because you knew
Its meat could not be sold!

MAULER:
No. 'Twas because the poor beast's bellowing
Sickened my heart.

GRAHAM:
Oh, great Mauler, now at last I see
The full extent of your greatness. Even your heart
Has foresight!

LENNOX:
Mauler, I'd like just once more . . .

GRAHAM:
Touch him in the heart, Lennox. Touch him in the heart.
'Tis a sensitive garbage pit!
He punches Mauler in the solar plexus.

MAULER: Ouch!

GRAHAM: You see, he *has* a heart!

MAULER:
That does it, Freddy. Now I'll fix it
So Cridle doesn't take a single can
Off your hands. Because you punched me.

GRAHAM:
No, Pierpy, no! That would be mixing
Private affairs with business.

CRIDLE:

Don't worry, Pierpy. Anything you say.

GRAHAM: I have two thousand workers, Mauler.

CRIDLE: Send them to the movies. But Pierpy, our contract isn't valid. (*He does some figuring in a small notebook.*) When you decided to pull out and we drew up this contract, the shares, that we each held a third of, were selling for three ninety. You let me have them for three twenty; that was cheap. Today it's too much, because the market is glutted and they're quoted at a hundred. I couldn't pay you without throwing any of my shares on the market. If I do that, they'll drop to seventy and I won't realize enough to pay you. I'll be through.

MAULER:

If that's your story, Cridle, I
Had better get my money out of you now
Before you're through.
Believe me, Cridle, I'm so frightened
I'm breaking out in sweat. Six days is all I
Can give you! No! Where's my head? Five days
If that's your situation.

LENNOX: Look at me, Mauler.

MAULER: You tell us, Lennox. Does the contract say anything about a slump?

LENNOX: No.

Lennox goes out.

MAULER (*looking after him*):

Methinks some trouble is gnawing at his vitals
And I, immersed in business (more's the pity!)
Let it escape me. Oh beastly business!
It turns my stomach, Cridle.

Cridle goes out. Meanwhile Joan has motioned one of the detectives over to her and said something to him.

THE DETECTIVE: Mr Mauler, there are some people over there who would like a word with you.

MAULER: A shabby bunch? Envious looking? Violent? Tell them I'm busy.

THE DETECTIVE: It's two members of the Black Straw Hats.

MAULER: What's that?

THE DETECTIVE: It's an organisation with numerous branches and a large membership. The lower classes think the world of them and call them the Soldiers of the Lord.

MAULER: I've heard of them. 'Soldiers of the Lord'; that's an odd name. What do they want of me?

THE DETECTIVE: They say they would like a word with you.

Meanwhile the roar of the Livestock Exchange goes on: Steers 43, Hogs 55, Calves 59, etc.

MAULER:

Very well, tell them that I'll see them.
But tell them too that they are not to say
A single word unless I ask them first.
I want no tears or hymns
Especially no maudlin blubber. Also tell them
Their best advantage lies in
Impressing me as peaceful folk without
Prison records, who don't want anything
Out of me that I haven't got.
And one more thing: Don't tell them that I'm Mauler.

The Detective goes over to Joan.

THE DETECTIVE:

He'll see you, but you're not
To ask him any questions, only
To answer those he asks.

Joan steps up to Mauler.

JOAN: You're Mauler!

MAULER: No, no. Not I! (*Points to Slift.*) It's him.

JOAN (*pointing to Mauler*): You are Mauler.

MAULER: No, it's him.

JOAN: It's you.

MAULER: How do you come to know me?

JOAN: Because you have the cruellest face.

Slift laughs.

MAULER: Laughing, Slift?

In the meantime Graham has run off.

MAULER (*to Joan*): How much do they pay you girls for a day's work?

JOAN: Twenty cents, but we're fed and clothed.

MAULER:

Flimsy clothing, Slift, and watery soup, I'll wager.
Yes, undoubtedly, flimsy clothing and not much nourishment in the soup.

JOAN:

Why, Mauler, have you locked the workers out?

MAULER: (*to Slift*):

Isn't it odd, their working without pay?
I've never heard of such a thing, people
Working for nothing and not minding it.
And in their eyes I see no fear
Of misery and destitution.
(*To Joan*:)
You Black Straw Hats are funny creatures.
I won't ask what you want of me. I know
What people – the simpletons! – say of me. They call
Me ruthless, they say I've ruined Lennox
And driven Cridle, who between you and me
Is not the best of men, into a corner.
But these are business matters and unlikely
To interest you. There's something else, though, which
I'd welcome your opinion about.
I'm planning to give up this bloody business
As soon as possible. Completely.
The other day – this ought to interest you –
I saw a steer being killed. I was so shaken
I'm going to drop it all. I've even sold
My share in the plant. Twelve million dollars worth.
I gave it to him for ten.
Don't you
Think I did right? Don't you approve?

SLIFT:

He saw a steer being slaughtered and resolved
To slaughter the wealthy Cridle
Instead of the poor steer.
Wasn't that right?
The packers laugh.

MAULER:

Laugh and be damned. It doesn't bother me.

I'll see you crying yet.

JOAN:

Just tell me, Mr Mauler, why you've closed
The packing plants. I've got to know.

MAULER:

Doesn't it beat all records that I've pulled
Out of a thriving business just because it's cruel?
Say it was right and meets with your approval.
No, don't say anything. I know. I admit
My act has brought misfortune on some people.
They're out of work. I know. Unfortunately
That part could not be helped. But they're
A lot of no-good riff-raff anyway. My
Advice is: don't go near them. But tell me:
My pulling out of the business –
Wasn't it right?

JOAN:

Strange question, I wonder if you're serious.

MAULER:

That's because my accursed voice
Is so accustomed to dissembling.
I know, it makes you
Dislike me. Don't say anything.
(*To the others*:)
I feel as though a breeze from another world had touched me.
Give me your money, you hog butchers, give me your money!
(*He takes money from their pockets and gives it to Joan.*)
Here, girl. Take this for the poor.
But mind you, I feel no obligation.
I sleep most soundly. Why am I helping? Maybe
Because I like your face, because it's so
Innocent, though you've lived for twenty years.

MARTHA (*to Joan*):

I wouldn't trust that man.
Forgive me, Joan. I too am going to leave you.
Frankly, I think you too
Had better quit all this!

Martha goes out.

JOAN: This is only a drop in the bucket, Mr Mauler. Can't you do something that will really help them?

MAULER:
Publish it far and wide, I heartily
Approve of what you're doing, and wish there were
More like you. But you're wrong about the poor.
They are evil. People don't move me.
They are not guiltless. They themselves are butchers.
But enough of that.

JOAN: Mr Mauler. In the stockyards they're saying that you're to blame for their misery.

MAULER:
For steers I feel compassion. Man is evil.
Men are not ready for your plan.
Before the world can be changed
Man must be changed.
Just a moment.
(*He speaks to Slift in an undertone.*)
Get her alone and slip her some more money.
Tell her it's for her poor, so she can take it without
Blushing, but then see what she buys herself.
And if that doesn't work – I hope it doesn't –
Then take her to the stockyards. Show her
Those poor of hers, how base, how bestial
They are, how cowardly and treacherous.
Get her to see that they themselves are to blame.
That ought to do it.
(*To Joan*:)
Sullivan Slift, my broker, has something
To show you.
(*To Slift.*)
You see, it's almost more than I can bear
To know there are people like this girl
Possessing nothing but a black straw hat
And twenty cents a day, yet fearless.
Mauler goes off.

SLIFT (*to Joan*):
I wouldn't want to know what you're so keen on knowing

But if you still insist, come here tomorrow.

JOAN (*looking after Mauler*):

That man's not wicked. He's the first
Our drums have flushed from the thickets of baseness
The first to hear the call.

SLIFT (*on his way out*): My advice to you is to keep away from those people in the stockyards. They're no good, if you ask me; they're the scum of the earth.

JOAN: I want to see them.

4

THE BROKER SULLIVAN SLIFT SHOWS JOAN DARK THE BASENESS OF THE POOR: JOAN'S SECOND DESCENT INTO THE DEPTHS.

The stockyard district.

SLIFT:

Now, Joan, I'm going to show you
The baseness of these people you
Feel sorry for, and show you that
Your sympathy is misplaced.

They walk along a factory wall with big letters on it, saying: Mauler & Cridle, Meat Packers. The name of Mauler is crossed out. Two men step out of a small gate. Slift and Joan listen to their conversation.

FOREMAN (*to a young fellow*): Four days ago a man by the name of Luckerniddle fell into one of the rendering tanks. We couldn't stop the machines fast enough and he ended up with the leaf lard; horrible. This is his jacket and this is his cap. Take them, get rid of them, they're only using up a hook in the cloakroom and making a bad impression. My advice is to burn them, the sooner the better. I'm asking you, because I know you're reliable. I'd be fired if they were found anywhere. Naturally, you'll get Luckerniddle's job as soon as the plant opens.

THE YOUNG FELLOW: You can count on me, Mr Smith.

The Foreman goes back through the small gate.

THE YOUNG FELLOW: It's a shame about that man, going out into the world in the form of leaf lard. But it's a damn shame too about his jacket, which looks hardly worn. Old man Leaflard won't need it any more, he'll have his can to shelter him, but I can make good use of it. Hell, I'll take it. *He puts it on and wraps his own jacket and cap in newspaper.*

JOAN (*swaying*): I feel sick.

SLIFT: That's the world for you. (*He stops the young fellow.*)

Where'd you get that jacket and that cap? They belonged to Luckerniddle, the man who had the accident.

THE YOUNG FELLOW: Oh please sir, don't tell anybody. I'll take them right off. I'm in a bad way. Last year the twenty cents extra they pay in the fertilizer cellars tempted me to work on the bone mill. It affected my lungs and gave me an eye inflammation that wouldn't go away. That cut down my efficiency and I've hardly worked at all since February.

SLIFT: Keep them on. And come to Canteen No. 7 at lunchtime. You'll be given a meal and a dollar if you'll just tell Luckerniddle's wife where you got that cap and jacket.

THE YOUNG FELLOW: But wouldn't that be cruel, sir?

SLIFT: Well, if you'd rather go without –

THE YOUNG FELLOW: You can count on me, sir.

Joan and Slift go further on.

MRS LUCKERNIDDLE (*is sitting outside the factory gate, ranting*):

Hey you in there, what have you done to my husband?
Four days ago he went off to work, saying:
Keep my soup warm for me tonight. And
He hasn't shown up yet. What have you done
To him, you butchers! Four days now I've been
Out here in the cold. And four nights too. Waiting
But no one says a word to me. And my husband
Doesn't come out. But get this straight. I'm going
To stand here till I get to see him, and
God help you if you've hurt him.

Slift steps up to her.

SLIFT: Your husband has left town, Mrs Luckerniddle.

MRS LUCKERNIDDLE: Left town? I don't believe it!

SLIFT: Look here, Mrs Luckerniddle, he has left town, and it's extremely disagreeable for the plant to have you sitting here shooting off your mouth. So we'll make you an offer, though the law doesn't require us to. If you'll stop making inquiries about your husband, you can eat in our canteen for three weeks free of charge.

MRS LUCKERNIDDLE: I want to know what's happened to my husband.

SLIFT: We've told you. He's gone to Frisco.

MRS LUCKERNIDDLE: He hasn't gone to Frisco. Something has happened to him and you're trying to hush it up.

SLIFT: If that's how you feel about it, Mrs Luckerniddle, you can't accept food from the plant and you'll have to bring suit. But think it over. I'll be at the canteen tomorrow if you want me.

Slift goes back to Joan.

MRS LUCKERNIDDLE: I've got to have my husband back. He's my only support.

JOAN:

She will never come.
Twenty meals may mean a good deal
To a hungry person, but they
Are not the whole story.

Joan and Slift walk on. They come to a factory canteen and see two men looking in through a window.

GLOOMB: That's the foreman who's to blame for my sticking my hand in the tin cutting machine. There he sits, stuffing his belly. Let's make sure it's the last time he stuffs at our expense. Better give me your blackjack. Mine looks too flimsy.

SLIFT (*to Joan*): Stay here. I'll talk to him. If he comes over, tell him you're looking for work. Then you'll see what these people are like. (*He goes over to Gloomb.*) Before you let yourself be drawn into something rash, as you seem to be doing, I'd like to make you a good proposition.

GLOOMB: I'm busy right now, sir.

SLIFT: Too bad. You'd have stood to gain by it.

GLOOMB: Make it quick. We don't want to miss the slave-driving bastard. He's going to pay for his part in their inhuman system.

SLIFT: I've got a suggestion that might help you. I'm an inspector in this plant. Your place at the machine hasn't been filled yet, and that is very inconvenient. Most of the men think it's too dangerous, and do you know why? Because of the stink you've been making about your fingers. I don't have to tell you how eager we are to find someone for the job. Now if you were to bring us somebody, we'd be glad to rehire you on the spot, in fact we'd give you an easier and better job than you had before. You might even get the foreman's job. You look intelligent to me. And it so happens that the guy in there has been making himself unpopular lately. You get the drift. Of course we'd expect you to keep the men on their toes. But the main thing, as I've said before, is to find someone to man the tin cutting machine which, I admit, lacks adequate safety devices. Say, that girl over there is looking for work.

GLOOMB: Can I bank on what you've said?

SLIFT: Yes.

GLOOMB: The one over there? She doesn't look strong. It's no job for a person who tires easily. (*To the other man*:) I've thought it over; we'll do it tomorrow night. Such jobs are best done at night. So long. (*Goes up to Joan.*) Looking for work?

JOAN: Yes.

GLOOMB: Eyesight okay?

JOAN: No. I worked in the fertilizer cellars last year, on the bone mill. It affected my lungs and gave me an eye inflammation that wouldn't go away. I've been unemployed since February. Is it a good job?

GLOOMB: The job is good. It's work that can be done by people like you, who aren't very strong.

JOAN: Are you sure there's nothing else available? I've heard that machine is dangerous for people who tire easily. Their hands start to shake and get caught in the blades.

GLOOMB: Lies. You'll be amazed to see what pleasant work it is. You'll shake your head and say: How can people tell such ridiculous stories about this machine?

Slift laughs and pulls Joan away.

JOAN: I'm almost afraid to go any further. What will I see next!

They go into the canteen and see Mrs Luckerniddle talking to the waiter.

MRS LUCKERNIDDLE (*reckoning*): Twenty lunches . . . then I could . . . then I'd go . . . and then I'd have . . . (*She sits down at a table.*)

WAITER: If you're not eating, you'll have to leave.

MRS LUCKERNIDDLE: I'm waiting for someone who said he'd be here today or tomorrow. What is there today?

WAITER: Lentils.

JOAN:

There she sits.
I thought she was as firm as a rock, yet feared
She'd come tomorrow. And now she's run here quicker than we have
And there she is, waiting for us.

SLIFT: Go bring her some food. Maybe she'll change her mind.

Joan gets some food and takes it to Mrs Luckernidddle.

JOAN: Here so soon?

MRS LUCKERNIDDLE: It's because I haven't had anything to eat in two days.

JOAN: But you didn't even know we'd be here today.

MRS LUCKERNIDDLE: No, I didn't.

JOAN: On the way here I heard someone saying your husband had an accident and the management was to blame.

MRS LUCKERNIDDLE: Oh. So you're taking back your offer? So I don't get my twenty meals?

JOAN: But they tell me you got along fine with your husband. And I hear you're all alone in the world.

MRS LUCKERNIDDLE: But I haven't had anything to eat in two days.

JOAN: Couldn't you wait until tomorrow? If you desert your husband, no one will give him another thought.

Mrs Luckerniddle is silent.

JOAN: Don't take it.

Mrs Luckerniddle grabs the plate out of her hand and starts eating greedily.

MRS LUCKERNIDDLE: He's gone to Frisco.

JOAN:

And the cellars and the warehouses are full of meat
And it can't be sold and it's spoiling
Because no one will buy it.

The Young Worker with the jacket and cap comes in at the rear.

THE WORKER: Good morning. So I can eat here?

SLIFT: Sit down with that woman over there.

The worker sits down.

SLIFT (*behind him*): Nice cap you've got there. (*The worker hides it.*) Where'd you get it?

THE WORKER: Bought it.

SLIFT: Where'd you buy it?

THE WORKER: I didn't buy it in a store.

SLIFT: Where did you get it then?

THE WORKER: I got it from a man who fell into the rendering tank.

Mrs Luckerniddle feels sick. She gets up and goes out.

MRS LUCKERNIDDLE (*on her way out, to the waiter*): Don't take my plate away. I'm coming back. I'll be coming every day. You can ask the gentleman. (*Goes out.*)

SLIFT: For three whole weeks she'll come here and eat like an animal without looking up. Well, Joan, now do you see that they're base beyond measure?

JOAN:

But how you harness
Their baseness! How you exploit it!
Don't you see how their baseness thrives on misfortune?
I'm certain that, like other women, she'd have kept
Faith with her husband as she should have
And gone on asking a little longer
About the man who gave her his support.
But the price was too high, it came to twenty meals.
And that young fellow
Who would run errands for any scoundrel
Would he have shown her the dead man's jacket
If he had been free to choose?
But he felt the price was too high.
And what makes you think that man without a hand
Wouldn't have warned me? If the price
Of so trifling a kindness hadn't been too high?
Why have they sold their indignation, which was righteous
  but too expensive?
If their baseness is beyond measure
So is their poverty. You have shown me not
The baseness of the poor but

The poverty of the poor.
Now you have shown me the baseness of the poor
Let me show you what suffering they endure.
Your tales of their debasement you will see
Refuted by the face of poverty.

5

JOAN INTRODUCES THE POOR TO THE LIVESTOCK EXCHANGE

The Livestock Exchange.

THE PACKERS:
We've got canned meat for sale!
Buy canned meat, you wholesalers!
Fresh and succulent canned meat!
Mauler & Cridle's Leaf Lard!
Graham's tasty loins of beef!
Wilder's Kentucky salt pork!

THE WHOLESALERS:
And there was stillness on the face of the waters
And sky-blue ruin among the wholesalers!

THE PACKERS:
Thanks to vast progress in technology
To engineering skill and managerial know-how
We are able to offer you
Mauler & Cridle's Leaf Lard
Graham's tasty loins of beef
Wilder's Kentucky salt pork
At a thirty percent reduction.
Buy canned meat, you wholesalers!
Strike while the iron is hot!

THE WHOLESALERS:
And there was stillness over the mountain tops
And the hotel kitchens covered their heads
And the food stores turned away in horror
And the middlemen paled!
We wholesalers puke at the sight of
A can of meat. The country's stomach
Has been stuffed too full of meat from cans
And is rebelling.

SLIFT:
What have your friends in New York been writing you?

MAULER:

Theories. If they're to be believed
The whole meat ring will topple to the ground
And lie there several weeks more dead than alive
And I'll be left with mountains of meat on my hands!
Blarney.

SLIFT:

Boy, would I laugh if those guys in New York
Really forced down the tariffs
And opened up the south, provoking
Some kind of boom, and we had stayed out in the cold.

MAULER:

Supposing all that happened, would you have
The gall to batten on such misery
When the whole country is watching like a hawk
What goes on here? I wouldn't have the gall.

THE WHOLESALERS:

Here stand we packers with mountains of canned goods
And cellars full of frozen steers
Trying to sell our canned steer meat
And nobody wants it!
And our customers, the restaurants and stores
Filled to the rafters with frozen meat
Are bellowing for purchasers and diners!
We're not buying any more.

THE PACKERS:

Here stand we packers with our slaughterhouses and packing plants
Our barns full of livestock, our machines
Day and night under steam, our pickling vats, our rendering tanks, our cauldrons
All raring to transform our bellowing, fodder-eating herds
Into canned meat, and nobody wants canned meat.
We're ruined.

THE STOCKBREEDERS:

And we the livestock breeders?
Who's buying cattle now? Our barns are full of
Bovines and hogs, devouring expensive corn.
They're headed here in trains and in the trains

They eat, and at the stations, waiting
In rent-devouring pens, they go on eating.

MAULER:
And now the knives reject them. Giving
Your livestock the cold shoulder, death
Has shut up shop.

THE PACKERS (*shouting at Mauler, who is reading the paper*):
Treacherous Mauler, fouling your own nest!
You think we don't know who's been knocking the bottom
Out of the market with secret sales of livestock!
Hell, you've been selling meat for days now!

MAULER:
Insolent butchers, playing the cry-baby
Because poor persecuted animals
Have stopped their bellowing! Run home and tell your mamma
One of your number couldn't bear to hear
The bellowing of cattle any longer and
Preferred your bellowing to theirs!
I want my money and my peace of mind.

A BROKER (*at the entrance of the Livestock Exchange in the rear, shouting*):
Disastrous stock market crash!
Frantic selling. Cridle's formerly Mauler's are
Dragging meat prices and the whole meat ring
Down with them.

Uproar among the Packers. They rush at Cridle, who stands there as white as a sheet.

THE PACKERS:
What is this, Cridle? Look us in the eye.
Have you been dumping shares on a falling market?

THE BROKERS:
At one fifteen!

THE PACKERS:
Where are your brains?
You're not the only one that's being ruined!
Bastard! Murderer!

CRIDLE (*pointing at Mauler*):
Ask him!

GRAHAM (*placing himself in front of Cridle*):
It isn't Cridle. It's somebody else.
Somebody fishing and using us for fish!
Somebody out to get the meat ring, and
Stopping at nothing. Speak up, Mauler. What have
You got to say for yourself?

THE PACKERS (*to Mauler*):
Mauler, the story is you've been demanding
Your money from Cridle, who's on the ropes.
Cridle's not talking, but he points at you.

MAULER: If I were to leave my money for one more hour with this man Cridle, who told me himself that he was on the skids, would a single one of you take me seriously as a business man? And there's nothing I want so much as to be taken seriously by you gentlemen.

CRIDLE (*to those around him*): Just four week ago I made a contract with Mauler. He wanted to sell me his shares, which came to a third of the total capital, for ten million dollars. From that day on, as I've just discovered, he has been secretly undermining an already declining market by selling large amounts of livestock cheap. He was entitled to demand his money whenever he pleased. I was planning to pay him by selling some of the shares, which were priced high at the time, and borrowing on the rest. Then came the slump. Today Mauler's shares are worth not ten but three millions, and the value of the whole plant has fallen from thirty millions to ten millions. The exact same ten millions that I owe Mauler and that he's demanding without delay.

THE PACKERS:
We're not in partnership with Cridle, but
You damn well know that if you drive him to
The wall, we too will suffer. You're wrecking
The whole meat market. It's your fault
Our cans are cheap as dirt, because it was
By selling canned meat cheap you ruined Lennox.

MAULER:
You should have slaughtered less, you meat-crazed butchers!
I want my money. Even if it beggars

The lot of you, I want my money back
For I have other plans.

THE STOCKBREEDERS:
Lennox KO'd and Cridle on the ropes.
And Mauler pulling out his capital!

THE SMALL SPECULATORS:
Ah, no one gives a hoot in hell for us
Small speculators. Those who scream
As the colossus falls don't stop to see
Which way it falls and whom it crushes.
Mauler, our money!

THE PACKERS: Eighty thousand cans at fifty. But hurry!

THE WHOLESALERS: Not one single can!

Silence. The drums of the Black Straw Hats and Joan's voice are heard.

JOAN'S VOICE: Pierpont Mauler! Where is Mauler?

MAULER:
What's that drumming I hear? Who's
Calling my name?
Here where we all
Show our bare fangs, dripping with blood!

The Black Straw Hats enter, singing their battle hymn.

THE BLACK STRAW HATS (*singing*):
Watchful, be watchful.
Look, there's a man going down.
Somebody crying for rescue
Some girl about to drown.
Stop all those motorcars, hold up that tram
So many people are sinking, and nobody gives a damn.
Have you no eyes to see?
Why throw a line to your brother and none to humanity?
Stand up and leave your dinner
The poor are getting thinner
How hungry they must be!
So never say that nobody can change things
That inequality is ours from birth.
For we're telling you it's time for action
To go ahead and sweep it from the earth.
We'll order those tanks to move up here

And warships shall mobilise
And bombers shall blacken the skies
Until they've won a bowl of soup for every poor man.
Right now is the time to go forward
Let everyone answer our call
And instantly do as we've ordered
For the forces of goodness are small.
'Tenshun! Fix bay'nits! Beat the drum!
Courage, all those who were sinking! Look this way! Here we come!

Meanwhile the battle of the Livestock Exchange has been going on. But laughter, provoked by shouted jibes, has spread to front stage.

THE PACKERS: Eighty thousand cans at half price. But hurry!

THE WHOLESALERS: Nary a one!

THE PACKERS: Mauler! That means we're sunk.

JOAN: Where is Mauler?

MAULER:
Don't go away now, Slift, Graham, Meyers.
You stand in front of me. I don't
Want to be seen here.

THE STOCKBREEDERS:
Impossible to sell a single steer in Chicago!
All Illinois is perishing this day.
With rising prices you conned us into raising
Steers. And here we are with steers
And no one buys them.
Mauler, you dog, we're sunk and you're to blame.

MAULER:
No talk of business now. Graham, my hat. I must be going.
A hundred dollars for my hat.

CRIDLE: Damn your hide! (*Cridle goes out.*)

JOAN (*behind Mauler*): You stay right where you are, Mr Mauler, and listen to what I have to say. You can all listen. Quiet! It doesn't suit you, does it, to have us Black Straw Hats turning up here in the dark and hidden places where you carry on your business! I've heard what you do here, making meat more and more expensive with your machinations and oily tricks. If you thought you could keep it secret, you had another think coming, now and on the day of His Judgment, for then it will all be made manifest, and what will you look like when our Lord and Saviour makes you line up in front of Him and glares at you out of His big round eyes and asks: Where are My oxen now? What have you done with them? Did you make them available to the people at reasonable prices, and if not what became of them? And when you stand there wriggling, casting about for excuses like in your newspapers that don't always tell the truth either, the oxen will set up a bellowing behind you in all the barns where you hide them to drive the prices sky-high, and with their bellowing they will bear witness against you before Almighty God!

Laughter.

THE STOCKBREEDERS:

We stockbreeders see nothing to laugh about!
Summer and winter at the mercy of the weather, we are
Much closer to the old-time God.

JOAN: And now for a parable. Suppose a man builds a dam against the capricious waters and a thousand people help him with the toil of their hands and he gets paid a million for it, but the dam collapses the moment the water rises, and all the people who'd been building it and a lot more drown – what is the man who builds such a dam? You can call him a business man if you like, or a scoundrel if you prefer, but we say unto you, he's a fool. And you, the whole lot of you, who raise the price of bread and make life such a hell for people that they all turn into devils, you're stupid; you're low-down contemptible fools, and nothing else!

THE WHOLESALERS (*shouting*):

With your unscrupulous profiteering
Driving prices out of sight
You're ruining yourselves
You blockheads!

THE PACKERS (*shouting back*):

Blockheads yourselves!

No one's to blame for crises!
Over us, changeless and inscrutable, rule
The laws of economics.
And natural catastrophes recur
In dreadful cycles.

THE STOCKBREEDERS:
Is no one to blame that you've got us by the throat?
It's wickedness, unadulterated wickedness!

JOAN: And why is there wickedness in the world? What would you expect? If a man has to hit his neighbour over the head with an axe for a slice of ham to put on his bread, for everything he needs to keep body and soul together, if brother has to fight brother over the barest necessities, does it surprise you that all feeling for higher things is stifled in the human breast? Just for a change, why not think of helping your neighbour as waiting on a customer? Then you'll understand the New Testament in a twinkling and how modern it still is. Service! What does service mean but loving thy neighbour? When you come right down to it. Gentlemen, I keep hearing that the poor are short on morals, and it's true. Because the slums breed immorality, and immorality breeds revolution. But now let me ask you just this: Where are these people's morals to come from when they have nothing else? Where are they going to get morals without stealing them? Gentlemen, there's such a thing as moral purchasing power. If you increase people's moral purchasing power, you'll get morality. And by purchasing power I mean something very simple and natural, I mean money, wages. Which brings me to a very practical point: if you meat producers go on like this, you'll end up having to eat your own meat, because the people out there have no purchasing power.

THE STOCKBREEDERS (*reproachfully*):
Here we stand with our steers
And nobody buys them.

JOAN: And here you sit, you high and mighty gentlemen, imagining that no one will ever see through your tricks and closing your eyes to the misery all around you. All right, now you can take a look at the people you've been abusing and trampling, the people you refuse to recognize as your brothers. Come on out, ye who labour and are heavy laden. Show yourselves. Don't be ashamed.

Joan shows the gentlemen of the Livestock Exchange the poor whom she has brought with her.

MAULER (*screaming*): Take them away! (*He faints.*)

VOICE (*in the rear*): Pierpont Mauler has fainted.

THE POOR: That's him. He's the guilty party.

The Meat Packers come to Mauler's assistance.)

THE PACKERS: Water for Pierpont Mauler! A doctor for Mauler!

JOAN:

You've shown me, Mauler, the
Baseness of the poor. Now I will show you
The poverty of the poor, for, kept at a distance
From you, and hence from life's necessities
Live the invisible people, whom you
Maintain in such poverty, so weakened and so desperately
Dependent on unattainable food and warmth that they
Can also be kept at a distance from all aspiration
To anything higher than base craving for food and bestial habits.

Mauler revives.

MAULER: Are they still here? Please, please, take them away.

THE MEAT PACKERS: The Black Straw Hats? Take them away?

MAULER: No. Those people behind them.

SLIFT: He won't open his eyes until they're gone.

GRAHAM:

Can't bear to see them, can you? But it's you
Who got them into this condition.
Closing your eyes won't make them go away.
Far from it.

MAULER:

Please, please, get rid of them. I'll buy!
Listen, everybody. Pierpont Mauler is buying!
To give these people work and make them go away.
All the canned meat you turn out in eight weeks
I'll buy it.

THE MEAT PACKERS:

He's bought it! Mauler has bought canned meat!

MAULER: At the current price.

GRAHAM (*stops him*): And what they've got in storage?

MAULER (*lying on the floor*): I'll buy it.

GRAHAM: At fifty?

MAULER: At fifty!

GRAHAM: He's bought it. Did you hear? He's bought it.

BROKERS (*in the rear, shouting through megaphones*): Pierpont Mauler is propping up the meat market. He has contracted to buy up the meat ring's entire stocks at the current price of fifty. In addition, he's buying two months' output beginning today, also at fifty. The meat ring will deliver a minimum of forty thousand tons of canned meat to Pierpont Mauler on November fifteenth.

MAULER: But now, my friends, I beg you, carry me away.

Mauler is carried away.

JOAN:

Sure, let them carry you away.
While we toil like farm horses at our mission work
Look at what you people do up here!
You sent word that I wasn't to speak
But who are you, trying to muzzle the Lord?
When nobody even has a right to muzzle the ox when he treadeth out the corn.
I will speak.
(*To the poor*:)
There'll be work for you on Monday.

THE POOR: We've never seen anybody like that. The two who were with him are more familiar. They look a lot worse than he does.

JOAN: Now before we go, open your hymn books at: 'Never will you want for bread.'

THE BLACK STRAW HATS (*singing*):

Never will you want for bread
If your trust is in your Maker.
In His bosom rest your head
Harm will spare your house and acre.
How should snow and how should sleet

Fall where He has set His feet?

THE WHOLESALERS:

The man is crazy in the head. This country's stomach
Is glutted with canned meat. It's in revolt.
And now he's making them can meat that
No one will buy. His name is anathema.

THE STOCKBREEDERS:

All right, you lousy butchers, raise the prices!
Until you double the price of livestock, you
Won't get a single ounce out of us. Now that you need it.

THE MEAT PACKERS:

Keep your old carcasses. We won't buy them.
The contract you've just witnessed is only
A scrap of paper. The man who dreamed it up
Was not in his right mind. For such a scheme
He won't succeed in raising one red cent
Between New York and Frisco.

The Meat Packers leave.

JOAN: If any of you are interested in God's word, if you care about what He says and not just what the financial pages say, and even here there must be a few decent people who do business with the fear of God in their hearts, which is perfectly all right with us, you'll be welcome at our Sunday services on Lincoln Street at 2 p.m., music from three o'clock on. Admission free.

SLIFT (*to the Stockbreeders*):

When Pierpont Mauler makes a promise, he keeps it.
Breathe easy, friends. The market's going to hum.
Employer and prospective employee
Atrophy at last is overcome.
Restored are confidence and harmony.
Ye hungry workers, eager to begin
Come to the gate, the boss will let you in!
Wise counsel, wisely given and wisely taken
Has bested those whom reason had forsaken!
The chimneys smoke. A happy sight indeed
For work, my friends, is what both parties need!

THE STOCKBREEDERS (*cornering Joan on the stairs*):

The things you've said and your way of saying them

Have made a big impression on us cattle breeders
And shaken some of us to the foundations
Because we too are having an awful time.

JOAN:

Listen to me, I've got my eye on Mauler
He's woken up. If you're in urgent need
Just come with me, he'll lend a helping hand.
As of today the man will know no peace.
Till everyone has been helped.
For help he can, so let's
Get after him.

Joan and the Black Straw Hats go out, followed by the Stockbreeders.

6

CATCHING THE CRICKET

Financial District. Home of the broker Sullivan Slift, a small house with two entrances.

MAULER (*inside the house, talking to Slift*): Lock the door, put on all the light you can, and now, Slift, take a good look at my face and tell me if it's true: would everyone know?

SLIFT: Know what?

MAULER: Well, what I am.

SLIFT: A butcher? Mauler, why did that speech of hers make you faint?

MAULER:

What did she say? I didn't
Hear her, because behind her
Stood people with such ghastly faces
Of misery – the misery which goes before
The anger that will sweep us all away –
That I saw nothing else. Now, Slift
I'm going to tell you what I really think
About our business.
It can't go on, this naked
Buying and selling, with one man coldly
Tearing the next man's skin off. Too many people
Are howling with pain, and there will be more.
That crowd besieging our bloody cellars
Can't be put off any longer. When they
Lay hands on us, they will
Dash us to the ground like rotten fish.
Not one of us will die in bed. Long
Before that they'll come in packs and
Stand us up against the wall and cleanse the world of us and
Our stooges.

SLIFT: They've rattled you! (*Aside*:) I'll get him to eat a rare steak. His old weakness has struck again. Maybe the taste of raw meat will bring him to his senses. (*He goes and fries a steak on a gas burner.*)

MAULER:

I often wonder why
That stupid unworldly talk so moves me
That cheap insipid babble they learn by heart.
I guess it's because they do it for nothing, eighteen hours a day
Through rain and hunger.

SLIFT:

In cities like this that are burning underneath
And freezing at the top, you'll always find
A few to carp at one thing or another
That's not exactly as it should be.

MAULER:

But what is it they say? When in these burning
Cities, amid the headlong streams of people
Bellowing as they tumble down to hell
I hear a voice like that, absurd I know
But utterly free from bestiality
I feel as if I'd been clouted on the backbone
With a stick, like a leaping trout.
But even that, Slift, so far, has been only
A subterfuge, for what I really fear
Is something else than God.

SLIFT: What then?

MAULER:

Not what's above but what's below me!
Those people in the stockyards, too weak
To last the night, but who will rise
Up in the morning, I know it.

SLIFT: Wouldn't you care to eat a piece of meat, dear Pierpont? Look, you can do it with a clear conscience now. As of today you have severed your connection with the murder of cattle.

MAULER:

You think I ought to? Maybe I could.
It must be all right now. Don't you think so?

SLIFT: Get some food under your ribs and think about your

situation, which isn't too hot. Do you even realize that you've just bought up all the canned meat in existence? I see, Mauler, that you're busy admiring your beautiful soul. Allow me to give you a simple, straightforward picture of the purely material situation, unimportant as it may be. For one thing you've bought fifteen thousand tons of the meat ring's stock. You'll have to unload them in the next few weeks on a market that can't absorb a single can. You paid fifty, and the price is sure to drop to thirty or less. Secondly, on November 15th, when the price is thirty or twenty-five, the meat ring will deliver forty thousand tons to you at fifty.

MAULER:

I'm ruined, Slift.
I'm through. Christ, I've bought meat!
O Slift, what have I done!
I've loaded all the meat in the world on my back
Like an Atlas I'm staggering
With tons of canned goods on my shoulders
Straight to the poorhouse. Only this morning
Some brokers were failing, and I
Went down to see them fail and scoff at them
And shout: How can anyone be such
A fool as to buy canned meat?
And while I'm standing there, I hear my own voice saying:
I'll buy it all.
Slift, I've bought meat. I'm ruined.

SLIFT: What have your friends in New York been writing?

MAULER: That I should buy meat.

SLIFT: Do what?

MAULER: Buy meat.

SLIFT: And you have bought meat. So what are you complaining about?

MAULER: Buy meat, they tell me.

SLIFT: But you have bought meat.

MAULER:

Yes, yes, I did buy meat, but I didn't
Buy it because of that letter and its advice
(Which is all wrong anyway, pure theory). I didn't

Buy it for sordid reasons, but because
That woman moved me so deeply I can swear
I hardly glanced at the letter, it only came this morning.
Here it is. 'Dear Pierpont . . .'

SLIFT (*continues to read*): 'We can now inform you that our money is beginning to bear fruit. A good many Congressmen are going to vote against the tariffs. It therefore seems advisable to buy meat, dear Pierpont. We shall write you again tomorrow.'

MAULER:
Such gross abuse of money is something else
That shouldn't be. How easily
Such crimes can lead to war
And thousands die for filthy lucre. Oh, dear Slift
I fear no good can come of news like this.

SLIFT:
It all depends. The question is: who wrote the letter?
Bribery, starting wars, repealing tariffs
Are not for every Tom or Harry. Are they good men?

MAULER: They're solvent men.

SLIFT: Who could that be, I wonder.
(*Mauler smiles.*)
The price then might pick up after all.
We'd get off with a broken nose or two.
I'd see some hope were it not for all that meat
In the farmers' hands, which, all too frantically
Thrown on the market, would make the prices
Come crashing down again. No, Mauler, I fail
To understand that letter.

MAULER:
Look at it this way. Somebody has stolen something.
Somebody catches him. The thief is lost
Unless he strikes the other dead. But if
He does, he'll go scot free. The letter (which
Is wrong) calls (to make it right)
For such a crime.

SLIFT: What kind of crime?

MAULER:
One that I can't commit. Because, from now on

I want to live in peace. So let them gain by
Their crime, and gain they will. They only need
To buy up meat wherever they find it
Convince the breeders that there's too much meat
Point out in passing how Lennox was laid low and
Buy up their meat. That's the main thing
Buy up their meat. But that of course is cheating
Them once again. No, Slift, I wouldn't touch it.

SLIFT:

Pierpont, you shouldn't have bought meat.

MAULER:

It was a big mistake.
But now you won't catch me buying a hat or a pair
Of shoes until I'm out of this. I'll be lucky
If I come off with a hundred dollars to my name.

Drums. Joan comes in with the stockbreeders and a few workers.

JOAN: We'll lure him out of his hole the way we'd catch a cricket. You stand over there, because if he hears me singing he'll try to avoid me by slipping out the other way. Because he doesn't want to see me. (*She laughs.*) Or the people with me for that matter.

The stockbreeders station themselves outside the right-hand door.

JOAN (*outside the lefthand door*): Come on out, Mr Mauler. I have a bone to pick with you about the plight of the stockbreeders of Illinois. I've got some workers here too, who want to ask you when you're reopening your packing plant.

MAULER: Slift, where's the other exit? I don't want to see her and certainly not the people with her. And I'm not opening any packing plant now.

SLIFT: Come this way.

They go inside to the righthand door.

THE STOCKBREEDERS (*outside the righthand door*): Come on out, Mauler. You're to blame for our troubles. There are more than ten thousand of us stockbreeders in Illinois and we're at the end of our rope. So buy our livestock.

MAULER:

Shut the door, Slift. I will not buy.
Am I, who bear the meat of the whole world
Upon my shoulders in so far as it's canned
To purchase all the livestock on Sirius as well?
It's as if someone came to Atlas, barely
Able to stagger beneath the weight of the world
And told him Saturn needed a carrier too.
Who's going to take this cattle off my hands?

SLIFT: Possibly the Grahams. They need livestock.

JOAN (*outside the lefthand door*): We're not leaving here until something is done to help the stockbreeders.

MAULER: Possibly the Grahams. Yes, they need livestock. Slift, go out and tell them to give me two minutes' time. I have to think.

Slift goes out.

SLIFT (*to the stockbreeders*): Pierpont Mauler is considering your proposition. He requests two minutes' time.

Slift goes back into the building.

MAULER: I won't buy. (*He starts reckoning.*) Slift, I'm buying. Slift, bring me everything that looks like a hog or a bovine, I'll buy it, or anything that smells of lard, I'll buy it, bring me every grease spot, I'm your buyer at the current price, which is fifty.

SLIFT:

You wouldn't buy a hat, oh no, but every head of cattle in Illinois you'll buy.

MAULER:

Yes, so I will. My mind's made up now, Slift.
Let me explain.
(*He draws an A on the door of a cabinet.*)
Somebody makes a mistake. Let's call it A.
It's a mistake because his feelings got
The better of him. Then he makes
Another move. We'll call it B. B too
Is wrong. But taken together A and B –
Two wrongs – will make a right.
Let the stockbreeders in, they are good men
Down on their luck but neatly dressed

The sight of them won't scare me.

SLIFT (*steps out. To the stockbreeders*): To save the state of Illinois and avert the ruin of its farmers and stockbreeders, Pierpont Mauler has decided to buy up all the livestock on the market. But the contracts will not be in his name; his name must not be mentioned.

THE STOCKBREEDERS: Hurrah for Pierpont Mauler, who has saved the livestock industry! (*They go into the house.*)

JOAN (*calls after them*): Tell Mr Pierpont Mauler that we Black Straw Hats thank him in the name of God. (*To the Workers.*) If the buyers and the sellers of cattle both get what they want, there'll be bread again for you too.

7

THE MONEY CHANGERS ARE DRIVEN OUT OF THE TEMPLE

The Black Straw Hat mission house.

The Black Straw Hats are sitting at a long table, emptying their tin boxes and counting the coins they have collected for the poor.

THE BLACK STRAW HATS (*singing*):

Singing we gather pence for the poor
They've got neither bed nor board
But the Almighty Lord
With his Eternal Word
Will somehow keep the wolf from their door.

PAUL SNYDER, MAJOR OF THE BLACK STRAW HATS (*stands up*): Very little! Very little! (*To some poor people in the background, among them Mrs Luckerniddle and Gloomb*:) You here again? Are you going to spend your life here? Didn't you know there was work at the stockyards?

MRS LUCKERNIDDLE: What work? The stockyards are closed.

GLOOMB: They were supposed to open, but they haven't opened.

SNYDER: Don't get too near my cash box.

He motions them to move further back. Mulberry, the landlord, comes in.

MULBERRY: Well, what about my rent?

SNYDER: Dearly beloved Black Straw Hats, friend Mulberry, ladies and gentlemen; with regard to the troublesome problem of fund raising – a good cause speaks for itself and what it needs more than anything else is propaganda – we have always addressed our appeals to the poor, because we believed that those most in need of God's help would be most likely to have something to spare for God, and that many a nickel makes a mickle. But to our sorrow we find that for some unfathomable reason the poorer classes are most ungenerous toward God. Maybe it's because they have nothing. For this reason I, Paul Snyder, in your name, have invited the wealthy citizens of Chicago to come here and make arrangements to join us next Saturday in a major campaign against godlessness and materialism in Chicago, especially among the lower classes. Out of this money we will pay our dear landlord, Mr Mulberry, the rent about which he has shown such infinite patience.

MULBERRY: I could use it all right, but don't let it worry you. (*Mulberry goes out.*)

SNYDER: Well, that's that, and now all of you, go cheerfully about your work, but first scrub down the front steps.

The Black Straw Hats go out.

SNYDER (*to the poor*): Tell me, are the locked-out workers still standing patiently in the stockyards, or are they starting to talk like subversives?

MRS LUCKERNIDDLE: They've been making a big noise since yesterday, because they know the plants have orders to fill.

GLOOMB: Some are saying the only way to get jobs is to take them by force.

SNYDER (*aside*): That's good. The meat kings will be more likely to come here and listen when the brickbats start flying. (*To the poor*:) Couldn't you chop our wood for us at least?

THE POOR: There isn't any more wood, major.

Enter the packers Cridle, Graham and Meyers, and the broker Slift.

MEYERS: I've been wondering, Graham: where's all the livestock?

GRAHAM: I've been wondering, too: where is the livestock?

SLIFT: So have I.

GRAHAM: Really? You have? And Mauler too, I suppose?

SLIFT: Yes, Mauler too, I should think.

MEYERS:

Some bastard has been buying it all up.
A bastard who's well aware that we've contracted
To deliver meat in cans and therefore need
Livestock.

SLIFT: Who could it be?

GRAHAM (*punches him in the pit of the stomach*):
You rotten stinker!

Who do you think you're kidding!
Tell Pierpy to lay off, he's touching
A vital nerve!

SLIFT (*to Snyder*): What do you want of us?

GRAHAM (*punches him again*): What do you suppose they want, Slift?

With an air of exaggerated slyness Slift makes the gesture of handing out money.

GRAHAM: You guessed it, Slift.

MEYERS (*to Snyder*): Fire away!

They sit down in the pews.

SNYDER (*in the pulpit*): We Black Straw Hats have heard that there are fifty thousand people standing around in the stockyards without work. We've also heard that some of them have started to grumble and say: we'll have to help ourselves. And your names are being mentioned as the ones to blame that fifty thousand people have no work and are standing around outside the plants. One of these days they'll take the factories away from you. They'll say: why not do like the Bolsheviks and take the factories into our own hands so everybody can work and eat? Because word has been going around that calamity doesn't come of its own accord like rain, but is brought about by certain people who stand to gain by it. But we Black Straw Hats will tell them that calamity does come like rain, from no one knows where, that suffering is their earthly lot and their compensation awaits them later on.

THE THREE PACKERS: Compensation? Why bring that up?

SNYDER: The compensation we have in mind is paid after death.

THE THREE PACKERS: How much are you asking for this service?

SNYDER: Eight hundred dollars a month, because we need hot soup and loud music. We'll also promise them that the rich will be punished, after death of course.

The three laugh uproariously.

SNYDER: And all that for only eight hundred dollars a month!

GRAHAM: You don't need anything like that much. Five hundred!

SNYDER: Well, we could do it for seven fifty, but then . . .

MEYERS: Seven fifty. That's more like it. All right, let's say five hundred.

GRAHAM: You definitely need five hundred. (*To the others*:) They've got to have it.

MEYERS (*front stage*): Admit it, Slift. You fellows have the livestock.

SLIFT: As true as I'm sitting here, Mauler and I haven't bought one cent's worth of livestock. God is my witness.

MEYERS (*to Snyder*): Five hundred dollars? That's a lot of money. How do you expect to raise it?

SLIFT: Well, all you have to do now is find somebody to give it to you.

SNYDER: I suppose so.

MEYERS: It won't be easy.

GRAHAM: Admit that Pierpy has the livestock.

SLIFT (*laughing*): They're all scoundrels, Mr Snyder.

All laugh except Snyder.

GRAHAM (*to Meyers*): The man has no sense of humour. I don't like him.

SLIFT: The main question, major, is where you stand. On this side of the barricades or the other?

SNYDER: The Black Straw Hats are above the battle, Mr Slift. So it's on this side.

Joan enters.

SLIFT: Here comes our St Joan of the Livestock Exchange.

THE THREE PACKERS (*bellowing at Joan*): We're not pleased with you! Look here. Can you give Mauler a message from us? We hear you've got influence with him. They say he eats out of your hand. All the livestock has disappeared off the market, so we can't help thinking of Mauler. They say you can get him to do anything you want. Get him to let go of the livestock. If you do that for us, we'll pay the Black Straw Hats' rent for four years.

JOAN (*has seen the poor people and is horrified*): What are you doing here?

MRS LUCKERNIDDLE (*steps forward*):
The twenty meals have been eaten.
Don't let it rile you, seeing me here again.

I'd gladly spare you the sight of me.
The cruel thing about hunger is that
However often you satisfy it, it always comes back again.

GLOOMB (*steps forward*):
I know you. I tried to persuade you
To work on the very same knife
That cut my arm off. Today I'd do something even worse.

JOAN: Why aren't you working? Now that I've made jobs for you.

MRS LUCKERNIDDLE: Where? The stockyards are closed.

GLOOMB: They were supposed to open, but they didn't.

JOAN (*to the packers*): So they're still waiting?
(*The packers are silent.*)
And I thought they'd been taken care of.
For seven days now the snow has been falling on them
And the selfsame snow that is killing them hides
Them from every human eye. For shame, that I forgot
So easily what everyone likes to forget, for the sake of his peace of mind!
If someone says, The trouble is over, no one looks into it.
(*To the packers*:)
But Mauler bought meat from you, didn't he? He did it because I pleaded with him. Can it be true that you still haven't opened your plants?

THE THREE PACKERS: It's true all right. We wanted to open.

SLIFT: But you wanted to cut the farmers' throats first!

THE THREE PACKERS: How can we slaughter when there's no livestock?

SLIFT: Mauler and I bought meat from you on the assumption that you'd open the plants so the workers could buy meat again. Who's going to eat the meat we took off your hands now? Who did we buy the meat for if the customer can't pay?

JOAN: It's bad enough that you should own the tools of the workers you employ in those great big factories of yours. But if that's the way it is, the least you could do is let them get at their tools, because if you don't they're sunk. The whole thing looks like exploitation to me, and it those poor tortured, agonizing devils, who are our fellow men, are driven to the point where they pick up clubs and start clouting their tormentors on the head, you shit in your pants, I've seen it before, and then all of a sudden religion looks good to you, you expect it to pour oil on the waters. But the Lord thinks a little too much of Himself to clean out your pigsty for you. I go running from pillar to post, I tell myself that if I help the people on top it will help the people under you too. Your interests are pretty much the same, I say to myself, so why wouldn't you all pull together? Man, was I stupid! It looks as if the only way to help the poor is to side with them against you. Have you lost all respect for the human countenance? If that's how it is, a time may come when you won't be looked upon as human any longer, but as wild beasts, and it will become necessary to destroy you in the interest of law and public safety. And you think you have a right to set foot in the house of God just because of your filthy Mammon, but we know where and how you got it, we know you haven't come by it honestly. This time, so help me, you've made a big mistake, and you're going to be driven out, driven out with a club. And take that dumb look off your faces, I know it's wrong to treat human beings like cattle, but you aren't human beings, so get out of here and make it quick or I'll clout you, don't try to hold me, I know what I'm doing, I was ignorant too long. (*Joan drives them out with a reversed flag, which she brandishes like a club. The Black Straw Hats appear in the doorways.*) Out! Do you think you can turn the house of God into a barn? Or another Livestock Exchange? Out! You have no business here. We don't need faces like yours. You're unworthy and I'm turning you out. Money or no money!

THE THREE PACKERS: As you wish. But with us, humbly, modestly and never to return, goes forty months' rent. We need every penny anyway, because we're heading for the worst times the market has ever known.

The Packers and Slift go out.

SNYDER (*running after them*): Wait, gentlemen, don't go, she had no authority! A muddle-headed woman! She'll be dismissed! She'll do anything you wish.

JOAN (*to the Black Straw Hats*): I admit that was stupid, on account of the rent. But we can't let that worry us. (*To Mrs Luckerniddle and Gloomb*:) Sit back there. I'll bring you some soup.

SNYDER (*coming back*):
Ask the poor to your table and treat them
To rain water and high-flown words
When even in heaven there's no compassion for them
But only snow!
Without the least humility you
Gave in to your first impulse! How easy it is
To turn up your nose and drive out the unclean.
Fastidious about the bread we must eat
Too curious about how it's made, you nevertheless
Want to eat! And now, angelic spirit, out
Into the rain with you! Out into the snowstorm with your self-righteousness!

JOAN: You mean I should take off my uniform?

SNYDER: Take off your uniform and pack your bag! Leave this house and take the riff-raff you've brought here with you. It's only scum and riff-raff that go chasing after you. And soon you'll be one of them. Go get your things.

Joan goes out and comes back with a small suitcase, dressed like a servant girl from the country.

JOAN:
I'll go and see Mauler, who's rich and not entirely
Devoid of fear and goodwill
And get him to help us. I won't
Put on this uniform and black straw hat again
Or return to this beloved house
Of hymns and awakenings until I
Can bring the rich Mauler, become
One of us, converted through and through.
I know their money, like a cancerous growth
Has eaten away their ears and human face
So that they sit apart but highly placed
Where no cry of help can reach them!
Poor mutilated creatures! But
There must be *one* righteous man among them!

(*Goes out.*)

SNYDER:

Poor ignorant thing!
What you don't see is that, ranged
In huge batallions, employers and employed
Confront each other irreconcilably.
Go on, run back and forth between them, trying
To reconcile, to arbitrate! And then, useless to either side
Go to the dogs!

MULBERRY (*comes in*): Have you got the money now?

SNYDER: God will find a way of paying for the meagre – meagre, I say it again, Mr Mulberry – lodgings He has found on earth.

MULBERRY: That's the ticket, Snyder, pay. You took the words out of my mouth. If the Lord pays up, good. If He doesn't pay up, no good. If the Lord can't pay His rent, He'll have to move out, on Saturday night to be exact. Got it, Snyder? (*Goes out.*)

8

MAULER'S SPEECH ON THE INDISPENSABILITY OF CAPITALISM AND RELIGION

Mauler's Office.

MAULER:

This is the day, Slift, when friend Graham
And all those with him who had thought they'd wait
For bottom livestock prices will be forced
To buy the meat they owe us.

SLIFT:

They'll pay a good price now, for every head
Of livestock bellowing in Chicago's pens
Is our livestock.
And every hog they owe us must be bought
From us, which makes it more expensive.

MAULER:

And now, good Slift, unleash your middlemen
And let them flay the market with their calls
For everything resembling hog or steer.
That will drive up the prices.

SLIFT:

What news of your Joan? It's rumoured on the
Livestock Exchange that you have bedded with her.
I told them there was nothing in it. We
Haven't seen hide nor hair of her since she
Threw us all out of the temple. It's as though
Black, bellowing Chicago had swallowed her up.

MAULER:

That tickled me, the way she chucked you out
Just like that. That girl's afraid of nothing.
If I had been there, she'd have driven me
Out too. I like that. And I like that house
Because it has no room for men like me.
Look, Slift. Drive the price up to eighty.
That will make Graham and company look like the mud

We tread on for the pleasure of seeing our footprints.
I won't let a single scrap of meat escape me.
I'll skin those characters alive
For that's my nature.

SLIFT:

I'm glad to see you recovered, Mauler, from
Your recent weakness. So now I'll run along
And watch them buying livestock.
Slift goes out.

MAULER:

It's time that someone took the skin off
This God-damned town and taught those bastards something
About the meat business. Let them yell 'bloody murder!'
Joan comes in with a suitcase.

JOAN: Hi, Mr Mauler. It's not easy to get hold of you. I'll leave my stuff over there for now. You see, I'm not with the Black Straw Hats any more. We had a disagreement. So I said to myself: why not go and see how Mr Mauler is getting along? Without that mission work to run me ragged, I'll have more time for individuals. So now I'll give you a bit of attention, I mean, if you don't mind. You see, I've noticed that you're more approachable than some people I can think of. That's a nice old horsehair couch you've got there, but why is there a sheet on it? And besides, it's all crumpled. My goodness, do you sleep in your office? I thought you must have one of those big mansions. (*Mauler says nothing.*) But you're right, Mr Mauler, to economize in little things, seeing you're a meat king. Isn't it funny? Every time I see you I think of the story about the Lord dropping in on Adam in the garden of Eden and calling out: 'Adam, where are you?' Do you remember? (*She laughs.*) Adam's in the bushes again, and both his arms are in a stag again, clear up to the elbows, so he's dripping with blood when he hears God's voice. What does he do? He pretends he's not there. But God sticks to His guns and calls out again: 'Hey, Adam, where are you?' So Adam blushes to the roots of his hair and says in a wee small voice: 'Why did You have to turn up at this particular moment, right after I'd killed a stag? Don't say anything, I know, I know I shouldn't have done it.' But I trust your conscience is clear, Mr Mauler.

MAULER: So you're not with the Black Straw Hats any more?

JOAN: No, Mr Mauler. And I don't belong there any more, either.

MAULER: Then what have you been living on?

Joan is silent.

MAULER: I see. On air. How long is it since you left the Black Straw Hats?

JOAN: A week.

MAULER (*weeping backstage*):

So changed, and in only a week!
Where has she been? With whom has she spoken? What has
Given her those lines around the mouth?
The city
She comes from is still unknown to me.
(*He brings her food on a tray.*)
You look so changed. Here's food.
I won't be wanting it.

JOAN: You see, Mr Mauler, after we drove those rich men out of our house . . .

MAULER: . . . which really tickled me and struck me as a good thing to do . . .

JOAN: . . . the landlord, who lives off the rent, gave us notice for next Saturday.

MAULER: I see, and the Black Straw Hats' finances are in bad shape at the moment?

JOAN: That's right, and that's why I thought I'd come and see Mr Mauler.

She starts eating hungrily.

MAULER: Don't worry. I'll go to the market and get you the money you need. Yes, indeed I will, I'll raise it at all costs, even if I have to cut it right out of this city's skin. For you I'll do it. Naturally money is hard to come by, but I'll get it. You'll be pleased with me.

JOAN: Yes, Mr Mauler.

MAULER: So go and tell them the money is on its way, they'll have it by Saturday. Mauler will raise it. He's just gone to the livestock market to raise it. The business with the fifty thousand workers didn't turn out very well, not quite as I'd have liked. I couldn't get jobs for them right away. But with you it will be different. Your Black Straw Hats shall be spared. I'll get you the money. Run and tell them.

JOAN: Yes, Mr Mauler.

MAULER:

There, I've written a note. Take it.
I too am sorry people have to wait for work
In the stockyards, and rotten work at that.
Fifty thousand, standing
Around in the stockyards, staying there day and night!
(*Joan stops eating.*)
But in this business it's a question of
To be or not to be, of whether I'm to be
Top man, or walk the dismal road to the stockyards myself.
Besides, riff-raff is pouring back into the yards
Kicking up trouble.
And now, I tell you frankly, I'd have liked
To hear you say that what I'm doing is right
And that my occupation is natural. Please
Back me up on this: wasn't I taking your
Advice when I ordered meat from the meat ring
And from the breeders as well, thereby doing good?
And well aware that you Black Straw Hats are poor
And that they're threatening to take the roof from over your heads
I also intend to give you a little something for that
As proof of my good will.

JOAN: So the workers are still waiting outside the packing plants?

MAULER:

What have you got against money?
When having none works such a change in you!
What *do* you think of money? Tell me
I want to know. But don't go thinking like an idiot
That money is something smelly. Consider the fact
Bitter perhaps – but that's the way with facts – that

Human affairs are uncertain and
Man the plaything of chance, one might almost say of the weather
While money is a means of making some things
A little better, if only for the few.
Consider the beauty of the edifice!
Under construction since Man's dim beginning
Repeatedly rebuilt after repeated collapses
And yet, in spite of the sacrifices exacted, enormous.
Most arduous to erect, built unremittingly
With unremitting groans, and yet at every turn
Squeezing the possible, now more now less
Out of a hostile planet, and therefore
At all times justified by men of worth.
Now think it over: even if I, who
Have grave misgivings about it and have trouble sleeping
Wanted to abstain from dealing in money, it would be the same
As if a gnat should abstain from holding back a landslide.
In that same moment, I'd be reduced to nothing
And the falling rock would pass right over me.
Were it not so, the whole shebang would have to be destroyed
And rebuilt according to a different plan
Based on a radical new concept of man
Which you reject and we reject because
Such building would be done without us and without God, who
Would be abolished as useless. Therefore you people
Must play the game and, even if you make no sacrifices, which
We don't expect of you, at least put your stamp of approval
On those required of others.
In short: you must
Rebuild God
The only salvation, and
Beat the drum for Him, to get Him a
Foothold in the slums
And make His voice resound in the stockyards.

That would be enough.
(*He holds out the paper to her.*)
Take what you get, but realize what you're getting it for, and
Then take it! Here's my I.O.U. It's good for four years' rent.

JOAN:
Mr Mauler, I don't understand what you've been saying
And I don't wish to understand.
(*She stands up.*)
I know I should be pleased to hear
That God is to be helped. But I
Am one of those this doesn't help. And who
Are being offered nothing.

MAULER:
But if you bring the Black Straw Hats the money
They'll let you stay with them. This unsettled
Life is no good for you. Believe me
They're out for money, which is all to the good.

JOAN:
If the Black Straw Hats
Accept your money, let them.
But I will sit down with the people in the stockyards
Waiting for the plants to open. I will eat
Nothing but what they eat, and if
Snow is what's handed out to them, then snow
And whatever work they do I'll do it too
For I too have no money and no other way of getting any
Not honestly at least. And if there is no work
Let there be none for me, and
You, who live on other people's poverty and
Can't bear to see the poor, who condemn
People you don't know, and arrange matters so
As not to see those people who stand
Condemned, abandoned and unseen in the stockyards:
If you want to see me again, it
Will have to be in the stockyards.
(*She goes out.*)

MAULER:

Ah, Mauler, you will rise
Every hour of the night and
Look out the window to see if it's snowing, for if it is
The snow will be falling on someone you know.

9

JOAN'S THIRD DESCENT INTO THE DEPTHS: THE SNOWFALL

a

Stockyard district.

Joan, Gloomb and Mrs Luckerniddle.

JOAN:

Let me tell you what I dreamed
One night last week:
In a small field
Too small for the shadow of a medium-sized tree
Because enormous buildings hemmed it in, I saw a
Crowd of people – I couldn't say how many, but surely
Many more than the number of sparrows that would fit in
So small a space – so dense a crowd
That the field buckled and rose in the middle. And now the
Crowd hung over the edge, clung fast
For a moment, pulsing, and then
Under the impact of a word, shouted somewhere
Signifying nothing in particular, began to flow.
Then I saw marching columns, streets, some known to me,
  Chicago! You!
I saw you marching, and then I saw myself
Saw myself striding silently at your head
With warlike steps and bleeding forehead, shouting
Martial-sounding words in a language unknown
Even to myself. And since many columns were
Marching on all sides, I marched in many
Forms at the head of many columns. Young or old
Sobbing or cursing, escaped at last from my skin!
Virtue and terror! Transforming everything
My foot touched, wreaking immoderate destruction
Perceptibly influencing the course of the stairs
But also changing neighbourhood streets

Known to us all, beyond recognition.
And so the column marched and I marched with it
Shielded by snow from enemy attack
Rendered diaphanous by hunger, presenting no target
Residing nowhere, hence impossible to lay hands on
Accustomed to every torment, hence
Impervious to torment.
And so the column marches, abandoning
Positions that cannot be held
For others will take their place.
That's what I dreamt.
And now I see the meaning.
This very night we shall
Leave these stockyards and reach
Their city of Chicago in the dawn.
We will display our misery on the streets and squares
And appeal to everyone who looks as if he might be human.
After that I do not know.

GLOOMB: Do you see what she's driving at, Mrs Luckerniddle? I don't.

MRS LUCKERNIDDLE: If she hadn't shot her mouth off at the Black Straw Hats, we'd have been sitting in a nice warm place, spooning up our soup.

b

Livestock Exchange.

MAULER (*to the packers*):
My New York friends have written me
That the tariff law in the south
Has just been repealed.

THE PACKERS:
Heavens! The tariff repealed, and we
Haven't so much as a shred of meat to our name! All of it sold at
Rockbottom prices. Must we now buy when they're rising?

THE STOCKBREEDERS:
Heavens! The tariff repealed, and we haven't
Got any livestock to sell! All of it sold at

Rockbottom prices!

THE SMALL SPECULATORS:

Heavens! Forever opaque
Stand the eternal laws of
Human econony!
Oh, without warning, giving no notice
Volcanoes erupt, laying waste the whole region!
Most unexpectedly our
Island of profit is blown out of the tempestuous sea!
Nobody notified! No one informed! But the hindmost
Gets his arse bitten.

MAULER:

Since a demand has now arisen for
Livestock in cans at reasonable prices, I
Demand immediate delivery of the
Canned meat our contract calls for.

GRAHAM:

At the old price?

MAULER:

As per agreement, Graham
Forty thousand tons, unless my memory
Deceives me about a moment when I was not in my right mind.

THE PACKERS:

How can we be expected to buy livestock with the prices rising?
When it has all been cornered by
An unknown buyer?
Release us, Mauler, from that contract!

MAULER:

Sorry, I need that canned goods. But there's
Plenty of livestock, expensive to be sure
But enough. Just buy it!

THE PACKERS:

Buy livestock now? Damn his hide!

c

Small bar in the stockyard district.

Working men and women, among them Joan. A troop of Black Straw Hats come in. Joan stands up and during the following motions to them desperately to go away.

JACKSON, LIEUTENANT OF THE BLACK STRAW HATS (*directing a perfunctory hymn*):
Brother, won't you eat the bread of Jesus?
Since we gathered at his board
What delights have come to please us!
Friend, come quickly to the Lord!
Hallelujah!
Martha, a rank-and-file Black Straw Hat, speaks to the workers, intermittently making a remark to her comrades.

MARTHA: (Is there really any point in this?) Brothers and sisters, there was a time when I myself stood sadly by the wayside like you, and all the old Adam in me wanted was to eat and drink, but then I found the Lord Jesus, and light and gladness came into my heart, and now (They're not even listening) I only have to think hard about my Lord Jesus, who redeemed us all with His suffering in spite of our many many sins and I'm not hungry any more and I'm not thirsty, except for the word of our Lord Jesus. (It's no use.) Where the Lord Jesus is, there's no violence but only peace; there's no hate, but only love. (This is a complete waste of time!) And so I say: Help us to keep the pot boiling!

THE BLACK STRAW HATS: Hallelujah!
Jackson passes the collection box around, but nothing is put into it.
Hallelujah!

JOAN:
Why must they come and bother people
Here in the cold, and worst of all, make speeches?
Indeed, I can hardly bear
To hear the words which

Were once such a joy and comfort to me! If only
They had a voice left, some little something inside them that would say:
This is a place of snow and wind: be still!

A WOMAN: Leave her be. That's what they have to do for the bit of food and warmth they get. I wouldn't mind being at their mission house myself.

MRS LUCKERNIDDLE: That was real nice music!

GLOOMB: Sort of.

MRS LUCKERNIDDLE: They're sweet people all the same.

GLOOMB: Sort of.

THE WOMAN: But why don't they talk to us and convert us?

GLOOMB (*making the gesture of paying out money*): Can you keep their pot boiling, Mrs Swingurn?

THE WOMAN: Their music is nice, but I thought maybe they'd give us a dish of soup, seeing they've brought a pot.

A WORKER (*amazed at her*): No kidding? That's what you thought?

MRS LUCKERNIDDLE: I'd rather see some action myself. I've heard enough talk. If certain people had kept their mouths shut, I'd know where to go for the night.

JOAN: Isn't anybody around here going to do something?

THE WORKER: Yes, the Communists.

JOAN: Don't they incite people to crime?

THE WORKER: No.

Silence.

JOAN: Where are they?

GLOOMB: Mrs Luckerniddle can tell you.

JOAN (*to Mrs Luckerniddle*): How do you know such things?

MRS LUCKERNIDDLE: Well, you see, in the days before I started relying on people like you, I went to see them a few times about my husband.

d

Livestock Exchange.

THE PACKERS:

We're in the market for livestock! Yearlings

Calves! Steers! Hogs!
Let's have offers!

THE STOCKBREEDERS:
There's nothing left. What could be sold
We've sold.

THE PACKERS:
Nothing left? The railroad pens
Are clogged with livestock.

THE STOCKBREEDERS:
All sold.

THE PACKERS:
Sold to whom?

Mauler comes in. The Packers besiege him.

THE PACKERS:
Not a steer to be had in all Chicago.
Mauler, you've got to give us more time.

MAULER: You signed a contract to deliver meat. Deliver it. (*He joins Slift.*) Bleed them dry.

A STOCKBREEDER: Eight hundred Kentucky steers at forty.

THE PACKERS:
Forty! Are you crazy?

SLIFT:
Sold. At forty.

THE STOCKBREEDERS:
Eight hundred steers to Sullivan Slift at forty.

THE PACKERS:
It's Mauler! See? We told you so. It's him!
You dirty dog! He makes us contract to deliver
Canned meat and buys up all the livestock, so
We have to buy the meat we need to fill
His cans from him! You lousy butcher! Here!
Take some of *our* flesh! Cut yourself a chunk!

MAULER: When you're a steer, the sight of you will whet people's appetite, you've got to expect it!

GRAHAM (*ready to rush at Mauler*):
I'll kill him. I'll kill him.

MAULER:
Okay, Graham, what I want from you is cans!
Stuff yourself into them for all I care!

You businessmen, I'll teach you how to
Sell meat! From this time on the price
Of every hoof of every calf from here
To Illinois gets paid to me. A good price too.
So for a start I'm putting up five hundred steers
For sale at fifty-six.
(*Silence.*)
Not much demand. All right, since no one here needs livestock
I'm asking sixty! And don't forget
My canned goods!

e

Another part of the Stockyards.

Placards reading: 'General strike in support of the locked-out stockyard workers!' Outside a shed two men from union headquarters are talking with a group of workers. Joan comes along.

JOAN: Are you the people who are running things for the unemployed? I can help. I've learned to speak on the street and indoors too, even in big halls. I'm not easy to intimidate, and if I've got a good cause to explain, I think I'm pretty good at it. If you ask me, something needs to be done quick. And I've got a few suggestions.

A LABOUR LEADER: Fellow workers! So far the meat bosses have shown no sign of reopening their plants. At first it looked as if the exploiter Pierpont Mauler was trying to get the plants opened, because he has been demanding delivery of some big lots of canned goods the packers owe him. Then it turned out that Mauler himself had bought up the meat they need for their canned goods and has no intention of parting with it. We now know that if the meat bosses have their way we workers will never get our jobs back, anyway, not at our old wages. Obviously, in this kind of a situation, only force can help us. The workers in the big light and power plants have promised to call a general strike no later than the day after tomorrow. We want this made known all over the stockyards, because if it isn't, some false rumour could make the workers drift away, and then if they want to come back it'll be on the meat bosses' conditions. Between now and tomorrow morning the meat bosses are sure to broadcast a lot of lies; they'll say everything's been settled and the general strike isn't coming off. That's why these letters, announcing that the light and power workers have called a sympathy strike, have to be delivered to the delegates who'll be waiting for instructions from us at various points in the stockyards at ten o'clock tonight. Stick this one under your shirt, Jack, and wait for the delegates outside Ma Schmitt's hashhouse.

A worker takes the letter and leaves.

ANOTHER WORKER: Give me the one for the Graham plant, I know the place.

THE LABOUR LEADER: Twenty-sixth and Michigan Park.

The worker takes the letter and leaves.

THE LABOUR LEADER: Thirteenth Street, outside the Westinghouse Building. (*To Joan*:) Hey, who are you?

JOAN: I've been fired from my job.

THE LABOUR LEADER: What kind of a job?

JOAN: I sold a magazine.

THE LABOUR LEADER: Who'd you work for?

JOAN: An agency.

A WORKER: She could be a stoolpigeon.

SECOND LABOUR LEADER: No, I know her. She's with the Black Straw Hats, so the police are used to seeing her around. Nobody'd ever suspect her of working for us. That's a good thing, because the cops are watching the place where the comrades from the Cridle plant are expected. She'll attract less notice than anybody else we've got.

FIRST LABOUR LEADER: How do you know what she'll do with the letter?

SECOND LABOUR LEADER: I don't. (*To Joan*:)
A net with one torn mesh
Is useless.
The fish swims through it at that point
As if there were no net at all.

Suddenly
All the meshes are useless.

JOAN: I sold papers on Forty-Fourth Street. I'm not a stoolpigeon. I'm heart and soul for your cause.

FIRST LABOUR LEADER: Our cause? You mean it's not your cause?

JOAN: Well, I don't see how it can be in the public interest for the plant owners to throw all those workers out on the street. It would almost make a body think the rich drew profit from the poverty of the poor! And that the rich people are to blame for all the poverty!

The workers laugh uproariously.

But that's inhuman!! What about somebody like Mr Mauler?

More laughter.

What are you laughing about? Why are you so resentful? I don't like it and I don't think it's right of you to assume without proof that a person like Mr Mauler can't be human.

SECOND LABOUR LEADER: Not without proof. Give her the letter, nothing to worry about. You know her, Mrs Luckerniddle? (*Mrs Luckerniddle nods.*) Wouldn't you say she's honest?

MRS LUCKERNIDDLE: Honest, yes.

FIRST LABOUR LEADER (*giving Joan the letter*): Go to the Graham plant, Gate 5. If you see three workers coming along and they look around, ask them if they're from the Cridle plant. The letter's for them.

f

Livestock Exchange.

THE SMALL SPECULATORS:

The stock market's falling! The packing plants in danger!
What's to become of us shareholders?
Us small investors who have risked our savings?
The middle class, already so sorely tried?
Somebody ought to blow such men as Graham
To bits before they make waste paper out of
Our stock certificates, our
Share in the profits of their bloody cellars.

Buy livestock, you bastards, buy at any price!

During the whole scene the names of firms that have suspended payments are called out: 'The following firms have suspended payment: Meyers & Co., etc.'

THE PACKERS: We can't go on. The price is over seventy.

THE WHOLESALERS: Damn big shots! Brain them, kill them. They aren't buying.

THE PACKERS: Two thousand steers wanted at seventy.

SLIFT (*to Mauler standing by a pillar*): Push them higher.

MAULER:

I see you fellows haven't kept the contract I
Concluded with you in the hope of making
Jobs for the workers. Now I hear that they're
Still standing idle in the yards. Well, you'll regret it:
I've bought canned meat and I want it now.

GRAHAM:

We couldn't help it. Meat had
Vanished completely from the market!
Five hundred steers at seventy-five!

THE SMALL SPECULATORS:

Buy it, you bloodsuckers!
They're not buying! They'd rather let
The packing plants go under.

MAULER:

No higher, Slift, I wouldn't advise it.
They're at the end of their tether.
Bleed them okay, but don't kill them
For if they bite the dust
We bite it too.

SLIFT:

There's life in 'em yet. Higher, higher!
Five hundred steers at seventy-seven.

THE SMALL SPECULATORS:

Seventy-seven. Hear that? Why didn't you
Buy when the price was seventy-five? Now
It's seventy-seven and still going up.

THE PACKERS: Mauler's buying our cans at fifty. How can we pay him eighty for his livestock?

MAULER (*to those around him*): Where are those men I sent to the stockyards?

A MAN: There's one of them now.

MAULER: Well, what's the story?

FIRST DETECTIVE (*reporting*): The crowds, sir, reach farther than the eye can see. If one were to shout the name of Joan, ten or a hundred might answer. Faceless and nameless, they sit waiting. Besides, a single voice could never make itself heard with all those people running around, shouting for members of their families who've gone astray. And in the districts where the unions are at work the excitement is at fever pitch.

MAULER: Who's at work? The unions? And the police look on while they agitate? Hell and damnation! Call up the police this minute, use my name, ask them what we're paying taxes for. Tell them to bash the agitators' heads in, don't beat about the bush.

The first detective goes out.

GRAHAM:

All right then, Mauler, if we die we die.
A thousand steers at seventy-seven. That's our death.

SLIFT:

Five hundred to Graham at seventy-seven.
Anything more will cost him eighty.

MAULER (*has come back*):

This business, Slift, amuses me
No longer. It could lead too far.
Drive the price up to eighty, but
Then let them go at eighty.
Give them their steers and let them off the hook.
Enough's enough, this city needs
A breathing spell and I have other worries.
This throttling, Slift, does not amuse me
Nearly as much as I expected.
(*He sees the second detective.*)
Have you found her?

THE SECOND DETECTIVE: No, I haven't seen anyone in the uniform of the Black Straw Hats. A hundred thousand people are milling around the stockyards, it's dark, and no one could shout above that bitter wind. Besides, the police are clearing the stockyards and starting to shoot.

MAULER:

To shoot? At whom? Yes, yes, of course.
How strange. In here one doesn't hear a thing!
So they can't find her, and there's shooting? Go
To the phone booths, find Jim and tell him not to phone
For if he does, they'll say as usual that we
Told the police to shoot.
The second detective goes out.

MEYERS:

Fifteen hundred at eighty.

SLIFT:

Only five hundred at eighty!

MEYERS:

Five thousand at eighty! Cutthroat!

MAULER (*has gone back to the pillar*):

Slift, I feel sick. Lay off.

SLIFT: I wouldn't dream of it. There's life in 'em yet. If you can't take it, I'll drive them higher.

MAULER:

Slift, I need air. You carry on. I can't.
Respect my wishes, though. I'd rather
Lose everything than have
Some new disaster on my conscience. Don't
Go above eighty-five! And
Respect my wishes. You know me.
He runs into some reporters on his way out.

THE REPORTERS: Hi, Mauler! What's new?

MAULER (*on his way out*): I want it made known in the stockyards that I've released livestock to the packers, so now they've got livestock. Otherwise there'd be violence.

SLIFT: Five hundred steers at ninety!

THE SMALL SPECULATORS:

We heard Mauler say
To let them go for eighty-five. Slift has no right.

SLIFT:

That's a lie. I'll teach you to
Sell meat in cans and

Have no meat!
Five thousand steers at ninety-five!
Uproar.

g

Stockyards.

Many people waiting, among them Joan.

PEOPLE: Why are you sitting here?
JOAN: I have a letter to deliver. Three men are coming.
A group of reporters come along, led by a man.
THE MAN (*pointing at Joan*): That's her. (*To Joan*:) These men are reporters.
THE REPORTERS: Hello, there. Are you Joan Dark of the Black Straw Hats?
JOAN: No.
THE REPORTERS: We were told in Mr Mauler's office that you've sworn not to leave the stockyards before the packing plants are opened. We've got the story right here, you can read it in bold type on the front page. (*Joan turns away. The reporters read aloud*:) Joan Dark, Our Lady of the Stockyards, says God is on the side of the packing house workers.
JOAN: I never said anything of the kind.
THE REPORTERS: We want to tell you, Miss Dark, that public opinion is with you. Except for a few unscrupulous speculators, all Chicago sympathizes with you. This'll give your Black Straw Hats a big boost.
JOAN: I'm not with the Black Straw Hats any more.
THE REPORTERS: That can't be. As far as we're concerned, you'll always be a Black Straw Hat. But we won't bother you. We'll just sit quietly over there.
JOAN: I wish you'd go away.
They sit down at some distance.
WORKERS (*offstage, in the stockyards*):
They will not open the packing houses
Until our affliction is at its height.
When our misery grows greater

They will open up.
But answer us they must.
Don't go away. Wait for the answer!

COUNTERCHORUS (*also offstage*):
Wrong! No matter how great our misery grows
They will not open the packing houses.
Not until their profits grow greater.
Their answer will come
From cannon and machine guns.
No one can help us but we ourselves
Only to our fellow workers
Can we appeal!

JOAN: Do you believe that, Mrs Luckerniddle?

MRS LUCKERNIDDLE: Yes, that's the truth.

JOAN:
I see the system. Its surface
Has long been known, but not
The inner workings. I see some people, a few, on top
And many down below, and those on top
Shout down to those below: Come up, then all
Of us will be on top. But if you look
Closely, you'll see a hidden something
Between the ones on top and those below. It
Looks like a path, but no, it's not a path.
More like a plank, and now you see it plainly, it's
A seesaw. That's it. This whole
System's a seesaw with two ends
Depending on each other. Those on top
Are where they are because the others
Are down below, and they will stay up top
Only so long as the others stay down. They'd be
On top no longer if the others, leaving their
Old place, came up. And so it is that those
On top inevitably want those below to
Stay there for all eternity and never rise.
And anyway, there have to be more people down below
Than up on top to keep the seesaw in position
For that's the way with seesaws.

The reporters stand up and go to the rear, because some news has just reached them.

A WORKER (*to Joan*): What did those men want of you?

JOAN: Nothing.

THE WORKER: But they spoke to you.

JOAN: They thought I was somebody else.

AN OLD MAN (*to Joan*): Say, you're shivering. Want a slug of whiskey? (*Joan drinks.*) Stop! Stop! You've had enough to kill a mule.

A WOMAN: Some nerve!

JOAN: Did you say something?

THE WOMAN: I sure did. Some nerve! Drinking up the old man's whiskey!

JOAN: Shut up, you ninny! Hey, where's my scarf? They've gone and stolen it. They stop at nothing! Stealing my scarf! Who swiped my scarf? Give it back this minute. (*She tears the sack off the head of the woman next to her, who defends herself.*) It's you all right. Don't start telling lies, and give me that sack.

THE WOMAN: Help, she's killing me.

A MAN: Take it easy!

Someone tosses her a rag.

JOAN:

If you people had your way, I'd be sitting here in this draught stark naked.
It wasn't this cold in my dream. When I
Came to the stockyards with great plans, encouraged
By dreams, I never dreamt that it could be
So cold here. What I miss more than
Anything else is my warm scarf. For you people
Hunger's no problem. You haven't any food.
For me they're waiting with a bowl of soup.
You're used to being cold, but I
Can go to that warm room at any time
Pick up the flag and beat the drum
And talk of HIM who dwelleth in the clouds.
What have you left behind you? I have left
A calling and what's more a job
A noble way of life, but also

A tolerable livelihood.
It seems almost like play-acting
Somehow disgraceful that I should stay out here when I
Don't absolutely have to. And yet:
I cannot leave, although, I tell you frankly
I'm choked with terror when I think of this
Not eating, not sleeping, not knowing where I'm at
This common hunger, this abysmal cold
And worst of all, this wanting to go away.

WORKERS:
Stay where you are! Whatever happens
Don't break ranks!
Only by staying together
Can you help yourselves!
You have been betrayed
By all your official spokesmen
And by your unions, which have sold out.
Listen to no one, believe nothing
But consider every suggestion
That might bring real change. Above all, learn
That force alone can help you
And that you yourselves must wield it.
The reporters come back.

THE REPORTERS: Hi, kid. You've swung it. We've just heard that the millionaire Pierpont Mauler, who has been holding enormous lots of livestock, has started selling to the packers in spite of the rising prices. The packing plants will be open tomorrow.

JOAN: Oh, that is good news!

MRS LUCKERNIDDLE: That's the kind of lies our people were talking about. It's a good thing we've got the truth in our letter.

JOAN:
Listen, there's work!
The ice has melted in their hearts. At least
The righteous man among them
Has proved himself. Appealed to as a man
He has responded as a man. There is
Such a thing as goodness.

Machine-gun fire is heard in the distance.

What's that?

A REPORTER: Machine guns. The army's been ordered to clear the stockyards, because now that the plants are being reopened, the agitators, who are inciting the masses to violence, must be silenced.

A WOMAN: Should we go home now?

A WORKER: How do we know that there's really going to be work?

JOAN: Why wouldn't it be true if these gentlemen say so? People don't joke about things like that.

MRS LUCKERNIDDLE: Don't be a fool. You have no sense at all. You know why? Because you haven't been sitting out here in the cold long enough. (*She gets up.*) I'm going over to our people now to tell them the lies have started in. But you stay right here with that letter, understand! (*She goes away.*)

JOAN: But they're shooting.

A WORKER: Don't worry. The stockyards are so big it'll be hours before the soldiers get here.

JOAN: How many are there?

THE REPORTERS: Maybe a hundred thousand.

JOAN:

So many?
Oh, what an unknown school, this lawless snow-
Filled world, where hunger teaches and need
Speaks perforce of necessity!
You hundred thousand pupils, what are you learning?

WORKERS (*offstage*):

If you stick together
They will slaughter you.
We advise you to stick together!
If you fight
Their tanks will crush you.
We advise you to fight!
This battle will be lost
And maybe the next one
Will also be lost.
But you will learn how to fight

And learn
That force alone can help you and
That you yourselves must wield it.

JOAN:
Stop! That's enough teaching!
Your teaching is too cold!
Force is not the answer to
Disorder and confusion.
True, the temptation is great!
Another night like this, another day of this
Oppressive silence and no one
Would hold himself back. True
You have stood together
For many nights and many years, learning
To think coldly and cruelly.
True, violence builds up in the darkness
Weakness and weakness build strength and
Unfinished business accumulates.
But who will sit down to the meal
You people are cooking?
I'm getting out of here. No good can come of violence.
I don't belong with these people. If hunger and the heel of poverty had taught me violence as a child, I'd be one of them and I wouldn't ask any questions. As it is, I'll have to be going. (*She remains seated.*)

THE REPORTERS: We advise you to leave the yards in a hurry. You've made the front page, but the show is over now.

They leave.

Shouting from the rear, coming closer. The workers stand up.

A WORKER: They've got the men from union headquarters.

The two labour leaders, handcuffed, are led past by detectives.

THE WORKER (*to one of the handcuffed leaders*): Don't worry, Bill. This isn't the end of the story.

ANOTHER WORKER (*shouts after the group*): Bloodhounds!

FIRST WORKER: If they think this'll stop us, they've got it wrong. Our boys are prepared for everything.

In a vision Joan sees herself as a criminal, outside the familiar world.

JOAN:

Those men who gave me the letter. Why
Are they handcuffed? What is in
That letter? I could never
Take an action requiring violence and
Breeding violence. He who does so
Would have to be moved by malice
Against his neighbour, and closed
To all the understandings
Customary among men.
Cut off from all community, he would find
No bearings in
A world grown unfamiliar. The movement of the stars
Over his head would no longer be governed by
The old rule. Words
Would change their meaning for him, innocence
Forsake him, the pursued pursuer
His vision would lose all candour.
I couldn't be like that. That's why I'm leaving.
For three days Joan was seen
In Packingtown, in the swamp
Of the stockyards, going down
Lower and lower, hoping to transfigure the muck
And be a light to the poorest of the poor.
For three days striding downward
She weakened on the third day and in the end was
Engulfed by the swamp. Say:
It was too cold.

She stands up and goes away. Snow is falling.

MRS LUCKERNIDDLE (*comes back*): Nothing but lies! Where's that woman who was sitting with me?

A WOMAN: Gone.

A WORKER: I knew she'd beat it when it really started snowing.

Three workers come along, look around and, not finding the person they are looking for, leave. As it grows dark, a sign appears:

The snow's blowing this way
So who would want to stay?
The same as always stayed before:
The stony soil and the very poor.

h

PIERPONT MAULER CROSSES THE BORDER OF POVERTY

Street corner in Chicago

MAULER (*to one of the detectives*):
No further, let's turn back. What's that you say?
You laughed, admit it! Let's turn back, I said
And then you laughed. They've started shooting again.
Seems to be some resistance. But get this through
Your heads. My turning back a couple of times
As we approached the stockyards doesn't mean
A thing. Stop thinking about it. I'm not paying you
To think. I had my reasons. I'm known there. Now
You're thinking again. Looks like I hired a couple
Of blockheads. Anyway we're turning back. I hope
Good sense has moved that girl I'm looking for
To leave the stockyards where all hell
Seems to have broken loose.
(*A newsboy passes.*)
Hey, paper! Let's see what's happening on the livestock market!
(*He reads and turns chalky-white.*)
Something has happened all right. This changes everything.
It's written here in black and white that livestock
Is down to thirty and that not a head
Is being sold, because, it says again
In black and white, the packers have gone bust
And left the livestock market. It also says
That Mauler and his sidekick Slift are flatter broke
Than all the rest. That's what it says. Which brings
Us to a situation which I didn't
Aim at, but welcome with relief.
I can no longer help them

For I put all my livestock
At the disposal of the public at large
And no one wanted it. So now I'm free.
No one has any claim on me. I
Hereby dismiss you
Once having crossed the border of poverty, I
Don't need you any more.
No one will want to kill me.

THE TWO DETECTIVES: Then we can go.

MAULER:

You can indeed, and so can I, wherever
I like. Even to the stockyards.
And as for the edifice of sweat and money
That we've constructed in these cities, it's
As if someone has put up a building
The biggest, most expensive, most efficient
In all the world
But by some oversight and to save money
Has built it out of dogshit, making it
A horrid place to stay in, so that in the end
His only claim to glory was that he had
Produced the biggest stink in all the world. The
Man who escapes from such a building
Has every reason to be happy.

ONE OF THE DETECTIVES (*as they are leaving*): Well, that's the end of him.

MAULER:

Misfortune crushes common men. They therefore fear it.
Not I, for it will raise me to the realm of spirit.

i

A deserted section of the stockyards.

Mrs Luckerniddle meets Joan in the snow storm.

MRS LUCKERNIDDLE: So there you are! Where are you going so fast? Did you deliver the letter?

JOAN: No. I'm leaving.

MRS LUCKERNIDDLE: I should have known it. Give me that letter!

JOAN: No, you can't have it. Don't come near me. I know it's just another call for violence. Now everything has been straightened out, and you people want to keep right on.

MRS LUCKERNIDDLE: Oh, you think everything's been straightened out, do you? And I told them you were honest, or they wouldn't have given you the letter. But you're a cheat and you belong on the other side. You're trash! Give me the letter they trusted you with. (*Joan vanishes in the snow storm.*) Hey, you! She's gone.

j

Another section of the stockyard district.

Hurrying towards the city, Joan hears two passing workers.

THE FIRST: First they launched a rumour that the packing plants were going to start up again and put everybody to work. Now that some of the workers have gone home so as to be ready to report tomorrow morning, it suddenly comes out that the packers aren't opening at all because P. Mauler has ruined them.

THE SECOND: The Communists were right. The masses shouldn't have broken ranks. Especially considering that every factory in Chicago would have struck tomorrow.

THE FIRST: Nobody told *us* that.

THE SECOND: That's bad. Some of the couriers must have lain down on the job. A lot of workers would have stayed on if they'd known. No amount of police brutality would have stopped them.

Joan, wandering about, hears voices.

VOICE:

For not getting there
You have no excuse. The cobblestones
Do not excuse those who fall.
Even if you get there
Don't bother us with talk of difficulties
But silently present

Yourself or what was entrusted to you.

Joan has stopped still and started walking in a different direction.

VOICE (*Joan stops still*):

We sent you on a mission.
Our situation was critical.
We didn't know who you were. Possibly
You would carry out our mission and possibly
You would let us down.
Did you carry it out?

Joan hurries on and is stopped by a new voice.

VOICE:

When someone awaits you, you must arrive.

Looking around for an escape from the voices, Joan hears voices on all sides.

VOICES:

A net with one torn mesh
Is useless.
The fish swim through it at that point
As if there were no net at all.
Suddenly
All the meshes are useless.

MRS LUCKERNIDDLE'S VOICE:

I vouched for you.
But when they gave you a letter with the truth in it
You didn't deliver it.

JOAN (*falling to her knees*):

O Truth, bright light, unseasonably darkened by a snow storm!
Never more to be seen! Oh, what force in a snowstorm!
Oh, weakness of the flesh! O hunger, what can withstand you?
What can outlive you, frost of the night?
I must turn back!

She runs back.

10

PIERPONT MAULER HUMBLES HIMSELF AND IS EXALTED

The Black Straw Hat Mission.

MARTHA (*to another Black Straw Hat*): Three days ago a messenger from Pierpont Mauler the meat king came and told us that Pierpont Mauler himself promised to pay our rent and help us to do something big for the poor.

MULBERRY: It's Saturday night, Mr Snyder. Would you kindly pay the rent, which is very low, or vacate my premises?

SNYDER: Mr Mulberry, we are expecting Mr Pierpont Mauler any minute; he has promised to help us.

MULBERRY: Hey, Dick, hey, Albert, put their furniture out on the street.

Two men start carrying the furniture out.

THE BLACK STRAW HATS:

Oh, they're taking the penitents' bench away
Already their rapacious claws are threatening
Harmonium and pulpit.
And all the more loudly we scream:
If only the rich Mr Mauler
Would come now and save us
With his money!

SNYDER:

For seven days now in the rusting stockyards
The masses have been standing, freed at last from work.
Delievered from all shelter they are standing
In rain and snow
While over them hangs an unknown fate.
Dear Mr Mulberry, some hot soup now
Hot soup with music and we've got them. In my mind's eye I see
The kingdom of heaven complete.
If only we can scare up a band and some decent soup

With some body to it, all God's worries are over
And Bolshevism will give up the ghost.

THE BLACK STRAW HATS:
The dykes of faith have burst
In our city of Chicago
And the muddy waters of materialism
Are threatening to engulf its last temple.
Look, it's tottering; look, it's sinking!
But stand fast, for the rich Mr Mauler is coming!
He's on his way with all his money!

A BLACK STRAW HAT: Where do we put the public now, major?

Three poor men come in; Mauler is one of them.

SNYDER (*shouts at them*): All they want is soup! There's no soup here! Only the word of God! That'll get rid of them!

MAULER: Here stand three men who have come to their God.

SNYDER: Sit down over there and keep quiet.

The three sit down.

A MAN (*enters*): Is Pierpont Mauler here?

SNYDER: No, but we're expecting him.

THE MAN: The packers went to speak to him and the stockbreeders are yelling for him. (*He goes out.*)

MAULER (*front stage*):
I hear they're looking for one Mauler.
I knew the man: a fool. And now they're searching
Heaven and hell, the heights and depths, for this
Mauler who all his life was stupider than
A dirty drunken bum.
(*Stands up and goes to the Black Straw Hats.*)
A certain man I knew was asked for
A hundred dollars. And he had ten million.
He didn't give the hundred dollars, but threw
The ten million away
And gave himself.
(*He takes hold of two of the Black Straw Hats and sits down with them on the penitents' bench.*)
I've come here to confess.
No one as base as I am, friends
Has ever knelt here.

THE BLACK STRAW HATS:

Don't give up hope!
Be not of little faith!
Surely he will come, even now he is near
With all his money.

A BLACK STRAW HAT:

Is he here?

MAULER:

A hymn, I beg of you. For I am light
Of heart, yet bowed with sadness.

TWO MUSICIANS:

One number, no more.

They strike up a hymn. The Black Straw Hats sing absently, looking towards the door.

SNYDER (*over his account books*):

Trying to figure something out. I'm not saying what.
Quiet!
Bring me the account book and the unpaid
Bills. Yes, it's come to this.

MAULER:

I have been guilty of exploitation
Misuse of force, expropriation of
Everyone in the name of property. For seven days
I held this city of Chicago by the throat
Till it croaked.

A BLACK STRAW HAT: That's Mauler!

MAULER:

I plead however in extenuation
That on the seventh day I cast everything
Away, and stand here penniless.
Not indebted, but repentant.

SNYDER:

You're Mauler?

MAULER:

Yes, and ravaged by remorse.

SNYDER (*screaming*): Without money? (*To the Black Straw Hats*:) Pack up our stuff. I hereby suspend all payments.

THE MUSICIANS:

If that's the man you were expecting money from

To pay us with, we might as well shove off.
Good evening.
They leave.

CHORUS OF THE BLACK STRAW HATS (*at the departing musicians*):
With prayers we awaited
Mauler the rich, but in walked
Mauler the penitent, bringing us
His heart
But not his money.
Therefore our hearts are moved, but
Our faces are long.
(*Sitting on their last chairs and benches, the Black Straw Hats sing their last hymns confusedly.*)
By the waters of Lake Michigan
Here we sit and weep.
Take the mottoes off the walls
Wrap the hymn books in the unvictorious flag
For we can pay our bills no longer
And against us rise the snowstorms
Of gathering winter.
In conclusion they sing: 'March Straight Into the Fight'. Mauler looks over the shoulder of one of the Black Straw Hats and joins in the singing.

SNYDER:
Quiet! And now get out, the whole lot of you (*to Mauler*:) and especially you!
Where are the forty months' rent from the unconverted
That Joan cast out? And instead brought *this* guy in!
Joan, give me back my forty months' rent!

MAULER:
I see, you thought you'd build your house beneath
The shade I cast. To you a man is one
Who helps you, just as to me a man was someone
To prey on. But even if none but those whom I helped
Deserved the name of man, it would be no different.
Then you'd need drowning men, and you'd be straws.
Thus in the mighty circuits of the stars
As of commodities, all remains unchanged.

Such wisdom, Snyder, would embitter some.
But I am willing to accept the fact
That in my present shape I'm not the man you need.
Mauler starts through the door. The meat kings enter and push him back. They are chalky-white.

THE PACKERS:
Exalted Mauler! Do forgive us for
Seeking you out and interrupting the complex
Tergiversations of your giant brain.
But we are ruined. Chaos blows around us
And over us unknown intention threatens.
What are your plans for us, Mauler? What
Are you going to do next? For
We are the victims of your rabbit punches.
Enter the stockbreeders in great agitation. They too are chalky-white.

THE STOCKBREEDERS:
Accursed Mauler! So this is where you're hiding.
Pay for our livestock instead of getting converted.
We want your money, not your soul. You wouldn't
Have to relieve your conscience here if you
Hadn't relieved our pockets of their contents!
Pay us for our livestock!

GRAHAM (*comes forward*):
Permit us, Mauler, to recount in brief
The battle which began this morning
Lasted for seven hours and swept us all
Into the depths.

MAULER:
Oh, eternal slaughter! In this day and age
No different than in times gone by when
Warriors bashed each other bloody with iron!

GRAHAM:
Remember, Mauler, how, through contracts obligating
Us to deliver meat, you forced us to
Buy meat from you, since you alone had meat.
Well, when you left at twelve o'clock, Slift squeezed
Our throats still tighter. With raucous cries he drove
The prices higher and higher, till they stood

At ninety-five. Whereat the dear old Fed
Stepped in and called a halt. Alive to her
Responsibility, that kindly lady threw
Canadian yearlings on the gutted market.
The prices trembled in the balance, but
Insensate Slift, no sooner had he glimpsed
Those yearlings from the distant north, than he
Grabbed them at ninety-five, much as a drunkard
Still thirsty after swilling up an ocean
Gulps avidly at one last drop. The old
Lady looked on in horror. Loew and Levi
Wallox and Brigham, bankers of highest repute
Sprang to her help, pledging their holdings and chattels
Down to the last eraser, in earnest of their promise to
Bring in from Canada, Argentina and so on
Every last quadruped dimly resembling a steer or hog.
'Not in three days!' cried Slift. 'I need them this minute.'
Upward the prices he drove. And bathed in hot tears, the
Banking establishments rushed into the final conflict
Since, to deliver, they were obliged to buy.
Levi in person, sobbing his heart out, poked
One of Slift's brokers full in the stomach.
Brigham gasped: 'Ninety-six' and tore out his beard. At
That point in time if an elephant had chanced to come in, that
Elephant would have been squashed like a berry.
Even the office boys, seized with despair, silently took
Bites out of each other, just as in olden times the fighting men's
Chargers would sink their teeth into each others' flanks.
Known for their air of boredom, office boys
Were heard this day to gnash their teeth.
And still we bought because we had to buy.
Slift said: 'One hundred!' And in silence
So thick you could have heard a pin drop
The banks collapsed like trampled mushrooms. Once
Mighty and firm, suspending payments as though
Breathing their last. Then old man Levi whispered
So everyone could hear: 'You'll have to fall back

On the packing plants themselves now, for we
Are powerless to meet those contracts.' Then
Morosely, packer after packer laid
His idle, useless plant at your feet and Slift's
And made his exit, while the brokers closed
Their order books. And at that very moment
Sighing as with relief, because no contract
Compelled its purchase, beef went down
And down and down.
Like water hurled from cliff to cliff, the prices
Fell from quotation to quotation, plumbing
Unfathomable depths. They stopped at thirty.
And so your contract, Mauler, is now worthless.
Aiming to lead us by the neck, you strangled us.
How can you lead a dead man by the neck?

MAULER:
So this, Slift, is the way you handled the mission
That I entrusted to you?

SLIFT:
Tear my head off.

MAULER:
What can I do with your head?
Give me your hat, it's worth a nickel.
What's to be done
With all this livestock that no one's forced to buy?

THE STOCKBREEDERS:
Without flying off the handle
We humbly beg you to inform us
Whether, when and wherewith you mean to
Pay for the livestock which
Was purchased but not paid for.

MAULER:
All right. I'll pay you with this hat and boot.
Here for ten millions is my hat, and here
One shoe for five. I need the other. Are
You satisfied?

THE STOCKBREEDERS:
Ah, when some moons ago
We led our frolicking calves

And lovingly fattened steers by the halter
To the railroad siding in far-away Missouri
Our families with voices cracked by toil
Shouted after us as the trains rolled away
Don't drink up the money, boys, and
Let's hope the livestock prices get better!
What can we do now?
How can we go back?
What will we say when they see
Our empty halters
And empty pockets?
How, Mauler, can we go home like this?

THE SAME MAN AS BEFORE (*enters*): Is Mauler here? A letter from New York.

MAULER: I used to be the Mauler such letters were addressed to. (*Opens it and reads it off to one side.*) 'Not long ago, dear Pierpont, we wrote advising you to buy meat. Today our advice is: come to an agreement with the breeders and get them to limit the livestock supply; then the market will recover. We shall be glad to give you all possible help. More tomorrow, dear Pierpont. Your friends in New York.' No, no. It's no good.

GRAHAM: What's no good?

MAULER: I have friends in New York, who claim to know a way out. It doesn't look possible to me. Here, what do you think?

He hands them the letter.

How very different everything
Seems now. Give up the struggle, friends.
Your wealth is gone. You'll have to face it: gone.
But not because we are no longer blessed
With earthly goods – which are not within the reach
Of all – but only because we have no feeling
For higher things. That's why we are poor!

MEYERS:

Who are these New York friends of yours?

MAULER:

Horgan and Blackwell. Sell . . .

GRAHAM:

That sounds like Wall Street.

A whispering spreads among those present.

MAULER:

The inner man, neglected and repressed . . .

THE PACKERS AND STOCKBREEDERS:

Exalted Mauler, kindly condescend
To step down from your lofty meditations
And think of us! Consider the chaos
That threatens to engulf the world.
You're needed, man. It's time that you resumed
The burden of responsibility!

MAULER:

I don't want to.
Alone I wouldn't dare. My ears still ring with
The grumbling in the stockyards and the rat-
Tat-tat of the machine guns. I would need
The backing of some lofty moral
Authority. I'd want our programme to be
Acknowledged as vital to the public welfare.
Then I might do it.
(*To Snyder*:) Are there many of these gospel mills?

SNYDER: Yes.

MAULER: And how are they doing?

SNYDER: Not very well.

MAULER:

Many and not doing well.
Suppose we were to invest big money in
You Black Straw Hats. Then, well supplied with soup
And music and appropriate
Bible quotations, lodgings too perhaps
In urgent cases, do you suppose that you
Could spread the gospel far and wide
That we were upright men, striving for the best
In evil times? For only by extreme
Measures, that may seem harsh, because they
Hit some people – quite a few, to tell the truth
Pretty near everyone in fact –
Can we now save this system of

Buying and selling, which is the only system
We have, though, true, it has its darker side.

SNYDER: For pretty near everyone. I see. We would.

MAULER (*to the packers*):
And I will merge your packing plants
Into one vast conglomerate and
Acquire half the stock.

THE PACKERS: What a brain!

MAULER (*to the stockbreeders*):
Listen, my friends!
They whisper to each other.
The difficulties that have weighed upon us
Are clearing. Poverty and hunger, crime
And violence, all have one cause, and this
One cause is being obviated.
There was too much meat. This year the market
Was glutted and the price of livestock
Fell through the floor. But now, to hike it up
And keep it up, we packers and we breeders have
Resolved by one accord to impose a limit
On hitherto unbridled livestock production
And to forestall the glutting of the market
By wiping out the present oversupply.
In a word, by burning a third of all our livestock.

ALL: How stunningly simple!

SNYDER (*speaks up*):
If all this livestock is indeed so worthless
That you consider burning it, then why
Couldn't you give it to those people
Standing out there? They'd make good use of it.

MAULER (*smiles*):
Dear Mr Snyder, you have failed to grasp
The essence of the problem. All those people
Standing out there *are customers*!
To the others:
It's almost unbelievable.
Prolonged smiles on all their faces.
They may seem worthless, superfluous
Even bothersome, but it cannot

Escape close scrutiny that *they* are customers
Though many will not understand, it is
Essential to lock out a third of all the work force
For labour too has glutted the market and must be
Curtailed!

ALL: The only way!

MAULER:

And wages cut!

ALL: Columbus's egg!

MAULER:

Our overriding purpose
In this dark time of cruel confusion
Of dehumanized humanity
When in our cities the unrest never ceases
(For once again Chicago is shaken by rumours of an impending general strike)
Is to prevent the brute force of the short-sighted people
From smashing their tools and destroying their livelihood
And to bring back peace and order. To this end we mean to
Encourage the order-fostering work of you Black Straw Hats by
Generous endowments.
Of course we'd be happier if your ranks once more included
People like that girl Joan, whose very looks
Inspire trust.

A BROKER (*rushes in*): Good news! The general strike has been crushed. The criminal desecrators of law and order have been thrown into jail.

SLIFT:

Breathe easy now, the market will recover
Once more the dreaded crisis has passed over
We've done the heavy task we had to do
Our calculations have again proved true
And things are running as we like them to.
Organ.

MAULER:

Fling open now your doors
To them that labour and are heavy laden

Fill the pot with soup and strike up music
And we ourselves will sit on your front benches
And get converted.

SNYDER:

Open the doors.
The doors are opened.

THE BLACK STRAW HATS (*look toward the doors and sing*):

Spread the net, for they are sure to come!
They've lost their lodgings and the night is wet.
God sets the cold upon them
God sets the rain upon them
Therefore they're sure to come, so spread the net.
Welcome! Welcome! Welcome!
Welcome to our place!

Bar the doors, let nobody escape
They're on their way, they're on their way
If there's no job they can find
If they're deaf and if they're blind
This is where they'll come, don't let them go astray.
Welcome! Welcome! Welcome!
Welcome to our place!

Pull 'em in as fast as they can come
Hat and head and shoe and foot and scab and sore.
If their last reserves are spent
And they've come here to lament!
Pull 'em in and hold 'em. Lock and bar the door.
Welcome! Welcome! Welcome!
Welcome to our place!

Here we are! They're coming. They are coming!
Misery drives them to our mission house like beasts at bay!
Look, they are coming, they're coming!
Look, they are coming, they're coming!
(Here they can't escape. For here we stay!)
Welcome! Welcome! Welcome!
Welcome to our place!

11

a

Stockyards. Outside Graham's warehouse.

The yards are almost deserted. Only isolated groups of workers pass by.

JOAN (*comes along and asks*): Have three men been here asking for a letter?

Shouts in the rear, spreading toward the front. Then, guarded by soldiers, five men enter: the two from union headquarters and the three from the power station. Suddenly one of the men from the union headquarters stops walking and talks to the soldiers.

THE LABOUR LEADER: If you're taking us to jail, there's something you ought to know. We did what we did because we want to help people like you.

A SOLDIER: If you want to help us, get a move on.

THE LABOUR LEADER: What's the hurry?

THE SOLDIER: You scared?

THE LABOUR LEADER: Yes. But that's not what I want to talk about. I want you to stop a second so I can tell you why you arrested us, because you don't know.

THE SOLDIERS (*laughing*): All right. Why did we arrest you?

THE LABOUR LEADER: Penniless yourselves, you help the wealthy, because you haven't yet glimpsed the possibility of helping the penniless.

THE SOLDIER: Okay. So let's get a move on.

THE LABOUR LEADER: Hold it! I haven't finished what I've got to say. But in this city the employed are already helping the unemployed. So the possibility is coming closer. Make good use of it.

THE SOLDIER: I suppose you'd like us to let you go?

THE LABOUR LEADER: Don't you understand? I'm only trying to tell you guys that your time is almost up.

THE SOLDIERS: Can we go on now?

THE LABOUR LEADER: Yes, now we can go on.

They go on. Joan stops and looks after the arrested men. Then she hears two men talking near her.

FIRST: Who are those men?

SECOND:

None of those men
Thought only of himself.
Never resting, they ran themselves ragged
For the sake of other people's bread.

FIRST: Why never resting?

SECOND:

The unjust man walks the streets openly
The just man hides.

FIRST: What will become of them?

SECOND:

Although they
Work for little pay and are useful to many
Not one of them lives out his natural life span
Eats his bread, dies with a full belly and
Is buried with honours. All
End before their time. They are
Struck down, trampled and buried in shame.

FIRST: Why do we never hear about them?

SECOND:

When you read in the papers that some criminals have been shot or
Thrown into jail, it's them.

FIRST: Will it always be like this?

SECOND:

No.

When Joan turns, the reporters speak to her.

THE REPORTERS: Isn't that Our Lady of the Stockyards? Hi there! Things have gone bad. The general strike has been called off. The packing plants are opening, but only for two-thirds of the work force at two-thirds of their old wages. But meat's going up.

JOAN: Have the workers accepted?

REPORTERS: Sure. Only a fraction knew that a general strike was planned, and the police drove that fraction away with their guns and nightsticks.

Joan collapses.

b

Outside the Graham warehouse.

A group of workers with lanterns.

A WORKER: This is where she must be. She came over from there, and she was here when she shouted to our people that the municipal power plants were going on strike. With all that snow coming down she probably didn't see the soldiers. One of them knocked her down with his rifle butt. I saw her clear as day for a second. There she is! There ought to be more like her. No, that's not her! She was an old working woman. This one's not one of ours. Let her lie, the soldiers'll pick her up when they get here.

12

DEATH AND CANONIZATION OF ST JOAN OF THE STOCKYARDS

The Black Straw Hat mission is richly furnished. Grouped in tiers stand the Black Straw Hats with new flags, the packers, the stockbreeders, and the wholesalers.

SNYDER:

So at last we have succeeded
God once more is on his legs
To the heights we have acceded
We have mingled with the dregs.
Folks, take pleasure in what we did
On the crest and in the trough.
Finally we have succeeded
Finally we've pulled it off.

A crowd of poor people come in, in the lead Joan supported by two policemen.

THE POLICEMEN:

Here is a homeless woman.
We found her lying
Unconscious in the stockyards.
This, it seems, was her last
Steady address.

JOAN: (*holds up the letter as if to deliver it*):

Never will the man who has gone under
Receive my letter.
My whole life told me to perform
This one small service in a good cause
And I did not perform it!

While the poor sit down on the benches to await their soup, Slift goes into a huddle with the packers and Snyder.

SLIFT: That's our Joan. Just when we needed her most. She rates a big promotion, because of the way she helped us through these difficult weeks with her kindly social work in the stockyards, her eloquence on behalf of the poor, and even her attacks on us. Our St Joan of the Stockyards, that's what she'll be. We'll publicize her as a saint and put her on a pedestal. The very fact that we're the ones who publicize her will prove to the world that with us humanity comes first.

MAULER:

May her simple childlike soul
Shine among us, bright and whole.
Likewise may her glorious
Voice speak out for you and me.
Castigating infamy
Let it speak for all of us.

SNYDER:

Arise, Joan of the Stockyards
Advocate of the poor
Consoler of the lowest depths!

JOAN:

What a wind in the depths! What cries are
You muffling, O snow?
Eat your soup, you!
Don't waste the last drop of warmth, you
Skunks! Eat your soup!
If only I had lived
As placidly as a cow
But delivered the letter that was entrusted to me!

THE BLACK STRAW HATS (*turning toward her*);

Undecided see her sway
By the sudden light distracted.
It was human how you acted!
Human how you lost your way!

JOAN (*while the girls dress her once more in the uniform of the Black Straw Hats*):

The factories are humming again, I can hear them.
Another chance to shut them down has
Been missed.
Once again
The world is back on its old course, unchanged.
When there was a chance to change it
I wasn't there; when unimportant as I am

My help was needed, I was
Absent.

MAULER:

Man with his high-flown intention
Jibs at living in the dark
And his arrogant ascension
Up from monotonous
Everyday rottenness
To unattainable
Regions unnameable
Tends to overshoot the mark.

JOAN:

I spoke in all the marketplaces
Countless were my dreams, but I
Brought injury to the injured and
Was useful to the injurers.

THE BLACK STRAW HATS:

Where there's spirit without matter
All our projects fall down dead
And we never get ahead.

THE PACKERS:

All the same there's nothing better
Than when cash and spirit wed.

JOAN:

One thing I've learned, and dying
I will tell you:
It makes no sense to say there's something deep inside you that
Won't come out! Can you think of *any*thing
That has no consequences?
I, for instance, have done nothing.
For nothing, however good it looks, should be termed good unless it
Really helps, and nothing counted honourable but what
Irrevocably changes the world, which is in need of change.
I was just what the oppressors wanted!
Oh inconsequential goodness! Oh negligible virtue!
I changed nothing.
Soon to vanish fruitlessly from this world

I say to you:
Take care that when you leave the world
You have not merely been good, but are leaving
A better world!

GRAHAM: We'd best be careful and only let the sensible parts of her speeches go through. Don't forget, she has been in the stockyards.

JOAN:

For there is a gulf between top and bottom, wider
Than between the high Himalaya and the sea
And what goes on at the top
Is not known at the bottom
Nor on top what goes on at the bottom.
And top and bottom have two languages
And two standards of measurement.
Both bear human faces
But have ceased to know each other.

THE PACKERS AND STOCKBREEDERS (*very loudly, drowning out Joan's voice*):

Any structure that goes up
Needs a bottom and a top
Consequently every man
Has to stay where he began
Till Kingdom come
Doing what he's always done.
Interfere with rules like these
And you'll wreck our harmonies:
Bigger wheels need smaller cogs
(Sometimes known as underdogs).
So be careful how you call
Those un-deferential
Ever essential
Quite indefensible
Yet indispensable
Throwouts from the deepest pit of all!

JOAN:

Those at the bottom are kept at the bottom
So that those on top may stay on top.
And the baseness of those on top is beyond measure.

And even if they got better, it wouldn't
Help, for the system they have
Created is flawless:
Exploitation and disorder, bestial and therefore
Incomprehensible.

THE BLACK STRAW HATS (*to Joan*):
Hold your tongue. Be good! Be wise!

THE PACKERS:
Those who hover in mid-air
Never will get anywhere.
Step on others if you'd rise
Then you'll have support enough.
Reaching up means treading down.

MAULER:
Those who act, alas, can wound.

THE BLACK STRAW HATS:
Look out for your bloody shoe –

THE PACKERS:
But don't try to take it off!
It will have to see you through.

THE BLACK STRAW HATS:
Aim forever at the skies
And repent of what you do.

THE PACKERS:
Do what you please!

THE BLACK STRAW HATS:
But always do
It with a guilty conscience
For as a spectator
And self-underrater
You *do* have a conscience.
Selling and buying
Ye merchants of meat
Don't forget the extensible
Greater than great
Quite indispensable
(Especially when your sale is fraudulent)
Eternal, undying
Word of God.

JOAN:

So anyone down here who says there's a God
And that even if no one can see Him
He can, invisibly, help us all the same
Should have his head bashed against the sidewalk
Until he croaks.

SLIFT: Hey, you people, shut that girl up! Say something, anything, but make it loud!

SNYDER: Joan Dark, aged twenty-five, contracted pneumonia in the Chicago stockyards in the service of God, warrior and martyr!

JOAN:

And those preachers who tell the people they can rise in spirit
Even if their bodies are stuck in the mud, they too should have their heads
Bashed against the sidewalk. The truth is that
Where force rules only force can help and
In the human world only humans can help.

ALL (*sing the first verse of the hymn to drown out Joan's words*):

Shower the rich with Thy treasure! Hosanna!
And virtue and leisure! Hosanna!
Pile high the rich man's plate! Hosanna!
Give him the city and state! Hosanna!
Give to the winner in full measure! Hosanna!

During these declamations loudspeakers announce disastrous news:

'POUND CRASHES! BANK OF ENGLAND CLOSES DOORS FOR THE FIRST TIME IN THREE HUNDRED YEARS!'

'EIGHT MILLION UNEMPLOYED IN THE USA!'

'FIVE YEAR PLAN SUCCEEDS!'

'BRAZIL DUMPS A WHOLE YEAR'S COFFEE CROP INTO THE OCEAN!'

'SIX MILLION UNEMPLOYED IN GERMANY!'

'THREE THOUSAND BANKS CRASH IN THE USA!'

'EVERY BANK AND STOCK EXCHANGE IN GERMANY CLOSED BY GOVERMENT ORDERS!'

'POLICE BATTLE UNEMPLOYED OUTSIDE HENRY FORD'S DETROIT FACTORY!'

'THE MATCH TRUST, THE BIGGEST TRUST IN EUROPE, FAILS!'

'FIVE YEAR PLAN COMPLETED IN FOUR YEARS!'

Under the impact of the disastrous news, all those who are not at the moment engaged in declaiming shout wild insults at one another, such as: 'Lousy hog butchers, why'd you have to slaughter so much?' 'No-good stockbreeders, why couldn't you raise more livestock?' 'You stupid skinflints, why didn't you hire more workers and pay decent wages. Who'd you expect to eat our meat?' 'The middlemen are to blame for the high price of meat!' 'The grain profiteers are to blame for the high price of livestock!' 'It's all the fault of the railroads with their freight rates!' 'It's all the fault of the banks with their high rates of interest!' 'Who can pay such rents for cattle barns and grain elevators?' 'Why don't you reduce your output?' 'We have reduced our output, but you haven't!' 'It's all your fault!' 'Nothing will get any better until they string you up!' 'You should have gone to jail long ago!' 'How come you're still running around loose?'

ALL (*sing the second and third verses of the hymn. Joan can no longer be heard*):

Give all Thy blessings to Croesus, Hosanna!
Love him to pieces, Hosanna!
Temper Thy wrath, Hosanna!
Do not deprive him that hath, Hosanna!
Give him whatever he pleases, Hosanna!

Joan can be seen to stop speaking.

Help Thine own class which hath helped Thee, Hosanna!
Not stinting their spending, Hosanna!
Throw Hatred overboard, Hosanna!
Laugh with the laughers, reward, Hosanna!
Criminal greed with a happy ending, Hosanna!

During the last verse the girls have tried to spoon some soup into Joan. Twice she has pushed the dish away. The third time she grabs it, holds it up and pours it out. Then she collapses and falls back into the girls' arms, mortally stricken, without sign of life. Snyder and Mauler go over to her.

MAULER: Give her the flag!

The flag is given to her. It falls out of her hands.

SNYDER: Joan Dark, aged twenty-five, died of pneumonia in the stockyards, in the service of God, warrior and martyr.

MAULER:

When purity
Unmarred and whole
And loving kindness beckoned
They shook vile men like you and me
Arousing in our hearts a second
And better soul!

All stand for a long while, speechless with emotion. At a sign from Snyder all the flags are lowered over her until she is entirely covered. The scene is suffused with a rosy glow.

THE PACKERS AND STOCKBREEDERS:

Mankind's inbuilt aspiration
From its primal childhood years
Is to win its soul a station
In the top celestial sphers.
While the stars of God's creation
Draw him to a higher level
Still his flesh must seek the devil
Dangling in the void downstairs.

MAULER:

A razor-sharp dichotomy
Cutting deep into my breast
Fashions two souls from my soul.
Though do-gooding suits me best
Meanwhile business interest
Also plays a certain role
Unconsciously.

ALL:

Man, two warring souls reside
Deep inside you.
No use trying to decide
For you can't help having two.
With your other self contending

Cleaving, clawing, splitting, rending
Keep the good and keep the evil
Keep the god and keep the devil
In a conflict never-ending!

Notes and Variants

LINDBERGH'S FLIGHT

Texts by Brecht, Hindemith and the organisers

FROM A LETTER TO ERNST HARDT

I've been thinking about the radio broadcast of *Lindbergh's Flight*, especially the planned public rehearsal. It could be used for an experiment, a way of showing, at least visually, how listener participation in the art of radio could be made possible. (I regard such participation as necessary if the radio play is to become an 'art'.)

I suggest the following little stage set for this demonstration:

The enclosed statement of principles concerning the use of radio is projected on a large canvas. This projection remains in place during the whole play. On one side of the stage (with the screen behind them) are the broadcasting apparatus, the singers, musicians, speakers, etc.; on the other side, screened off so as to suggest a room, a man sits at a desk in his shirt sleeves with a musical score and hums, plays and sings the part of Lindbergh. *This is the listener.* Since quite a few specialists will be present, it will probably be necessary to have on one side a sign saying 'The Radio' and on the other a sign saying 'Listener'. Before the thing starts, I should like to ask you, dear Herr Hardt, to say a few words about this experiment and the theory behind it, a statement of which I enclose and which we shall have an opportunity to discuss. This is a bother for you, but I know of no one else who could do it.

P.S. Enclosed also the complete manuscript.

The new parts are not set to music, they are just recited. The speaker of Lindbergh's part makes a caesura at the end of each line!

[From *Letters 1913–1956*, no. 148, thought to date from July 1929. Hardt was the former Intendant of the Cologne Schauspielhaus, and had worked with both Weill and Brecht. He became the first head of the West German Radio (Cologne) in July 1927. He would be removed by the Nazis in 1933.]

MUSIC FOR RADIO

Among the tasks of the radio one of the most extensive is its devotion to present-day musical creativity. The German Radio goes still further. For some time it has been actively involved in contemporary production, as animator and patron of a branch of literature especially intended for broadcasting. In addition to existing musical works of art that were created under different conditions it proposes to provide original music for radio.

Whereas up to now commissions have been given to individual composers, German Radio's cooperation with Deutsche Kammermusik Baden-Baden appeals 'to one and all' for the creation of specific radio music.

The task set was the creation of a musical work of art tailored to the present state of radio technology and the acoustic limitations of the microphone. This art can be acquired by observation and experience, and is not so difficult as meeting the other requirement of a work designed specifically for the radio: namely creating music stylistically suited to the medium. Radio music does not address itself to a particular stratum of society, but to humanity at large; it includes listeners whose lives owe their first experience of spiritual and artistic values to the radio. The formal and stylistic demands that have to be placed on any radio music will be so exhaustively handled by experts in the days to follow that there is no call for us to go into them further.

What we are presenting is experiments ('Versuche'), experiments that can by no means cover all the significant possibilities of this time – experiments that will limit themselves to the use of today's compositional and instrumental techniques to create a clear-sounding music suited to the radio.

[The programme for the 'First performance of original music for radio' then followed, with the names of the participants as follows:]

1. 'Lindbergh's Flight', by Brecht – Hindemith – Weill
   Lindbergh – Josef Witt
   'The Fogbank' and 'The City of New York' – Johannes Willy
   'The Snowstorm' – Oskar Kálmán
   'Sleep' – Betty Mergler
   Chorus – Hugo Holle's Madrigal Society
   Orchestra – Frankfurt Radio Orchestra
   Conductor – Hermann Scherchen
   Producer – Ernst Hardt

[Cited in Rudolf Stephan's introduction to Paul Hindemith's *Sämtliche Werke*, vol. 1,6 (Schott, Mainz, 1982).]

TO BE PROJECTED

In obedience to the principle that the State shall be rich and man shall be poor, that the State shall be obliged to have many possibilities and man shall be allowed to have few possibilities, where music is concerned the State shall furnish whatever needs special study, special apparatus and special abilities; the individual however shall learn all that is needed for enjoyment. The enjoyment of music demands that there should be no possibility of distraction. Free-roaming feelings aroused by music, special inconsequential thoughts such as may be entertained when listening to music, physical exhaustion such as easily arises from merely listening to music are distractions from music and take away from its enjoyment. To avoid these distractions the thinking man shares in the music, thus obeying the principle that doing is better than feeling, by humming the missing parts and following the music with his eyes as printed, or joining others in singing aloud. Thus the State provides incomplete music but the individual completes it.

[From an early typescript cited by Reiner Steinweg in *Brechts Modell der Lehrstücke* (Suhrkamp, 1976), p. 38. Sometimes headed 'Theory', this text is shown projected in the illustration in *Brecht on Theatre*, figure 9. A slightly modified version was included, along with this photograph, in *Versuche 1*, 'Explanations', cited below.]

INTRODUCTORY SPEECH

Most of you will have heard the radio broadcast of Brecht's *Lindbergh's Flight*, as a kind of acoustic depiction. The aim was to portray the experience of Lindbergh as a human being, with emphasis on what he felt. The listener's sensitivity was aroused, and the general effect was to subject him to an artistic suggestion that would give him illusions. Since this is only *one* possible way of realising such works, we want to hold a concert performance which will at the same time exemplify a different application such as would also mean a different use of the radio.

On one side of the stage you will see the position of the Radio, on the other side the listener. And you will see how Radio and listener together perform the work, playing into one another's hands, as it were, in such a way that the Radio delivers to the listener's home whatever the listener himself would have difficulty in producing but nevertheless needs in order to perform his own part. As for the listener, he takes the (central) leading part, i.e. that which is able to educate him.

In the case of *Lindbergh's Flight* he plays Lindbergh. The Radio supplies the voice of the opposing elements – the fog, the storms, sleep, the choruses of two continents encouraging the airman to take off and awaiting his arrival – but also various primitive noises to further the illusion, such as the sound of engine, wind and water.

You may retort that this experiment (tomorrow night) cannot be instantly realised (e.g. by broadcasting it from the German stations). To say nothing of the organisational problems – like sending musical scores to the listeners' homes, and (above all) launching a great propaganda campaign – or the paedagogical difficulties (the need to train broad masses of people in music).

Above all you will ask why should the listener make music just for himself, if nobody is going to listen to him. Well, he can be assured of the lift that a man will get from singing the Lindbergh part, and identifying himself with a tough character who battles to achieve his end. (To tell the truth, this is not how Brecht himself sees it. His theorising does *not* lead him to take the slightest interest in the listener's emotional life.) At the same time Brecht would reject any involvement for enjoyment's sake, because in this case [a qualification added by Brecht] it is a matter of paedagogy. So his answer to the question of what compels anyone to join in and get educated is: simply, the State.

To get some idea of the paedagogical value of such an artistic exercise from the State's point of view, try to imagine the boys' schools joining with the Radio to perform a work like this. Thousands of young people would be brought in their classrooms to adopt that heroic attitude which this work shows Lindbergh adopting in his flight.

Of course our little demonstration cannot be other than incomplete, since we are forced to make use of yesterday's performance without further rehearsal; that is to say, a performance which was not conceived for this new objective. Brecht may call for essential changes at certain points.

[Cited by Reiner Steinweg in *Brechts Modell der Lehrstücke* (Suhrkamp, 1976) from TS in the Brecht Archive. Steinweg suggests that it may have been dictated by Brecht as material for Ernst Hardt's talk to the audience at the performance on 28 July. Alternatively it may have been written by Hardt himself.]

NOTE TO THE TEXT

The first of the *Versuche*, *Lindbergh's Flight*, is a radio Lehrstück for boys and girls. It is not an account of a flight across the Atlantic, but a paedagogical operation. At the same time it is a hitherto untested application of the radio: not the most important by a long way, but one of a series of experiments ('Versuche') in which a piece of imaginative writing is used as an exercise.

The photograph is reproduced so as to stimulate new applications of this kind.

[From Brecht: *Versuche 1*, 1930, introducing the text with his additions and the Explanatory Notes which follow. By then the play had been revised so as to replace the hero Lindbergh by 'The Lindberghs', plural, a collective personality.]

EXPLANATORY NOTES

The Lindberghs' Flight *for instruction, not for pleasure. The Lindberghs' Flight* is valueless unless learned from. It has no value as art which would justify any performance not intended for learning. It is an *object of instruction* and falls into two parts. The first part (songs of the elements, choruses, sounds of water and motors, etc.) is meant to help the exercise, i.e. introduce it and interrupt it – which is best done by an apparatus. The other, *paedagogical* part (the Flier's part) is the text for the exercise: the participant listens to the one part and speaks the other. In this way a collaboration develops between participant and apparatus, in which expression is more important than accuracy. The text is to be spoken and sung mechanically; a break must be made at the end of each line of verse; the part listened to is to be mechanically followed.[. . .]

The radio not to be served but to be changed. The Lindberghs' Flight is not intended to be of use to the present-day radio but to alter it. The increasing concentration of mechanical means and the increasingly specialised training – tendencies that should be accelerated – call for a kind of resistance by the listener, and for his mobilisation and redrafting as a producer.

The Baden-Baden radio experiment. The employment of *The Lindberghs' Flight* and the use of radio in its changed form was shown by a demonstration at the Baden-Baden music festival of 1929. On the left of the platform the radio orchestra was placed with its apparatus and singers, on the right the listener, who performed the Flier's part, i.e. the paedagogical part, with a score in front of him. He read the sections to be spoken without identifying his own feelings with those contained in the text, pausing at the end of each line; in other words, in the spirit of an *exercise*. At the back of the platform stood the theory being demonstrated in this way.

Why can't The Lindberghs' Flight ***be used as an object of instruction and the radio be changed?*** This exercise is an aid to discipline, which is the basis of freedom. The individual will reach spontaneously for a means to pleasure, but not for an object of instruction that offers him neither profit nor social advantages. Such exercises only serve the individual in so far as they serve the State, and they only serve a State that wishes to serve all men equally. Thus *The Lindberghs' Flight* has no aesthetic and no revolutionary value independently of its application, and only the State can organise this. Its proper application, however, makes it so 'revolutionary' that the present-day State has no interest in sponsoring such exercises.

Here is an example of the effect of this application on the text: the figure of a public hero in *The Lindberghs' Flight* might be used to induce the listener at a *concert* to identify himself with the hero and thus cut himself off from the masses. In a concert performance (consequently a false one) at least the Flier's part must be sung by a *chorus* if the sense of the entire work is not to be ruined. Only *concerted I – singing* (I am so-and-so, I am starting forth, I am not tired, etc.) can save something of the paedagogical effect.

> [From *Versuche 1*, 1930, as published in *Brecht on Theatre*, but omitting the second paragraph, a revised version of the text 'To be projected' (given above). Signed 'Brecht. Suhrkamp' – Peter Suhrkamp being a former progressive schoolmaster who was now an editor for Kiepenheuer, Brecht's publishers. A draft cited by Steinweg in *Brechts Modell der Lehrstücke* (item 49) suggests that Elisabeth Hauptmann also contributed, writing for instance that 'lindbergh's flight was performed by the radio in the framework of the baden-baden music festival 1929 as a work about the glorification of the airman lindbergh whose sheer artistic merit justifies its performance. the following day brecht demonstrated what he considered to be the right way to use such a play *and also the radio*. here he did not cater for the listener's wish for undisturbed musical appreciation, but would frequently interrupt the performance . . .'.]

TO THE SOUTH GERMAN RADIO, STUTTGART, 1950

Gentlemen,

If you wish to broadcast *Lindbergh's Flight* as part of a historical survey, I must ask you to add a prologue and to make a few slight changes in the text. Lindbergh is known to have had close ties with the Nazis; his enthusiastic report on the unconquerable German air force had a paralysing effect in several countries. L also played a sinister role as a fascist in the USA. The title of my radio play must therefore be changed to *The Ocean Flight*, the prologue must be spoken and the name of Lindbergh expunged.

1) in 1 (Appeal to all) 'Captain Lindbergh's Ocean Flight' is replaced by 'The First Flight Across the Ocean'

2) in 3 (Introduction of the Flier, The Take-off) 'My name is Charles Lindbergh' is replaced by 'My name doesn't matter'

3) in 10 (All through the flight the people said . . .) 'of Captain Lindbergh will succeed' is replaced by 'of Captain So-and-so will succeed'

4) in 16 (Arrival of the Flier . . .) 'I am Lindbergh. Please carry me' is replaced by 'I am So-and-so. Please carry me.'

If this version is acceptable to you, I have no objection to your broadcasting the play. The changes may detract slightly from the poetry, but the removal of the name will be instructive.

N.B. If the titles are read, it must always be 'The Flier' [or 'The Airman'].

[From *Letters 1913–1956*, no. 626, dated 2 January 1950. This radio station had asked on 19 December 1949 for permission to broadcast the work. The new Prologue follows below.]

PROLOGUE, TO BE SPOKEN BEFORE BROADCASTING 'THE OCEAN FLIGHT'

You are about to hear
A report of the first ocean flight
In May 1927. Achieved by a
Young man. He conquered
Storm, ice and the voracious water. And yet
His name must be blotted out, for
He who found his way across the trackless waters
Was lost in the mire of our cities. Storm and ice
Could not defeat him, but his fellow-man
Defeated him. Ten years
Of fame and riches, and the wretch
Showed Hitler's butchers how to fly
With deadly bombs. Therefore
Let his name be blotted out. You, though
Be warned: neither courage nor knowledge
Of engines and charts can promote society's enemy
To the rank of a hero.

[From the Suhrkamp-Verlag republication of *Versuche 1–12*, 1959, in which the changes are made in accordance with Brecht's letter. The current Berlin and Frankfurt edition (1988), however, follows the 1930 *Versuche* text and only cites the changes in its notes, along with this prologue. In the view of the Brecht Estate they remain mandatory for performance; in that of the Kurt Weill Foundation 'Kurt Weill's music may only be performed in the original version without any alteration or cuts'.]

Editorial Notes

Brecht's text appears to have been written in stages, starting at the latest in January 1929, during the Berlin run of *The Threepenny Opera*. The playwright was in Cologne on the 10th and 11th of that month, for a broadcast discussion under the direction of Ernst Hardt; this was unrelated to the theme and form of the new work, though he and Hardt may well have talked about it then. The first six scenes (nos. 1–6) were ready in time to appear in the magazine *Uhu* in mid-April, under the title 'Lindbergh. A radio play for the Baden-Baden Festival, with a score by Kurt Weill'. Weill however was under considerable work pressure, and this is presumably why Hindemith, the moving spirit of these festivals, composed nearly half the work as originally performed, notably (in our numbering) scenes 5 (fog), half 6 (snowstorm), 7 (sleep), 12 (the French press), 15 (le Bourget) and 17 (last scene). The rest of this first performed version was composed by Weill, viz. 1–4, the second half of 6, 10 (the American press), 13 (the engine), and 14 (nearing Scotland). Three scenes were without music: 9 (water), 11 (thoughts) and 16 (arrival), which were read aloud. The title was now *Lindbergh's Flight. Radio Play by Bertolt Brecht. Music by Paul Hindemith and Kurt Weill*. The word 'Lehrstück' was not used.

The orchestral forces used by the two composers were the same throughout. Weill, however, was not happy with Hindemith's settings, and during the following October he wrote his own versions of the Hindemith numbers, adding music to the two silent or spoken numbers (11 and 16) and rescoring the whole work for a larger orchestra. This had its première at the Kroll Opera in Berlin on 5 December under Klemperer, and was published in 1930 as *Lindbergh's Flight. Words by Brecht. Music by* KURT WEILL. An English translation was made by the American composer George Antheil.

Late in 1930 Brecht's text was published under his name alone as the first of his new grey paperbound series of *Versuche* (or Experiments), along with three pages of his apothegmatic 'Keuner Stories' and fragments of his unfinished play *Fatzer*. By then he had decided to make various changes which, while they made little difference to the individual numbers as set by Weill, introduced two new numbers – 2 (the American press) and 8 (ideology) – and altered the thrust of the work so as to play down the heroism of the individual and emphasise the contribution of his helpers. Accordingly Lindbergh throughout became 'the Lindberghs', to be represented by more than one voice, still however speaking as 'I'. The numbering was also altered after the first seven scenes, the new, spoken, 'ideology' coming in as number 8 and 'water' as number 9, so that the previous number 8 (the press on Lindbergh's luck) becomes 10, and so on to the end of the work. Reflecting Brecht's awareness of the whole new genre, the title was further changed to *Lindbergh's Flight (A radio 'Lehrstück' for boys and girls)*, which relates it to the other works in the present volume. At the end were the names of the three collaborators: Brecht Hauptmann Weill.

We have taken the present text, as given in the Berlin and Frankfurt (1988) edition of Brecht's plays, and made a typographic distinction between that part of it which constitutes the work as set by Weill (and fits the music), and Brecht's subsequent additions, which are not sung and are in some cases only one or two lines long. The Weill/Hindemith version (which cannot be publicly performed for copyright reasons) is textually very close to the 1930 Weill score.

Following Brecht's letter to the South German Radio some twenty years later, some editions of the text appeared under the title *The Ocean Flight*, omitting all mention of Lindbergh's name. Thus 'The Fliers' appear and announce 'My name is irrelevant' or (in 16) 'I am So-and-so'. The consequent changes are most clearly conveyed in the 1959 Suhrkamp reissue of *Versuche 1–12*. Brecht's reason for making them is given in the new prologue appended to his letter and printed on p. 356 of that volume. While understandable at that time, they do not improve the work.

THE BADEN-BADEN LESSON ON CONSENT

Texts by Brecht and Hindemith

ABOUT THE 'LEHRSTÜCK'

The 'Lehrstück', product of various theories of a musical, dramatic and political nature aiming at the collective practice of the arts, is performed for the self-orientation of the authors and of those actively participating, and is not meant to be an experience for all and sundry. It is not even finished. The audience, therefore, *inasmuch as it is not involved in the experiment*, would fulfil the role not so much of a recipient as of a mere bystander.

[From the programme of the Deutsche Kammermusik, Baden-Baden, 1929, reprinted by Reiner Steinweg, 1976. At that point the *Badener Lehrstück* was called simply *lehrstück*, as in Hindemith's 1929 piano score. As yet that term was not applied to *Lindbergh's Flight*.]

MUSIC FOR AMATEURS

In our concern to draw the attention of the creative artist to the demands of our time and the musical requirements of the various strata of our population, we have decided to devote an evening to compositions for the amateur, ranging from chamber-scale works to community music involving singers and intended for large groups of performers. This is a kind of music intended not so much to be immediately effective in the concert hall as to take account of the demands of the players and singers themselves. The 'Lehrstück' is intended to be a community play on the same plane as such community music.

[From an article signed by the Artistic Directors – i.e. Heinrich Burkhard, Josef Haas and Hindemith himself – in the same programme, reproduced by Rudolf Stephan in Hindemith's *Sämtliche Werke*, vol. 1,6 (Schott, Mainz, 1982), p. xiii.]

PROGRAMME OF THE PREMIÈRE

Sunday 28 July
20.00 hrs, City Hall, Leopoldstrasse 18

Lehrstück

with solo singers, small and large chorus, amateur orchestra, brass band, spoken and acted episodes and a film interlude

by Brecht-Hindemith

Male Voice 1 – Josef Witt

Male Voice 2 – Oskar Kálmán

Three clowns – Theo Lingen, Karl Paulsen, Benno Carlé

Small chorus – Hugo Holle's madrigal singers

General chorus

Orchestra – amateurs

Brass band – the Lichtental Band

Film *Dance of Death* by Valeska Gert (cameraman: Karl Koch)

Conductors – Alfons Dressel, Ernst Wolff

Director – Bert Brecht

Costumes – Heinz Porep

[Source as for 'Music for Amateurs' above.]

INTRODUCTION TO HINDEMITH'S PIANO SCORE

For the performance of this work the requirements are:

Male Voice 1 (tenor) – taking the part of the crashed airman.

Male Voice 2 (baritone or bass) – can be a member of the chorus.

Speaker (male or female).

Chorus – numbers according to the size of the room in which the performance takes place.

Orchestra – size and composition at the director's discretion. The purposely vague division of the score into high, middle and low voices enables the conductor to allocate them according to the wishes and capabilities of the performers and the limitations of the room. The high voices can be doubled at the octave above, the low voices at the octave below. In the use of brass instruments caution is advised; they should be used mainly in the loud passages and can double the voice parts in accompanied choruses. The layout of the score is not meant to be followed exactly; it has been presented in simplified form so that it can also be used as a piano score.

Offstage orchestra – designed for brass instruments: 2 trumpets, 2 Flügelhorns, 2 (tenor) horns, 2 trombones, 1 bass trombone. These can be extended or replaced by waldhorn, saxophone and euphonium; or single-woodwind instruments would be permissible. The parts have been written for the nine named instruments. For other instruments the parts may be transposed as necessary.

Dancer (male or female).
Three clowns.
Various singers (male and female) in the crowd.
The Crowd.

Positioning
[Hindemith here gives the disposition as at the beginning of Brecht's text, but with 'Male Voice 1' – i.e. the Airman – in place of the later 'The singers of the Airmen's or Mechanics' parts'.]

Performance
The work is not designed for theatre or concert performances of the kind where specific persons entertain or instruct an audience with their own productions. The audience is an active partner in the performance. It sings the passages scored for the Crowd. Voices in the Crowd have previously been rehearsed in their parts and sing these to the Crowd under the direction of the chorus master. The passages are then repeated by the Crowd (i.e. audience). For performances using a relatively small group the preliminary singing of the passages in this way should be adequate. For a larger gathering it would be advisable to use a projector, showing the words and notes on a screen. In the same way the titles and captions of the various sections of the work can be projected. It is very possible that the integration of soloists, chorus and crowd will not be immediately achieved to everyone's satisfaction. In communal artistic achievements of this sort a flawless rendering of each piece can never be expected. For that reason, adequate preparation is to be preferred to a straight run-through.

Since the only purpose of the Lehrstück is to bring everyone present into the performance of a work and not directly to arouse artistic impressions in others, the form of the piece should be adapted as far as possible to the actual aim. The order in the score should consequently be regarded as a suggestion rather than a command. Cuts, additions and changes in the running order are permissible. Whole musical numbers can be omitted, as well as the dance, and the clowns' scene can be shortened or left out entirely. Other musical pieces, scenes, dances or readings can be introduced, if these are felt to be necessary and not to clash in style with the rest. Simpler exercises could consist of performing the Examination alone, or the beginning and Examination together. Other parts could equally well be practised on their own. It is left to the person in charge of the exercise and to the group of performers themselves to find the most practical form for their own purposes.

The choral and orchestral parts are so simple to perform that almost any amateur group can master them, provided they go about it seriously. Two trained singers for the solo parts should be easy enough to find anywhere. Where no dancers or actors are available, the relevant scenes, as stated above, should be left out.

No costumes or stage settings should be used in a performance of the work. The only exceptions to this rule might be the clowns' scene and the dance.

[From Hindemith: *lehrstück* piano score (Schott, Mainz, 1929), translated by Geoffrey Skelton. 'The Examination' is scene 8 (7) in our text, the 'clown scene' scene 3 (Third Inquiry) (6); the Dance (4) had no text and was replaced by 6. To judge from the following Note, it is extremely unlikely that the above Introduction was agreed with Brecht.]

NOTE

Without going any further into the particular rules of the Lehrstück genre (which will be done in a detailed 'Theory of Paedagogics') I must at least briefly correct the erroneous indications of the composer Hindemith (in the piano score of the *Lehrstück*, which is based on the first, wholly incomplete version of the text. Hindemith suggests:

[Brecht then cites the second paragraph under the heading 'Performance' in Hindemith's Introduction above, and continues:]

This misunderstanding is attributable probably to my own readiness to provide an incomplete and easily misread fragment of text for purely experimental purposes, as was the case with the version performed at Baden-Baden, with the result that the only conceivable educational purpose was one of purely musical form. But of course the Baden-Baden production was intended just for self-orientation, as a one-off. It is clear that the educational value of such a musical exercise on a 'meditative text that corresponded to the imagination of the director' was far too slight. Even if it was expected that the individual was going 'to commit himself in some way', or that certain intellectually formal correspondences would emerge, such insipid and artificial harmony could never for one moment provide a really broad and energetic basis from which to oppose those collectivities whose very different kind of force is now tearing the people of our time apart.

[From *Versuche 2*, 1930. Brecht's revised text of the play, as printed in that publication, differs considerably from the 1929 version as set by Hindemith. See the Editorial Notes that follow.]

NOTE TO THE TEXT PRINTED IN 'VERSUCHE 2'

Experiment number seven, ***The Baden-Baden 'Lehrstück'***, is a further essay in the Lehrstück genre following ***Lindbergh's Flight***. On its completion the piece turns out to be unfinished: too much importance is given to death in relation to its doubtless rather slight utility. The work is printed here because, when all is said and done, its production creates a collective apparatus. For some parts of it there is a musical score by Paul Hindemith.

[From *Versuche 2*, as above.]

Editorial Notes

It was on 10 March 1929, when Brecht's writing of *Lindbergh's Flight* was already under way, that Hindemith told his publishers he was planning a 'People's Oratorio' for Baden-Baden with Brecht. By 25 June, said his wife, it was nearly finished. Brecht however still considered the result to be a fragment, as he said in his programme note at the time, and he seemed all along to have in mind the completion of the work independently of Hindemith's share in it, possibly with some other composer or with no music at all. This was agreed between the two men and stipulated after the Festival in Brecht's correspondence with Schott the music publishers, who were, however, anxious to bring Hindemith's setting out as it stood while there was some interest in further performances. After giving Brecht a month in which to object, Hindemith accordingly sent off score and text, along with his own Introduction as above.

As with the companion piece *Lindbergh's Flight*, Brecht would soon be making radical changes both in the thrust of what he had written and in the nature of the two works, which would appear in his new *Versuche* series during the following year as linked examples of a new genre, the teaching play or 'Lehrstück'. Unclear as it still is who actually originated that term, it came to dominate Brecht's theoretical thinking in the last phase of the Weimar Republic. At the same time his revisions demythologised both his airmen-heroes by making them collective figures who could stand also for the workers and helpers in their exploit, which was no longer to conquer 'the unattainable' but to reach 'the not-yet-attained'. Finally he introduced a new concept which, again, would recur in the works that followed. This was the idea of 'Einverständnis' – of Acquiescence, Agreement or Consent – a kind of understanding-cum-acceptance of the extreme pains and penalties of living in our age such as we find in modern examples of stoic self-sacrifice.

During the months following the Baden-Baden performances these affected both works. The major difference however was that, whereas Weill felt that he had been unable to finish composing the 'Radio Play', and wanted to complete it as originally intended, Hindemith was content to leave the 'Lehrstück' as it was, concluding with the Crowd's verdict in scene 8 (7) of 'The Examination', on the line 'Now is his smallest dimension attained'.

It is not clear if Brecht ever sent Hindemith his four new numbers or his many other changes of order and wording, but clearly the composer had no wish to set them, or to limit the considerable – almost aleatory – freedom given to director and performers in his Introduction to the score. What Brecht particularly objected to there was the suggestion that the clown scene and the filmed 'dance of death' by Valeska Gert might be omitted, and he reacted by insisting that future performances must be agreed by himself as well as the composer. In the event Schott would inform him of the dozen or so subsequent applications to perform the work before the Nazis took power, giving him each time a month in which to make any objection. This he seems not to have done. And any further chance of collaboration between the two men was destroyed when Hindemith's next 'Neue Musik' Festival in 1930 rejected Brecht's new 'Lehrstück' with Hanns Eisler for political reasons.

* * *

Our aim in the present volume has been to start with a singable translation of the 1929 text, add the extra passages written by Brecht during the following months (but not composed) and put the ensuing whole in the scene order of volume 3 (1988) in today's current Berlin and Frankfurt edition. The main changes undergone by our text can be seen from our typographic differentiation between the original work and the later additions, which follows the same principle as that for *Lindbergh's Flight*, along with the numbering of the scenes: 1929 numbers in brackets, 1930 (*Versuche* and subsequent) numbers without brackets.

Broadly speaking, Brecht moved the clown scene forward from the penultimate position to the middle of scene 3, to form the third 'Inquiry' (as to whether men help one another), switching the previous scene 3 ('The Chorus speaks to the Crashed Airman') to take the clown scene's place and become scene 10. The 'Dance of Death' film was dropped, to be replaced as second 'Inquiry' by the present display of photographs, while that Inquiry's conclusion – from 'I cannot die' to 'For the way of truth is easy' – became redistributed between a repeat display of photographs (scene 6) and the opening of 'Instruction' (scene 7). Scenes 4 and 5 were new, introducing the concept of necessary force, as were the Airman's twelve closing lines to 8, following the end of the Hindemith version. Scenes 9 and the final 11 ('Agreement' – or 'Einverständnis') were also new. No option was given to cut any scene.

In lieu of Male Voice 1 there were now to be four performers sharing what had been the Airman's part, while Male Voice 2 continued to act as 'The Leader of the [Trained] Chorus'. The Chorus of the Hindemith score, namely, was now described throughout as 'Der gelernte Chor': the trained or rehearsed chorus, as opposed to the Crowd (i.e. the participating audience). We have not followed this added description. As for the four performers, they speak sometimes as one man, using 'we', the first person plural, where the original Airman spoke of 'I'. From scene 5 on, however, they divide into two parts: the Crashed Airman and the Three Crashed Mechanics, of whom only the Airman, it seems, is killed. This entails substituting plural for singular in those parts set by Hindemith, as follows:

Scene 2: *we, our, us* for *I, my, me*
they, them for *he, him*
four men for *a man*
They're for *he's*
Scene 3(1): *They are* for *he is*
Scene 7: *We* for *I*
Scene 8(1): *Airmen* for *Airman*
we for *I*
raised ourselves for *raised myself*
(2): *We, our, they* for *I, my, he*
were for *was*
(3): *we are, ones* for *I am, one*
they who have for *he who has*
(4): *us* for *me*
our fathers and mothers for *my father and mother*
(5): *we* for *he*
ourselves for *himself*
you have, you die for *he has, he dies*
your for *his*

HE SAID YES/HE SAID NO

Texts by Brecht, Waley, Weill, Hauptmann

NOTE TO THE TEXT

The school operas *He Said Yes* and *He Said No*, with music by Weill, are intended for schools. If possible the two little plays should always be performed together.

[From Brecht: *Versuche 4*, 1931, introducing the two texts – the former in his revised version. Weill wrote *no* music for the latter. A footnote to the title of *He Said Yes* says 'After the Japanese play *Taniko* in Arthur Waley's English version.]

NOTE ON 'TANIKO' AND IKENIYE'

Both of these plays deal with the ruthless exactions of religion; in each the first part lends itself better to translation than the second. *Taniko* is still played; but *Ikeniye* [. . .] has probably not been staged for many centuries.

The pilgrims of *Taniko* are Yamabushi, 'mountaineers' [. . .]. They called themselves Shugenja, 'portent-workers', and claimed to be the knight-errants of Buddhism. But their conduct seems to have differed little from that of the Sohei (armed monks) who poured down in hordes from Mount Hiyei to terrorise the inhabitants of the surrounding country. Someone in the *Genji Monogatari* is said to have 'collected a crowd of evil-looking Yamabushi, desperate, stick-at-nothing fellows'.

Ikeniye, the title of the second play, means 'Pool Sacrifice', but also 'Living Sacrifice', i.e. human sacrifice.

[From Arthur Waley: *The Nō Plays of Japan* (Allen and Unwin, London, 1921), p. 229. The first of these was by Zenchiku, the second by his father-in-law Seami.]

FROM AN INTERVIEW WITH ELISABETH HAUPTMANN

Q: So how did Waley lead on to *He Said Yes*?

EH: I translated a number of Nō plays into German on the basis of Waley's adaptations. These translations were not meant for publication. I am against translating via an intermediate language. But not long afterwards I learned from some Japanese students who translated some Nōplays for me along with parts of Seami's *Kvadensho* that Waley's translations, while very beautiful, took considerable liberties. I did this work purely for fun, primarily so as to be able to discuss these fascinating matters with one or two friends. The editor of a theatre magazine persuaded me to let him publish *Taniko or The Valley-Hurling*. I subsequently wrote a radio feature on the life and work of Seami, which was broadcast by Berlin Radio in 1931.

[From an interview of 1966, reproduced in Hauptmann's *Julia ohne Romeo* (Berlin, 1977). The magazine was the Essen theatre publication *Der Scheinwerfer*, edited by Hannes Küpper.]

FROM AN INTERVIEW WITH KURT WEILL

Q: . . . Mr Weill, may I ask how you arrived at that kind of simple, popular music.
KW: I think I share my aim of writing such music with a good number of present-day composers. We no longer want music to be a private, backroom affair but are seeking new and wider outlets. In the *Threepenny Opera* I already tried to do something of the sort, with a fair measure of success. [. . .] In *Lindbergh's Flight* Bert Brecht and I had the schools in mind for the first time. I am hoping to develop this direction further in my latest play, the 'Lehrstück' *He Said Yes*.
Q: What is the formal structure of your latest work? Does it include self-contained forms?
KW: I am glad you have raised this point. In the 'Lehrstück' *He Said Yes* I no longer want to offer 'songs' so much as self-contained musical forms. In the process I want to take over whatever I hitherto found right, like what I once termed the gestic approach to music. The melody must give clear expression to the gest. It is clarity, not lack of clarity that has to prevail in all that the composer wishes to express. And [. . .] this 'Lehrstück' has to be a fully authentic work of art, not a secondary piece.
Q: [. . .] I greatly like the text, from the pedagogical point of view too. It is good that the obedience demanded of the schoolboy should be repeatedly emphasised. The text brings this out very well. Another pedagogically valuable point is the picture given of the teacher-schoolboy relationship. And a third attractive element in the text is its portrayal of the son's love for his mother.
KW: Incidentally, the motive of the medicine which the boy wants to

bring back to save his sick mother's life was first introduced by Brecht. I am particularly glad that you should have stressed the importance of obedience. This message of 'agreement' gives the Lehrstück its political impact – in an elevated sense, not of course in that of party politics.

[From 'Aktuelles Zwiegespräch über die Schuloper', prefacing the play's first publication in *Die Musikpflege*, April 1930, and reproduced by David Drew in *Kurt Weill Ausgewählte Schriften*, Suhrkamp, 1975. The interviewer was Dr Hans Fischer, editor of the *Zeitschrift für Schulmusik*. The Prussian Zentralinstitut für Erziehung und Unterricht would present the work in Berlin on June 24, after a broadcast performance the day before. For this première Kurt Drabek was the conductor, while Otto Hopf directed and also played the Teacher. The boy performers were drawn from various schools.]

WEILL ON HIS SCHOOL OPERA

I have arranged *He Said Yes* in such a way that each part (chorus, orchestra, solo voices) can be performed by schoolchilden, and I likewise imagine sets and costumes being designed by them too. The work is scored so as to take account of a school orchestra's possibilities: a basic orchestra of strings (without violas) and two pianos, then ad lib. three wind instruments (flute, clarinet, saxophone), percussion and plucked instruments. Not that I think the music for a school opera should be over-simplified, or that it needs to be particularly 'childish' and easy to sing along with. The music for a school opera definitely has to involve a long and careful period of study. For it is *precisely in such study that the practical value of a school opera consists*, and its performance is a good deal less important than the education which it gives the performers. In the first place, the character of such education is purely musical. But it has to be at least equally philosophical. Music's pedagogical effects may also consist in its leading the student by means of the study of music to some specific idea which makes a more vivid impression in its musical form and becomes more firmly rooted in him than if he had to read it in books. *For this reason the aim for any school play, over and above the pleasure of making music, has to be that of giving boys the chance to learn something.* The old Japanese play which we (that is, Brecht and I) chose as the text for our first school opera seemed to us well fitted for school use so far as its basic attitude went, but to lack any motivation for its events that might make it pedagogically applicable. We accordingly introduced the concept of 'agreement', and altered the story to correspond with this: instead of the boy being hurled willy-nilly into the valley, as in the old play, they first of all ask him, so that when he declares his consent he shows that he has learned to take full responsibility for a community or an idea with which he has chosen to associate himself.

[Extract from Weill's article 'Über meine Schuloper' in *Die Szene* (Berlin), August 1930, reproduced by David Drew in *Kurt Weill Ausgewählte Schriften*, Suhrkamp, 1975.]

FROM A REPORT OF DISCUSSIONS ABOUT 'HE SAID YES' AT THE KARL MARX SCHOOL, NEUKÖLLN

Subject of the discussion was a version of the play close to the Japanese original, where the expedition was a scientific one (which the Boy joins in order to get medicine and consultation for his Mother) and the killing of the Boy takes place in response to a traditional Great Custom. (The Boy gives his agreement to this.) The two versions printed in the *Versuche* were made in accordance with this report. Criticisms and suggestions in italics were taken into account.

> . . . The play is inappropriate for our school, because the Teacher is very cold-blooded and this might be thought to refer to it . . . Science is less important than a human life . . . The play stops: the Boy can't go on, he stays there waiting. Hunger overcomes him and he plunges voluntarily into the depths . . . There should be a legal footnote . . . Play stops; Boy taken along with great effort. On the way two of them slip and fall . . . *Put the Boy on a rope and take him along.*
>
> Form Upper 3a

> . . . We find the discrepancy between music and text in this play quite new. At the end, after the death of the Boy, another composer might well have a number of prolonged, ceremonious chords accompanying the Chorus. The result being to make this scene seem so shattering that one retains only it in one's head and remains vague about the others. Bertolt Brecht's cheerful approach avoids this. The music in his opera is consistently cheerful. When the Boy dies and the Chorus sing 'And he was dead' the music was strongly reminiscent of a contemporary dance. Brecht's light and cheerful approach gives us a very useful view of the opera, since it is never so gripping as to squeeze actual tears out of us, nor so reserved that one can say there are passages where one gets no view, but can only treat the opera as a whole . . . Unfortunately there is one place where the

text is not all that convincing. *The Boy is presented almost as a martyr, because he goes to his death voluntarily and without resistance.* One might almost think the Boy is obeying the wishes of his comrades, because they are also his own wishes, though he does not express them. How about having the Boy hesitate a bit? *In our view the opera would also be highly effective if the Boy started by hesitating a bit* . . . Generally we feel that this is one of the rare plays that schoolchildren can perform without straining . . .

. . . Either the student should fall ill too and the expedition turn back, despite the Boy's wish to be hurled down the cliff. Or else *they should try to get past the track*, and either the Boy or the whole lot should fall, so that nobody bears the guilt for the Boy's death . . .

W. Berg, form 4a, age 12

I am simply setting down what the pupils say. 'This opera is very sad.' 'It doesn't sound good.' 'In opera people are supposed to sing.' 'The arrangement of the sentences is odd, and the verse doesn't fit it.' 'I like the play a lot, but *the business with the Custom strikes me as wrong*.' 'It's just as well the sick boy is hurled down, or he'd suffer worse.' 'But that's murder.' 'I've been in the Alps where there were huts, and we always found something to eat there, every evening someone came who had pots and pans.' 'I don't understand that about the one who says Yes.' 'The point is, he says Yes without knowing about it, and it's the same with the Mother.' 'But apparently they picked him up and carried him, and I don't believe anyone can be carried.' 'Only as far as the precipice.' 'It's more a play for grown-ups.' 'We aren't Weeping Willies.' 'I think he should write more clearly.' 'That stuff with the chorus is for kids, I'd say.' 'I think he said Yes because he wanted his mother to get well, and if he'd said No the rest of them wouldn't even have got to the doctors.' 'What are they on about? It's not clear.' 'Once his mother hears of his death I'd say she'd get even more ill.' 'How are they going to hurl him down?' 'That's just cruel.' 'Suppose he's tough enough to survive it.' 'I'd say a young life was worth more than an old one.' '*It'd be better if he said I'll think it over*, then you hear the Boy talking to himself, and you'll understand his motives.'

B. Korsch, form 6b, age 10

. . . We had two suggestions that would rather alter the sense of the play. 1. Give the Boy malt extract (but where does one get it?); 2. Give the Boy a check-up beforehand.

Form 5a, age 11

. . . There was considerable support for the view that *the fate of him that said Yes is not portrayed in such a way that one sees its necessity. Why didn't the whole group turn back to save the stricken member instead of killing him?* . . . This led to the suggestion that the scene of the climb and the fall should be more strongly depicted in the hope of creating the essential understanding. *The mysticism that permeates the opera is a cause of discomfort* . . . *The story's motivation is not sufficiently clear (i.e. real).*

Group from Upper 1, age 18

. . . *The play could be used to show what damage is done by superstition.* It might be understandable in its own Japanese context, but here it is only for aesthetic connoisseurs.

M. Tautz, Lower 3a, age 14

. . . Most of the form feel that the play should definitely remain as it is. At most there should be an introductory note in the programme to convince the audience of the necessity of this brutal yet not unrealistic affair.

H. Zeschel, Lower 1b, age 17

. . . The group must act in solidarity to bring the inadequate invalid home . . . The rest of the group must on no account exert any moral pressure on the Boy to secure his agreement . . . *The question is that of testing whether the advantage secured is great enough to justify the Boy's sacrificing his life.*

Gerhard Krieger (Workers' Course), age 20

[From Brecht: *Schriften 4*, Berlin and Frankfurt edition, edited by Peter Kraft and others, Suhrkamp, Frankfurt, 1991. Brecht may also (as suggested by Ernest Borneman in his slightly hazy account in *Die Urszene*, S. Fischer, 1977) have consulted participants from other schools.]

Editorial Notes

The message of agreement

After Kurt Weill's death in 1950 his widow Lotte Lenya would suggest that it irked him to compose such severely didactic plays under Brecht's (by that time undesirable) influence, and that he needed 'sich auszumusizieren', to discharge the music in him, by composing operas or symphonic works instead. His remarks quoted above show that she was wrong. It was in the first place Weill who was drawn to Waley's text when Elisabeth Hauptmann translated it, and who wished to set it as a radio or school opera. And despite its unpretentious style and scale, he did not want it considered a 'Nebenwerk', a secondary work.

The changes made to Waley's version represent two stages in their shared conception of this highly successful piece (which had two or three hundred performances in Germany before Hitler came to power). First came the introduction of the notion of 'Einverständnis', Consent or Agreement – a combination of understanding and approval or acquiescence. Then there were the further alterations which Brecht made following the first (1930) production and its critical treatment by liberals like his old friend Frank Warschauer, who saw this supposed virtue as entailing mere obedience and conformism among the country's youth. These are the changes made in autumn 1930 before the play's appearance in the 1931 *Versuche*, as indicated in our translation and taken into account by Weill in his two musical additions.

But beside what we may call the Brecht/Weill changes there is the alternative text offered in *He Said No* – to which the composer was *not* a party, so that it can only be performed without his music and is wrongly termed a school opera. And finally, lying almost ignored beneath the original Waley text, there are Waley's annotations which Hauptmann did *not* translate: the first at the end of Act 1, the second at the end of the play. The former says: 'Here follows a long lyric passage describing their journey and ascent. The frequent occurrence of place-names and plays of word on such names makes it impossible to translate.' The second, following after 'And . . . flat stones they flung', reads:

> I have only summarized the last chorus. When the pilgrims reach the summit, they pray to their founder, En no Gyoja, and to the God

> Fudo that the boy may be restored to life. In answer to their prayer a Spirit appears carrying the boy in her arms. She lays him at the Priest's feet and vanishes again [. . .].

There is no mention of these in the *Versuche* edition of 1931 or in Weill's piano score (UE 8206). Only in Peter Szondi's 'Materialien' volume (Suhrkamp, 1968) is the Hauptmann translation followed by an unattributed footnote, to say, less ambiguously, that 'The ending of the Japanese original tells how the boy was awakened to a new life.'

From Hauptmann's translation to the double text

Szondi's useful publication also shows what the three collaborators had added to Hauptmann's translation to make the text of the first performances and piano score. In brief these changes were, taken scene by scene:

Act One

1 The chorus on 'consent' is new.

3 So is the term 'Forschungs-' (scientific), as applied to the expedition.

4 The Teacher's speech was originally in prose. The Boy's four lines following, with their reference to 'doctors in the town. . . , medicine and consultation', are new.

5 Similarly with their reiteration in the Teacher's speech. The Mother's speech was in prose. The four concluding lines of the scene are also new.

6 The four lines for the Teacher and the Mother (mentioning 'consent') are new.

Act Two

7 This whole chorus has been developed from the Boy's two lines at the end of 6.

8 Waley's 'Leader' and 'Pilgrim' have become the Three Students. 'Pilgrims' are now the Full Chorus. Substance of the scene is the same up to the '*Long pause*'. Then the three lines from 'Once past the hut' to 'one's to cross it' are new, as is the exchange from 'down to the valley?' to '*Boy sits down*'.

9 Up to 'tell him tenderly of this Great Custom' it is effectively Waley's text apart from the interpolated phrase 'Also he has sat down'. Thereafter the Three Students' intention to ask the Boy's agreement, and the Full Chorus's repetition of this are both added to Waley's text.

10 Is mainly new, apart from the Teacher's first two sentences, the Boy's response from 'I knew quite well' down to 'drove me on to join you', and the concluding Full Chorus, except for its opening mention of the jug. The crucial addition is where the Boy says 'Yes'. To which the Teacher adds 'He says yes to me' and the Three Students echo 'He says yes to us'.

To summarise these, we may say that the idea of 'Einverständnis' or agreement was inherent in the original play by Seami's son-in-law Zenchiku, where it is expressed by the Boy, on hearing of his unavoidable fate, saying 'I understand' (Waley p. 235, our scene 10). The collaborators sought to spell this out, starting with the new opening chorus and hoping to secularise the idea, but it remains rooted in a religious discipline, though certainly an un-Christian one. Doctors, medicine, the town beyond the mountains, the jug, are so many accessories to the original notion of praying for the sick mother: non-religious ways of motivating the Boy's understanding and reconciling it with what Brecht saw as 'the scientific age'.

This did not work. Not only critics like Warschauer, but also some of the schoolchildren for whom the play was intended objected to what Weill and Dr Fischer (above) saw as its stressing of 'the importance of obedience'. It was Warschauer who attacked this concept most strongly in his review for *Die Weltbühne* (8 July 1930), comparing it with the attitude of supporters of the First World War and accusing the work of

> subtly but very effectively embracing every nasty ingredient of reactionary thinking grounded in irrational authority.

The order of events

Brecht himself was not at the première, but among those who attended was one of the music teachers at the Kaiser-Friedrich Realgymnasium in the Neukölln (south central) district of Berlin – a progressive school then in the process of changing its (imperial) name to that of Karl-Marx-Schule. This was Paul Hermann, who then seems to have raised the possibility of performing the work with some of his senior students. His first discussions with them and his fellow-teachers revealed a mixture of approval and scepticism, notably (reports Albrecht Dümling in Dorothea Kolland's symposium *Rixdorfer Musen, Neinsager und Caprifischer*, Edition Hentrich, Berlin, 1990) with regard to the need for the Boy's self-sacrifice. Since Brecht himself appeared open to suggestions, Hermann that autumn brought a group of students round to the writer's flat to talk their problems over.

'At an early stage', writes Dümling, 'Brecht put forward the idea of *He Said No*: an alternative version to be performed along with *He Said Yes*, leaving the audience to decide the matter for itself. This would have been 'a similar pairing to that of *Lindbergh's Flight* and the *Baden-Baden Lesson on Consent* in 1929'. The students however wanted a clear-cut solution, and so 'a few weeks later [Brecht] came up with a third version of the play, which at once met with their approval' (see p. 128 of the cited article). This took into account a number of the points raised in further discussions held throughout the school following the autumn meeting, ranging from the views of ten-year-olds like Karl Korsch's daughter Barbara (whose mother was on the staff) to those of young adults of eighteen or twenty. A full report of these discussions was sent to Brecht by Hans Freese, the school's head of Arts, on 9 December. The selection which we print above was immediately given by him and Hauptmann to be published in the *Versuche* edition of 1931, where they constitute his only notes on the play.

The new version was publicly performed by the school on 18 May of that year; the conductor was Willi Linow, a senior student who had rehearsed under Kurt Weill; the director Heinz Kuckhahn, another student who would be an assistant to Brecht in 1948. *He Said No* was *not* then performed, despite the suggestion in the *Versuche* note, nor do we know of any performance before Hitler came to power two years later. Brecht's German editors, including Elisabeth Hautpmann in later years, all treat it as having been written after the new version, but the Dümling account is much more plausible. Otherwise why was it derived from the first *He Said Yes*, rather than the second? And why does it by-pass points emphasised in the school discussions?

During Brecht's lifetime it seems that *He Said No* was only once staged in tandem with *He Said Yes*. This was a studio performance by the Living Theater in New York in 1951. The first German production of both plays was in Düsseldorf in 1958.

THE DECISION

Texts by Brecht and Eisler

NOTE TO THE TEXT

The Decision, with music by Hanns Eisler, is an attempt to practise a particular attitude of intervention by means of a 'Lehrstück'.

[From Brecht: *Versuche 4*, 1931.]

OPEN LETTER TO THE ARTISTIC BOARD OF THE 'NEUE MUSIK', BERLIN, 1930: Heinrich Burkhard, Paul Hindemith, Georg Schuenemann

Berlin, 12 May 1930

You have refused to take responsibility for our 'Lehrstück' as agreed between us, and referred the matter to a 'Programme Committee' of unknown membership. You ask us to submit our text to this committee to dispel political reservations. (You add that this check is required for all works.) We have refused, for the following reasons:

If you wish to continue your very important performances aimed at opening up new applications of music, then you should on no account make yourselves financially dependent on persons or institutions that are out to forbid you a number of applications (possibly not the worst) on other than artistic grounds. Just as it is not your artistic task to criticise the police, so is it inadvisable for you to let the police of all people finance your artistic performances; you might then be having them prejudged by the police. There are some tasks for the new music that cannot be forbidden by the state, but cannot exactly be financed by it. Grateful as we should be if the police president does not forbid our works, we don't have to go on and call for a police band!

Apart from that, we have at last reached the position we always wanted; didn't we always call for amateur art? Haven't we long had our doubts of these huge institutions whose hands are tied by a hundred reservations?

We are cutting these important performances clear of all kinds of dependence, and allowing them to be realised by those they are meant for, who alone have a use for them: by workers' choruses, amateur dramatic groups, school choruses and school orchestras, in other words those people who neither can pay for art nor are paid for art, but just want to take part in it.

We hope you realise that as things are, your resignation from the artistic board of Neue Musik Berlin 1930 as a protest against all attempts at censorship would do more for new music than any staging of a further music festival in summer 1930.

(Signed) Bertolt Brecht. Hanns Eisler

In the event the festival was held and performance of *The Decision* was refused 'due to formal inadequacy of the text'.

[From Notes in *Versuche 4*, 1931. First published in the *Berliner Börsenkurier* on 13 May 1930 along with a response by the addressees to say that the work had *not* been rejected, as only the text had been sent them and the Programme Committee still had to see the music. Asked by the paper about this new body, they stated two days later that it had no role in the planning of the festival programmes, and they would permit no censorship by it. 'From what we have learnt of the text however, we must assume that the music takes a subordinate place. We have neither the right nor the obligation to use our events for the experimental staging of literary trends or intentions.' Their board, they said, 'bases its decisions on strictly artistic viewpoints, just as it did in Donaueschingen and Baden-Baden'. At this the paper commented that it was odd for a Programme Committee to have no influence on the programme. Brecht's letter 153 to Eisler from France a month or two later shows him calling this episode an 'Edelpleite', a splendid fiasco.]

NOTE TO THE AUDIENCE

The 'Lehrstück' *The Decision* is not a play in the normal sense. It is an event put on by a mass chorus and four players. In today's performance, which is meant to be more like a kind of demonstration, the role of the players is taken by four actors. But it can of course also be performed in a perfectly simple and primitive manner, and this is its primary aim.

Briefly the story is as follows: four Communist agitators are facing a Party inquiry, represented by the mass chorus. They have been conducting Communist propaganda in China, and in the course of this they had to shoot their youngest comrade. In order to convince the court of the need for their decision to shoot him, they show how the Young Comrade behaved in a number of different political situations. They show him as revolutionary in his feelings but inadequately disciplined and too reluctant to listen to his reason, so that in the end he became a real threat to the movement. The 'Lehrstück''s aim is to show incorrect political attitudes and thus to teach correct ones. The performance is meant to provoke discussion of the political usefulness of this type of event.

[Cited in Reiner Steinweg: *Die Massnahme. Kritische Ausgabe*, Suhrkamp, 1972, p. 237. Steinweg thought this was probably a programme note for the first performance on the night of 13 December 1930, but had so far been unable to locate a printed copy.]

REHEARSING 'THE DECISION'

The dramatic presentation has to be simple and sober; there is no need for special energy or particularly 'expressive' acting. The players simply have at any moment to show the attitude on the part of the four which one must know in order to understand and judge the situation. (The three agitators' text can be shared out.) Each of the four players must have at least one chance to show the attitude of the Young Comrade; hence each should play one of his principal scenes.

The performers (players and singers) have the task of teaching as they learn. As Germany has half a million worker-singers, what occurs in the process of singing is at least as important as what occurs in that of listening. However, no attempt to derive recipes for political action from *The Decision* should be made without knowing the ABC of dialectical materialism. Some of the ethical concepts occurring in the play are subject to Lenin's remark about morality: 'We base our morality on the interests of the class struggle of the proletariat!'

['Einübung der *Massnahme*', from Notes in *Versuche 4*, 1931.]

SOME TIPS FOR REHEARSAL OF 'THE DECISION'

1 First and foremost it is essential to break with the 'lovely singing' typical of choral societies. The profound murmur of the basses, the poetic resonance (not to say Schmalz) of the tenors – these have no place in *The Decision*.
2 The aim has to be a very precise, tight, rhythmic kind of singing. The singer must try to sing without expression; that is to say, he must not put his feelings into the music as in a love song, but present his notes as a reporter, like a report at a mass meeting, i.e. cold, sharp and trenchant.
3 Above all the aim must be to perform not with feeling but with clarity.

4 The whole audience must be able to understand the text throughout. The best thing is for the chorus to speak the text in the rhythm of the setting before learning the musical notes. Above all so as to secure consistent pronunciation of the words.
5 The basic tempo of *The Decision* is that of walking, marching; above all the tempi must not drag.
6 It is very important that the singers should not treat the text as self-evident, but should discuss it during the rehearsals.
7 Each singer has to be quite clear about the political content of what he is singing, and should criticise it.
8 The choruses in *The Decision* are a mass report, communicating a specific political content to the masses.

[Article by Eisler in the Berlin magazine *Kampfmusik*, March/April 1932, republished in his *Musik und Politik. Schriften 1924–1948*, edited by Günter Meyer, Leipzig, 1973, p. 168.]

QUESTIONNAIRE FOR THE AUDIENCE

1 Do you think an event like this is politically instructive for the audience?
2 Do you think it is politically instructive for the performers (players and chorus)?
3 To which lessons embodied in *The Decision* do you object politically?
4 Do you think our choice of form is right for your political objectives? Can you suggest alternatives?

[From Reiner Steinweg, as for the 'Note to the Audience' above. The ensuing public discussion was reported in the *Welt am Abend* on the 22nd, when speakers objected that the Young Comrade could have been expelled from the Party rather than shot. According to the reporter, 'Brecht replied that the play was so constructed that changes could be made at any time. Sections could be added or taken out as in a montage. There had been many amendments in response to the answers received.'

At the same time 'Brecht's and Eisler's view that the whole work was intended to instruct producers rather than consumers met with sharp disagreement.'

'Wittfogel [the Marxist China specialist who chaired the meeting] summed up the results, and clarified the issues debated, including the undialectical question of the relative weight to be given to reason and feeling [of the Young Comrade]. The conclusive point was that all were convinced by the necessity of the decision to shoot him on security grounds.']

LETTER OF 21.4.1956 TO PAUL PATERA

Dear Mr Patera,
The Decision was not written for an audience but exclusively for the instruction of the performers. In my experience, public performances of it inspire nothing but moral qualms, usually of the cheapest sort. Accordingly, I have not let anyone perform the play for a long time. My short play *The Exception and the Rule* is better suited to performance by non-professional groups.

[Letter 865 from Brecht: *Letters 1913–1956*, Methuen, 1990. Patera's allegedly anti-Communist production at the Uppsala Chamber Theatre in Sweden would open five days later. In the same way as in the United States and elsewhere, this prohibition was ignored, as was the importance of Eisler's music. Nonetheless the letter was subsequently cited to other applicants for performance rights, together with a note by Brecht to say that 'The playwright has always refused to let *The Decision* be performed to an audience, since only the Young Comrade can learn from this, and then only if he has also played one of the Agitators and sung in the Chorus'. We know of no record of this condition ever having been fulfilled in Brecht's lifetime. In 1998, Brecht's centenary year, his forty-year-old refusal is to be waived.]

Editorial Notes

From 'He Said Yes' to 'The Decision'

The Decision followed so closely on *He Said Yes* that Brecht and his collaborators were sometimes working on both plays at once; and only the subsequent pairing of the second with the more perfunctory *He Said No* has come to obscure the importance of their relationship. By Eisler's account (as reported by his friend Notowicz) he and others had been dismissing *He Said Yes* as 'a feeble-witted feudal text', when Brecht offered to write a 'counter-play' in which a man would agree to be 'excluded from the collective'. Eisler, who had not previously worked with Brecht, came round to discuss its writing, which directly or indirectly relates both to the Meyerhold production of Tretiakov's *Roar China* (which came to Berlin that spring) and to some of the experiences of the composer's brother Gerhart, who worked as an undercover Comintern agent in Canton (the 1927 rising) and Shanghai (between 1929 and 1931). It is not clear when this collaboration on the text began, but the Brecht/Eisler letter to the Neue Musik board was written in mid-May 1930 – six weeks before the *He Said Yes* première – while Eisler's main work on the music took from 7 July to 2 August. The actor Ernst Busch, who was to play the Young Comrade, told Reiner Steinweg forty years later that Eisler was then staying in Busch's lodgings. Brecht was away in the south of France.

The first surviving sketches by Brecht have the Leader of the Party House as a separate role, under the name of Herr Keuner. The Young Comrade was 'a boy', 'ein Knabe' as in *He Said Yes*, and the (three) Agitators ask him why he is not at school. This follows from what appears to be the earliest title, thus –

> he said yes
> (rendered concrete)
> 1
> at the party house three agitators visit herr keuner to collect the chinese ABC of communism. mr k. makes a speech asking if they are in agreement with the idea of supporting the revolution of the chinese proletariat by every means. they answer yes. a boy who is writing in the outer office says yes too. as the agitators leave with the documents the boy asks them to take him along, and shows them a radio

set which he could bring and that might come in useful. mr keuner agrees, after asking a few questions and stipulating that the boy's yes 'applies only to those who bring knowledge'.

items:
i know chinese
the way the coolies speak it
i learnt this for the world revolution
and i have learnt
from the writings of karl marx
for the world revolution and
have built a radio set
for it too.

The Chinese City of this first conception was Urga (in Outer Mongolia), later changed to Mukden (Manchuria, taken over by Japan in 1932). *The ABC of Communism* was the title of Nikolai Bukharin's book of Marxist theory, which is presumably what Brecht meant by his references in the play. Bukharin had been expelled from the Soviet Politburo in 1929, and thereafter slowly slid into disgrace until his death following the last of Stalin's great show trials in March 1938. Neither in Brecht's theoretical writings in vols. 16–20 of the 1967 *Gesammelte Werke* nor in the play itself is his name mentioned.

The order of events

In May 1929 Brecht was strongly influenced towards the KPD (i.e. Communist Party) by police violence during the Berlin May Day demonstrations. The Berlin police were then under Socialist control. The theatre holidays followed, as did the Baden-Baden Festival (with the original *lehrstück*). At the beginning of the new theatre year in Berlin there were two notable failures: the one by Brecht, Weill and Elisabeth Hauptmann (*Happy End*); the other by Piscator, Walter Mehring and Eisler (*The Merchant of Berlin*). The Wall Street crash occurred in October, with disastrous consequences for Germany, and Weill completed *Lindbergh's Flight*, re-setting the Hindemith numbers.

Weill took up the commission to write a piece for radio (and/or schools) for the next Festival on a Hauptmann/Brecht version of the Waley *Taniko*. Work started in January 1930, involving a new focus on 'Einverständnis'. Brecht and Eisler agreed to write a companion play which would be a 'concretisation' of the same theme; they set it in China. With their letter of 13 May they withdrew it from the Festival before Eisler began on the music; and Weill with his piece followed suit. *He Said Yes* was then performed separately in late June by the Berlin schools under the auspices of a Prussian State institute, after which Eisler set *The Decision* for three left-wing workers' choral societies to rehearse that autumn and perform in the Philharmonie (concert hall) on 13 December, then again in the Grosses Schauspielhaus on 18 January 1931. Both pieces were conceived to be worked on for the benefit of the (non-professional) participants, performing to an unorthodox audience. The first performances were followed by public discussions, after which amendments were made to the texts and the composers made adjustments accordingly.

Universal-Edition, who published both composers, brought out Weill's piece in 1930, without waiting for the changed text of Brecht's *Versuche* and Weill's consequent adjustments. Eisler's however appeared in mid-1931 with a text corresponding to the revised *Versuche 4* (also of that year). Meantime Brecht had tacked *He Said No* on to the former, seemingly without consulting the composer. As a result it is necessarily the first *He Said Yes* that gets performed if the music is to play its part. Both Weill's and Eisler's are music-theatre works of the highest quality.

THE MOTHER

Texts by Brecht and Eisler

'THE MOTHER'

The Mother, with music by Eisler, is the fifteenth of the 'Versuche', a dramatisation of the novel by Maxim Gorky. It also made use of a dramatisation by G. Stark and G. Weisenborn. It was performed on the anniversary of the death of Rosa Luxemburg, the great revolutionary.

The Notes to *The Mother* are part of the ninth 'Versuch', 'Concerning a non-aristotelian dramaturgy'.

[From *Versuche 7*, Kiepenheuer, Berlin, 1933. Stark was then a director at the Berlin Volksbühne, Weisenborn a playwright, later associated with the Harnack-Boysen resistance group, which was linked to the Red Orchestra.]

SONG OF THE MOTHER ON THE HEROIC DEATH OF THE COWARD VESSOVCHIKOV

So what was he like?
Whatever it was
When he went to the wall
He could die.
Nor did he compare it with others
Or himself with other people, but
Set about changing himself, under threat, into
Indestructible dust. And whatever
Still occurred, he performed
Like an agreement, as though fulfilling
A contract. Extinguished too
Were the wishes within him. Strictly he denied himself
The slightest movement. His inside
Caved in and vanished. Like an empty page
He escaped all
But description.

['Lied der Mutter über den Heldentod des Feiglings Vessovchikov', from p. 127 of *Gedichte 4* (vol. 14) of the Berlin and Frankfurt edition, 1993. The editors' note dates the typescript 1931 and says that Brecht passed it to Eisler, but it was never set. Neither of the two Vessovchikov brothers is shown by him as dying or as a coward, so it must have been written before the play took shape.]

NOTES

I

Written in the style of the didactic pieces, but requiring actors, *The Mother* is a piece of anti-metaphysical, materialistic, non-aristotelian drama. This makes nothing like such a free use as does the aristotelian of the passive empathy of the spectator; it also relates differently to certain psychological effects, such as catharsis. Just as it refrains from handing its hero over to the world as if it were his inescapable fate, so it would not dream of handing the spectator over to an inspiring theatrical experience. Anxious to teach the spectator a quite definite practical attitude, directed towards changing the world, it must begin by making him adopt in the theatre a quite different attitude from what he is used to. The following are a few of the means employed in the first production of *The Mother* in Berlin.

II *Indirect impact of the epic stage*

In the first production of *The Mother* the stage (Caspar Neher) was not supposed to represent any real locality: it as it were took up an attitude itself towards the incidents shown; it quoted, narrated, prepared and recalled. Its sparse indication of furniture, doors, etc. was limited to objects that had a part in the play, i.e. those without which the action would have been altered or halted. A firm arrangement of iron piping slightly higher than a man was erected at varying intervals perpendicularly to the stage; other moveable horizontal pipes carrying canvasses could be slotted into it, and this allowed of quick changes. There were doors in frames hanging inside this, which could be opened and shut. In New York the set (by Max Gorelik) was similar but more solid. A big canvas at the back of the stage was used for the projection of texts and pictorial documents which remained throughout the scene, so that this screen was also virtually part of the setting. Thus the stage not only used allusions to show actual rooms but also texts and pictures to show the great movement of ideas in which the events were taking place. The projections are in no way pure mechanical aids in the sense of being extras, they are no *pons asinorum*; they do not set out to help the spectator but to block him; they prevent his complete empathy, interrupt his being automatically carried away. They turn the impact into an *indirect* one. Thus they are organic parts of the work of art.

III *Projections*
See below (page 363).

IV *Epic method of portrayal*
The epic theatre uses the simplest possible groupings, such as express the event's overall sense. No more 'casual', 'life-like', 'unforced' grouping; the stage no longer reflects the 'natural' disorder of things. The opposite of natural disorder is aimed at: natural order. This order is determined from a social-historical point of view. The point of view to be adopted by the production can be made more generally intelligible, though not properly characterised, if we call it that of the genre painter and the historian. Scene 2 of *The Mother* includes the following incidents which have to be brought out by the production and kept separate from one another.

1. The young worker Pavel Vlassov is visited by revolutionary comrades who want to do an illegal piece of work in his quarters.
2. The Mother is disturbed to see him in the company of revolutionary workers. She tries to chase them away.
3. During this illegal work the worker Masha Khalatova explains in a little song how, in order to gain bread and jobs, workers need to 'turn the whole State upside down for ever'.
4. A police search makes the Mother realise the danger of her son's new activities.
5. Though horrified by the brutality of the police, the Mother declares that she finds her son, not the State, to be guilty of violence. She blames him for this, and his leaders even more so.
6. The Mother sees her son being chosen for a dangerous operation, distributing pamphlets, and offers her own services in order to save him from being involved.
7. After a moment's discussion the revolutionaries hand the pamphlets over to her. She cannot read them.

These seven incidents must be portrayed as emphatically and significantly as any well-known historical episodes, though without sentimentalising them. In this epic theatre serving a non-aristotelian type of drama, the actor will at the same time do all he can to make himself observed standing between the spectator and the event. This making-oneself-observed also contributes to the desired indirect impact.

V *For example: a description of the first portrayal of the Mother*
Here are a few examples of what epic acting brought out, as shown by the actress who created the part (Helene Weigel):

Scene 1: In the first scene the actress stood in a particular characteristic attitude in the centre of the stage, and spoke the sentences as if they were in the third person; and so she not only refrained from pretending in fact to be or to claim to be Vlassova (the Mother), and in fact to be speaking those sentences, but actually prevented the spectator from transferring himself to a particular room, as habit and indifference might demand, and imagining himself to be the invisible eye-witness and eavesdropper of a unique intimate occasion. Instead what she did was openly to introduce the spectator to the person whom he would be watching acting and being acted upon for some hours.

Scene 2: Vlassova's attempts to scare off the revolutionaries were shown in such a way that, if one paid attention, it was not difficult to glimpse her own enjoyment of the situation. Her way of reproaching the revolutionaries was shocked rather than angry; her offer to distribute the pamphlets was full of reproach.

Scene 3: By muscling into the factory yard she showed what an asset it was for the revolutionaries to gain such a fighter.

Scene 4: She received her first lesson in Communism with the attitude of a great realist. She showed a certain amicable energy in her argument with her partners, treating them as idealists who were loth to recognise reality. A proof for her had to be not only true but also probable.

Scene 5: The May Day demonstration was spoken as if the participants were before a police-court, but at the end the actor playing Smilgin indicated his collapse by going down on his knees; the actress playing the Mother then stooped during her final words and picked up the flag that had slipped from his hands.

Scene 6: From this point on, the Mother was played so as to be much friendlier and more in command of the situation, apart from the very beginning of the scene, where she showed fright. 'Praise of Communism' was sung softly and calmly. The scene where the Mother and other workers learn to read and write is one of the most difficult for the actor. The audience's laughter at one or two sentences must not prevent him from showing how difficult learning is for the old and unadaptable, thus achieving the stature of the real historical event, the fact that a proletariat which had been exploited and restricted to physical work was able to socialise knowledge and expropriate the bourgeois intellectually. This event is not to be read 'between the lines'; it is directly stated. A lot of our actors, when something has to be stated directly in a scene, get restless, and at once look there for something less direct which they can represent. They fall on whatever is 'inexpressible', between the lines, because it calls for their gifts. Such an approach makes what they can and do express seem banal, and is therefore harmful.

In the short scene 'Ivan Vessovchikov can no longer recognise his brother', the actress managed to convey how, without believing the teacher's nature to be unalterable, the Mother was at the same time not going to point a finger at the changes that had taken place.

Scene 7: The Mother has to discuss her revolutionary work with her son under the enemy's nose: she deceives the prison warder by displaying what seems to him the moving, harmless attitude of the average mother. She encourages his own harmless sympathy. So this example of a quite new and active kind of mother-love is herself exploiting her knowledge of the old familiar out-of-date kind. The actress showed that the Mother is quite aware of the humour of the situation.

Scene 8: This is another scene where the actress showed that not only she herself but Vlassova too could appreciate the slightly comic aspect of her make-believe. She made clear her conviction that a quite passive, if flexible attitude (that of a justifiable injury) should be enough to make the butcher aware of his class origins. She acted as the modest little drop that causes the bucket to overflow. 'Praise of the Vlassovas' (an instance of limited praise) was recited in front of the half-curtain and in her presence, standing to one side at a little distance.

Scene 11: The Mother's mourning for her son can be shown by her hair having turned white. It is strong, but is merely sketched. And of course it does not destroy the humour. This must permeate the description of the denunciation of God.

Scene 12: Here the actress not only set herself against the workers she was addressing, but also showed herself to be one of them; she and they together made up a picture of the proletariat at the start of the war. Notably the long drawn-out 'yeees' four lines from the end of the scene was very carefully spoken, so that it virtually became the scene's climax. Bent like an old woman, she raised her chin and smiled, dragging the word out and speaking it softly in the head-voice, as if she understood the temptation to let everything go, but at the same time the necessity to do her very utmost in the situation confronting the workers.

Scene 14: At first the actress conducted her anti-war propaganda bent over, turned away and with her head wrapped in a big scarf. She showed that the work was like that of a mole. In every case she picked, out of all conceivable characteristics, those whose awareness promoted the most comprehensive political treatment of the Vlassovas (i.e. special, individual and unique ones), and such as help the Vlassovas themselves in their work. It was as if she was acting to a group of politicians – but none the less an actress for that, and within the framework of art.

VI *Choruses*

See below (pages 358–360).

VII *Is non-aristotelian drama primitive, as typified by* The Mother?
[. . .] Far from believing for one instant that they were being offered a portrayal of certain historic events in Russia with a view to 'spiritual participation' in an adventure story, 'a distillation of eternal human nature' etc.; far too from wanting to forget the inhuman conditions of their own lives – special, alterable conditions – these spectators were prepared to mobilise their entire experience, intelligence and fighting spirit, to acknowledge objectives and handicaps, to make comparisons and objections, and to criticise the conduct of the characters or to generalise so as to apply it to their own situation and learn from it. This is a kind of psychology they can understand, an *applicable, political psychology*. The spectator is here considered to be faced with images of men whose originals he has to deal with – i.e. make speak and act – in real life, and cannot treat as finally and exactly determined phenomena. His duty to his fellow-men consists in ranging himself with the determining factors. In this duty the drama must support him. The determining factors, such as social background, special events, etc. must be shown as alterable. By means of a certain interchangeability of circumstances and occurrences the spectator must be given the possibility (and duty) of assembling, experimenting and abstracting. Among the differences that distinguish individuals from each other, there are quite specific ones that interest the political being who mixes with them, struggles with them and has to deal with them (e.g. those which the leaders of the class-struggle need to know). There is no point for him in stripping a given man of all his peculiarities until he stands there as Man (with a capital M), i.e. as a being who cannot be altered further. Man has to be understood in his role as man's (the spectator's) own fate. It has to be a workable definition.

VIII *'Direct', flattening, impact*
In calling for a direct impact, the aesthetics of the day call for an impact that flattens out all social and other distinctions between individuals. Plays of the aristotelian type still manage to flatten out class conflicts in this way although the individuals themselves are becoming increasingly aware of class differences. The same result is achieved even when class conflicts are the subject of such plays, and even in cases where they take sides for a particular class. A collective entity is created in the auditorium for the *duration of the entertainment*, on the basis of the 'common humanity' shared by all spectators alike. Non-aristotelian drama of *The Mother*'s sort is not interested in the establishment of such an entity. It divides its audience.

IX *Is Communism exclusive?*

[. . .] A great many intellectual workers have a strong feeling that the world (their world) is off balance, but do not behave as if this were so. If we exclude those who construct a world intellectually which is inherently unbalanced (and lives by that) then we are left with those who more or less know about this imbalance but behave as if it were not so. Since the thought processes of such people are not much affected by the world, it is hardly surprising if their thoughts have no effect on it. This however means they consider thinking to be ineffective: hence we have the 'pure intellect' which exists for its own sake, more or less impeded by 'external' circumstances. For such people the arguments of a working-class woman, as sparked off by *The Mother*, cannot be classed as intellectual. They send in the politicians. Just as they themselves are cut off from practical matters, so are the politicians nothing to do with intellect. Why should the head bother what the hand does when it fills his pocket for him? These people are against politics. Which means in practice that they support the politics that affect themselves. Their behaviour is utterly political, even in their own profession. Setting up one's home outside politics is not the same as being forcibly settled there, and to be beyond politics is not the same as to be above them.

Some think they could become perfect in an imperfect State, without trying to perfect it. But it is in the nature of our State to do without any perfect people, or people who are trying to become perfect. We see plenty of institutions which can use the handicapped, those missing an arm or one or both legs. Public administration is best mastered by blockheads. To do their job properly, our policemen should be criminal and our judges blind. Research workers deaf and dumb, or at least the latter. While book and magazine publishers rely on the illiterate to save them from bankruptcy. What we call cleverness shows itself not in finding and expressing the truth, but in finding untruth and saying nothing, with greater or less sensitivity. Some complain of the lack of great works, which they ascribe to the absence of major talents. But no Homer and no Shakespeare could make poetry of what they want to hear. And those who miss the great works can get along quite well without them, and might be unable to live with them.

X *Resistance to learning, and contempt for the useful*

One of the chief objections made by bourgeois criticism to non-aristotelian plays like *The Mother* is based on an equally bourgeois distinction between the concepts 'entertaining' and 'instructive'. In this view *The Mother* is possibly instructive (if only for a small section of the potential audience, the argument goes) but definitely not entertaining (not even for this small section). There is a certain pleasure to be got out of looking more closely at this distinction. Surprising as it may seem, the object is to discredit learning by presenting it as not enjoyable. But in fact of course it is enjoyment that is being discredited by this deliberate suggestion that one learns nothing from it. One only needs to look around and see the function allotted to learning in bourgeois society. It amounts to the buying of materially useful items of knowledge. The purchase has to take place before the individual enters the process of production. Its field is immaturity. To admit that I am still incapable of something that is a part of my profession, in other words to allow myself to be caught learning, is equivalent to confessing that I am unfit to meet competition and that I must not be allowed credit. The man who comes to the theatre for 'entertainment' refuses to let himself be 'treated like a schoolboy' once again because he remembers the fearful torments with which 'knowledge' used to be hammered into the youth of the bourgeoisie. Libellous things are being said about the learner's attitude.

In the same way most people have taken to despising the useful and the instinct for the useful ever since men first took to making use of one another exclusively by means of underhand tricks. Nowadays utility derives only from abuse of one's fellow men.

['Anmerkungen' to the play in *Versuche 7*, 1933, with small amendments (1938) and abridgements. Translation largely taken from *Brecht on Theatre*, 1964. The many quotations from the Berlin 1932 and New York 1935 press criticisms have been omitted; they can be found in the German editions of the play, notably in vol. 24 of the Berlin and Frankfurt edition, 1991.]

OPTIONAL CHORUSES

To prevent 'free' association and the 'carrying away' of the spectator, it is possible to place small choruses in the auditorium which would demonstrate the proper attitude, invite him to make up his own mind, call on his experience and exercise control. Such choruses constitute an appeal to the spectator's practical side: to liberate himself from the world depicted, and also to depict himself. Here are a few examples of their texts. They are meant to be adaptable to the situation and may be supplemented or replaced by the reading of quotations or documents.

Chorus 1:

Observe mother and son. Between them
Is an estrangement. Outside circumstances
Have made her almost his enemy: it is a struggle between

Friendly mother and hostile son.
So you see:
The struggle raging outside carries on in the parlour
And a space full of struggle cannot be entered unscathed.

Chorus 2:
He is discontented; he understands his position.
And on his discontent
The whole world is waiting.

Chorus 3:
See how far she is from
Understanding her task, so gigantic! Still she considers how
To divide his dwindling pay-packet, so it could
Grow still smaller, unperceived thanks to her art!

Chorus 4:
Everyone seems to the mother a natural enemy, who
Strengthens her son in his rebellion. Far preferable
Would she find it, if he kept to his engagement: welcome
To the eyes of his oppressors, he might perhaps
Crawl through under the poverty line, or even
Join the side of the exploiters to his own advantage. This way however
By trying to improve his lodging, he merely
Puts that lodging at risk.

Chorus 5:
Stop! Don't go on! what you are portraying is peculiar!
Here she is, condemning those who fight her, for their cruelty.
Just the application seems cruel to her, not the law!
And there are others who forgive those who put cruel laws into effect.
Both views are wrong! Never dissociate
This law from its servant or this
State from its rulers!
It is exactly as they are! For it was made
By men. It consists of people, and for
People it was planned
And by no means for all
But just for a few – and those unlike yourself.
Easily the rumour grows and proves long lasting
That the State is somehow different from those that run it
And of a nobler kind than those that use it for their own ends.

Much as one says: those are good people in a bad business
One likewise says: bad people serve a good cause.
But in reality whoever acts badly is bad, and bad too
Is the bad ones' business.
Therefore do not say: the State is good that treats you badly
And it could become better. No: if it were better it would be a State
no longer.

Chorus 6:

See, now she realises: this is my business
And the struggle is useful. Soon
She will join it. And then she can
Say aloud: this struggle is useful
Always in a loud voice: especially for me!

[These constitute section 6 of the 'Anmerkungen' to *Versuche 7*, above. Their suggested places in the first three scenes of the play are indicated by the figures (1) to (6) in our text. There is no record of any setting by Eisler, or of their actual performance.]

HANNS EISLER ON THE THEATRE UNION'S PRODUCTION OF 'MOTHER'

The experience with the music in the Theatre Union's production of *Mother* again shows the difficulties encountered in introducing a new use of music to the theatre. The conventional man of the theatre uses music in only two ways: for singing and dancing (as in musical comedy) or for music emphasising and illustrating a drama. With these two outmoded methods, however, the newer music can not be made use of. An artistically wrong presentation of the music leads, strangely enough, to serious political errors. Therefore the political content cannot be separated from the artistic as one conditions the other. To present music of the *Mother* type properly, it is necessary first of all to realise that it is an independent part of the production. It must therefore be clearly separated from the action.

As to the purely musical performance, such as the accompaniment on two pianos and the studying and recitation of the choruses by the actors, it must be made clear in the first place that music of the type written for *Mother* does not express a state of the soul but is meant to force the interpreters into a certain attitude, a certain gesture.

When composing the score of *Mother* the limited possibilities of the revolutionary theatre and the actors lack of musical training, was in general taken into consideration. This means, that difficulties of a purely technical nature, such as the playability of the accompanyment, the correct reading of the notes, could be overcome more or less easily. An interpretative musician, approaching this music with conventional standards may however make the mistake of underrating its peculier difficulties of a sort new to him, or may not even note them at all.

In the Theatre Union these problems caused great difficulty: singing without sentimentality or pathos, coldness of recitation without dryness, exact understanding of the tempo, the avoiding of accelerandos or ritenutos where they are not marked. The differences between the various ways of playing such as portamento and non legato, light staccato etc. etc. In the studying of such music it is absolutely necessary to avoid all rigid conceptions of tempi. To get the proper tempo it is necessary to try out various tempi. In the beginning this naturally causes great difficulties for the musicians. A revolutionary theatre, if it is to make progress, must demand much more of its musicians than the bourgeois theatre. In the American working-class musical movement there is so much talent and so many important manifestations that the workers' theatres will soon be able to overcome these difficulties.

[Shortened from the uncorrected English-language original in Eisler's *Musik und Politik 1924–1948*, Leipzig, 1973, pp. 358–360. This was written at the request of the US Communist Party for publication in their *Daily Worker*, but may not have appeared. The concert performance at the New School took place on 3 May 1936. That of *The Decision* never materialised. See Brecht's letter 287 to Lee Strasberg, dated New York City, 27 January 1936.]

RECOMMENDATIONS TO THEATRE UNION

Act I

I am very glad you have decided to use the more stylised form of the original for the first two Acts. I lay particular store by the monologues and the curt conversations and closing lines, as for example the Mother's uninterrupted monologues and the conclusion 'No, I can't read' to the first scene. In scene 3 the tautness of the conversation about property. As for the conclusion of this scene I beg you above all to cut the last words, where the Mother promises to join the march. This destroys the surprise of Act 4.

Act II

This is where the projection of the scene titles is particularly important. In scene 6 there are some changes to be made. Pavel has not escaped. He has served his sentence in Siberia and must now travel on to Finland on a new mission for the Party. Just a few phrases will suffice for this. E.g. for the start of the scene, project:

IN THE YEARS PRECEDING WORLD WAR ONE THE BOLSHEVIK PARTY WAS TIRELESS IN ITS PROPAGANDA. PELAGEA VLASSOVA IS ACTIVELY INVOLVED IN AN ILLEGAL PRESS

Act III
Scene 1
Projection: 1914 THE TSAR MOBILISES
Scene in the railway compartment. Version attached.

Scene 2
The bible scene. Back to the original text:

Comrade Vlassova, your son
Has been shot. But . . .

Sole change:

THE THREE WOMEN *at the door*: Pavel Vlassov has been arrested and shot for revolutionary agitation among the troops.

The Mother, very white make-up. We see the great effort she has to make in the conversation with the three women. Following her closing sentence 'Whatever happens I'd advise you to insure your harvest!' she faints.

Scene 3
The Schoolmaster's flat.
Before and during the scene, large background projections of the Tsar, Poincaré, Grey and the Kaiser, the powers whom the Mother must fight. This scene must show how the Mother, after the terrible blow represented by the death of her son, is brought to her feet again by the threat to the Party and the cause of the workers, and the necessity for redoubled work. All the same she has greatly aged.

Scene 4
Street corner. Original scene 12.

Scene 5
Conclusion. The demonstration. Before it starts there must be a big projection saying:

IN NOVEMBER 1917 THE RUSSIAN PROLETARIAT SEIZED POWER

The projections are of the utmost importance for the play. They are the only way by which it can acquire the character of a History. It must on no account function like a story.

The less colourful the set, the more successful the establishment of the play's background as a historical one. In Berlin we performed against white canvases (with a lot of light on the stage) and virtually nothing else apart from projected inscriptions and photographs.

[From Brecht: *Werke: Schriften*, Berlin and Frankfurt edition, vol. 24, 1991, pp. 135–137. From Brecht's German typescript, sent to Paul Peters from Denmark as an annex to his letter no. 274 of 3 October 1935. This was four days before he sailed for New York.]

PROJECTIONS, 1932 AND 1935

(a) Berlin production

Scene 1: THE VLASSOVAS OF EVERY COUNTRY

Scene 2: BATTLE FOR THE KOPECK

Scene 3: Photograph: P.SUCHLINOV, OWNER OF THE SUCHLINOV WORKS

Scene 4: THEORY TURNS INTO A MATERIAL FORCE WHEN IT GETS HOLD OF THE MASSES (Marx)

Scene 5: MAY 1ST. WORKERS OF ALL COUNTRIES, UNITE!

Scene 6: MEMBERSHIP CARD OF THE RUSSIAN SOCIAL-DEMOCRATIC PARTY (BOLSHEVIKS) IN THE NAME OF PELAGEA VLASSOVA FROM TVERSK

Scene 6: THE WORKERS STRIVE FOR KNOWLEDGE BECAUSE IT IS ESSENTIAL FOR THEIR VICTORY

Scene 7: SHOW THAT YOU CAN FIGHT! (Lenin to the women)

Scene 8: The hammer and sickle emblem taken apart, to show hammer and sickle next to one another linked by the word 'and'

Scene 8: Hammer and sickle linked by superimposition

Scene 9: THE SOCIAL IMPACT OF WOMEN MUST BE PROMOTED SO THAT THEY SHAKE OFF THEIR DOMESTIC AND FAMILY PSYCHOLOGY (Lenin)

Scene 10: RELIGION IS THE OPIUM OF THE PEOPLE (Marx)

Scene 11: Photograph of the war leaders: THE TSAR, THE KAISER, POINCARÉ, WILSON, GREY

Scene 12: AGAINST THE STREAM!

Scene 13: Photograph of Lenin alongside inscription: FOR THE TRANSFORMATION OF THE IMPERIALIST WAR INTO A CIVIL WAR

Scene 14: 1917

Scene 14, the ending: IN NOVEMBER 1917 THE RUSSIAN PROLETARIAT SEIZED POWER

Film with documentary shots of the October Revolution (forbidden by censors)

Auditorium, a banner saying: THERE CAN BE NO TRUE MASS MOVEMENT WITHOUT THE WOMEN (Lenin)

(b) New York production

Before Scene 1

Title: THE LIFE OF THE REVOLUTIONIST PELAGEA VLASSOVA OF TVERSK

Picture of the Mother

Scene 1

Title: IN 1907. THE WORKERS OF THE CITY OF TVERSK LIVED UNDER CONDITIONS OF EXTREME HARDSHIP

Picture: Shopping list in large handwriting of untutored person:

bread	4 kopeks
lard	7 "
cabbage	3 "
potatoes	5 "
onions	2 "
tea	5 "
	26 kopeks

Scene 2

Title: PELAGEA VLASSOVA SEES WITH SORROW THAT HER SON IS IN THE COMPANY OF REVOLUTIONARY WORKERS

Picture: Four poor women of different nations including Negro and Chinese with caption: IN EVERY COUNTRY OF THE WORLD THERE ARE WOMEN LIKE PELAGEA VLASSOVA

Scene 3

Title: THE MOTHER HERSELF DISTRIBUTES LEAFLETS IN THE SUCHLINOV PLANT TO KEEP HER SON OUT OF THE REVOLUTIONARY ACTIVITY

Picture: Leaflet:

Workers:
Don't let Mr Suchlinov
Cut your wages! Don't
Negotiate!
Strike!
Suchlinov Factory Committee

Scene 4

Title: THE MOTHER RECEIVES HER FIRST LESSON IN ECONOMICS

Picture: Factory with picture of factory-owner in oval shape; caption under the whole: THE SUCHLINOV WORKS and under the photograph of the man: P. SUCHLINOV, THE OWNER

Scene 5

Title: ON MAY 1ST THE WORKERS OF TVERSK DEMONSTRATE AGAINST THE WAGE CUT. THE MOTHER RECEIVES A LESSON IN POLITICS

Picture: A demonstration

Scene 6

Title: 1908. PAVEL IS IN PRISON. IVAN VESSOVCHIKOV BRINGS THE MOTHER TO THE HOME OF HIS BROTHER NIKOLAI, THE TEACHER, WHO LIVES IN THE CITY OF ROSTOV

Picture: Reproduction of Vlassova's membership card with picture of the Mother superimposed and caption: MEMBERSHIP CARD OF PELAGEA VLASSOVA IN THE RUSSIAN SOCIAL DEMOCRATIC LABOR PARTY

Title: THE TEACHER SURPRISES HIS HOUSEKEEPER IN THE MIDST OF A MEETING

Title: THE MOTHER LEARNS TO READ AND WRITE

Picture: KNOWLEDGE IS POWER (Francis Bacon)

Picture: The words: CLASS STRUGGLE – WORKER – EXPLOITER

Title: IVAN VESSOVCHIKOV DOES NOT RECOGNIZE HIS OWN BROTHER

Picture: Framed picture of the Czar

Scene 7

Title: THE MOTHER MAKES USE OF A VISIT TO HER SON IN PRISON TO GET THE ADDRESSES OF PEASANTS SYMPATHETIC TO THE MOVEMENT

Picture: Prison

Scene 8

Title: IN THE YEARS 1909–13 THE WORKERS TRIED REPEATEDLY TO DRAW THE POOR PEASANTS INTO THEIR MOVEMENT

Pictures of workers on one side and peasants on the other side

Scene 9

Title: PAVEL RETURNS AFTER A LONG EXILE IN SIBERIA

Picture: Lines from the Third Thing

Scene 10

Title: CROSSING THE FINNISH BORDER, PAVEL VLASSOV HAS BEEN CAUGHT AND EXECUTED

Picture: Photograph of Pavel. Later Rogues Gallery picture of him

Scene 11

Title: WAR IS DECLARED

Picture: Photograph of the Czar and his generals

Scene 12

Title: DURING THE FIRST YEARS OF THE WAR THE WORKERS WOULD NOT LISTEN TO THE REVOLUTIONISTS

Picture: Line of text: IF YOU SHOULD FAIL!

Scene 13

Title: THE MOTHER CARRIES ON ANTI-WAR PROPAGANDA

Picture: Casualty list (three battles on the Eastern Front)

Scene 14

Title: JANUARY 1917, IN THE TUMULTUOUS RANKS OF THE STRIKING WORKERS AND MUTINYING SOLDIERS MARCHES PELAGEA VLASSOVA, THE MOTHER

Picture: Photograph of armed demonstrations

End

Title: IN NOVEMBER 1917, THE RUSSIAN PROLETARIAT SEIZED POWER

[(a) From *Versuche 7*, 1933, 'Anmerkungen', para. III, expanded to include (b) in para. III of the Malik-Verlag *Gesammelte Werke*, vol. 2, London, 1938.]

MEMORANDUM ABOUT THE DISTORTION AND MUTILATION OF THE TEXT

In view of the stylistic problems involved in performing *Mother*, Brecht for some weeks refused to allow its production unless he could be involved in the rehearsals and have complete control of the integrity of his text. In Denmark both these points had been guaranteed to him by Manuel Gomez on behalf of the theatre. While there was a contractual agreement to use a particular version which departed from the book version, the theatre was to have no right to cut its text without Brecht's approval. On arriving in New York Brecht took part in the work on the third act of that version, but got the theatre's permission to show the board his own earlier version based on the book. The board formally opted for this (i.e. Brecht's) version of the third act.

On Saturday 9 November 1935 the theatre told Brecht and Eisler that cuts were needed in Act 3. The shortened version would have to be put before the board on the following Monday (11.11). Brecht protested against the cuts, saying the weaknesses of the third act were due not to the text but to inadequacies in the acting. To protect the principle of textual integrity he and Eisler approached Comrade Jerome of the Agitprop department and called on the Party for an explanation.

On the Monday evening Comrade Jerome went with Eisler to see the performance of the play as cut without Brecht's approval. (The cuts in question added up to about half a page of text; they were points of dramaturgical and political significance.)

Tuesday 12.11 saw a meeting with the Theatre Union fraction which led to a Party resolution calling on the theatre to respect the integrity of the text as approved by Brecht and last performed on the evening of Friday 8.11. The theatre accepted this resolution nem. con.

On Wednesday 13 and Thursday 14, Brecht tried to reinstate the Friday 8 version as had been agreed. As the second of these was already the opening night Brecht volunteered the suggestion that, to reduce the strain on the actress, the cuts should be retained for one last time on condition that from the next performance on they would finally be abandoned.

Once again this Thursday evening performance was most inadequate. Once again the theatre blamed this on the text of the third act. Brecht's and Eisler's efforts to correct the true errors, which lay in the acting, had been sabotaged by the theatre during the Thursday afternoon, and it became impossible to resume them on Friday. Friday evening also saw the maintenance of the cuts that the Agitprop department had agreed to cancel. On Saturday Brecht and Eisler managed to reach Jerome and begged him to enforce the Party resolution. Moreover Brecht asked his permission to inform all the critics invited to the première that the play had been butchered. Comrade Jerome wanted Brecht at all costs not to do this, and promised to get the Party resolution put into effect. He went to the Saturday night performance, only to discover that on top of the previous unauthorised cuts a whole scene (the farm workers) had now been cut too.

Early on Sunday morning (17.11) Comrade Jerome told Comrade Eisler that the fraction had promised him to let the authors join in the work once more; they would be 'invited into the theatre'. Manuel Gomez did indeed telephone them that morning, and the result was a session in Brecht's apartment, where a number of improvements were suggested by Eisler and Brecht, and discussed. Brecht once again insisted on the integrity of his text.

On Sunday evening the previous cuts and the farm workers scene were once again missing.

On Monday morning the authors were told that the theatre was now proposing to cut a further scene, the bible scene. They informed Comrade Jerome, who immediately rang the theatre and angrily forbade the cutting of the bible scene. Jerome did however criticise as politically questionable one passage in that scene, where the bible is torn in half, whereupon Brecht submitted to Party orders without demur and agreed that the passage should be deleted.

That same evening Manuel Gomez rang Brecht with respect to a technical detail which would make this feasible.

On Tuesday morning (19.11), as they could not raise anybody on the telephone, Brecht and Eisler came to the theatre and discussed various technical details with Gomez. They were extremely surprised to learn from Gomez that yet another scene might have to be cut, namely the anti-war propaganda scene which forms the core of the third Act. Once again the authors invoked the Party resolution. An hour later Jerome invited them to a meeting in the Agitprop department, where the Theatre Union fraction were waiting, and informed them that the theatre did indeed wish to cut the anti-war propaganda scene. Comrade Jerome referred to the authors' protest and the Party resolution guaranteeing the text's integrity. It was clear that the fraction had made their cuts without Brecht's approval, indeed against his explicit refusal. Their attempt to accuse Brecht (and Eisler too) of failing to take an interest in the production was a piece of impertinence in view of the authors' repeated efforts to have a say in it by means of writing and telephone calls. Brecht had continued to make written suggestions to the leading actress and gone on conferring with the designer even after he had been denied all possibility of working personally in the theatre. As late as Sunday, Brecht and Eisler had been supplying practical suggestions. The final decisive cutting of the anti-war propaganda scene had been concealed from Comrade Jerome and the authors until an allegedly technical fait accompli had been prepared. Thus in Tuesday's discussion the fraction explained that 'technical grounds' (impossibility of altering the lighting plot again) made it quite impossible for them to include the anti-war propaganda scene. And indeed it was omitted at the première that evening, along with the farm workers scene and all the passages the Agitprop department had ordered to be restored. On top of that, various other politically and dramaturgically most important points had been cut. At subsequent performances too, though there could now be no technical pretexts, all that had been cut remained cut.

To sum up, the cuts were:

In the bible scene [scene 10], a speech by the Mother with an anti-religious message, ideologically the key point of the whole scene.

In the scene 'The Party is in Danger' [scene 11], the phrase 'If the Tsar is mobilising, us workers must mobilise too'. (The decisive phrase that foretells the Bolsheviks' preparation of civil war.)

In the street-corner scene [12], the slogans spread among the masses by the Bolsheviks in 1914 ('Down with the war, long live the Revolution!').

The whole scene [8] of the Mother and the farm workers, raising the issue of the alliance of the workers with the poor peasants.

The whole anti-war propaganda scene [13]. If this scene is cut, then the refusal of the workers to listen to the Bolsheviks' slogans at the start of the war leads directly to the triumph of the 1917 Revolution, which then appears as a gift from the gods for which no revolutionary effort was needed.

On the pretext of political incorrectness the theatre changed the song 'Praise of Communism' to one in 'Praise of Socialism', and the Mother's declaration in the anti-war scene that 'I am a Bolshevik' (in all performances where the scene was played) to 'I am a revolutionary'. Then on the last day the costumes were Russianised in defiance of all agreements, and this in the clear understanding (stressed more than once by the theatre) that it would turn the revolutionary cause into an exotic, specifically Russian affair. When the authors, together with the designer Gorelik, suggested that the workers in the final scene (Demonstration, 1917) should be armed, that too was rejected.

All these cuts represented a sad mutilation of the play from a political and artistic point of view. The theatre was behaving exactly like the average Broadway theatre, which treats a play simply as a commodity, or as raw material for some commodity that can be easily marketed. The Theatre Union fraction had moreover received a clear resolution by the Party to say that the integrity of the text must be respected as a basic right of the author. The authors were respecting the Party's wishes when they agreed not to withdraw play and music if these got mutilated and distorted. Brecht, despite not belonging to the Party, even agreed not to tell the critics invited to the première that his play had been so treated. Thanks to the Theatre Union fraction's lack of discipline, the Party's undertaking to protect the integrity of the text could not be fulfilled.

[Typescript signed 'Brecht' and dated 22 November 1935, as published in vol. 24 of the Berlin and Frankfurt edition, pp. 137–141. This is the document quoted in Lee Baxandall's account 'Brecht in America, 1935' in Erika Munk's symposium *Brecht*, Bantam Books, New York, 1972. Two points are somewhat overlooked in Brecht's account: (i) Theatre Union were interested in Gorky's novel and largely unaware of the work of Brecht, and (ii) only a few of their members belonged to the Communist Party. Manuel Gomez was a board member who conducted the negotiations with Brecht.]

DISCUSSION JEROME/BRECHT/EISLER

[A partial transcription by Elisabeth Hauptmann (says James Lyon), taken down on 23 November 1935 and starting with V.J. Jerome's remark 'I would like to write an article on comparative dramaturgical methods of MacLeish and Brecht. I see certain points of contact between you. It would help me very much if you would give me some information on specific points . . .'.]

J: MacLeish, too, has a chorus, he, too, uses verse. His verse method is also unique. He uses symbolism. Do you use symbolism?

B: No.

J: Symbolism is very strong in MacL, a metaphysical element. Would it be so with you?

B: I hope not.

J: You say, you do not employ any method of symbolism?

B: No – but – there is a certain method that I use once in a while – but that is not symbolism – that is the parable – I don't use it in 'Die Mutter', but in other play, i.e. 'Heads Round and Heads Pointed'.

J: You mean a simile –

B: Yes, think of the simile of the vineyard in the bible, the similes of Buddha, Marx, Engels, Lenin –

E: Lenin 'On Climbing High Mountains' – or when he speaks about Rosa Luxemburg – (eagle).

B: Or about Paul Levi (fox-hunting, red flags).

E: Or that with the car, the robbers, the guns and robbing the money.

J: The Prodigal Son. Or the lamb of the poor, the story that was told David to demonstrate the Uria-case.

B: That is the method I use.

J: How do you use it? But may I first say this: I have seen one dramatist also use the simile, Strindberg in The Father, it is the opening of the play – the dialogue between the Father and the stableman etc. culminating in the sentence of the stableman: 'How do I know it is my child?'

B: Yes, that is a 'parable'.

J: A prologue in the form of a parable.

B: You have it also in 'The Dream Play' – the story of Indra's daughter.

J: Also Ibsen's 'The Master Builder'.

B: But executed (carried out) too naturalistically. Let me say this: The purpose of a 'parable' is to clearly demonstrate the relations of men to and among each other and their attitudes towards each other. In the simile you can see very distinctly whether their attitude is useful or not. I am interested in the relations and behaviour of men. Therefore I build up before you Men that behave in the right or wrong way. You see him doing wrong and the outcome is a failure.

J: That is a cinematographic method.

B: Well, but the cinematographic method is not essentially interested in the behavior of people. I shall give you an example. Take my play 'Heads Round and Heads Pointed'. I invent a country that is inhabited by two kinds of people, two races, those with round heads and those with pointed heads. One day there comes a man – at a very lucky moment – and says I shall divide this country into two kinds of people, the r.h. and the p.h., that is according to a racial standpoint. This division proves to be very good for the rich and very bad for the poor. The form of the play is the 'parable'.

J: You do not use this method in 'Die Mutter'.

B: No, there is no simile in 'The Mother'.

J: Do you employ a chorus in all your plays, or only in 'The Mother'?

B: Not in all.

J: Why do you use the chorus in 'Die Mutter'?

B: In reality it is no special chorus. The chorus can take many parts. In the Commentary to the play 'Die Mutter' I add other kinds of choruses that are not in the play. (B. reads the passage out of the Commentary on the chorus.)

J: In other words, the chorus is the teacher.

B: Yes – the chorus determines i.e. the attitude of the spectator. In the examples for the use of the chorus as given in the Commentary small choruses are placed among the audience. Suppose you are in the theatre and a man sits beside you. He, in the course of the play, asks questions, criticizes, praises – informs you –

J: So the chorus is a mentor –

B: Yes – and then kind of measurestick. The experiences on the stage there in front and above you must be generalized, the processes there before you must be criticized –

J: I am interested in the didactics of the chorus, let me put this question: You do not take it over from antiquity and use it in the same form? –

B: No.

J: – That would be a mechanical superimposition. I would like now to reason in terms of another category and you will tell me how you feel about it.

B: Let me say this first: The antique chorus is principally idealistic. Take even Euripides. Even Aristophanes in his comedies has idealistic choruses though the processes are very realistic.

J: I will take the following things of which Engels speaks in his 'Origin of Family', the question of 'armed forces'. In primitive communism the armed forces were not a specialised group, they were the people. It was the people who fought the forces of nature and the people were armed. In the society of private property the property owners because they are in the minority have to have an armed army to protect their property from the disinherited majority, the disarmed people. This constellation: armed minority vs disarmed people is true of Slavery, Feudalism, Capitalism. Sometimes army is recruited, or mercenary like in China –

B: Levée en masse –

J: In the dictatorship of the proletariat you have in that transient phase towards scientific communism the Red Army representing the armed forces and the Red Army must be identified with the movement in the direction where the army is the people. They are not a force to protect the property but an army that has come into the possession of property. In the (future) state of communism when the need for international and civil wars will be abolished then the army will again be used against forces of nature as in primitive communism, Thesis – antithesis – synthesis on a higher plane. Now I want to know this. You have the Greek drama with the chorus from which later developed the chorusless drama. Now you bring back the chorus. What is the synthesis?

B: That is a very important question. But first: we must speak of the development of the antique drama into the bourgeois drama – we will call it this way – the drama with a hero – we must not make the distinction whether there is the drama with or without chorus. The first phase of the drama known to us shows only the chorus. Then there was the chorus leader. Aeschylos. Then two chorus leaders. I will not try right now to construct a scheme and will speak later about the manifoldedness what concerns the use of the chorus. But I will say that right now we see again that the choric element is brought to the foreground and that the individual is brought more into the background. We have perhaps the phase where the individual is on the way back into the collective. Where this leads to we cannot say yet. I would like to say something about the various kinds of choruses that I have used. You know the chorus in 'The Mother'. There is a different kind of chorus in 'Die Massnahme'. A third version you find in 'Saint Joan of the Stockyards'. Here the chorus whenever it appears represents collectives, you have the chorus of the workers, but also of the capitalists, you have the chorus of the dealers and you have the chorus of the wholesale buyers – all groups with common interests. Each group has its own language. So that if you look at it this way you in the end have an exhibition (demonstration) of idioms. The big meat packers for instance use the Shakespearian blank verse as the language of the rich bourgeois individuals. It is the slang of this society as it has already fixed it in its literature in a classic way. As an example I read to you from the first scene of the play the first lines of dialogue between the great Pierpont Mauler, meat packer, and his partner Cridle.

CRIDLE: Why so sinister, my dear Pierpont?
MAULER: Remember, Cridle, 'twas some days ago –

> We were walking through the slaughter-house, 'twas evening
> And how we stood beside our brand-new cannery etc., etc.

That is how the great free (what's on reason of exploitation) individuals speak. The 'people' on the contrary speak in verses like those of Aristophanes – somewhat hasty syncopated verses – and they speak only in verses when they are in groups, the single one speaks prose.

J: How do you recognise the different kinds of verse?

B: The great individuals speak in the iambic metre, irregular iambics –

J: Pentameter –

B: Yes – but modernised.

J: And what here?

B: Those are free verses, syncopated.

J: MacL also uses mixture of metres. Basic rhythm of American folk diction very different from British. British rhythm is iambic, American Folkrhythm trochaic.

B: With us the rhythm is determined by the class standpoint.

J: Is this to be interpreted that you want to give more dignity to the one group?

B: No. The function is only to be class-distinctive.

J: MacL does not use metric divisions, he uses so to say 'quantity of division'. Units of syllables, units of accents instead of metric arrangements. (Examples: He'll say / properly so / Never again will it come / everywhere I looked for him). 'Panic' is extremely interesting. MacL gives to the chorus 3 accents, to the bankers 5 accents. Because of the five accents the bankers of course get a fuller characterization whereas the chorus of the unemployed remain anonymous. The bankers are by far better drawn, individuals of flesh and blood – the unemployed which he treats sympathetically are shown in the twilight of becoming. Their leader is a blind man.

E: With Brecht the leader would have the best eyes.

J: It is his theory of the leader being a prophet, to see into the future he needs no physical eyesight. His lines are very beautiful. Example: that passage 'Like pebbles into a pool'), beautiful cadence.

B: Eliot has that, too. There are beautiful things in Eliot's works, for example in 'Waste Land'.

J: But he uses not the same method.

B: Yes, this whole method is very strange. I would always prefer the historical method. I would give the various classes that diction that historically belongs to them.

J: I'll ask you this, how would you meet this problem? Suppose you were writing in English – here in the United States – a play about negroes, a historic drama, not 1905, but 1800, and you were writing a heroic drama with an epic sweep, a drama of the revolutionary tradition of the Negroes – what would you do what regards language? What language would you use for characterization? First, would you write it in verse?

B: No, certainly not. The single one would always speak prose. In groups they would speak in that free, syncopated language, gestic rhythm – I would make no exception with the Negroes, not a difference between Negroes, Chinese or Irish.

J: But when the Negroes speak a dialect – the South, about 1800 – would you write the play in dialect?

B: No.

J: How would you meet the need for verisimilitude? Here verisimilitude requires dialect.

B: I would use a dialect when it plays a political part. For instance, there are plantation owners, they speak while doing business pure English. Those that intend to rob (fool, exploit) might speak dialect. If the spectator is supposed to learn that a dialect separates various classes, only then would I use dialect. Nowhere else.

J: Lets take for example, well a drama about a slave insurrection. Only in the first scene you have the slaveowners who speak a cultivated English. They only appear in this first scene, later there are only slaves, practically illiterate. Only one of the slaves is cultured. How would you meet then the language problem?

B: If there is then this cultured negro, this kind of leader, I would use dialect in the first scene and later pure English. If there is this Negro leader I had to investigate first, whether the difference in the diction is important. Perhaps whether there is a ressentiment against the leader because of the difficulty to understand him, whether he is forced to learn their language or they are forced to learn his etc. In all this cases the language problem would be a central one, it would not be accidental.

J: Suppose they understand him, there is no language problem – how shall the slaves speak? Standard English?

B: Standard English, throughout.

J: Verse or prose?

B: Prose.

J: The leader, too?

B: All. In the first scene the owners perhaps speak in verse, but the whole then is in prose.

J: Verse for the slave owners, prose for the slaves, of course their vocablary limited according to their cultural standard. But here is the question: The American people are attuned to hear slaves speak dialect.

B: That's excellent! Then the introduction of standard English is very important. That is revolutionary to let the Negroes speak standard English.

J: You are considering how you would write it – according to your epic theory or as a natural drama?

B: I would not write it as a natural drama. A naturalistic writer could write it in dialect. Not I. You know the 'Weavers' [by Gerhard Hauptmann (1892)], they are written in a beautiful dialect. The play is based on facts. I always wanted to rewrite the play using the documents of the trial, in standard German.

J: As a naturalistic play, without abbreviations?

B: No. I don't like naturalistic plays. A natural play with an idea (ideology) is a perversity. The naturalistic drama is like a piece of earth dug out, a material quantity exposed before your eyes and investigated – of course investigated from a certain standpoint.

J: According to your theory – would you have a chorus of slaves?

B: Perhaps a chorus of white workers.

J: There are there no white workers.

B: Right now I see no chance a chorus there, without really missing the chorus I do not need it.

J: You would make the dialect-concession?

B: No, only as an expression of class-struggle.

E: What do the negroes think of dialect?

J: The emancipated Negro looks upon the dialect as a hangover of slavery.

[B: Do they use the Negro dialect in 'Porgy and Bess'?

J: No, that is not the real Negro dialect.

E: In 'Green Pastures'?

J: Not standard English.]

B: I think, the whole approach to the language problem must be the historic-political one.

J: Of course. But the modern bourgeoisie and blank verse?

E: The bourgeois class with Brecht speaks in blank verse as a means to deride them.

B: (points to the last scenes of 'Saint Joan of the Stockyards' where the verses are written in the manner of 'Faust' as the adequate language form for the capitalists that show the same dualism as Faust: Strive upwards, kick downwards.)

E: To use Goethean verses here has a mean and aggressive effect.

B: The position in the whole process of production determines the language of a person.

E: (shortly tells the story of 'Saint Joan': Like Indra's daughter a Salvation Army girl sets out to help arbitrate in a strike with goodness – she only helps the capitalists.)

J: Religion as enabling Capitalism.

[Über Dramatik vom Typ Mutter', 1935, published in Werner Hecht (ed.): *Brecht im Gespräch*, Suhrkamp, 1975, pp. 44–52. That text was translated from ours in the Brecht Archive. The original was taken down in New York in 1935 by Elisabeth Hauptmann, and includes handwritten amendments or additions to his own remarks by Brecht. We have barely edited it apart from restoring the four bracketed lines, 12–15 lines from the end, and have left her punctuation and US spellings as she typed them. V.J. Jerome was the American Communist Party's intermediary between Brecht and Eisler on the one side and Theatre Union on the other.]

LETTER TO THE NEW YORK WORKERS' COMPANY 'THEATRE UNION' ABOUT THE PLAY 'THE MOTHER'

1

When I wrote the play *The Mother*
On the basis of the book by comrade Gorky and of many
Proletarian comrades' stories about their
Daily struggle, I wrote it
With no frills, in austere language
Placing the words cleanly, carefully selecting
My character's every gesture, as is done
When reporting the words and deeds of the great.
I did my best to
Portray those seemingly ordinary
Countless incidents in contemptible dwellings
Among the far too many-headed as historical incidents
In no way less significant than the renowned
Acts of generals and statesmen in the school books.
The task I gave myself was to tell of a great historic figure
The unknown early champion of humanity
To constitute an example.

2

So you will see the proletarian mother take the road
The long and winding road of her class, see how at the start

She feels the loss of a penny on her son's wages: she cannot
Make him a soup worth eating. So she engages
In a struggle with him, fears she may lose him. Then
Reluctantly she aids him in his struggle for that penny
Ever fearful now of losing him to the struggle. Slowly
She follows her son into the jungle of wage claims. Thereby
She learns to read. Quits her hut, cares for others
Beside her son, in the same situation as he, those with whom she
Earlier struggled over her son; now she struggles alongside them.
Thus the walls around her stove start to tumble. Her table welcomes
Many another mother's son. Once too small for two
Her hut becomes a meeting place. Her son, though
She seldom sees. The struggle takes him from her.
And she herself is among the throng of those struggling. The talk
Between son and mother grows into a rallying-cry
During the battle. In the end the son falls. No longer was it
Possible for her to provide him with his soup by the one
Available means. But now she is standing
In the thickest turmoil of the vast and
Unceasing battle of the classes. Still a mother
Now even more a mother, mother of many now fallen
Mother of fighters, mother of unborn generations, she embarks
On a spring-clean of the State. Gives the rulers stones
In their extorted feast. Cleans weapons. Teaches
Her sons and daughters the ABC of struggle
Against war and exploitation, member of a standing army
Covering the entire planet, harried and harrying
Untolerated and intolerant. Defeated and relentless.

3

So too we staged the play like a report from a great epoch
No less golden in the light of many lamps than the
Royal plays staged in earlier times
No less cheerful and funny, discreet
In its sad moments. Before a clean canvas
The players entered simply with the characteristic
Gests of their scenes, delivering their phrases
Precisely, authentic words. Each phrase's effect
Was awaited and exposed. And also we waited
Till the crowd had laid those phrases in the balance – for we had noticed
How the man who owns little and is often deceived will bite
A coin with his teeth to see if it is genuine. Just like coins then

Must the actors' phrases be tested by our spectators
Who own little and are often deceived. Small hints
Suggested the scene of the action. The odd table and chair:
Bare essentials were enough. But photographs
Of the great opponents were projected on the screens at the back
And the sayings of the socialist classics
Painted on banners or projected on screens, surrounded the
Scrupulous actors. Their bearing was natural
Yet whatever said nothing was left out in the
Carefully considered abridgement. The musical numbers
Were lightly presented, with charm. Much laughter
Filled the house. The unconquerable
Good humour of the resourceful Vlassova, grounded in the assurance of
Her youthful class, provoked
Happy laughs from the workers' benches.
Keenly they took advantage of this rare chance
To experience the usual incidents without urgent danger, thus
Getting the leisure to study them and so prepare
Their own conduct.

4
Comrades, I see you
Reading the short play with embarrassment.
The spare language
Seems like poverty. This report, you reckon
Is not how people express themselves. I have read
Your adaptation. Here you insert a 'Good morning'
There a 'Hullo, my boy'. The vast field of action
Gets cluttered with furniture. Cabbage reeks
From the stove. What's bold becomes gallant, what's historical normal
Instead of wonder
You strive for sympathy with the mother when she loses her son.
The son's death
You slyly put at the end. That, you think, is how to make the spectator
Keep up his interest till the curtain falls. Like a business man
Investing money in a concern, you suppose, the spectator invests
Feeling in the hero: he wants to get it back
If possible doubled. But the proletarian audience
At the first performance never missed the son at the end.
They maintained their interest. Not out of crudeness either.

And then too we were sometimes asked:
Will the workers understand you? Will they renounce
The familiar opiate: the spiritual participation
In other people's anger, in the rise of others, the whole deception
That whips one up for two hours, to leave one still more exhausted
Filled with hazy memories and yet vaguer expectations?
Will you truly, offering
Knowledge and experience, get an audience of statesmen?

Comrades, the form of the new plays
Is new. But why be
Frightened of what's new? Is it hard to bring off?
But why be frightened of what's new and hard to bring off?
To the man who's exploited, continually deceived
Life itself is a perpetual experiment
The earning of a few pennies
An uncertain business which is nowhere taught.
Why should he fear the new rather than the old? And even if
Your audience, the workers, hesitated you should still
Not lag behind it but show it the way
Swiftly show it the way with long strides, its final power inspiring
you
With unbounded confidence.

[Written between August and October 1935. First published in *Gesammelte Werke*, vol. 1, Malik-Verlag, London, 1938.]

Editorial Notes

Maxim Gorky wrote his novel *Mother* (called *Comrades* in its first English edition) under the impact of the 1905 Revolution; his friend Lunacharsky, who was Commissar for Enlightenment (i.e. education and the arts) for twelve years after the Bolshevik Revolution of 1917, termed it a 'Lehrbuch' for the European working class. It was filmed by Pudovkin in 1926 for Mezhrabpom-Russ, and shown successfully in Germany. Around 1930 it was dramatised by Günther Stark of the Berlin Volksbühne in collaboration with the playwright Günther Weisenborn, but seemingly without the support of that theatre's Socialist management, whose younger subscribers were even then splitting away to form a more radical 'Junge Volksbühne' in the wake of Piscator. Stark, who staged Friedrich Wolf's *The Sailors of Cattaro* at the Volksbühne's main house in November, was reluctant to give the Gorky project further time, but Weisenborn was intrigued by the idea of an 'epic theatre' and decided to bring in a new collaborator in the shape of Brecht. Eisler agreed to write the music, and work began in the summer of 1931.

Gorky's book had been written in 1906, and the Stark/Weisenborn adaptation stuck fairly closely to the original. Thus scene 1 is inside the Vlassovs' hut and shows the Mother agreeing to distribute leaflets in the factory. Scene 2 is the factory yard. Scene 3, a barn in the country, where the comrades plan the May Day demonstration. In scene 4 they demonstrate and are arrested. Scene 5 is the Mother visiting Pavel in prison to get the names of rural sympathisers. In scene 6 she distributes leaflets in the village of Nikolskoye. In scene 7 she is involved in an attempt to free the comrades from prison. Scene 8, the last, is the courtroom where they are tried; the set revolves to show the crowd outside. The Mother announces the verdict from within: penal servitude for life, in Siberia. But 'An idea cannot be suppressed by force. Siberia for life . . . what does it matter? Cheer up, my dear friends.' She weeps, all start singing and in the background the windows of the court building light up. The songs in the adaptation are traditional ones of the Socialist movement.

It is not clear how far Weisenborn contributed from that point on, but the play was radically rewritten, and the surviving accounts of its thirty-odd performances at different Berlin venues during 1932 attribute this entirely to Brecht, who certainly regarded it as his play. In the 1933 *Versuche* edition the collaborators are given as 'Brecht Eisler Weisenborn'; in the 1938 Malik-Verlag edition Weisenborn was not mentioned – he had remained in Germany as one of the 'Red Orchestra' network – but the Bulgarian Slatan Dudow was mentioned instead; he had been directing the Brecht/Eisler/Ottwalt film *Kuhle Wampe* during the rewriting of the play. Then the name Weisenborn was again added in the *Gesammelte Werke* of 1967. If Elisabeth Hauptmann, Brecht's aide and editor, did not mention herself (as she did in the case of all the Lehrstück collaborations apart from *The Decision*) it could be because she remained in Germany as a member of the Communist underground till the end of 1933.

Structure and characters

The first five of the eight scenes outlined above served as a basis for Brecht's version as far as the end of the prison scene. From that point on he altered and extended the story, which Gorky had confined to the events of 1905, so as to take it up to the eve of the Bolshevik revolution in 1917. There was thus no court scene; Pavel escapes from exile and is shot after his appearance as a fugitive in scene 9; in scene 11 we hear that the First World War has broken out, and the play ends with the Mother leading an anti-war demonstration in scene 14. Her evolution from an unpolitical sceptic into a self-confessed Bolshevik is therefore at the centre of the play, while Pavel (who in Gorky developed from a sullen young drunkard into an exiled hero) is a secondary and, in the last quarter of the play, liquidated figure. Not surprisingly, Russian and Soviet critics have shown little enthusiasm for this approach, and even if it is true that Brecht was hoping to counter the increasing anti-Soviet propaganda in Germany – whether in 1931 or after 1945 – it is widely agreed that the characters are more German than Russian, while the problems finally tackled are those of the KPD on the collapse of the Weimar Republic rather than of the Russians after 1905.

Brecht's *The Mother* has been essentially the same play since it was first written, but its text and production are marked by three phases of intense interest: 1932, Berlin's last year of Left theatre and active agitprop; 1935, when it was staged in New York during the 'New Deal'; and 1951, when Brecht staged it in Max Reinhardt's old theatre with his new Berliner Ensemble. These correspond roughly to the three main book editions: the *Versuche* of 1933, the émigré Malik *Gesammelte Werke 2* of 1938 and the Suhrkamp *Gesammelte Werke 2* of 1967 – though the last was a final text in accordance with Brecht's and Hauptmann's wishes rather than the acting script of 1951. Each time the nature of the exercise was different, starting with the terse, agitational nature of the first, with its echoes of *He Said Yes* in the opening scene, its thinly orchestrated Eisler settings and its easily dismantled and transportable Neher sets. It seems seldom to have played more than two or three nights in any of its provisional venues, and in one famous production for the IAH (or International Workers' Aid) in a community hall the police forced it to dispense with costumes, sets and even acting; it became a reading.

In New York the Theatre Union embarked on Brecht's text under a misapprehension; clearly they would sooner have used their own, more naturalistic version of it, as being closer to Gorky. Here again there were some thirty-five performances, all in their conventional proscenium house, the Civic Repertory Theatre; instead of the original piano, trumpet, trombone and percussion the band there consisted of two pianos; for Brecht's and Eisler's frustrated interventions see pp. 366–369 above. The agitprop element seems to have been preserved – this was the theatre where Odets's *Waiting for Lefty* was performed the same year – but Brecht's ideas of 'epic theatre' were not seen as acceptable.

Finally in 1951, just nine years after its Berlin première, Brecht directed a long-running production in the old-established Deutsches Theater, with his wife Helene Weigel in her original part as the Mother, music once again by Eisler and sets by Neher, but with richer orchestration, a new naturalism in costumes and décor and a greater concern with the Russian background. This was not so surprising in a State where Soviet Russia was regarded as a model, not least in the theatre. The main textual changes were due to the new prominence given to Smilgin, along with a shuffling of characters to fit the Ensemble's actors; not all of this was transferred to the 1967 edition.

In the stage directions and projections, dates were amended to accord with history. Thus scene 5 (1 May 1900 in the original dialogue, 1908 in 1938) was changed to 1905; scene 8 (1909–1913) to summer 1905; scene 9 (1913) to 1912; scene 11 (undated) to 1914; scene 13 (undated) to 1916. The names of the characters also varied. In the 1951 production the Vessovchikov brothers were called Lapkin, but this was changed back in the 1967 edition. The unemployed worker Sostakovitch became Sigorski, and new names were given to some of the minor figures, then likewise dropped in 1967.

In 1933 the central figure is called 'The Mother' throughout. The 1938 edition always prints her names – Pelagea Vlassova – and this was followed in 1967.

Details of changes and cuts since 1933

Scene 2: The song 'The Answer' (also 'Lied von Ausweg' or 'Lied von der Suppe') was added in 1935/37.

Scene 3: Smilgin, who in 1933 did not appear until his entrance carrying the red flag in scene 5, is introduced as 'an old worker' in 1967, answering the First Worker's 'So what?' with: 'I'm against handing out leaflets like that while negotiations are going on'. In the stage direction he is named as one of the works committee. One or two lines are then shuffled.

The 'Song of the Patches and the Coat' (or 'The Whole Loaf') was added in 1935. Following that song all Karpov's lines except the exclamation 'A strike, then!' became given to Smilgin in 1967; before 1951 it was Karpov that was arrested. In the 1951 production Smilgin was played by Friedrich Gnass.

Scene 4: The Mother's initial allusion to Smilgin was originally to Karpov; and Ivan said nothing about his being released.

Scene 5: The spoken chorus in 1933 ended 'With our sides's conclusive triumph/In every town and every country/Where workers are found'.

Scene 6: The subdivisions of this long scene into (a), (b), (c) and (d) are not marked by letters before 1967. In the New York production 'Praise of Communism' was called 'Praise of Socialism'. In 1933 the Teacher's flat was not situated.

In the song 'Praise of the Revolutionary' lines 4–6 were not included in 1933, then substituted for lines 1–3 in 1938. However all six were in Eisler's *Neun Balladen* version of 1932, and this is followed in the 1967 text.

The lines in square brackets from the Teacher's 'they'll make a revolution' to '*Ivan laughs*' were added in 1938.

Scene 8: Again, the letters marking the sub-division were added in 1967. For the second half of (a) we have followed the two earlier versions. The 1967 dialogue has been slightly altered.

Scene 9: Vassil Yefimovitch, the Butcher from the previous scene, did not appear again in 1933. By 1938 he had taken over and expanded the lines of the Second Worker in this scene, and would also appear in the demonstration of scene 14.

The Small Store or The Paper Overcoat: This was scene 10 in the 1933 version, but appears to have been omitted from the 1932 production, and is not known ever to have been played. Appended on pp. 384–386 below.

Scene in a Railway Carriage: by Paul Peters. Appended on pp. 386–394 below. This was included as an additional scene in Peters's 1935 translation. Brecht liked it, made his own draft version in German and suggested that it should be the opening scene of Act 3, preceding scene 10 (and the announcement of Pavel's death). It was unpublished till 1988, and is not known to have been played.

Scene 10: Of the three commiserating women only the Landlady was named in 1933. In 1938 the others became the Peasant Woman and the Poor Woman, of which the former was described by the Landlady as 'My relative is visiting here'. Then in 1967 she was named as the Niece Up From the Country.

For Pelagea's final remark (which she '*Calls after them*') we follow the two earlier versions. The bracketed sentence is cut in 1967.

Scene 11: In 1933 this came after scene 12, so that the attack on Pelagea, rather than the news of Pavel's death, was the reason for her taking to her bed. The opening exchange between doctor and teacher was accordingly shorter, the former saying 'She has been badly beaten up, and is no longer young'. Nor is the word 'war' mentioned.

Scene 12 (originally scene 11): In the Mother's recitation the last line about the 'class enemy' was added in 1935/37.

Scene 13: Is virtually the same in all versions apart from the initial specification of the date.

Scene 14: In 1933, beside the Mother and the Maidservant from the previous scene, Ivan Vessovchikov and the butcher Vassil Yefimovitch are marching. The (projected) heading to the scene says that they were 'in the ranks of the striking workers and mutinous sailors'. Photographs show how this was suggested in the 1951 production.

Appended scenes

(a) THE SMALL STORE OR THE PAPER OVERCOAT

Even in small everyday matters the Mother battles with the indifference of the exploited towards their sufferings. The paper overcoat.

WORKING-CLASS WOMAN *with a child*: How much does that come to?

THE STOREKEEPER: 5 for the sausage, flour 12, jam 10, tea 20, 2 kopecks for the matches. That's 49 kopecks altogether.

WORKING-CLASS WOMAN *to the child*: There you are, Ilyitch, 49 kopecks, and I've still got to get you a coat. *To the other women in the shop*: He's always freezing.

THE WOMEN: He's much too thinly dressed. It's not surprising he's cold. How can you let him go around like that when it's snowing so hard?

WORKING-CLASS WOMAN: I've only 20 kopecks left. Do you have any coats?

The Storekeeper shows her a rack with six children's coats on it.

WORKING-CLASS WOMAN: That's quite a few. *She feels the material.* The right size too. That one's not all that expensive. Not so warm of course. But it's not bad. The one with the lining would be better.

THE STOREKEEPER: It's also dearer.

WORKING-CLASS WOMAN: So how much is the thin one?

THE STOREKEEPER: Five and a half rubles.

WORKING-CLASS WOMAN: Right, then I can't buy it. I've not got that much money.

THE STOREKEEPER: Death's free. *To another woman*: What can I get you?

THE WOMAN: Half a pound of semolina.

WORKING-CLASS WOMAN: They cut wages again last week in the Muratov works.

THE MOTHER: I heard that too: and the workers agreed.

WORKING-CLASS WOMAN: Only because Mr Muratov would have closed his works down if they hadn't. If you ask me to choose between low wages and shutting down the factory I'd take the low wages.

THE MOTHER: There you are, Ilyitch, you always have to go for the lesser evil. After all it's the lesser evil for Mr Muratov too. He'd rather pay less than more. If Mr Muratov is to make a profit, Ilyitch, then he must cut your father's wages. There's no reason why your father should go on working if he doesn't want to. But you need a coat. And not a coat for 20 kopecks but a coat. If he needed a 20-kopeck coat then this would be it. *She picks a paper pattern off the counter and puts it on little Ilyitch.*

THE STOREKEEPER: Just leave my paper patterns where they are.

THE WOMAN: It's only in fun.

SECOND WOMAN: Why are you making the child ridiculous?

THE MOTHER: Who's making Ilyitch ridiculous? Me or Mr Muratov and the man who made the coat? Ilyitch wants a coat for a few kopecks. Now he's got one. Isn't it warm enough? He should have asked for a warm one!

THE STOREKEEPER: That's right: tell me it's my fault for not giving the coat for nothing.

WORKING-CLASS WOMAN: That's not what I asked for. I know you can't do that.

FIRST WOMAN *to the Mother*: You weren't saying anything of the sort, were you – that it's the storekeeper's fault?

THE MOTHER: No. It's nobody's fault but Ilyitch's.

WORKING-CLASS WOMAN: Anyway I can't buy the coat.

THE STOREKEEPER: You don't have to buy it if the price is too much for you.

THE MOTHER: That's right, Ilyitch, you don't need a coat if the price is too much for you.

WORKING-CLASS WOMAN: I've got just 20 kopecks left, and that's all.

SECOND WOMAN: I know her. She goes around spreading discontent.

FIRST WOMAN *indicating the Storekeeper, who is now in tears*: And she's still got to pay the man who made the coat.

THE MOTHER: Of course that's not a coat, there's no warmth in it. And those – *pointing to the six coats on the rack* – are not coats either; they're goods. If the coatmaker is to make his profit, then there can be no other coat for Ilyitch. This coat, Ilyitch, is the lesser evil, no coat at all would be the greater. Take your coat and go outdoors, Ilyitch; tell the snow to take care of you, as Mr Muratov doesn't want to. You have got the wrong coat and the wrong parents, Ilyitch; they don't know how to get coats for you. Go and tell the snow and the wind they should be snowing in here; it's where the coats are.

[From *Versuche* 7, 1933, where it was included in the play as scene 10.]

(b) SCENE IN A RAILWAY CARRIAGE (from the 1935 New York production)

ACT THREE

Scene 1

A compartment in a railroad. Two wooden benches face each other, with racks for luggage overhead. In the rear is the hallway which runs the length of the train, and a window. It is a cold day, in the early winter of 1916.

The Mother enters dressed as a peasant woman with a kerchief over her head. She looks around, sees nobody in the compartment, sits down and waits.

THE MOTHER: I'm early. The train's almost empty. This is my first important (Party) assignment. It's dangerous, but I mustn't be afraid. Pavel wouldn't like it if he thought I was afraid. If only I could hear once in a while from Pavel! All I know is that he's organising in the army at the front. That's the most dangerous work there is, but it's got to be done. All right, it's got to be done. You must keep your wits together now, Pelagea Vlassova.

The Worker passes in the corridor, sees the Mother, comes in, looks cautiously about, and sits down beside her. For a moment they act as if they don't know each other. Then:

THE WORKER *blurting it out*: The teacher's gone!

THE MOTHER: Gone?

THE WORKER: I look behind and all of a sudden he isn't following me any more. Gone, just like that.

THE MOTHER: But the grip!

THE WORKER: Grip's gone too. Oh, these intellectuals, comrade. Crammed full of learning, everything from tree to fish. But they can't do the simplest thing right; can't even follow a man down the street.

THE MOTHER *alarmed*: Maybe something happened to him. There are so many spies these days.

THE WORKER: All the more reason why he shouldn't *let* anything happen to him.

THE MOTHER: But we can't lose our literature. We better go back.

THE WORKER: Sure. Go right back and say: 'Hoy, you spy. You can't have that. We sat up all night printing it on our illegal presses. It's our anti-war literature. It's for the soldiers. What do you want with it? You're a spy. Give it back.'

THE MOTHER: Don't talk so loud. They'll hear you in the next compartment. *She gets up, goes to the hallway and looks into it.*

THE WORKER: Anybody there?

THE MOTHER: No. *She looks out the window.* We walked too fast for him, maybe. He's getting to be an old man. *She sees something out the window; then she breathes in relief.* There he is now: looking for us. *You* better signal him.

The Worker goes to the window, while the Mother returns to the bench. He whistles sharply, then makes a quick jerk of the head. He returns to the seat. After a moment the Teacher comes in, puffing, excited, carrying a large yellow grip. He sets it down, takes off his hat and wipes his face.

THE TEACHER: No, no, no. You have no right to ask this of me. It's too dangerous. I'll lose my position, and then I'll be of no use either to you people or to myself. I won't be able to give you any advice when I'm in jail, you know.

THE WORKER: It's more important for you to carry our literature.

THE MOTHER: Be quiet, Sostakovich. We thank you for bringing the grip, Nikolai Ivanovich. You see: you can carry it through the streets without suspicion. We can't. When they see you everybody says: 'The poor man, he has so much learning he can't carry it all in his head any more.'

THE TEACHER: I was followed.

THE MOTHER: Followed?

THE WORKER: You're sure?

THE TEACHER: I looked behind, and here's a fellow with a dark coat following me. I cross the street. He crosses the street. I turn the corner: he turns the corner. I walk faster: he walks faster. I think I've seen him around the house before. There was something familiar about the look in his eyes. He has two warts on his cheek running up from his mouth, so he looks like he's sneering all the time.

THE MOTHER: What did you do?

THE TEACHER: I jumped in a cab.

THE WORKER: And the spy? Did he jump in a cab too?

THE TEACHER: I didn't see him any more. *He takes a bundle of pamphlets out of his grip, wrapped in the green shawl, like a peasant's bundle.* Here are the pamphlets, Mrs Vlassova. I must go now.

THE MOTHER *as voices are heard outside*: You must both go. There are people getting on the train.

THE WORKER *rising*: Now remember: at the first stop Andrei will get on the train and say: 'Is there room for me beside your bundle, mother?' And you say: 'There's always room for one of the Czar's soldiers.' That's the password. Then you take his bundle, and he takes yours, and it's done.

THE MOTHER: Go, go. I'll remember.

THE WORKER: But what if they catch you?

THE MOTHER: I'll say I don't know anything about it. Somebody just smuggled them into my bundle.

THE TEACHER: They won't believe that.

THE MOTHER: Then I'll think of something. I've passed out literature before. Now go.

THE WORKER *hesitating*: You won't be afraid, Pelagea Vlassova?

THE MOTHER: Nobody asks any other member (of the Party) if they're afraid. Why do you ask me?

THE TEACHER: Goodbye, Pelagea Vlassova. Take care of yourself.

Other people come into the compartment, one at a time: first a big burly soldier; then a man with a dark coat, the collar of which is turned up over his face; then a middle-aged working woman.

THE MOTHER: Goodbye, Nikolai Ivanovich. Goodbye, Sostakovich. *For the benefit of the newcomers*: Tell your wife if she makes any more lace to send it to me. In my village I'll always be able to sell such fine lace.

The two men leave. The train passengers begin to settle down. The bell rings and a voice cries: 'All aboard!'

THE SOLDIER: Well, we're moving.

THE MOTHER *relieved*: Yes, we're moving.

THE WORKING WOMAN: It's so cold in here.

THE MOTHER: They've got to save on coal, haven't they? What would the generals and the big people have, if they used up all the coal on us? *The Soldier is beating his arms and stamping his feet.* You soldier: are you cold, too?

THE SOLDIER: What do you think? I carry a stove with me?

THE MOTHER: But you're going to the front, aren't you?

THE SOLDIER: Yes, and you freeze plenty there, too.

THE MOTHER: But you'll be fighting for the Czar. That should warm your heart.

THE SOLDIER: It don't warm your toes, grandma. Especially when this is the kind of shoes you got on your feet – *Showing her the holes in his soles.* And this is the kind of coat you got to wear. *Showing her his torn overcoat.*

THE MOTHER: What do you care if you freeze? The important thing is that the generals don't freeze. Plain people like you and me: couple of frozen toes don't hurt them much.

THE SOLDIER *ripping off a piece of loose leather from his torn shoe*: I wonder how the Czar would like to fight in shoes like this.

THE WORKING WOMAN: I have two sons at the front. I hate to think of them lying in the snow and ice all winter with torn coats and holes in their shoes.

THE MOTHER: Oh, a few common soldiers like that: that don't make no difference. If they freeze, there are always plenty more. What we've got to think about is beating the Germans so we can get Turkey.

THE SOLDIER: Get what?

THE MOTHER: Turkey. And Galicia and Armenia too. But first of all we've got to pay the bankers back for their loans. Why should you want a new coat and shoes when we've got to pay the bankers?

The man in the dark overcoat gets up and crosses the compartment.

THE MAN: Excuse me. I don't like to ride backwards. *He stands looking down at the Mother.* Do you mind if I move your bundle?

THE MOTHER: Sit over there. I don't want my eggs broken.

THE MAN: I thought it was lace you had.

THE MOTHER *looking up at him, cautiously*: Eggs too.

THE MAN: I'd like to sit near the window. I'm not feeling well. *Suddenly reaching out for the bundle.* I'll put it overhead for you.

THE MOTHER *rising and snatching the bundle from him*: Don't you – *His coat collar has dropped down and now she sees the two warts on his face running up from his mouth, so that he looks as if he were sneering. She stands in confusion a moment.* You leave my bundle alone.

THE MAN: What makes your eggs so heavy?

The Mother has an impulse to run out; she even looks toward the door; then she conquers it, sets the bundle down squarely on the same spot on the bench, and sits down.

THE MOTHER *loudly*: Such fresh people you meet on the trains these days. No respect, not even to an old woman like me. After five minutes, they want to look through your bundle. They want to know how many eggs you've got and how big they are. I suppose now I have to take out the wood-carvings I bought to sell in my village and show them to every stranger in the car.

THE MAN: So it's wood-carvings now.

THE MOTHER *feigning to grow more furious*: I tell you, you can't trust nobody these days. The country's full of German spies. They count every bite we put in our mouths so they can write back and tell the Kaiser we're starving. It's true we don't get the right food to eat, and the cost of living's so high poor people can't eat at all, but why should the Germans know about it?

THE SOLDIER *looking at the man with hostility*: You better sit down where you were, mister.

THE MAN: But I just –

THE SOLDIER: Sit down and leave the old woman alone.

The Man sits down on the opposite seat. The Mother smiles at the Soldier.

THE MOTHER: Thank you.

The train has meanwhile slowed up. The conductor's voice calls out 'Nijni. Nijni.' And a moment later: 'All aboard for Gulityan. All aboard!'

THE WORKING WOMAN *looking out on the platform*: More soldiers. They look so young.

THE SOLDIER: It's them kids they're getting in the new draft. Poor kids: they don't know what they're getting into.

THE WORKING WOMAN: Pretty soon there won't be any young men left in the country at all.

A soldier with his coat collar up comes into the coach. He looks into the compartment, enters slowly, and then walks over to the Mother.

SECOND SOLDIER: Is there any room for me beside your bundle, mother?

At the voice the Mother starts and looks up quickly. It is Pavel. A long pause. Then she masters herself and answers slowly.

THE MOTHER: There's always room for one of the Czar's soldiers.

He sits down beside her, placing a large bundle which looks very much like hers, between his feet.

PAVEL *stretching, and sighing in relief*: Agh! Thank God I'm here.

THE SOLDIER: Just back from a furlough, buddy?

PAVEL: Furlough! I haven't had a furlough for three years. How would you feel, mother, if you hadn't seen your son for three years?

THE MOTHER: If I believed in my son, I could wait.

PAVEL: And what would you say to him when you saw him, mother?

THE MOTHER: I'd say: 'It's good to see you, son. I know you had work to do and you couldn't come any sooner.'

PAVEL: I think a man would like a mother like that.

THE SOLDIER: Have you got a son at the front, grandma?

THE MOTHER: Me? No! But I've got a nephew. A fine boy! He's a lieutenant now. If only the war lasts long enough, he's sure to be a captain. Two or three more battles – that's all it takes and he gets gold braid on his shoulders. That is, if enough people get killed, of course.

PAVEL: Aren't you afraid he might be shot, mother?

THE MOTHER: Who? My nephew? Oh, no! Not him. They'll never send him to the front-line trenches. His father's a rich man: a big textile manufacturer in Kostroma. My nephew, he's got it good. He's in the commissary department.

PAVEL: Do you think it's right for the rich people to buy safe places for their sons?

THE MOTHER: Excuse me, it's their war, isn't it!

PAVEL: But we fight it.

THE MOTHER: You've heard the old expression: a rich man's war and a poor man's fight. Sure, you fight it; but just for that reason don't think it's your war. It isn't. It's the rich people's war. Be glad you're allowed to fight in it, but don't claim too much.

THE WORKING WOMAN: Oh, now I'm all confused. They told us the war's for all of us, to save us from the Germans.

THE MOTHER *looking over at the man with the dark coat*: That's just spies. Spies! The country's full of German spies.

THE WORKING WOMAN *shaking her head bewildered, sighing*: If only we had peace!

THE MOTHER: The poor are always crying for peace. The rich are more patriotic. They don't want peace.

PAVEL: There was a man in my company who was shot for saying that, mother.

THE MOTHER: Saying what?

PAVEL: It's a rich man's war. He was organising soldiers' councils and told them that. So smack up against the wall he went. 'Company, fire!' And that was the end of him. Nice fellow, too. His name was Andrei.

The Mother makes a little involuntary gesture, but controls herself.

THE SOLDIER: Are there lots of those councils in your sector, soldier?

PAVEL: Yes, lots of them.

THE SOLDIER: There don't seem to be any in mine.

PAVEL: What division you in?

THE SOLDIER: Ninth. Company C, light artillery.

PAVEL *looking at him to fix the face in his mind*: They'll show up by and by. I hear they're spreading like wildfire. Officers don't seem to like them. But the soldiers: they eat them up and yell for more. *A little pause.* Yes, nice young fellow. Smart too. When he died he yelled: 'Long live the working class! Long live the workers' and soldiers' Soviets!' His name was Andrei.

There is a long tense pause. Everybody in the car looks at him. The Mother, conscious of the staring of the Spy, breaks the silence with:

THE MOTHER: Well, all I say is that if only the war lasts long enough, my nephew will be a captain.

The train has slowed down and the conductor outside cries: 'Gorodskoy! Gorodskoy! Change to Kiev.'

PAVEL *picking up the Mother's bundle, and leaving his at her feet*: Well, here's where I get off. *To the Soldier*. Goodbye, soldier. Give my regards to the Ninth Division, Company C, light artillery. *Turning to the Mother.* And mother, here's hoping your nephew becomes a captain.

The Spy suddenly gets up and seizes Pavel by the arm.

SPY: Here, wait a minute. He's got her bundle.

PAVEL: Whose bundle?

SPY *shouting at the top of his voice*: He's a thief. He stole her bundle. Hey, police! Police!

THE MOTHER: He's crazy. Here's my bundle. He hasn't got my bundle. This is my bundle right here.

SPY *bellowing*: He's a thief! Police! Police!

The compartment is instantly thrown into confusion. Everybody rises. The Spy grapples with Pavel for the bundle. Pavel thrusts the man back and runs out of the compartment. Outside the cry: 'All aboard! All aboard!' Bells, and the train moves again.

SPY *struggling to his feet*: Hold him! He's a thief, a thief! Hold him!

The Mother runs to the door and blocks it against the Spy who now attempts to pursue Pavel.

THE MOTHER: No, you! You're the thief. That soldier didn't take anything from me. But you, you took my money. *Appealing to the others in the compartment.* When he sat down beside me he took my money away.

THE SPY *savagely*: Get out of the way, you old witch.

He gives her a shove, but she clings to him desperately.

THE MOTHER: Soldier! Help me! hold him! He's got my money, soldier.

The Soldier gets up, swings the Spy around, and pins him against the bench.

THE SOLDIER: Now, wait a minute, brother . . .

THE SPY: Let go. He's getting away. I've got to get out here.

THE SOLDIER *very deliberately, holding him helpless*: Well, what's your hurry? Take it easy. *He searches the man's pockets.*

THE SPY *struggling*: You . . . you fool! Get your hands out of my pockets. They're revolutionists! They're Bolsheviks!

THE SOLDIER *calmly pulling out some money*: Is this it, grandma?

THE MOTHER: No. It was tied up in a handkerchief.

THE SPY: Let go, I tell you!

THE SOLDIER *calmly completing his search*: Well, there don't seem to be any handkerchief, grandma. You sure this ain't it? *Holding the Spy down viciously with his knee, and holding up the money.*

THE MOTHER: No. No, it was a big red handkerchief with a knot.

THE SOLDIER *lifting his arms*: Well . . .

The Spy breaks out of his relaxed grip, rushes to the aisle, and shouts:

THE SPY: Police! Police! Hurry up! In here, in here!

The conductor and a policeman come rushing in. The train is moving fast now.

THE POLICEMAN AND CONDUCTOR: Who's shouting? What's the matter?

THE SPY: Illegal literature. They're giving it to the soldiers. Bolsheviks, that's what they are. Traitors! The man got away. That old devil there, she was carrying it in her bundle.

THE MOTHER: In my bundle? But there's nothing in my bundle but a few pieces of lace. Look, I'll show you . . .

She goes to open the bundle, but the Spy snatches it away.

THE SPY: Yeah, so light all of a sudden. The wood carving all sold, I suppose. *He pulls it apart and holds up a few dirty old rags.* You're a clever old jailbird, aren't you? Lace!

THE MOTHER *feigning modesty*: Well, it didn't seem nice to say it was dirty linen.

THE SPY *snorting with rage*: Nice! *He stands indecisive a moment; then he flings the rags furiously down.* Next time I'll know how to handle you, grandma. *He stalks out, flinging after the conductor and policeman.* Come on.

The conductor and policeman leave, spreading their hands in bewilderment to one another.

THE WORKING WOMAN: So he really was a spy.

THE MOTHER: Yes. He really was a spy.

THE SOLDIER: Are you a revolutionist, grandma?

THE MOTHER: Yes, I'm a revolutionist.

THE SOLDIER: I thought as much. *He thinks a moment.* Too bad you didn't save some of that lace for me.

THE MOTHER: There's always a bit extra for one of the Czar's soldiers. *And stooping down, she pulls out a pamphlet from under her skirt and gives it to him.* Don't forget to pass it on.

Blackout.

[Brecht Archive 443/43–52, text of the Theatre Union adaptation by Paul Peters. Brecht then made a German version which, say the notes in *Stücke 3* in the Berlin and Frankfurt edition of 1988, remained unpublished and unperformed. This was titled 'Eisenbahnszene' (Railway Scene) in Margarete Steffin's handwriting, and is included on pp. 391–398 of that volume under the heading 'Annex: draft scene 1935'. Among other things it cuts down the American stage directions and eliminates some characters.]

THE EXCEPTION AND THE RULE

Texts by Brecht

'THE EXCEPTION AND THE RULE'

– a short play for schools . . . was written in 1930. Collaborators: Elisabeth Hauptmann and Emil Burri. There is a musical setting by Paul Dessau.

[Prefixed to the text in *Versuche 15*, 1950. Dessau is not termed a 'collaborator', because his music was not written till 1948.]

NOTES

The 'Lehrstück' *The Exception and the Rule* is supposed to have been written in 1931. It is meant to show how relentlessly the possessive class conducts the class war, even where large sections of the productive class are not yet fighting. The possessive class acts in every situation as directed by the assumption that the productive class will resist it.

It is good if one of the two choruses provides an example from history. At the present day, for instance, the Right chorus can perform the following:

[Note for an incomplete project *c.* 1936 for a version with two choruses. The speech that follows is in another typescript of the same date. Both are in *Schriften 4*, Berlin and Frankfurt edition, 1991, pp. 109 and 490.]

SPEECH

I take the following examples from the history of my own country. When Hitler seized power, a profound discontent prevailed among the lower levels of the populace – the coolies of my country. Nevertheless there was no rebellion. In less time than it takes to build a house, Hitler destroyed the coolies' power by throwing all their leaders into prison and cancelling all their rights. In other words he treated them exactly as if they had made a bloody rebellion. He even set fire to a public building and treated the lower orders exactly as though they had burned it themselves. He did this on the ground, so he said, that because they were hungry they had every reason to rebel bloodily.

They might not have put that into practice, but who can say? Let us treat them as rebels, then there will be no rebellion. That was wise. A year later there was discontent among those who had won the power for him, because they had not got what they had been promised. However, before they could rebel he had their leaders arrested and shot, and threw many of them into prison, with the result that a rebellion was avoided. He told himself: are they not hungry, and did I not make promises to them? They have cause for rebellion. I shall treat them as rebels. That again was wise. It is the only possible way to act if one wishes to rule.

Editorial Notes

Brecht's first idea for this play is thought to date from the time of *He Said Yes* and the writing of *The Decision*. It was inspired by a full-length Chinese play of the Yüan dynasty which Elisabeth Hauptmann had just translated from the French. This was a nineteenth-century version, made by M. Bazin *aîné*, and his title was *Ho-Han-Shan ou la tunique confrontée* ('confrontation' here meaning 'matching'). Hauptmann called it *Zwei halbe Mäntel* after the coat which is torn in half and given to a father and a son so they can identify one another. It really has very little to do with Brecht's play apart from involving a journey and a judicial verdict at the end. But it seems that Hauptmann and Emil Hesse-Burri, who together had been working on *Saint Joan of the Stockyards*, were now given the task of developing her Chinese kernel on a smaller and simpler scale, under the initial title *The Story of a Journey*. This work coincided with the Brecht/Eisler/Dudow collaboration on *The Decision*, which clearly took precedence. The new play would involve choruses and songs, but we do not know how much thought was given to the question of music.

Like *The Decision* it was set in a never-never China; the one meaningful place-name being Urga, the old name for the Mongolian capital, Ulan Bator. And at first it seemed to rely largely on confrontation and contradiction: setting two choruses, Left and Right, to argue with one another, and even introducing a counter-title, *The Rule and the Exception*, along with two contradictory verdicts at the end, like the 'dialectical' opposition of *He Said Yes* and *He Said No*. So the opening chorus, now delivered by the Actors, was given to the Left Chorus, after which the Right Chorus came in with:

We confirm
The truth of these events. But
We see them as an unfortunate hitch
In the story of oil exploitation
By the Western pioneers.
We point out what is behind these things:
The conquest of the earth
By the race of Man.

Similarly at the end, the epilogue now spoken by the Actors was spoken by the Left Chorus only, and preceded by the Right Chorus with:

The law has spoken. The judgement seems harsh.
But oil must be extracted
And the load must be carried.
It is not for his own happiness
That Man is born. So let these events now
Be forgotten.

Another sketch for the antiphonal use of the two choruses comes from the same source, pp. 474–475 of the Berlin and Frankfurt *Stücke 3*, 1988. This raises an issue of some relevance today:

THE RIGHT CHORUS:
Forward! Merchant! Our cities were born
Of massive competition! Oil
Is delivered cheaply and in rich profusion
To the poorest hut, thanks to competition! Civilisation
Progresses through competition! The swift
Are beaten by the shrewder. So forward! The shrewd
Give in to the more shrewd. So forward! To him who brings the greater usefulness
The reward will be given. So forward!

THE LEFT CHORUS:
Oh, he is running too fast!
Slow, coolie! Their cities are great
But not good. In the leaky hut
Oil lights up hunger. Competition
Increases the brutality. The shrewd porter
Is slow. He fights
The haste which will finish him. Every step
That can be saved is a gain.
Competition between your exploiters
Is not yours. The most useful
Get the least reward.

Here the 'Right' and 'Left' were to have a political connotation. But this more ritualistic approach was discarded, perhaps around the time when Brecht went into exile and the collaboration with Hauptmann was interrupted. There was no more Chorus. The planned publication in the *Versuche* series had to be put off (till 1950, as it turned out) and from now on he would revise and simplify the play with

Margarete Steffin. It first appeared in 1937 in the German edition of the Moscow magazine ***Internationale Literatur***, without the label 'Lehrstück', after which Brecht checked it again before its definitive publication as a 'Lehrstück' in volume 2 of the Malik-Verlag *Gesammelte Werke*. This has been the basis of all subsequent printings, and there is no evidence of Brecht having worked on it again since 1938. It is unmentioned in his *Journals*.

In that year it was performed in Hebrew in Palestine (as the country was then called) by the actors of a kibbutz at Givat Chaim, directed by Alfred Wolf. The music, for voice and clarinet, was by the little-known Bulgarian-born Nissim Nissimov. Then after the Second World War Jean-Marie Serreau staged it in Paris in 1947 at the little Théâtre de Poche in a translation by Geneviève Serreau and Benno Besson, who would also play the Guide; they then toured it in the French Occupation Zone of Germany, until the military government began objecting. With this tour in mind Brecht had asked Paul Dessau to compose the songs, apparently for performance in German, and such a performance was given, still under Serreau, at the Comédie des Champs-Elysées in July 1949. The first purely German production was in September 1956, a few weeks after Brecht's death, at the Düsseldorf Kammerspiele; the Dessau music (later to become mandatory for any production) was not used. According to Carl Weber, then one of Brecht's assistant directors, Brecht had become more interested in the play than his recommendation of it as a substitute for *The Decision* (see his letter to Paul Patera on p. 347 above) might suggest.

In England it was staged by Unity Theatre in October 1956, following the Ensemble's first London season, and there have been a number of productions in schools and colleges, where its straightforward simplicity has made it one of the most acceptable of Brecht's works.

THE HORATIANS AND THE CURIATIANS

Texts by Brecht

NOTE TO THE TEXT

The Horatians and the Curiatians, written in 1934, is a Lehrstück for children about dialectics. It is part of the 24th experiment (plays for schools).

[Prefixed to the text in *Versuche 14*, Berlin, 1955. 'Dialectics' for Brecht was a way of thinking about processes – historical, social, scientific – which Karl Marx had developed on the basis of the philosophy of Hegel.]

PREPARATORY WORK ON 'THE HORATIANS AND THE CURIATIANS'

1

Can the story be constructed on the basis of 'parity' of forces? In real life such parity does not exist. But at given moments it does, and can be brought about by inequality of the terrain and so on. Moreover wars do not take place, or do not develop without the presence of a certain parity. Guile is more easily demonstrated if one assumes parity; then it is guile that is decisive. But perhaps it is best brought about by exploiting one's own peculiarities (weakness or superiority) along with those of the other man. Tricks alone prove nothing; they are accidental and difficult to teach, leaving an inadequate recommendation of guile as such.

2

Can the story be constructed on the basis of inequality of forces? Awkward. Here the victor loses two of his three battles. Intellectual superiority wins him the third. So the stronger has to succumb. Then in what respect was he the stronger? Was he better armed – that too would have called for intelligence. (Better production . . .) More powerful? That depends on good economy. And so on.

3

The first battle could be won by better exploitation of the peculiarities of one's equipment. The second by exploiting the terrain. The third, then, by organisation.

[From vol. 24 of the Berlin and Frankfurt edition, Suhrkamp, 1991, edited by Peter Kraft *et al.*, p. 220. Written in 1934, at the planning stage.]

TRADITIONAL CHINESE ACTING

It is well known that the Chinese theatre uses a lot of symbols. Thus a general will carry little pennants on his shoulder, corresponding to the number of regiments under his command, Poverty is shown by patching the silken costumes with irregular shapes of different colours, likewise silken, to indicate that they have been mended. Characters are distinguished by particular masks, i.e. simply by painting. Certain gestures of the two hands signify the forcible opening of a door, etc. The stage itself remains the same, but articles of furniture are carried in during the action.

[A passage from Brecht's 'Verfremdungseffekte in der chinesischen Schauspielkunst', written in 1935/36 and included in *Brecht on Theatre* (1964) as 'Alienation Effects in Chinese Acting'.]

INSTRUCTION FOR THE ACTORS

1

At the same time the Generals stand for their armies. Following a convention of the Chinese theatre, the elements of those armies can be indicated by little flags which the Generals wear on wooden shoulder-frames. They stick above the shoulder. The actors' movements have to be slow, due to their awareness of supporting the shoulderframes, and of a certain breadth. The actors show the destruction of their army units by pulling a number of flags out of their shoulderframes with a great gesture and throwing them away.

2

The landscape is fixed to the floor of the stage. Actors and spectators alike see the river or the valley drawn there. If the stage is raked a complete structure can be built on it, the entire battlefield, knee-high forests, hills and so on. This décor must not be too prodigal (e.g. not coloured) but the kind of thing seen on old maps. In the chapter called 'Seven conversions of a spear' the obstacles (such as Crevasse, Snowdrift etc.) can be indicated on small panels fixed to the bare scaffolding.

3
The positions of footsteps also need to be fixed; to some extent the actors follow one another's footprints. This is necessary because the time has to be measured. In the first battle the clock is the actor carrying the sun. During the 'Seven conversions' in the second, it is the Curiatian. The portrayal of the events must move as slowly as if it were under a magnifying glass.

4
In the battle of the archers no arrows are needed.

5
To indicate a blizzard a few handfuls of torn paper are thrown over the spearmen.

6
About speaking the verse: the voice starts each line afresh. But the recitation must not seem jerky.

7
One can make do without music by just using drums. After a while the drums will become monotonous, but not for long.

8
The titles should be projected or painted on banners.

[Written for the play's first publication in *Internationale Literatur (Deutsche Blätter)*, 1936, no. 1, and included with corrections in the Malik-Verlag *Gesammelte Werke*, vol. 2, 1938. Also in the subsequent collected editions.]

Editorial Notes

1934 may have been the year of the play's conception, but the main work was done in 1935. This was when Brecht and Eisler had both visited Moscow. The former saw the private performance by the Chinese actor Mei Lan-fang which led him to write the essay 'Alienation Effects in Chinese Acting' where he first used the term 'Verfremdungseffekt' and also made the reference to the use of little flags which we cite above. Eisler, who had just been appointed chairman of the Comintern's International Music Bureau, left Moscow after Brecht, bringing with him a commission from the Red Army to write a 'Lehrstück' for children, for which Brecht assumed Eisler would compose the music. Thus Brecht's letter 267 of 29 August says that he has started work on the play 'on your initiative'. This happened when the New York *Mother* production was already impending, and Eisler (though not as yet Brecht) was due to go over there.

The idea of a stylised playlet on a military theme seems to have come from a nineteenth-century translation of Livy's history of Rome, which Brecht owned and subsequently drew on for his adaptation of *Coriolanus*. On the eve of a war in the seventh century BC between Rome and the nearby Alba Longa (Castel Gandolfo) the two cities decided that the rival armies should be represented each by three warriors, chosen from their leading families, the Horatii for Rome and the Curiatii for the Alban city. Each family put a trio of brothers, supposedly triplets, all skilled in one of the three military weapons of the time: the crossbow, the spear or lance, and the sword. On the face of it, then, there was parity of forces and equipment on the two sides, and at first the battle seemed equal. But then two of the Horatii were brought down and the third was expected to surrender. He however chose to run away, and in so doing to kill his three opponents one by one. Whether this put Brecht in mind of Napoleon's Russian campaign we do not know – he mentioned it incidentally in the cited article – but the military symbolism clearly intrigued him, and the Chinese use of flags and a bare set accorded well with it. There is also Corneille's tragedy *Horace* (1640), which centres on the victorious brother and his love for his wife Sabine, a sister of the Curiatians, together with his own sister Camille and her love for Curiace (of the rival family), whom he kills. The account of the fighting is much the same, but it is hearsay; we never see it; nor do the other brothers on each side appear. Nor have we any idea whether Brecht knew that classic work in rhyming couplets.

A number of commentators attribute the absence of any music, or specific provision for music, to an unexplained quarrel between Eisler and Brecht. If there was indeed such a quarrel it can hardly have provoked Eisler's failure to stay with Brecht in Denmark in early September, but may rather have been the result of it. Brecht's letter cited above suggests that the plan was thrown out by Eisler's going off to Prague, as he felt bound to spend the first half of the month there in his new IMB capacity. This left virtually no time for visiting Brecht, before his boat left for New York, and so he chose to spend his two spare days in Paris rather than make the long detour from Prague via Denmark. This, at least, is what he eventually told Hans Bunge. Meanwhile Brecht, with Margarete Steffin's help, had finished the revised version of the text by September 15th, nor were there any major changes before its publication in Moscow the following spring. Eisler seems not to have composed any music for it, apart from an unpublished sketch or two in the Eisler Archive, dating possibly from before September 1935. Some five years later Brecht discussed a collaboration with the Finnish composer Simon Parmet, but this too led to nothing. Only in the last year of Brecht's life would there be a setting by the East German composer Kurt Schwaen, scored for woodwind, brass, percussion, piano and double-bass.

Brecht treated the Soviet commission as urgent and was plainly disappointed that it led nowhere. Yet he resumed the partnership with Eisler seamlessly almost at once, getting him to set further songs for the forthcoming *Round Heads and Pointed Heads* production, and presenting a common front to the Theatre Union over *The Mother*. All the same, there is no sign of his having pressed Eisler further about the school play, or even of having sent him the finished script. And he made none of his radical attempts to rework or transform it. Rather he suggested an unusually free treatment of the text: the Generals could introduce speeches or harangues of their own; there could be dialogues between one of the choruses and a member of the audience; and finally, the label 'Lehrstück' was dropped in favour of 'Schulstück' or 'Play for schools'. The text remained unwanted until shortly before Brecht's death in 1956. Then it was taken up by the music department of Halle university, where Hella Brock had been asking for a work of this kind. At Brecht's suggestion Kurt Schwaen composed thirty musical numbers for it. The emphasis was on mime and dance, and the première was on 26 April 1958. The impact appears to have been slight.

ST JOAN OF THE STOCKYARDS

Texts by Brecht

PRELIMINARY NOTE TO THE STAGE SCRIPT (1931)

Place: Chicago
Time: c.1900

A screen in the background can carry statements detailing the course of business. This consists of a crisis of several weeks affecting the meat trade, during which the workers in the big packing yards are locked out. In view of the symptoms of an impending saturation of the market (falling prices, heightened competition, the threat of protective tariffs in the adjoining states) Pierpont Mauler decides to take his money out of the meat business. His shares are transferred to his crony Cridle in exchange for the elimination of his rival Lennox. This is achieved, but at the same time the by now fully developed crisis forces the Mauler-Cridle group to shut down. Once meat prices have fallen till they can hardly go further, Mauler places huge orders with the meat plants. Simultaneously, to keep his control of meat prices, he buys up the stockbreeders' livestock. From then on the packing plants can only meet his orders by buying livestock from himself. The crucial battle is fought out on the Exchange, with Mauler's agent Slift so tightening the screw by driving up prices that the packing plants go bankrupt, with the result that Mauler's contracts, which should have guaranteed him a market, are void, and his livestock proves impossible to unload. The eventual answer to the whole dilemma is found when all concerned join together and decide to maintain prices at a profitable level by destroying part of the livestock while at the same time permanently eliminating part of the workforce from the production process. In other words, in the course of the crisis Mauler has united the packing plants under his control and cut wages and livestock prices alike.

In all this the Black Straw Hats personify public opinion.

[*Gisela E. Bahr: Die heilige Johanna der Schlachthöfe Bühnenfassung, Fragmente, Variante*, pp. 9–10. Edition Suhrkamp, Frankfurt-am-Main, 1971. The specified date of 1900 was later omitted.]

NOTE TO 'SAINT JOAN OF THE STOCKYARDS'

To clarify the course of business events, headlines can be called out by newsboys running across the stage or through the auditorium.

p. 208, before 2(d):
'Meat Kings in Bloody Battle!'
'Meat Price Plummets!'
'Mauler and Lennox – Battle of the Meat Titans!'
'Mauler – Lard Ten Cents a Kilo!'
'Lennox Offers Eight! Warned by Banks! Will Lennox Hold Out? Lennox or Mauler: Who'll Win?'

p. 212, after 'Where are we to turn?':
'Disaster hits Stockyard Workers!'
'Lennox Shutdown, Mauler Next! Half Chicago's Yard Workers Jobless! Winter Threatens!'

p. 243, before scene 6 'Catching the Cricket':
'Pierpont Mauler a Speculator!'
'Guarantees Buy Up Total Meat Production!'
'Stockbreeders Flummoxed! Buyers Holding Back! Expect Fall in Stock Price!'

p. 250, before scene 7 'The Money Changers are driven out of the Temple':
'Strange Developments on Livestock Exchange!'
'Secret Buying of Illinois and Kansas Stock!'
'Stock Price Rises! Yard Workers Uneasy after Five-Week Lockout!'
'Meat Packers Plan Aid! Frantic Activity of Charitable Groups!'

p. 258, before scene 8 'Mauler's Speech on Indispensability':
'Still No Work at Yards!'
'Growing Poverty Hits Masses! Shopkeepers Stuck for Rent! Who's Cornering the Stock? Mauler Interviewed – Does Not Know Secret Buyer!'
'Snow Coming! Chicago Under Snow!'

p. 265, before 'Joan's Third Descent into the Depths':
'Storm at Livestock Exchange! Stock Prices Rocket!'
'Black Hat Girl Joan Dark Says Won't Quit Yards Till Work Resumes!'

p. 266, before The Packers: 'Heavens! The tariff repealed . . .':
'Tariffs Cut in South! Export Stock in Sudden Demand!'
'Unforeseen Collapse of Tariffs!'

p. 267, after 'Get his arse bitten':
'Tariff Cuts in South! Export Stock Sought! Where Has The Stock Got To? No Livestock in Ill and Ark!'

p. 271, before 9(e) 'Another part of the Stockyards':
'The Secret Buyer? – MAULER!'
'Socialists Step Up Yards Action!'
'Agitators Exploit Agony of Locked-Out Workers!'
'The Locked-Out Workers – City Utilities Employees Plan Sympathy Strike! Police Chief Forsees Chicago Anarchy If Livestock Chaos Lasts!'

p. 273, before 9(f) 'Livestock Exchange':
'Amazing Sensation on Livestock Exchange!'
'Pierpont Mauler's Giant Corner Sinks Packing Plants!'
'Bankrupting Threatens Major Plants! Thousands of Shareholders' Savings Lost!'

p. 274, after 'How can we pay him eighty for his livestock?':
'General Strike Threat! Scores Livestock Exchange Manoeuvres! Chicago Without Light and Power in Four Hours! Can Wall Street Destroy Chicago?'

p. 280, after 'selling to the packers in spite of the rising prices':
'Pierpont Mauler Unblocks Livestock! New Swing on Livestock Exchange!'
'Packing Plants To Return To Work Tomorrow! Labour Unions Call Off General Strike!'

p. 284, before 9(h) 'Street Corner in Chicago':
'Mauler Sales Rumour Denied. Stock Price Still Going Up!'

p. 285, before 9(i) 'A deserted section of the stockyards':
'Latest from the Livestock Exchange: Chicago Meat Business Busted!'
'Mauler Went Too Far – Is Bust Too! Plants Stay Shut. Workers Quit Yards, Expect Work Tomorrow! Firms Not Opening, But No General Strike!'

p. 300, before 11 'Stockyards':
'Result Of Meat War: Main Packing Plants Merge! President: Pierpont Mauler! Labour To Be Rationalised, Meat Pile Slashed! It's Back To Work!'

[Appendix to *Gesammelte Werke Band 1*, Malik-Verlag, London 1938.]

MEANING OF 'SAINT JOAN OF THE STOCKYARDS'

In times when the prevalent social system, controlling the employment and livelihood of vast masses of people, is the cause of intolerable hardships, it should surprise no one if those same masses (whether in person or by the medium of those who speak for them) question the great intellectual systems which set out to shape the moral and religious aspects of their living standard. From the point of view of the institutions embodying these systems – churches, schools and so forth – it looks thus. Great sections of the working class, discontented with the prevalent social system, see the institutions in question as intellectually and organisationally bound up with a social order that denies them all possibility of life. And so they turn their backs on certain moral and religious trains of thought.

IS 'SAINT JOAN OF THE STOCKYARDS' A REALIST WORK?

Persons uncertain of the difference between realism and materialism are unlikely to consider this a realist work. It is even doubtful if they would describe it as a materialist one.

The formal aspect alone might well mislead them.

Apart from the nature of its subject-matter, it sets out various historical methods of representing this, with the result that the work incidentally becomes an investigation of such methods – something that is clearly a confusing factor. To link a particular kind of human behaviour with its means of expression (to be found in art – as notably in the final scene) may indeed be a source of confusion; but this is how certain forms of representation get demolished, in that their social function is made manifest. And this is an act of realism.

At the same time stylisation is in itself a factor which operates against realism, particularly when it is our own time that is being stylised. (Whereas earlier imaginative works often appear realistic when they contain a strong dash of stylisation.) Incidents in the natural world take a recognisably different course – recognisably so because their portrayal is unhampered by the tacit short-cuts of the normal draughtsman's perspective. Stylisation lacks an element of multiplicity that is present in the real world. It is removed because ambiguity is to be avoided. But ambiguity too is an essential part of reality.

Without dialectics, indeed, stylisation cannot produce realistic works. A certain superficial abstraction is no business of the realist.

All the same he abstracts. The formula 'transformation of the imperialist war into the civil war' along with its corollary 'imperialist war as a manifestation of civil war' is a stylisation. Only its expression in more concrete detail will characterise the realist; its association with practice – his own or other people's – be realism.

Investigating the effectiveness of behaviour such as that of Joan and Mauler in our own time is unquestionably the enterprise of a realist, even when the field where it all happens is artificially constructed.

NOTES TO 'SAINT JOAN OF THE STOCKYARDS'

The play was evolved from Elisabeth Hauptmann's play 'Happy End', with the collaboration of Hauptmann, Borchardt and Burri. Use was made of classical models and stylistic features: certain episodes were portrayed in the form historically assigned to them. In this way the aim is to show not only the episodes but also the kind of literary-theatrical treatment to which they have been subject.

1

'Saint Joan of the Stockyards' is a piece of non-aristotelian dramaturgy. This is a dramaturgy that demands a quite specific approach on the part of the spectator. He has to be in a position to adopt a specific and learnable attitude, absorbing the events on the stage and grasping them in their multiple relationships and complete progression. This with a view to a radical review of his own conduct. He is not allowed to identify himself spontaneously with particular characters in order merely to partake of their experience. So he does not set out from their intuitively grasped 'Being', but uses their statements and actions to piece together the overall process. (He is not always led suggestively to this approach by the work of art itself; he may have to get at it by some other route, by first hand experience or study or whatever.)

2

So what is being discussed in the play 'Saint Joan of the Stockyards', as an instance of this dramaturgy, is not 'the inner being of religion', faith, the existence of God. It is rather the approach adopted by religious persons (in so far as it can be understood from outside), the talk of God, the efforts people make to instil belief. The aim of the play – to communicate a profound and practically active awareness of the great social processes of our time – would be distorted by blaspheming 'God' or showing the religious approach in a contemptible light. For what matters from this point of view is tracing the effects of the religious approach as seen in quite specific situations of our time, along with those of a quite specific and *currently* observable historical approach.

3
The play claims to be necessary if one is to judge religious institutions and their conduct (e.g. the sect of the Black Straw Hats), or grasp such a movement as a *whole*. This movement is shown as inherently full of contradictions. Inseparable among them are religious inspiration (Joan Dark) and the apparat (Paulus Snyder and the rest of his group). But the spectator should not get too involved in the clash between them. For instance he must not approve Joan and reject the apparat, nor vice versa. He must make his criticisms of the totality of the institution, for it is as a totality that the social process encounters it along with its inherent contradictions. Neither Joan nor the apparat in isolation could bring about those effects which are to be felt in reality. Similarly the 'other world' of the stockyards forms a self-contradictory whole, and there is a sense in which Joan and Mauler, particularly when confronted with the locked-out workers – which is where the play first establishes its main critical point about the intolerable nature of our conditions – join with the Black Straw Hats and the owners of the chief means of production to form a single unit.

4
Catholics have reacted to Joan Dark's last desperate warning –

> So anyone down here who says there's a God
> And that even if no one can see Him
> He can, invisibly, help us all the same
> Should have his head bashed against the sidewalk
> Until he croaks –

with various degrees of outrage, but one cannot understand it unless one takes it literally and sees that she is not speaking about God at all but about talk of a God, or, more precisely, about specific talk in a specific situation, and specific remarks about God. She is in fact speaking about talk to the effect that God need have no function whatever in social matters, and that those who believe in such a God are called on to accomplish nothing in particular. It is enough if they have certain inner sensations.

The faith thus recommended is without effect on the world around us, and Joan defines such recommendation as a social crime.

[From *GW* 17, 1968. *Schriften zum Theater* 3, *zu 'Die heilige Johanna der Schlachthöfe'*. The introductory section of the last of these three items is adapted from the first edition of the play in *Versuche* 5, 1932. In the 1938 Malik edition Emil Hesse Burri figures under the pseudonym 'H. Emmel', to hide his identity from the Nazis. Hans Hermann Borchardt, whose name is omitted there, seems to have been an intermittent adviser, particularly concerning the business manipulations. He took refuge in the USSR, taught at Minsk University from 1934–36, was deported to Nazi Germany at the time of the purges, interned at Dachau and extricated by the efforts of his friends. He settled in New York.]

ABOUT THE DRAMA'S WAY OF DEPICTING BUSINESS MATTERS

There are two kinds of people: those that do business and those that read books. Those that do business do not understand much about reading books; those that read books, not much about business. This is one reason why it is so difficult to write books about business – and to make a business of doing so.

The mutual incomprehension of the two categories usually swells into positive contempt. The history of the German republic provides an example worth thinking about.

A certain political party thought (quite rightly) that one of the most effective arguments for its candidate in a presidential election was to suggest that he had never read a book. He was promptly elected, after which the other section, the book-reading category, obstinately refused to acquaint itself with his policies. The result was devastating.

Suppose a writer nowadays writes a dramatic (or belle-lettristic) work featuring business matters, then he must accept that anyone capable of understanding what his play (or book) is about is not going to read it, while anyone who reads it is not going to understand what it is about.

Business people at least are not quite so bad as the art experts. They may also take an occasional interest in art, but they have their reservations: there has to be no element of business. This insistence links them psychologically with the art lovers who otherwise are their opponents. We will leave aside the business lovers' objection to any representation of business in art, since it is to all intents and purposes the same as that of the art lovers. One principal argument for instance is that art is too serious to concern itself with anything so mundane as business. (In these sacred halls business is not recognised.)

depiction of pierpont mauler's business affairs
phase 1
the meatpacker mauler senses an impending sellers' crisis on the meat exchange. he sells his shares in the yards to his crony, while undertaking to knock out his competitors before he leaves the business. (I)
phase 2
the lennox yards are knocked out by the competition of mauler and cridle, and they close. (II)
phase 3
cridle also closes, with a view to rationalising his yards. at the same time he wants to wait till prices recover.

mauler now calls on cridle to pay the money for his shares. however, since prices are very low because of the great masses of meat coming on the market, cridle will be ruined if he has to pay.

[Fragments compiled by Gisela Bahr in her *Die heilige Johanna der Schlachthöfe. Bühnenfassung, Fragmente, Varianten*. Suhrkamp, Frankfurt 1972]

BUILDING UP A PART BY THE INDUCTIVE METHOD

An instance of the search for an expression: how does one rehearse Joan's phrase 'because you have the cruellest face' in scene 3?

For a start one should follow the usual practice involved in reading the part with amazement, and look for other possible answers that Joan could make to the meat king's question 'how do you come to know me?' For example 'because God showed me your face in a dream' or 'because I've seen it in your corned beef advertisements' or 'because you have the cleverest face'. These or similar sentences should be spoken with the appropriate expression in each case. Then the phrase 'because you have the cruellest face', as the part has it, should be spoken in a distinctively different way.

[Published by Gisela Bahr, as above.]

DRAFT FOR A RADIO TALK

Fascism cut short the development of the German theatre and German playwriting, which had already been obstructed by the last democratic or semi-democratic governments. Piscator's theatre, that had harnessed a whole generation of playwrights, was ruined; the Theater am Schiffbauerdamm closed, which had introduced a number of innovations and grouped such gifted actors as Oskar Homolka, Peter Lorre, Lotte Lenya, Carola Neher and Helene Weigel in an ensemble; the Volksbühne, which had remained a quality theatre for some time after Piscator left it, fell into the hands of empty-minded hacks. Small groups carried on the fight against the growing reaction, in the teeth of financial problems and difficulties with the police. The time was full of contradictions. Even as our own theatres were closing, the State Theatre staged a new production of one of my earlier plays; but it cost the Intendant his job. Even the radio performed scenes from my play 'Saint Joan of the Stockyards' – the organisers were artistically inclined intellectuals who shortly afterwards disappeared into the concentration camps.

The reaction had gone too far for any camouflage. There was already a ban on anything that stood for progress, even of a purely artistic kind. We replied by sharpening our political message. A dramatisation of Gorky's 'Mother' gave lessons in illegal resistance, the production and distribution of leaflets, conspiracy in the prisons, covert campaigning against war ideology. Helene Weigel, who played the mother, was hailed by the bourgeois press as one of the greatest German actresses, but the audience contained more and more policemen until finally she was arrested on stage. What a tribute by the bourgeois state to a great performer! Likewise the big workers' choral organisations fought up to the end. The producers of a central German performance of 'Die Massnahme' with Eisler's music were arrested. Their trial was extended to include the authors, and opened at the Reich's Supreme Court. Then came naked Fascism. Actors and directors were seized, others went into emigration.

For an actor, director or theatre writer to emigrate meant the virtually complete loss of his profession. His means of production were removed at a single blow. Actors had to learn a new language. Thus Ernst Busch, one of the best proletarian actors, had to perform in Dutch; Oskar Homolka learned English. As for the plays, outside Germany they are difficult to understand and difficult to put on. 'Saint Joan of the Stockyards' for instance, a play on non-aristotelian lines, was the object of one or two attempted productions abroad, but none of them came to anything. Both actors and directors for this kind of work were lacking. The German theatre had attained a pretty high standard. The political objections to its production are strong ones and growing stronger.

[Draft for a radio talk 'On German revolutionary dramaturgy, 1935'. Published by Gisela Bahr, as above. Among the Berlin theatres referred to, it is rare for Brecht to mention the Volksbühne, or formerly Socialist-managed 'People's Stage'. The State Theatre Intendant who put on Brecht's *Man equals Man* in 1931, and was sacked for it, was Ernst Legal. The Brecht/Eisler 'Lehrstück' *Die Massnahme* is known in English as *The Decision* or *The Measures Taken*.

Another version of this text is given under the same title in *GW* 15, p. 234: this ends on a more optimistic note with praise of the Soviet theatre as 'the most progressive in the world', while the émigré agitprop director Maxim Vallentin is termed 'outstanding'. It seems likely that the talk dates from Brecht's 1935 visit to Moscow.]

Notes of Uncertain Authorship

(a) *Inscriptions for the Black Straw Hats' meeting-house*

Can God knock out Jack Dempsey?
What does an unemployed office worker need to know about God?
Is God a bluff?
Does God accept the bootlegger's mite too?
Is God also capable of waiting?
What is worth more than a million dollars?
What has God achieved so far?
God locks nobody out
Can Henry Ford make automobiles without God?
Can Bolshevism become a business?
Does Bolshevism have a future?
Is God's word a best-seller?
Fear of God – the little man's capital
Make guns for God!
Must I pay my taxes to God too?

['Tafeln bei den SS', from Gisela Bahr, as above. From early material, typed by an unidentified hand and related to scene 7.]

(b) *Bert Brecht* Saint Joan of the Stockyards – *Extracts for radio*

'To assuage the misery of the stockyards, the Black Straw Hats sally forth from their mission house. At their head Joan Dark.'
Speaker: Joan

'Pierpont Mauler leaves the Livestock Exchange. Surrounded by meat kings, he is questioned by Joan. Pierpont Mauler feels the breath of another world.'
Speakers: Mauler, Detective, Joan, Slift

'The walk to the stockyards. Sullivan Slift shows Joan Dark the baseness of the poor'.
Speakers: Slift, Foreman Smith, Young Worker, Joan, Mrs Luckerniddle, Gloomb, Waiter

'Pierpont Mauler and his agent Sullivan Slift, having made their arrangements, gloat at the prospect of a black day for the Chicago Livestock Exchange.'
Speakers: Mauler, Slift

'Pierpont Mauler instructs Joan Dark about the indispensability of capitalism and religion.'
Speaker: Mauler

'Joan Dark, sitting in the stockyard district, unemployed among the unemployed, narrates a dream.'
Speaker: Joan

'The meat king Pierpont Mauler hears the report of the course of the great war on the Exchange, in which his agent causes him to lose his entire fortune.'
Speaker: Graham

'The chorus of butchers and stockbreeders answer the dying Joan'. (?text taken from scene 11)

Pierpont Mauler	Fritz Kortner
Joan Dark	Carola Neher
Mrs Luckerniddle	Helene Weigel
Foreman Smith	Ernst Busch
Speaker	Paul Bildt
Sullivan Slift *and* Graham	Peter Lorre
Young Worker *and* Gloomb	Friedrich Gnass
Detective *and* Waiter	Otto Kronberger
Director	Alfred Braun

[Quoted by Gisela Bahr, pp. 217–8, from the radio magazine *Berliner Funkstunde*, 11 April 1932. There is no surviving script for this adaptation. It appears to have been some 40 or 50 pages long. A recording is in the radio sound archives in Frankfurt.]

Editorial Notes

General structure

There are four principal scripts or versions prior to 1945: (a) a loosely assembled sequence of scenes and episodes, incomplete as to scenes 9 and 10; (b) the 11-scene duplicated stage script sent out by Felix Bloch Erben, the agents, in 1931; (c) the published text in *Versuche* no. 5 (Kiepenheuer, Berlin 1932), likewise with 11 scenes; (d) the 13-scene text in the Malik-Verlag *Gesammelte Werke*, Band 1 (London 1938). Of these (b) is published in Gisela Bahr's critical volume in the Edition Suhrkamp, no. 427 (Frankfurt a/M, 1971), as are selections from (a); while (c) is the text used by the editor Manfred Nössig in volume 3 of the *Große kommentierte Berliner und Frankfurter Ausgabe* (Berlin, Weimar and Frankfurt a/M, 1988) which also appends the different version of the last scene from (b). For the 8-scene radio version of 1932 see Brecht's note above.

The 11 scenes of the stage script are divided into Acts as follows: Act 1 = sc. 1 to 3; Act 2 = sc. 4 and 5; Act 3 = sc. 6 to 8; Act 4 = sc. 9, including what later became 11 (a); Act 5 = sc. 10 and 11. These Acts are not marked in the published texts, though the Malik version of 1938 uses roman numerals for its scenes, and arabic for the subdivisions marked elsewhere by letters. In the *Versuche* version the last section of scene 9 of the script is added to the end of scene 10 following the 'Welcome' chorus of the Black Straw Hats. In the Malik version of 1938 this section is renumbered scene XI, a new short (prose) scene XII is added (where the workers bring lanterns to identify the dead), and the final canonisation scene then becomes XIII. In *GW*, whose text was edited by Elisabeth Hauptmann in the 1950s and generally follows Malik, XI and XII become two parts (a and b) of a single scene 11, and the last scene becomes 12. The 1988 'Berlin and Frankfurt' edition, edited for Suhrkamp-Verlag by an East-West team, goes back to the eleven-scene structure of the previously abandoned *Versuche* text of 1932. See our comments below (pp. 427–432).

Neither the 1932 nor the 1938 published version includes a list of the characters' names.

Incomplete material

The early incomplete sequence of scenes and episodes analysed by Gisela Bahr varies widely from the subsequent texts, frequently containing passages written by Hauptmann and/or Burri to which Brecht made handwritten amendments. Characters figure under other names: Joan for instance is sometimes Joan Farland, Mauler is amended from Cracker (the gang leader of *Happy End*, or perhaps a relative – at one point there is a Zachary Cracker), Slift seems to have started as Swift. Hannibal Jackson the Salvationist lieutenant is another legacy from *Happy End*; probably by oversight, he survived right into the final *GW* text. Gloomb is Gloomp (not that there is much to choose between two such dreadful names). Most of the dialogue appears to be in prose.

But the most startling feature of what appears to be an incomplete early version is the presence of a subsequently expunged major character – God, also called The Old Gentleman. Somewhat giving the lie to Brecht's disclaimer of all blasphemous intention, He makes His appearance in the Salvationists' citadel rather diffidently in a draft of scene 7, after Snyder has prepared his listeners for the divine entrance, saying:

SNYDER: We have managed to win for our humble mission house One who has helped in the most difficult situations, who has demonstrated His power to attract the public, who can fill the biggest hall, who is familiar to every child, yet at the same time referred to with respect by every business man in the city [... etc., down to 'scrub down the front steps', then a short exchange with his secretary Barbara, a character not found in later versions.]

Enter God: am I intruding?

SNYDER: And where have you been?

GOD: I stepped outdoors for a moment.

SNYDER: O, I know where you were.

GOD: Getting a breath of air.

SNYDER: Outdoors indeed. You've been down to the Livestock Exchange again. How often do I have to tell you not to stroll around, with all those workers out on the streets? Just wait till they catch you, get out your new tunic. I've invited all the richest men in Chicago here to ask what they propose to do for you. It's no good my pretending our position is anything but critical since our benefactor Lennox went broke.

GOD: The same old story.

SNYDER: I wish you'd stop sounding so fed up. You've been grumbling ever since we opened this place. But times have changed.

GOD: Anyway let's hope they're respectable people.

SNYDER: Do you imagine we can pick and choose our benefactors? And you so insistent on humility.

The new tunic is brought in.

SNYDER: Sh. The staff mustn't know about this. I was meaning to tell you.

They put the new tunic on him.

SNYDER: How do you like this plain tunic? It was all we were allowed to give you.

A BLACK STRAW HAT: The old gentleman's going to look so handsome he'll put all the rich meat-kings in the shade.

ANOTHER BLACK STRAW HAT: Only last night I had another happy experience. A poor widow came up and gave us her savings book, saying 'this way God'll look after me and my five kids.'

GOD: Bravo! So where's the book?

SNYDER: You can take a breather now, my dear friends. *Aside.* The book . . . so he can have a quiet bet on prices falling!

GOD: Well, I imagine it'll be all right for me to be seen in public, and by the way, I hope I'll be getting the second room you promised me today. I was originally led to expect a second Saint Peter's, I hope you realise.

SNYDER: Indeed? What are you suggesting now? We're doing our best, you know. Here's me working myself to the bone, and the staff so poorly paid that the left-wing press has begun taking it up.

GOD: Yes, yes, I'm simply saying it's all very worthy. But there has to be some progress. We can't go on for ever in such modest surroundings.

SNYDER: Just you go into your room and wait there till I tell you the visitors have arrived. I'll explain our situation to them beforehand so you don't have to get directly involved in the business side.

GOD (*leaving*): Don't keep me waiting too long. (*He sits down behind a wall with the newspaper.*)

SNYDER (*to Jackson*): Someone had better tell the old man that absolutely nothing's being done for him anywhere else.

Following the appearance of the four meat-packers in the mission house (whence Joan will expel them) and Snyder's request for $800,

God asks one of the Black Straw Hats 'How're things going in there?'

BLACK STRAW HAT: Tough.

God shakes his head.

CRIDLE (*downstage*): Admit it, Slift, you fellows have the livestock.

SLIFT: True as I'm sitting here, Mauler and I haven't bought one cent's worth of livestock, as God's my witness.

CRIDLE: 200 dollars? That's a lot of money.

GOD (*gets up and puts a new record on the gramophone. To a Black Straw Hat*): Looks to me as if they're going to be quite a while in there. My dear Eliza [Joan], read me something about the old days, you know the sort of thing I enjoy.

Joan then reads Him the account of the building of King Solomon's Temple at Jerusalem. Gloomb and Mrs Luckerniddle do not appear, and Joan drives out the packers without making her long speech. Snyder tells them he will sack her, and does so, saying 'pack your bag, Joan, you have made the old gentleman homeless'. His verse speech, turning her out into the rain and blizzard, follows. Then:

GOD: Am I intruding? Do I keep this tunic on? Are you going to introduce me?

SNYDER: Oh, you're still waiting, are you? You heard what this Joan of yours has done?

GOD: Anything my Joan does is well done.

SNYDER:

I've chucked her out.
Yes, that's the way, just as I say, and really it's quite simple
The rich think it no joke
Once chase the money changers from the temple
The temple will go broke.

Enter the landlord.

[MULBERRY]: Have you got the money now?

SNYDER: God will be able to pay for the wretched – I repeat, wretched, Mister Mulberry – lodging which he has found on this earth. (*Exit.*)

MULBERRY: Yes, pay, quite right, that's what it's about. You picked the right word there, Snyder. If God pays, well and good, but if he doesn't pay, not well and good at all. If God fails to pay his rent then he must move out. That'll be Saturday night, Snyder, right? *Exit.*

GOD: Am I to move out then, Joan?

[*Joan says she will go and see Mauler, as in our text.*]

GOD:

Mauler, how will you get to see him?
He's the biggest of the lot. I too
Would like to speak with him. I'll come with you, Joan.
He takes his hat, turns to a Black Straw Hat, says
Elisa, tell the major I'm going out for a breather. I don't care for these business practices here. They really shouldn't be necessary.
[*And this ends the scene.*]

Two other short exchanges seem to be set in the mission house. In the first, God, under his earlier name of The Old Gentleman, points to an old man with a fiddle:

OLD GENTLEMAN: So who is that?

MARTA: He's the famous scientist who plays for the poor people here.

THE OLD GENTLEMAN (*gives him a smile and, when he returns the smile, shows him a sign which says*): LATEST DEVELOPMENTS OF SCIENCE ACKNOWLEDGED HERE.

THE FAMOUS SCIENTIST: That's easily done.

THE OLD GENTLEMAN: What d'you mean?

THE FAMOUS SCIENTIST: For instance, we now know there are three distinct cosmic laws. One for the great bodies, one for the middling, and one for the small ones. That's life, wouldn't you say?

THE OLD GENTLEMAN: Incredible . . .

[*Then a brief exchange with Joan.*]:

JOAN: What was the business with Jesus, by the way?

THE OLD GENTLEMAN: Wait a moment. Yes, I remember him. A little tubby fellow. I'm greatly indebted to Saul, who drew my attention to him. But there was a nasty incident: if I'm right, Saul once called him a Christian, and at that he turned the other cheek . . .

Scene 8 in what seems to be the same incomplete version starts with Mauler's short episode in the Livestock Exchange near the start of our scene 9. Following on this Joan appears outside the building, with The Old Gentleman. They are still looking for Mauler.

THE OLD GENTLEMAN: You must make every effort to speak to your Mr Mauler today, Joan. We've been tramping the streets for over a week while you tried to get hold of him.

Our Scene 8 then follows, though the location where Joan visits Mauler is his own office, not Slift's. Mauler makes his speech about money with some changes, and the confrontation ends with Joan speaking the closing four lines now given to Mauler, and Mauler soliloquising.

MAULER:
Nothing can get in my way, money attracts money.
And even if they wait seven years for a job, I shall
Not let a single scrap of meat escape me, so that
This time I shall skin them for good
As is natural to me.

Joan then addresses God, who has been waiting on the lower part of what is evidently a two-level stage:

JOAN: You come with me. We are going down to the stockyards to see the workers; they've been standing there for the past ten days.

THE OLD GENTLEMAN: Really? Then why aren't they working? Just taking it easy, I suppose?

JOAN: Don't you know nowadays it's the kings of finance and the lords of industry that rule the world? And do whatever they want with the workers?

THE OLD GENTLEMAN: Nobody tells me anything.

JOAN: The capitalists are exploiting the workers.

THE OLD GENTLEMAN: Are they really allowed to?

In a long speech thought to belong to scene 9, Joan harangues the workers. The Old Gentleman is sitting among them. It seems however that she has not yet been dismissed by Snyder, which suggests that it might belong earlier.

JOAN: We Black Straw Hats wish to tell you that help is on its way. God is in Chicago. God has appeared among you in the stockyards. God is with you, God is in your midst, God who led the children of Israel through the Red Sea, in a pillar of cloud by day, in a pillar of fire by night, He will lead you too. What are meat kings to Him? He will drive them two by two if need be. He who overthrew the Tower of Babel in a single day when it became too big for Him, He will also deal with the Chicago Livestock Exchange. He who made the world in seven days and saw that it was good (*A catcall.*) will also create order in the city of Chicago. And He who was able to lead the children of Israel into the Promised Land, flowing with milk and honey, He will also open the factory gates for you and lead you within them. And He who conjured manna out of the air for His people, He will feed you too when His hour comes, I'm referring to travelling kitchens and cheap foodstuffs. And you, the humblest of all as you sit there, a tiny group in the tempest, you will be the greatest in His Kingdom (*Catcalls.*) You have only to persevere and commit no foolishness, or the police will come, and that will be the finish. Just think what He has accomplished. For a start, He created the whole world as we know it, with all its accessories. With its mountains and lakes and the lovely sun and every kind of beauty. (*Catcalls.*) Then He led the people of Israel and indeed all the peoples so mildly and considerately yet so strictly through the ranks of their enemies that it was a real pleasure, and He smote those enemies with the pestilence till the welkin rang. And with no thought of His own advantage. And finally it isn't always winter. Summer too sometimes arrives. He was always stronger than His opponents, and the great kings acknowledged Him – just think of King David. And He was always for the economically disadvantaged – that can be found in plenty of places in the Bible. It's common knowledge. Of course one shouldn't just sit and wait for Him, for roast pigeons to fly into one's mouth. Now and again, for instance, one has to appeal to the public if things seem too difficult. Just try that.

PEOPLE (*below, to God*): D'you mind keeping your cigar smoke down?

A MAN: It's getting dreadfully cold again.

THE OLD GENTLEMAN: Just listen. Shut up!

A WOMAN: Who's that fellow with the starched collar? I bet you're warm enough under that topcoat.

SECOND WOMAN: What's he doing down here in any case?

THE OLD GENTLEMAN: If my face doesn't fit I can go away.

A MAN: Stop! Stay there! Let's know where you're from.

THE OLD GENTLEMAN: I'm having no truck with you. Rude people.

WOMAN: He started walking, and now he's running like a ferret. What kind of dirt is he trying to pick up?

Joan comes down.

PEOPLE: Your companion has left you, Miss.

JOAN: Has he? (*She goes off to look for him, returns alone.*) I couldn't catch up with him. He's got a longer stride than me, and he's scared.

An anonymously typed outline for scene 10, leading up to Joan's death against the background of the blazing city, reintroduces God under His proper name once more. It starts –

> Major Snyder's last effort to stop God being driven out of Chicago for good and all. He asks the removal men to wait a few hours before taking away the furniture; he also pacifies the bandsmen, who think they are not going to be paid.

Mauler then appears 'dirty, shattered, full of new awareness, liberated and happy' and pushes his way to the penitents' bench. He confesses and Snyder breaks down, asking where all his money has got to?

There must be a way of showing that it is money alone that thinks and that survives. However, 'the happy end begins' and God comes back to hear Mauler tell Slift and the others his plan for burning the surplus livestock. Two short fragments affirm God's ignorance of such matters:

> I oughtn't to come back, but last night I learnt a lesson. Conditions are truly wretched. (*He is given soup.*) How kind. Forgive the intrusion. Am I intruding? Of course I am all-knowing. But the prices on the exchange are more than I can foresee. Nobody can do that.

The second is headed 'God's outburst' and goes:

> I've been reading a book about the trade cycle. It says crises depend on natural laws. But tell me, surely I'm supposed to know something about those? Absolutely not! I've never had anything whatever to do with economics. Economics just doesn't exist for me. I've never interfered with it and I don't propose to.

A passage of dialogue fleshes this out:

> *Snyder, Mauler and a stockbreeder are talking to The Old Gentleman.*
>
> SNYDER: This is Mr Pierpont Mauler, our beloved meat king.
>
> THE OLD GENTLEMAN: Delighted.
>
> SNYDER: Mr Mauler has a suggestion to make to You for the benefit of the general welfare.
>
> MAULER: I don't wish to give offence, but before discussing details with You I would like to ask where You stand on the labour question.
>
> THE OLD GENTLEMAN: Er.

MAULER: So where do You stand?
THE OLD GENTLEMAN: Well, that's a strictly economic problem.
MAULER: Thank You. And now to the details.

Sound of whispering.
There is a prolonged conversation in the course of which The Old Gentleman's initial head-shaking starts changing to a nod of acquiescence.

THE BLACK STRAW HATS:

See, He shakes His head!
See, He doesn't like it!
Oh, we must leave our happy home
The organ and the penitents' bench, yes we too
Are economically at risk.
Oh, if only His glance would fall on us!

THE STOCK BREEDERS:

At least He has abandoned
That terrible head-shaking! If only He would agree
And we could go back bearing the happy message:
'The price of meat is going up!'
If only He would look across at us!

SNYDER:

Thank God! He is nodding! Everything is for the best
Both for Him and for us.

[All these and other incomplete scenes and passages are published in Gisela Bahr's 'edition suhrkamp' volume *Bertolt Brecht. Die heilige Johanna der Schlachthöfe. Bühnenfassung, Fragmente, Variante* (Frankfurt a/M, 1971).]

Final scene of the stage script

Much as in Caspar Neher's stage design for the finale of *Happy End*, which likewise centres on the chorus 'Hosanna Rockefeller', the setting here is not the refurbished mission house of all subsequent versions, but as follows:

In the background are big illuminated church windows portraying Rockefeller and Mauler. A screen depicts a steer being burned.
[Snyder and Joan deliver their opening verses, but the two policemen do not appear. Nor does Mauler speak until the last page of the play. Instead the chorus of Black Straw Hats have

other stanzas as a counterpoint to Joan's speeches, thus after 'entrusted to me' on p. 304:]

So at last we're almost there
So we fold our hands in prayer
May God bless us every day
Moth-like by His light attracted.
As a human here she acted
So it's here she lost her way.

[continuing with the words later given to Mauler, from 'Man with his high-flown' (p. 305). Then Joan's speech 'The factories are humming again', followed by the chorus:]

Man should moderate his pacing
Deserts match the planets' motions
And the coasts define the oceans.
All depends which way one's facing!

[Thence approximately as now from 'I spoke in all' to 'When cash and spirit wed'. Then the cattle raise their voice:]

FIVE OXEN:

Food can only come our way
When your hunger needs relief,
Sympathise with us, we pray:
Eat more
Beef!

[Thence as now from Joan's 'One thing I've learned!' (p. 305) to 'a better world', followed by Snyder's announcement of her illness (p. 308). Then Joan continues 'For there is a gulf' to 'ceased to know each other'. The first verse of 'Hosanna Rockefeller' is sung, leading on to 'Those at the bottom' and 'Any building that goes up', in reverse order to our text. From 'Be good! Be wise!' (p. 307) to 'Word of God' (p. 307) is omitted, as are Slift's three lines. Joan therefore continues 'So anyone down here' to 'until he croaks', followed by verse two of the chorus, then her 'And those preachers' followed by verse three. Then, in lieu of the loudspeaker slogans,]

During the third verse the girls have been trying to make Joan eat a plate of soup. She twice pushes it away. The third time she takes hold of it, raises it up and tips the soup out. Then she collapses.

[Snyder announces her death, as on p. 310, then the cattle are heard again:]

FOUR PIGS:

You are people, we are gammon
God says you can't be mistaken

If you go on eating bacon
And serving Mammon!

THE BUTCHERS:
Man, two warring souls reside
Deep down in you!
Once you realise that's true
One must be the other's bride!

WORKERS:
If no food can come our way
And you bring us no relief
We who want to live must pray
There'll be jobs for man and wife.
Buy us!

BUTCHERS:
And what is it binds us so?
It's love!
What unites us, friend and foe?
It's love!
Love that the calf feels for its butcher
Love of the butcher for his calf.
Love that leaves the mean man richer
And makes him laugh.
Calf and butcher see the picture:
Both go straying off the path.
Both alike depend on science
God's prescribed to make them big.
Hence the permanent alliance
Between Christian, ox and pig.

THE BLACK STRAW HATS:
He whose mouth's not just a slot that
Stays tight shut to higher things
Let him use the mouth he's got that
Sometimes eats but often sings.

[continuing 'Selling and buying' as on p. 307. Then the Packers and Stockbreeders speak the first of the three closing stanzas ('Mankind's inbuilt') followed by Mauler's 'A razor-sharp dichotomy'; but instead of the last stanza as we now have it, they all speak the quatrain:]

May to link them both together
Become his aim
Merge their qualities for ever
Pig and human just the same.

During the closing stanzas we come to see the basis on which all are standing: the whole stage is being carried by a dark mass of workers. End of Act Five.

From the stage script to the Versuche *edition of 1932*

Apart from the different last scene and the introduction of the scene titles, the 1932 publication is very largely the same as the stage script of the previous year. It is also to a great extent the final version, since the amendments for the Malik edition were not very substantial and of doubtful value to the play, and the editors of the extensive new 'Berlin and Frankfurt' edition of 1988 have accordingly decided to use it in lieu of the hitherto canonical *GW* text. Perhaps the articulation is slightly less clear than in the stage script, since the sub-scenes – notably in Joan's first and third 'descents into the depths' are not distinguished by letters nor are the scenes grouped into Acts. It adds the brief scene 2(b) 'P. Mauler', the singing of 'Watchful, be watchful' from *Happy End* in scene 2(d) and rearranges the latter so as to end with the Black Straw Hats' chorus and Joan's last line as now.

Scenes 3, 4 and 5 are practically unchanged. In Scene 6 Joan's simile 'the way we'd catch a cricket' is added after 'We'd lure him out of his hole' on p. 247 echoing the scene title (which is also new). Her singing of the Brandy-peddler's (or Grog-seller's) song from *Happy End* while Mauler is thinking on p. 248 is now omitted. An earlier suggestion that she should sing the Sailors' Song from the same work had been dropped.

In scene 7 there is some uncertainty as to the number of Packers mentioned, but clearly in fact they are four. Scene 8 has some small changes and rearrangement of lines but is essentially unaltered. Joan's dream speech in 9(a) loses its last sentence: 'I am/Hungry', and she speaks it alone. 9(b) is unchanged. 9(c) was previously much longer; Jackson seems to be a leftover from *Happy End* who is otherwise replaced by Snyder. The episode ends with the start of a new theme: the four lines where Joan and A Worker discuss the Communists as the only people doing anything. This is expanded slightly in the Malik text.

9(d), the Livestock Exchange, is unchanged and constitutes the final version. In 9(e), Another Part of the Yards, where Joan is given the strike letter, she now appears before the Workers' Leader speaks; she is looking for ways to help something to happen. The Leader's speech itself is rewritten, and close to the final text, though Mrs Luckerniddle is not yet present. 9(f) also is barely changed, apart from the resetting of some verse passages to read as prose. In 9(g), the Stockyards, the exchanges between Joan and the Reporters are new, and lead into her speech about 'the system' which was previously near the end of 9(c). The noise of shooting and the appearance of the arrested workers are pushed back towards the end of the episode, along with a new verse exchange about the use of force (which Joan discourages and the workers think inevitable). This too is subsequently expanded. 9(h) with Mauler and his two detectives remains the same all through. In the 'Deserted section' which follows as 9(i), Joan has to hear two workers saying that 'the communists were right' and that not all the messages can have been delivered, before hearing her 'Voices' as in the stage script. In the final (*GW*) version a different 9(i) is inserted, and the 'Voices' episode follows the same encounter with the two workers as 9(j) 'Another section', bringing the scene to an end.

The penultimate Scene 10 in the mission house is virtually unchanged right through, apart from some minor rearrangements, up to the beginning of the Black Straw Hats' 'Welcome' chorus on p. 299. This is the point in the stage script where the final canonisation scene begins. In the *Versuche* version the chorus is included, and is followed by an additional episode 'Stockyards. Area outside the Lennox plant's warehouses', which ends with Joan falling in a faint. In the Malik edition this episode becomes scene XI and a new, even shorter episode which follows it (where workers with lanterns identify Mrs Luckerniddle's body) is scene XII. In *GW* these two additions are strung together as scene 11, (a) and (b). The texts remain the same, and in each case the final 'Death and Canonisation' scene follows, numbered 11, XIII or 12.

The final scene was largely rewritten for *Versuche*, and thereafter not changed. It is as given in our text.

Svendborg amendments and additions

The need to make further changes around 1937 was presumably due partly to the proposed Copenhagen production and partly to the preparation of the new Malik edition. At the same time Brecht evidently did feel some obligation to strengthen the hand of the workers' spokesmen and distinguish between socialist gradualism and the more militant attitude of the Communists. It also seems likely that his exile from the German theatre made him want to write a better part for Helene Weigel, who had played Mrs Luckerniddle in the 1932 radio production. She is the character whose unseen husband fell into one of Mauler's rendering tanks in scene 4, apart from which she barely figures in the stage script except when eating the twenty (implicitly cannibalistic) canteen meals she is given as compensation. Now she becomes a political activist and Communist sympathiser for whose dead body the workers in the new scene XII send out a search party – a rather sketchy Chicago equivalent to Pelagea Vlassova, the part played by Weigel in Brecht's *The Mother*. The mixture of these conflicting features hardly displays conviction: an awkward piece of dramaturgical cross-breeding.

Presumably to stress the husband's fate, Mauler's aide Slift in scene 3 describes the 'new system' of killing hogs in a verse speech based clearly on the account in chapter III of *The Jungle*. Other touches are introduced to emphasise Joan's failure to deliver the workers' letter of warning during the strike. Not all Joan's hesitations are new, however, nor every reference to Communism or Bolschewismus; some are suggested in the *Versuche* or even the stage script. But the new role given to Mrs Luckerniddle in the second half of the play does seem designed to make Socialist reformism appear more suicidal, the language of the ending more bitterly farcical, and Joan's eventual canonisation that much more ironic.